Contemporary Computer-Assisted Language Learning

ALSO AVAILABLE FROM BLOOMSBURY

Contemporary Applied Linguistics, Edited by Li Wei and Vivian Cook

Contemporary Corpus Linguistics, Edited by Paul Baker

Contemporary Stylistics, Edited by Peter Stockwell and Marina Lambrou

Task-Based Language Learning and Teaching with Technology, Edited by Michael Thomas and Hayo Reinders

Contemporary Computer-Assisted Language Learning

Edited by

Michael Thomas,
Hayo Reinders and
Mark Warschauer

BLOOMSBURY
LONDON • NEW DELHI • NEW YORK • SYDNEY

Bloomsbury Academic
An imprint of Bloomsbury Publishing Plc

50 Bedford Square
London
WC1B 3DP
UK

175 Fifth Avenue
New York
NY 10010
USA

www.bloomsbury.com

First published 2013

British Library Cataloguing-in-Publication Data
A catalogue record for this book is available from the British Library.

ISBN: HB: 978-1-4411-9362-9

Library of Congress Cataloging-in-Publication Data
Contemporary computer-assisted language learning / edited by Michael Thomas, HayoReinders and Mark Warschauer.
p. cm. – (Contemporary studies in linguistics)
Includes bibliographical references and index.
ISBN 978-1-4411-9362-9 (hardcover : alk. paper) – ISBN 978-1-4411-1300-9 (ebook : alk. paper) – ISBN 978-1-4411-3450-9 (pdf : alk. paper) 1. Language and languages–Computer-assisted instruction–Research. 2. Language and languages–Research–Methodology. 3. Language acquisition–Research–Methodology. I. Thomas, Michael, 1969- II. Reinders, Hayo. III. Warschauer, Mark.
P53.28.C678 2013
418.0078'5–dc23

2012034908

Typeset by Newgen Imaging Systems Pvt Ltd, Chennai, India
Printed and bound in Great Britain

As this book project was beginning, the Tohoku Earthquake took place on 11th March 2011 in Japan. One year later, those events remain very much in our minds. All three editors and a number of contributors have a long-standing relationship with Japan, where many of us have taught English and/or computer-assisted language learning (CALL) over a number of years. In remembrance of those events, all proceeds from this book will be donated to the Japanese Red Cross.

Michael Thomas

Hayo Reinders

Mark Warschauer

2nd March 2012

Contents

Notes on contributors

James Dean Brown is Professor and Chair of Second Language Studies at the University of Hawai'i at Manoa. He has spoken and taught courses in more than 30 countries ranging from Brazil to Yugoslavia. He has also published numerous journal articles and book chapters (on language testing, curriculum design, research methods, and program evaluation) and authored or co-authored numerous books (on reading statistical language studies, language curriculum, language testing, language testing in Japan, testing L2 pragmatics, performance testing, criterion-referenced language testing, using surveys in language programs, doing research, language test development, ideas for classroom assessment, connected speech and heritage language curriculum).

Graham Davies began his career as a teacher of German and French in secondary education in the 1960s. He was employed as a Lecturer in German at Ealing College (later integrated into Thames Valley University) and then as Director of the Multimedia Language Centre. He has lectured and run ICT training courses for language teachers and has sat on numerous national and international advisory boards. In 1982 he wrote one of the first introductory books on computers in language learning, and he was conferred with the title of Professor of Computer-Assisted Language Learning in 1989. He was the founder president of EUROCALL from 1993 to 2000 and retired from full-time academic work in 1993.

Melinda Dooly is a teacher educator at the Science Education Faculty of the Universitat Autònoma de Barcelona, Spain. She teaches English as a Foreign Language Methodology and research methods courses, focusing on telecollaboration in education. Her research addresses teacher preparation and the use of CALL and CMC. She has published in the areas of teacher education and the use of technology in journals including *ReCALL, Language Learning and Technology, ELT-Journal and Teacher and Teaching Education.* She is co-editor of the book series *Telecollaboration in Education* (Peter Lang). Dr Dooly's current research interest is in project-based telecollaborative language learning and very young learners.

Dafne Gonzalez has been an ESP/EFL teacher for more than 30 years. She holds a Masters degree in Applied Linguistics and a PhD in Education with a major in E-course design. She is a Full Professor at Universidad Simon Bolivar, in Caracas, Venezuela, where she teaches blended and online English for Architecture and Urban Planning courses at the undergraduate level and graduate technology-related courses. She has been part of the TESOL Electronic Village Online (EVO) coordination team since 2003, and has co-moderated the EVO workshop 'Becoming a Webhead' since 2004.

Mirjam Hauck is a Senior Lecturer and Associate Head of the Department of Languages at the UK Open University. She has written numerous articles and book chapters on the use of technologies for the learning and teaching of languages and cultures covering aspects such as task design, tutor role and training and e-literacy skills. Apart from regular presentations at conferences, seminars and workshops in Europe and the United States, she serves on the CALICO executive board and the EUROCALL executive committee. She also chairs the EUROCALL Teacher Education Special Interest Group. She is the co-editor of the *EURODL* journal and a member of the editorial board of *CALL* and *ReCALL*.

Volker Hegelheimer Associate Professor in Applied Linguistics and Technology at Iowa State University, teaches courses on technology in language teaching and research, language assessment and research methodology. His research interests include applications of the WWW and emerging technologies in language learning, teaching and testing. He has presented his research and held academic workshops at numerous national and international conferences. His publications have appeared in journals such as *Language Learning & Technology*, *Language Testing*, *System*, *Computer-Assisted Language Learning*, *ReCALL*, *CALICO Journal*, and he has contributed to several edited volumes on computer-assisted language learning.

Trude Heift is Professor of Linguistics in the Department of Linguistics at Simon Fraser University, Canada. Her main research areas combine aspects of SLA and ICALL with a focus on the design as well as the evaluation of ICALL systems. From an SLA perspective, her work focuses on studies of human-computer interaction (e.g., navigation patterns, learner strategies and responses within intelligent systems, learner and task variables), corrective feedback and error analysis. From a computational point of view, she is interested in automatic analysis of learner language and learner modelling. She is currently Associate Editor of *Language Learning & Technology*.

Philip Hubbard is Senior Lecturer in Linguistics and Director of English for Foreign Students in the Stanford University Language Center. He has been active in computer-assisted language learning for over 25 years. He co-edited *Teacher Education in CALL* (2006) with Mike Levy and edited a four-volume series covering the whole field, *Computer Assisted Language Learning: Critical Concepts in Linguistics* (2009). His most recent book, co-authored with Deborah Healey and four colleagues, is *TESOL Technology Standards: Description, Implementation, Integration* (2011). He is an associate editor of *Computer Assisted Language Learning* and *Language Learning & Technology* and serves on the editorial boards of the *CALICO Journal*, *ReCALL* and *Writing & Pedagogy*.

Greg Kessler is Assistant Professor of Computer-Assisted Language Learning in the Department of Linguistics and Director of the Language Resource Center at Ohio University. His research addresses CALL teacher preparation, student language use in collaborative language learning, the role of students and teachers in innovative pedagogical contexts, student and teacher autonomy, and the relationship between technology and change in the English language. He has served as a leader in the teachers of English to speakers of other languages (TESOL) and was president of Ohio TESOL from 2007–8. He is currently interim co-director of the computer assisted language instruction consortium (CALICO).

Chun Lai is an Assistant Professor at the University of Hong Kong and currently teaches undergraduate and graduate courses in second language education. Her interests include technology-enhanced language learning, task-based language teaching and technology integration. She has published various articles on the design of online courses and online learning environments, and task-based language teaching in technology-enhanced environments.

Marie-Noëlle Lamy is Professor of Distance Language Learning at the UK Open University, where in the mid-nineties she led a team in charge of developing the University's first ever program of distance-taught languages. Her research focuses on the implications of using multimodal tutoring environments for distance learning and teaching. She has co-authored *Online Communication in Language Teaching and Learning* (2007), an overview of the field now considered a key read for researchers and post-graduate students. She is currently working on critical appraisals of Web 2.0 tools and networks for language and culture learning, a theme reflected in her co-edited book, *Learning Cultures in Online Education* (2009).

Joshua Lawrence is an Assistant Professor of Language, Literacy, and Technology at the University of California, Irvine. His research focuses on: (1) understanding adolescent language and literacy development, and (2) creating and testing interventions and teaching methods to improve adolescent literacy outcomes. He is particularly interested in understanding the achievement gap between students from low- and high-socioeconomic backgrounds, second language development, interventions that support reluctant adolescent readers, and individual differences in learning from in-school and out-of-school activities.

Jooyoung Lee is a PhD student in the Applied Linguistics and Technology program at Iowa State University. Her research interests include second/foreign language writing, computer-assisted language learning and language assessment. She is currently working on a research project, which aims to investigate and evaluate the use of an automated writing evaluation tool in University ESL courses from a pedagogical perspective.

Carla Meskill is Professor in the Department of Educational Theory and Practice at the University at Albany, State University of New York. Her research and teaching explore new forms of technology use in language education as well as the influences of new technologies on developing language and literacy practices. In tandem, her work explores the nature of electronic literacy and its centrality in teacher professional development. On these and related topics she has published widely. Dr Meskill is the former Director of the Technology Assisted Language Learning (TALL) project, Language Advocacy Project (LAP), co-editor of MERLOT and currently serves as associate editor of *Language Learning & Technology*.

Gary Motteram is a Senior Lecturer in Education at the University of Manchester. He has an M.Ed. in Teaching English Overseas and an Ed.D. in e-learning. He set up and still runs the innovative Masters in Educational Technology and TESOL, which is taught both on-site in Manchester and by e-learning. He has presented at conferences and published regularly in the fields of technology in language learning and technology supported distance teacher education. He has recently managed a number of international projects for the University of Manchester including: eChinaUK and AVALON and ran a two-year research project for Cambridge University Press exploring what teachers do with technology.

Ruhui Ni is a Research Associate at the College of Education, Michigan State University. She has been the co-director for the project of Zon, a Massive Multiplayer Online Role Playing Game (MMORPG) for learning Chinese as a foreign language for four years. Her research interests include innovative technology adoption in schools, digital gaming for foreign language learning and comparative education.

Robert O'Dowd teaches EFL and Applied Linguistics at the University of León, Spain, and is also the University's Secretary for International Training. He has a PhD from the University of DuisburgEssen, Germany. He has authored a book on telecollaboration, *Telecollaboration and the Development of Intercultural Communicative Competence* (2006), and has edited the volume *Online Intercultural Exchange: An Introduction for Foreign Language Teachers* (2007). He has also published on the topic in various academic journals. He has coordinated national and international projects about telecollaboration and has held two Eurocall Regional Workshops on telecollaboration and Computer Mediated Communication.

Zeynep Onat-Stelma is currently working in the School of Education, at the University of Manchester. She is teaching in the areas of language teacher education, bilingualism and research methods. She is also currently involved in a research project called Euroversity funded by the European Union. Her research interests lie in teacher professional development. She has previously been involved in research projects where she worked with language teachers in different international settings, funded by Cambridge University Press and the European Union.

Sue E. K. Otto holds a PhD in Spanish from the University of Iowa. She is Director of the University of Iowa Language Media Center and Adjunct Associate Professor of Spanish & Portuguese and International Programs. She is Past Chair of the Executive Board of the Computer Assisted Language Instruction Consortium (CALICO) and Past President and Past Executive Director of the International Association for Language Learning Technology (IALLT). She is a faculty member of the FLARE PhD program in Second Language Acquisition and teaches courses on multimedia and SLA.

Youngmin Park is a PhD student in Education at the University of California, Irvine, specializing in Language, Literacy and Technology. Previously a high school teacher and teacher trainer in Korea, she has published and presented on topics related to English teaching and learning in English as a Foreign Language environments. As a recipient of a fellowship from Korean Ministry of Education, she is using her studies at UCI to advance practical knowledge that she brings from her previous posts. Her research focuses on the use of digital media for English language learning, especially adolescent reading instruction. She is currently participating in research on Visual Syntactic Text Formatting (VSTF).

Joy Quah is a doctoral student at the University at Albany. Her interests include integrating multimedia, social media and project-based approaches in language learning. Her current projects involve examining various models of online and blended in-service ESL teacher education courses which prepare teachers to enable students to engage productively and creatively with emergent technologies in rapidly evolving literacy environments. Prior to commencing her doctoral studies, Joy worked with the Ministry of Education where she developed technology-integration courses for ESL teachers in Malaysia.

Hayo Reinders is Head of Learning Support at Middlesex University in London and Adjunct Professor at the University of Groningen, the Netherlands. He is also Editor of *Innovation in Language Learning and Teaching* and Convenor of the AILA Research Network for CALL and the Learner. His interests are in CALL, autonomy and out-of-class learning. He is a speaker for the Royal Society of New Zealand. He has edited or authored over 12 books and his most recent books are on teacher autonomy, teaching methodologies and second language acquisition. Dr Reinders edits a book series on 'New Language Learning and Teaching Environments' for Palgrave Macmillan.

Richard M. Robin is Professor of Slavic Linguistics and the Russian Language Program Director at the George Washington University. He has authored or co-authored numerous sets of materials for Russian, from textbooks with technological components to entirely Web-based resources. Much of his work has centred on listening comprehension. In the 1980s, he became the first to distribute listening comprehension exercises through the nascent internet. Among his current projects is the Simplified News – semi-authentic 'bridge' Web-based newscasts to allow listeners at the ACTFL Intermediate level move towards the Advanced threshold. Professor Robin is currently working on a case-based intermediate-level Russian multimedia packet with a business orientation.

Bernd Rüschoff studied English and Slavonic Languages at the University of Münster in Germany. He continued his studies at the University of Alberta in Canada and at the University of London, where he obtained a PhD in Russian Linguistics. Since then, his research focus has been in applied linguistics and second language acquisition as well as Technology Enhanced Language Learning (TELL). From 1993 to 1998 he held a professorship in TELL at the Pädagogische Hochschule in Karlsruhe, where his research focused on aspects of second language acquisition and TELL exploitation based on cognitive-constructivist approaches. Currently, Prof. Dr Rüschoff is chair and head of the didactics section of the Institute of Anglophone Studies at the University of DuisburgEssen.

Randall Sadler is an Associate Professor of Linguistics at the University of Illinois at Urbana-Champaign, where he teaches courses on Computer-Mediated Communication and Language Learning (CMCLL), Virtual Worlds and Language Learning (VWLL) and Teaching of Second Language Reading and Writing. His main research focus is on the role of technology in language learning, with a particular focus on how Virtual Worlds may be used to enhance that process. He has published in these areas in journals including the *Journal of English for Academic Purposes, CALICO Journal* and *Computers & Education.* His latest book, *Virtual Worlds, Telecollaboration, and Language Learning: From Theory to Practice* is published by Peter Lang.

Mathias Schulze is an Associate Professor of German at the University of Waterloo and the Director of the Waterloo Centre for German Studies. His research focuses on the application of Complexity Science to ICALL. He is also interested in second language development, particularly the acquisition of grammar, and online foreign-language learning and teaching. Together with Bryan Smith he edits the CALICO Journal, a peer-reviewed, online journal on Computer-Assisted Language Learning (http://calico.org). After he came to Waterloo in 2001, he developed a secondary research area in issues of individual and social English-German bilingualism.

Diane Slaouti is a Senior Lecturer in the School of Education, University of Manchester, where she has worked for 16 years, teaching and researching in the field of language teacher education (TESOL). A career which has taken her from the teaching of foreign languages in UK secondary schools to TESOL in international settings and then back to EAP in the UK Higher Education context has provided her with a variety of opportunities to explore technology in language education and it is this that forms her teaching and research focus. She is particularly interested in how teachers articulate the role of technology in language teaching and learning, and its relationship to situated practice and teacher beliefs.

Rubena St. Louis is a Senior Lecturer at Universidad Simón Bolívar in Caracas, Venezuela, where she designs and teaches blended courses in English for International Trade and English for Science and Technology at undergraduate level and Design and Evaluation of Learning Materials at graduate level. She holds a Masters degree in Applied Linguistics and her areas of interest are materials design, language learning and learner autonomy. Her work has been published in books and she has presented at both national and international EFL conferences.

Glenn Stockwell is Professor in Applied Linguistics at Waseda University, Tokyo, Japan. He teaches a range of English language subjects and several applied linguistics subjects. His research interests include computer-mediated communication, mobile learning and the role of technology in the language learning process. He is co-author of *CALL Dimensions* (2006) with Mike Levy, editor of *Computer-Assisted Language Learning: Diversity in Research and Practice* (2012), and has published widely in international journals in the field of CALL. He is the General Editor of *The JALT CALL Journal*, Associate Editor of *Computer Assisted Language Learning*, the *CALICO Journal*, and the *International Journal of Computer Assisted Language Learning and Teaching*.

Michael Thomas is Senior Lecturer in Language Learning Technologies at the University of Central Lancashire. He has taught at universities in the United Kingdom, Germany and Japan. His research interests are in task-based learning and CALL and distance and online learning. He is editor of two book series, 'Digital Education and Learning' (with J. P. Gee and J. Palfrey) and 'Advances in Digital Language Learning and Teaching' (with M. Peterson and M. Warschauer). Among his recent publications are *Handbook of Research on Web 2.0 and Second Language Learning* (2009), *Task-Based Language Learning & Teaching with Technology* (with H. Reinders) (2010), *Digital Education* (2011) and *Online Learning* (2011).

Paige Ware is Associate Professor in the Department of Teaching and Learning at Southern Methodist University, United States. Her research addresses technology and writing instruction at the secondary and post-secondary levels, issues of culture in telecollaboration, the integration of digital media into language exchange projects, and the use of online mentoring for pre-service teacher education. She has worked in Spain, Germany, Bangladesh and Guatemala and has co-developed online exchange projects in several countries. She is the principal investigator of Project CONNECT, a federally funded professional development grant that provides secondary teachers with additional training to support their work with recently immigrated second language learners.

Sylvia Warnecke is an Associate Lecturer in the Department of Languages at the UK Open University and Course Director at the Goethe Institute in Glasgow. She has extensive experience as a tutor, course designer and auditor in the field of online learning in distance and blended learning contexts. In 2011 she was appointed as supervisor of all virtual-learning environment-based courses produced at the 150 Goethe Institutes worldwide. She has undertaken research, presented papers and published articles and book chapters on matters of synchronous vs asynchronous online facilitation, identity, participation, task design, tutor role and training in connection with the use of technologies for the learning and teaching of languages and cultures.

Mark Warschauer is a Professor in the Department of Education and the Department of Informatics at the University of California, Irvine. Dr Warschauer's research focuses on the integration of information and communication technologies (ICT) in schools and community centres; the impact of ICT on language and literacy practices; and the relationship of ICT to institutional reform, democracy and social development. His most recent book, *Learning in the Cloud*, was published by Teachers College Press in 2011. His previous books have focused on the development of new electronic literacies among culturally and linguistically diverse students; on technology, equity and social inclusion; and on the role of ICT in second language learning and teaching.

Yong Zhao is currently Presidential Chair and Associate Dean for Global Education, College of Education at the University of Oregon, United States, where he also serves as the Director of the Center for Advanced Technology in Education (CATE). He is a fellow of the International Academy for Education. Until December 2010 he was University Distinguished Professor at the College of Education, Michigan State University, where he also served as the founding Director of the Center for Teaching and Technology, executive director of the Confucius Institute, as well as the US-China Center for Research on Educational Excellence. His research interests include educational policy, computer gaming and education, diffusion of innovations, teacher adoption of technology and computer-assisted language learning.

Binbin Zheng is a PhD student with a specialization in Language, Literacy, and Technology at University of California, Irvine. She has a Masters degree in Educational Technology and her research interests focus on using new technologies to facilitate teaching and learning. She has participated in several research projects on examining the effect of one-to-one laptop programs on student learning processes and outcomes. Her most recent project investigated social media and literacy, examining how blogging facilitates student participation and literacy development in a linguistically diverse fifth grade classroom environment. She has previously published her research on technology and writing in the *Journal of Adolescent & Adult Literacy*.

Foreword

For those readers with some familiarity concerning the topic of this book, it is perhaps surprising that the term 'computer-assisted language learning' (CALL) has survived to take its place in the title. This descriptive label certainly has been challenged over the years with numerous alternatives making an appearance, some briefly, others longer lasting, such as WELL for Web-enhanced language learning, MALL for mobile-assisted and even MTALL for machine-translation-assisted language learning. On this precarious topic, in an editorial entitled, 'Why call CALL "CALL"?' (Levy & Hubbard, 2005), Phil Hubbard and I argued in support of the term because of: the distinctiveness and complexity of language learning that was mediated by a computer, in some form; the need for an overarching term that could be readily employed to describe what we do; and the *de facto* existence of a substantial, international group of individuals and established professional organizations that have continued to use the term for well over two decades. These are perhaps some of the reasons why the label is useful. But reading this new book on contemporary CALL has prompted me to think about this question further.

First, what the new volume amply displays is that CALL now more than ever before has its own history. This is evident not only in Chapter 2, which focuses explicitly on historical perspectives on CALL, but also in many of the other chapters where individual authors have chosen to include their own topic histories, such as the chapters on telecollaboration, virtual worlds, intelligent CALL, distance CALL and language testing. Clearly, CALL includes persistent areas of attention and endeavour that have grown to become part of its profile. In fact, one of the earliest books on CALL by Higgins and Johns (1984), written almost 30 years ago, included sections on feedback, language learning games, language testing and artificial intelligence: these topics are represented anew in this volume, although, not surprisingly, with a great deal more sophistication. The point is that while the latest technologies may provide new avenues for exploration, collaboration and research, the interests of many of those who have dedicated themselves to CALL have been long-standing and, while new topics inevitably arise, there are many others that have been with us now for some considerable time. Also, incidentally, and because it is so tempting, we should not fault those of the past because their technologies were rudimentary, just as perhaps we hope those in the future do not dispatch our efforts too readily for exactly the same reason.

Second, and related to the earlier point, CALL does not represent one narrow topic area, but many. As CALL has grown and matured, it has increased in its size and complexity, and specializations have emerged. The range of topics under the CALL banner and represented in this volume are indeed impressive, and I am sure many of us will appreciate the scale of the vision that this collection entails. Commentators and critics sometimes attempt to circumscribe CALL too narrowly without appreciating the breadth of its interests and endeavours. This is evident sometimes in the desire to pull the field together under a unified, monolithic descriptive umbrella, be it philosophical, historical or theoretical. Happily this has proved rather difficult in CALL, as the genie continues to find a way to escape from the bottle.

Third, the current volume amply demonstrates that CALL has developed massively in terms of the expertise it can draw upon. The authors in this book are highly regarded experts and most if not all have spent long years researching their chosen topics. If we were to compare this work with one of even a decade ago, the differences would be resounding. Now there are fewer sweeping statements or assumptions, and a much greater capacity to absorb and respond to complexities, and then to attempt to resolve them through more finely gauged research questions and designs. Procedures for data capture are a case in point. For example, Meskill and Quah (Chapter 3) derive their understandings of student interactions in social media spaces by employing multiple datasets, such as focus groups, interviews, classroom and face-to-face learner video recordings, digital records of learner content development, open-ended questionnaires, learner self-reports and questionnaires and transcripts of collaborative work. Researchers like O'Dowd (Chapter 7) note that it was once common to read that intercultural learning could easily be achieved through tandem arrangements between international student partners. The reality turned out to be far less straightforward. Now instead of simply assuming that online partnerships will proceed unproblematically, interactional 'breakdowns' are investigated and factors contributing to sustainability in online interactions and relationships are examined. This contextual understanding and attention to detail is evident chapter by chapter, topic by topic in this volume. Cumulatively, the text represents a huge resource for anyone involved in the research and practice of CALL, both old hands and newcomers alike.

Finally, to once again return to reflect upon our name, label, moniker or tag, perhaps in the future a new term will emerge that better encompasses and represents our efforts in what we now call CALL. But whatever that term may be, I hope that it does not diminish CALL's body of work by omitting key areas, especially those that may appear to be on the edge of current mainstream practice. This includes some of the more established areas like intelligent CALL or distance CALL, as well as some of the more recent arrivals such as language learning that involves highly elaborated virtual worlds and multiplayer online gaming. This now leads me to what has impressed me so much about this new book on contemporary CALL. Not only are all the key topics present and accounted for, the discussion is state-of-the-art and written by top experts in the field. It will not surprise you, therefore, that I wholeheartedly recommend it to you.

Professor Mike Levy
The University of Queensland, Australia

References

Higgins, J., & Johns, T. (1984). *Computers in language learning*. London: Collins.
Levy, M., & Hubbard, P. (2005). Why call CALL 'CALL'? *Computer Assisted Language Learning, 18*(3), 143–9.

List of figures and tables

Figures

Tables

1

Contemporary computer-assisted language learning: The role of digital media and incremental change

Michael Thomas, Hayo Reinders and Mark Warschauer

Summary

This chapter introduces the main themes of contemporary computer-assisted language learning (CALL), and establishes a context for this volume as a whole. Over the last 20 to 30 years language learning has become one of the most popular and dynamic areas of education for the application of learning technologies. During this period CALL has consolidated itself as an innovative field of research and practice with the emergence of a series of refereed journals, annual conferences and national and international organizations. CALL courses and modules are now an integral part of taught undergraduate and graduate programmes around the world, as well as taught and research-based doctoral degrees. In addition to courses delivered in face-to-face settings, the last ten years in particular have also seen the emergence of a plethora of distance and online CALL courses. Technology is increasingly a core component of teacher training courses for language teachers across all educational levels, in both the state and private sectors. Most language teaching positions now require knowledge of the theory and practice of learning technologies and digital literacy skills. This chapter discusses these trends and considers how lessons learned from CALL can be instructive for wider developments in educational technology and the role of digital media.

Introduction

During the writing of this book, Steve Jobs, founder and CEO of technology company Apple died in October 2011. Rather surprisingly, and against the grain of educational technology advocates and vendors around the world, Jobs once said in an interview with *Wired* that 'What's wrong with education cannot be fixed with technology' (Wolf, 1996, n.p.). Given that Apple has played a significant role in the development of educational computing this is a strikingly honest appraisal. Although the interview took place in 1996, Jobs' comments remain significant for debates about contemporary educational technology for a number of reasons. As well as highlighting the perceived problem with the current system of Western education at the turn of the twenty-first century, they also imply that the standard government response of throwing technology at the problem is not the best way of solving it. Throwing technology at the problem of education today based on the use of highly emotive and often ambiguous terms such as, for example, the 'digital divide', 'digital education revolution' and 'digital natives', does little to address the underlying social, economic and pedagogical challenges that instead deserve the full attention of education reformers (see discussion in Gee, 2003, 2004; Gee & Hayes, 2011; Selwyn, 2011a, 2011b).

When Jobs was interviewed in 1996, an estimated 36 million people had access to the internet, instructors and learners used a dial-up connection and video was typically only available on CD-ROMs via a desktop computer in a dedicated computer lab. In 2012 the Web is 24/7 and 'always-on' and streaming video and digital content can be delivered to portable laptops, netbooks, media tablets and smartphones in real-time. Although technologies have changed in the intervening period and 36 million has grown to approximately 2.2 billion internet users worldwide (internetworldstats, 2012), the underlying structures of education have changed little in the post-industrial era. Indeed, while technologies can provide greater access to information and educational content, form online communities and aid learners in constructing their own learning environments, education with digital media is about much more than merely *delivering* the technology. The need to find the appropriate *sociotechnical infrastructure* remains, namely, the realistic educational design for integrating digital media in authentic environments, as does the need to understand the multiplicity of roles required of instructors and how to learn *with* digital media rather than merely *via* digital media (Jenkins, 2009; Lee, Dourish & Mark, 2006; Papert, 1993; Thomas, 2012; Warschauer, 2011).

Technology alone cannot improve the delivery of knowledge then; a new computer cannot make a teacher better. Nor can it provide a magic formula to improve learning; a new pencil does not make a child better at writing essays (Cuban, 1986, 2001). Technology itself 'does not bring about reform, but instead tends to amplify extant beliefs and practices' (Warschauer, 2011, p. 115). Teachers who believe in behaviourist principles without technology in the form of drills and cloze exercises are probably likely to replicate them through their use of digital media. Likewise, teachers influenced by constructivist principles are more likely to use digital media in the form of problem-solving approaches utilizing simulations and task-based approaches. Two decades of more empirical research on educational technology than ever before suggests that its successful implementation will be an incremental, uneven and complex process involving a variety of stakeholders rather than the much desired plug-and-play solution (Cuban, 2001).

Contemporary CALL: An exemplary case study

When it comes to these wider debates about the future of education and the role of technology within it, CALL has occupied somewhat of a niche location. Indeed, in its early decades, CALL was little more than a specialist interest within the wider field of language education in general (Chapelle, 2001, 2003; Motteram & Brett, 2000). Computer-assisted language learning is still quite a recent area of instruction, scholarship and research (see Davies, Otto and Rüschoff, this volume), and it has often been considered rather too technical and not pedagogically informed enough by classroom teachers, or alternatively, not technically sophisticated enough by those from a computing background.

Nevertheless, with the inevitability of change and the speed of innovation in new technologies, the emergence of the World Wide Web and related forms of Web-based learning, CALL has recently become more widely accepted as a recognized area of scholarship. Over the last decade the widespread availability of portable digital devices like laptop computers has consolidated this trend, and the more recent ubiquity of smartphones, tablets and e-readers seem likely to extend rather than reverse this trend over the next ten years.

Whereas only two decades ago language learners would have had to access CALL applications and foreign language tutorial programs on CD-ROMs, the growing centrality of digital media to peoples' everyday lives, both within and outside of formal teaching and learning contexts, has put thousands of language learning applications (or apps), electronic dictionaries and e-books in reach of everyone's pocket. During this period language learning has also become a strategically important subject area as Western universities turn away from their saturated domestic markets to build campuses overseas in the Middle and Far East with which to attract a new generation of international students. Indeed, today's foreign language learners in particular take for granted that any educational institution almost anywhere in the world will support interoperability and enable them to seamlessly integrate their digital devices and identities into their new personal learning environments (Bruns, 2008; Ito et al., 2009). Far from being marginal to educational reform, then, when understood in this trajectory, contemporary CALL represents an important example of long-term technological innovation, incorporating successes, failure and blind alleys, that ought to be of considerable value to anyone concerned with these macro-level debates. From this perspective contemporary CALL not only affords us a valuable vantage point from which to explore more established educational practices in language learning, but one from which we can interrogate normalized assumptions about the nature of education in general and the extent to which it can adequately prepare learners for the skills and knowledge necessary for the twenty-first century (Thomas, 2011a, 2011b).

Aspects of contemporary CALL

From its beginnings in mainframe technologies, through to personal computers (PCs), and the emergence of digital and latterly social media, CALL has developed to the point that it is now supported by a range of prominent international associations such as CALICO, EuroCALL, IALLT, IATEFL and JALT. These associations often oversee peer-reviewed journals, frequent international and national conferences, and maintain professional networks for an increasingly global group of interconnected CALL researchers and practitioners.

Whereas early forms of CALL often relied on amateur specialists, contemporary CALL is associated with a wide range of professional activities including designing and developing appropriate environments for learners, innovating in terms of the format and style of pedagogy and developing a rigorous research culture grounded in an evidence-based approach (Levy & Stockwell, 2006). CALL therefore embraces a wide array of stakeholders, from designers and classroom practitioners to researchers and commercial materials developers. With the advent of Web 2.0 technologies and applications (blogs, wikis, podcasting, photo and videosharing etc.), it may include learners themselves, who are increasingly able to *produce* as well as merely *consume* content and learning materials (Warschauer & Grimes, 2007).

In terms of its local influence and based on an increasingly rich range of research approaches, contemporary CALL can play a significant role in testing many of the assumptions of second language acquisition and understanding the processes of language learning. CALL research and practice today is positioned at the intersection of language learning and technology, and draws on a range of other fields such as psychology, sociology, natural language processing, linguistics, artificial intelligence, human-computer interaction and computer science for pedagogical and technological innovations. This positioning represents a change from the early days of CALL research when technological limitations and the restricted availability of resources and opportunities to develop CALL hardware and software significantly limited user involvement. From early beginnings with large mainframes beyond the budgets of schools and educational institutions, CALL technologies have developed as portable and mobile technologies have become more freely available. CALL pedagogies have changed accordingly, from those based on behaviourist principles to those supporting highly interactive and collaborative learning environments in which learners and instructors use technologies to enhance participation and communication by integrating combinations of the four main skills. To this we must also add that learners in today's CALL environments can potentially improve their technology and digital literacy skills as well as collaborate with language learners from other cultures to improve their understanding of cross-cultural communication in a globalized world. New broadband and mobile technologies are increasingly leading to opportunities that had earlier been envisaged but could not be realized by previous generations of technology. New trends in open access and open educational resources are likewise being facilitated by a Web 2.0 infrastructure built on sharing and collaboration thereby allowing access to digital materials and resources in online archives and communities (Warschauer & Grimes, 2007). Moreover, through dedicated social networking sites likes *Livemocha* and *Busuu*, the boundaries between instructors and learners are being deconstructed, with communities of *prosumer* learners simultaneously engaging in language learning, peer mentoring and instruction (Brick, 2012; Bruns, 2010; Harrison & Thomas, 2009).

Digital media and social CALL

While this vision incorporates some of the potential rewards from utilizing digital media, the history of CALL is also a cautionary tale that runs 'counter [to] the excessive mainstream eulogising of digital technologies in education' (Selwyn, 2011b, p. 154). In turning to consider what lessons contemporary CALL can learn from its own past a number of recent changes must be taken into account. In 2003, Bax hypothesized that CALL technologies are likely to achieve a state of normalization – a phase representing a high level of integration in everyday classroom environments (Bax, 2003). While many language educators make use of digital technologies, the reality remains that the vast majority may use little more than a computer attached to a projector to display presentation slides. This is even more the case in low-tech CALL contexts (see Gonzales & St. Louis, this volume), where although Web 2.0 technologies are becoming more visible, there are still significant barriers to entry (Thomas, 2009).

On the other hand, there is little doubt that a new generation of language teachers and educators currently completing their entry-level qualifications and acquiring teaching experience will have grown up using many aspects of digital media in their daily lives. While professional development is still required to understand how these technologies can be operationalized in formal educational contexts, the lack of expertise now required by digital media holds great promise for overcoming these initial barriers in professional development terms.

Previous CALL research identifies a number of important factors that influence the range and extent to which digital media can be integrated into any pedagogical context. These factors therefore present threats as well as opportunities in that a CALL solution may be adopted for spurious reasons. From its earliest beginnings it has rarely been the case that commercially available or locally made CALL resources can be operationalized in every classroom or learning context to the same effect. Such factors include financial constraints, as well as the extent to which the educational leadership exists to accompany the technology with substantive curriculum development or whether the technology is merely a sign of the need to innovate or market the institution.

The last three decades have seen a growing importance placed on the role of research in the process of content development and contemporary CALL reflects this, in that it consists of a range of fairly independent subfields, from ICALL (see Schulze & Heift, this volume) to the growing areas of online and distance learning and mobile learning – trends that have brought with them the consolidation of key terms and acronyms that are consistently used across these diverse areas (see Stockwell, this volume).

Contemporary CALL benefits from a firmer orientation towards empirical research, focusing less on providing justification for its use in relation to, for example, face-to-face instruction, and more on analysing the sociocultural context of learners and instructors involved in the process of language learning (see Motteram, Slaouti & Onat-Stelma, this volume). From earlier quantitative-based studies, CALL has increasingly developed to incorporate rich case studies and ethnographic research using qualitative data techniques and approaches (see Meskill & Quay, this volume). Through its evaluative and developmental frameworks it can contribute knowledge and experience to new environments driven by the latest pedagogical innovations.

Consequently, extending the research on the collaborative potential of digital media will be a concern of CALL researchers over the next decade. While the various attempts to describe a generation of new learners, from digital natives to Generation X, remain flawed, digital media are more widely used than ever before (Thomas, 2011a). Nevertheless, it is clear that whatever learners' competence level, they need assistance in understanding the responsibilities that accompany digital media, particularly in the area of privacy, copyright and security, rather than a 'guide on the side' approach. Raising consciousness among language learners of these issues is now an additional responsibility of language educators and such areas sit comfortably beside wider skill sets such as intercultural communication.

Earlier attempts to historicize CALL identified a number of different phases (see Davis, Otto & Rüschoff, this volume). From the vantage point of contemporary CALL, it is clear however that these phases did not emerge as a consequence of rejecting earlier phases; indeed, change does not occur at an identifiable point. Changes such as these occur over time and with a great deal of unevenness and overlap rather than as a result of a smooth and linear process of historical transition; the words 'revolution' and 'transformation' remain two of the most overused and inappropriate terms to describe change processes in education.

Building on Warschauer and Healey (1998) and Bax's (2003) three phases of CALL, we can perhaps identify a fourth social phase that distinguishes contemporary digital media. This shift towards social technologies is underpinned by developments in portable digital devices, from smartphones to tablets and e-readers, as well as by constructivist principles promoting collaborative learning on the social Web. Learning via a transmission mode of pedagogy has been rejected as a central mode of instruction in favour of participative experience. In terms of language learning, this view has become particularly influential and the process is now allied with the need to make learners active agents and users of the target language. Replacing the purely form focused pedagogies of the past, language learning is now focused more on communicative ability. The Common European Framework (CEF) as well as the Standards for Foreign Language Learning published in the United States both recognize this important shift. Contemporary CALL has a positive role to play in this process by promoting the use of a rich multiplicity of target language input as well as by creating authentic tasks in real-world environments that learners can relate to. Developments in Web-based instruction can produce authentic learning environments utilizing a task-based approach in which learners have been given a much more productive rather than passive role in the process (Thomas & Reinders, 2010).

In terms of the barriers to CALL integration noted earlier – these also include the overreliance on textbook-based curricula, the absence of technical or administrative support structures, encouragement and educational leadership, as well as the perceived risks of attempting to use technology in the first place – social technologies can help to address each of these areas as more of us establish and maintain important relationships via computer-mediated technologies in our daily lives.

Throughout its history CALL applications have sought to develop ways of transferring knowledge by developing interactive and visually stimulating environments that draw on multimedia technologies. Activities in such environments have developed around game-like quests and their natural affinities with problem-based learning, as well as the use of intelligent applications for providing feedback and assessment. Social CALL promises to add a new dimension to these environments, aiding rich forms of Web-based synchronous and asynchronous communication. Underlying engagement with these social technologies is the potential for enhanced learner engagement, collaboration and learner motivation within more decentralized, democratic and learner-centric environments (Reinders & Darasawang, 2011). At the heart of social CALL are pedagogies allied to encouraging higher-order critical thinking rather than a narrow subset of discrete skills like grammar, spelling and text decoding. Such applications of digital media are related to project-based research and rich open-ended activities not directly focused on narrower aims of raising standardized testing scores. These types of research-based activities require language learners to develop rich skill sets incorporating collecting and analysing data; evaluating results and solving problems as well as collaborating, sharing and disseminating information in ways that will be productive for others (Schafer, 2008; Warschauer, 2012). Twenty-first-century skills and learning require contemporary CALL applications and environments that will enable them to engage with creative practices in classroom environments with the aid of simulations and research-based tasks. Social CALL is therefore about more than the drill and practice tutorials that distinguished earlier phases in CALL applications, though a focus on these discrete skills will continue to develop and be part of a learner's personal learning environment, but in ways which are supplementary rather than central to developing learners' creative communication skills.

CALL enters the second decade of the twenty-first century in an era very different to that in which it was born in the middle of the last century. Learners today must engage with innovative educational practices if they are to be successful in a knowledge economy, driven as it is by how we access information and how it can be applied to create and sustain value for organizations.

CALL in the information era relies on new digital archives leading to greater interoperability between applications and platforms. Within a context of globalization, this necessitates collaborative practices. Contemporary multimedia technologies are becoming more interactive and responsive to learners (see Ware & Kessler, this volume). CALL is always open to future technologies. Research on virtual worlds suggests that they can replicate physical environments for learners as well as enable them to participate in creative experiences by building their own environments (see Sadler & Dooly, this volume). Digital games offer opportunities for collaboration and interaction difficult to achieve in other contexts (Reinders, 2012). On the horizon, as Google's augmented reality (AR) glasses suggest, is the potential for language learners to experience hybridized perception in both their L1 and desired foreign language by viewing the real world overlaid with digital information (Bilton, 2012).

Part of contemporary CALL is the realization that merely referencing success with small-scale projects and arguing that they can be generalized and applied in uniform ways across language learning environments is no longer feasible. CALL technologies do not provide a panacea for all of the challenges facing language learners and educators; integration cannot be seamless, nor can it be applied by all language educators in all contexts. The naïve optimism that suggested computers would replace language teachers has come and gone. Educational technology and contemporary CALL within it needs to be realistic. As articulated in Steve Jobs' comment noted at the beginning of this chapter, technology alone cannot change anything. This applies similarly to the euphoria surrounding Web 2.0 technologies, where for every blog started and maintained by a learner of a foreign language, there are many more left abandoned in the digital graveyard. Technologies produce potential affordances and frequently small-scale CALL projects do not last long enough to prove if the advances respond to little more than the immediate 'wow factor' (Bax, 2011b). It is essential for contemporary CALL to provide a pedagogical rationale that understands how people learn and how they learn with technology. So many CALL applications in the past have merely replicated behaviourist principles rather than fulfil expectations of greater interactivity. Educators need to work with programmers to produce the right kind of applications, building in opportunities for learner creativity as well as broader topics such as intercultural awareness. A key principle of Web 2.0 and mobile technologies is their intuitive design so that users do not need to spend a great deal of time understanding the complex functions required to use the application, at the expense of time available for engaging with the learning content. The promise of contemporary CALL is much more sensitive to applications that provide detailed feedback (see Ware & Kessler, this volume); maintain and develop applications that mirror authentic environments found in the real world (see Sadler & Dooly, this volume); provide users with opportunities for greater control, creativity and freedom to navigate content material; maintain and develop interoperable standards and consistency of quality; advance effective principles of design (see Hauck & Warnecke, this volume); and enable users to understand errors and react to them (see Brown, this volume).

Conclusion

As CALL progresses in the twenty-first century, it is important that it rids itself of a number of characteristics it has inherited from wider discourses on educational technology. These include adopting a more evenly balanced understanding of its potential, one which rejects technological determinism as well as the overly optimistic tone adopted by many educational technology advocates (see discussion in Cuban, 2001). While CALL, like other educational technologies, has promised significant advances in cross-cultural understanding, digital equity or collaborative communication, these remain potential gains which have yet to be conclusively realized. As Selwyn notes (2011a, 2011b; Selwyn, Potter & Cramer, 2010), this need not mean adopting a pessimistic tone in contemporary educational technology, but it means understanding the history of technological and pedagogical innovation, rather than trying to avoid its challenges as every new technology appears.

In this new era of social CALL, it is important to listen more to the voice of learners, to learn from the mistakes of the past, to remain cautious but optimistic for change. If the history of CALL were a case study for educational technology in general, then it would emphasize the genuine need to produce more effective spaces for our learners; that it ought not to result in ill-thought-out projects, all too quickly implemented; and that when grant funding is gone, worthwhile projects are sustainable. Contemporary CALL is not about replacing teachers with intelligent machines, or dispensing with all formal education altogether. It recognizes the importance of the teacher's role as *difficultator* rather than a mere facilitator or guide on the side (Bax, 2011b). It realizes that it is in and through effective teaching that CALL as well as education in general will prosper.

This volume represents an attempt to map the parameters of contemporary CALL and incorporates 18 previously unpublished chapters on topical areas authored by leading international researchers in the field. It is intended that the collection will provide a reference work for upper-level undergraduates, graduate students and researchers by giving them a more focused and clearer overview of how the different areas of contemporary CALL are shaping the field, as well as an understanding of the latest research approaches being developed to explore them. The contributors present accessible, yet detailed, analyses of recent methods and theory in the field, including recent applications in social media, second language teacher education, computer-assisted language testing, online and distance language learning, telecollaboration, 3D virtual worlds and digital games, mobile learning, CALL in low-tech contexts, intelligent CALL, technology-enhanced reading and writing, digital feedback and learner autonomy. It is intended that the volume will fulfil a range of aims and objectives, with the following being explicitly and comprehensively addressed:

(a) To provide a historical overview of the ways in which language learning technologies have been interpreted and to identify the antecedent conceptualizations, and relationships with other disciplines, that have contributed to current usages;

(b) To provide a critical overview of contemporary research in the field and the ways in which such research is leading to a clearer, and more coherent, theoretical understanding;

(c) To document research designed to explore the relationship between theory and practice in the promotion of technology-mediated learning in a range of formal and informal educational settings;

(d) To identify and explore new directions and approaches to research that can both extend and challenge existing models and paradigms within language learning technologies.

Given that it has passed through earlier phases in which technology was typically integrated without a clear pedagogical rationale, contemporary CALL, as this volume argues, has much to recommend it to debates about the wider process of technology integration. While promising 'incremental change' might not grab a passing reader's interest as much as the promise of a 'digital education revolution', such a vision remains more realistic and ultimately more well-attuned to the history of learning with technology.

References

Bax, S. (2003). CALL – past, present and future. *System, 31*(1), 13–28.

— (2011a). Normalisation revisited: The effective use of technology in language education. *International Journal of Computer-Assisted Language Learning and Teaching (IJCALLT), 1*(2), 1–15.

— (2011b). Beyond the wow factor. In M. Thomas (Ed.), *Digital education: Opportunities for social collaboration* (pp. 239–56). London & New York: Palgrave.

Bilton, N. (2012). Behind the Google goggles, virtual reality. Retrieved www.nytimes.com/2012/02/23/technology/google-glasses-will-be-powered-by-android.html

Brick, B. (2010). Social networking sites and language learning. *International Journal of Virtual and Personal Learning Environments, 2*(3), 18–31.

Bruns, Axel. (2008). *Blogs, Wikipedia, Second Life, and beyond: From production to produsage*. New York: Peter Lang.

Chapelle, C. (2001). *Computer applications in second language acquisition: Foundations for teaching, testing, and research*. Cambridge: Cambridge University Press.
— (2003). *English language learning and technology: Lectures on applied linguistics in the age of information and communication technology*. Amsterdam: John Benjamins Publishing.
Cuban, L. (1986). *Teachers and machines: The classroom use of technology since 1920*. New York: Teachers College Press.
— (2001). *Oversold and underused: Computers in classrooms, 1980–2000*. Cambridge: Harvard University Press.
Gee, J. P. (2003). *What video games have to teach us about learning and literacy*. New York: Palgrave Macmillan.
— (2004). *Situated language and learning: A critique of traditional schooling*. New York: Routledge.
Gee, J. P., & Hayes, E. (2011). *Language and learning in the digital age*. London & New York: Routledge.
Harrison, R., & Thomas, M. (2009). Identity in online communities: Social networking sites and language learning. *International Journal of Emerging Technologies and Society, 7*(2), 108–23.
Internetworldstats (2012). Internet growth statistics: Usage and poplulation statistics. Retrieved from www.internetworldstats.com/emarketing.htm
Ito, M., Baumer, S., Bittanti, M., Boyd, D., Cody, R., Herr-Stephenson, B. et al. (2009). *Hanging out, messing around, geeking out: Living and learning with new media*. Cambridge, MA: MIT Press.
Jenkins, H. (2009). *Confronting the challenges of participatory culture: Media education for the 21st century*. Cambridge, MA: MIT Press.
Lee, C. P., Dourish, P., & Mark, G. (2006). *The human infrastructure of cyberinfrastructure*. Proceedings of CSCW '06. Retrieved from http://portal.acm/org
Levy, M., & Stockwell, G. (2006). *CALL dimensions: Options and issues in computer-assisted language learning*. Mahweh, NJ & London: Lawrence Erlbaum Associates.
Motteram, G., & Brett, P. (2000). A special interest in computers. *Learning and teaching with information and communications technologies*. Whitstable: IATEFL Publications.
Papert, S. (1993). *The children's machine: Rethinking school in the age of the computer*. New York: Basic Books.
Reinders, H. (2012) (Ed.). *Digital games in language learning and teaching*. Basingstoke: Palgrave Macmillan.
Reinders, H., & Darasawang, P. (2011). Diversity in language support. In G. Stockwell (Ed.), *Computer-assisted language learning: Diversity in research and practice*. Cambridge: Cambridge University Press.
Selwyn, N. (2011a). *Education and technology: Key issues and debates*. London & New York: Continuum.
— (2011b). *Schools and schooling in the digital age: A critical analysis*. London & New York: Routledge.
Selwyn, N., Potter, J., & Cranmer, S. (2010). *Primary schools and ICT: Learning from pupil perspectives*. London & New York: Continuum.
Shaffer, D. (2008). Education in the digital age. *The Nordic Journal of Digital Literacy, 4*(1), 39–51.
Thomas, M. (2009) (Ed.). *Handbook of research on Web 2.0 and second language learning*. Hershey, PA: Information Science Reference.

— (2011a) (Ed.). *Deconstructing digital natives: Young people, technology and the new literacies*. London & New York: Routledge.
— (2011b) (Ed.). *Digital education: Opportunities for social collaboration*. London & New York: Palgrave Macmillan.
— (2012). Contextualising digital game-based language learning: Transformational paradigm shift or business as usual? In H. Reinders (Ed.), *Digital games in language learning and teaching* (pp. 11–31). Basingstoke: Palgrave Macmillan.
Thomas, M., & Reinders, H. (2010) (Eds.). *Task-based language learning and teaching with technology*. London & New York: Continuum.
Warschauer, M. (2011). *Learning in the cloud: How (and why) to transform schools with digital media*. New York & London: Teachers College Press.
Warschauer, M., & Grimes, D. (2007). Audience, authorship, and artifact: The emergent semiotics of Web 2.0. *Annual Review of Applied Linguistics, 27*, 1–23.
Warschauer, M., & Healey, D. (1998). Computers and language learning: An overview, *Language Teaching, 31*, 57–71.
Wolf, G. (1996). The Wired interview. Steve Jobs: The next insanely great thing. *Wired*. Retrieved from www.wired.com/wired/archive/4.02/jobs_pr.html

PART ONE

The CALL context

Section introduction

Michael Thomas, Hayo Reinders and Mark Warschauer

In order to understand the development of computer-assisted language learning (CALL) over the last three decades it is necessary to begin by considering a number of its most important dimensions (Levy & Stockwell, 2006). During this time CALL research has evolved from a relatively narrow area of specialist interest to a more widespread activity characterized by an increasing range of subfields. These developments are a product of numerous factors including in particular advances in technologies that have enabled earlier pedagogical aims to be realized as faster broadband speeds have produced more sophisticated multimedia applications and environments (Pegrum, 2009).

The five chapters in the first section of this volume map the parameters of CALL, focusing on how the field has developed historically over this period as it has moved towards discussion of technology integration and normalization (Bax, 2003, 2011; Warschauer & Healey, 1998); the emergence of different research trends and the current state of CALL research in the age of digital and social media (Tudini, 2010); the importance of second language teacher professional development and CALL (Hubbard & Levy, 2006); an overview of the key area of language testing and the role of digital technologies in driving forward advances in intelligent testing platforms (Brown, 1997); and a focus on CALL materials design in an era in which instructors with limited expertise can harness Web 2.0 technologies to create sophisticated technology-mediated language learning environments based on increased social presence and community (Kehrwald, 2008, 2010).

Chapter 2 is a particularly important one in the context of the whole volume and it provides an authoritative overview of the historical perspectives that have shaped CALL during the last three decades since digital technologies started to become more widespread. Davies, Otto and Rüschoff discuss how developments in the field of CALL have been shaped by available technologies as much as by important trends in second language acquisition and theories of language education. Discussing previous notable attempts to historicize CALL by Warschauer and Healey (1998) and Bax (2003, 2011), the authors describe how invariably any attempt to produce such a narrative risks being too linear, whereas the underlying reality is more complex with overlapping and often contradictory dimensions. The history of CALL that emerges from the chapter covers the period from the dominance of cognitive and psycholinguistic approaches through to more recent developments focusing on participation and the social turn in SLA. In the language classroom such developments have seen CALL technologies focused on one discrete skill, to more integrated approaches combining interactive engagement in reading, writing, speaking and listening. In this chapter pedagogical developments are read against a background of increasingly sophisticated technologies, and the transition from large mainframes through to the widespread availability of the World Wide Web and more recently, portable digital devices.

Developments from the most recent phase of the World Wide Web and social media are positioned at the centre of Chapter 3 which discusses research trends in CALL, focusing in particular on the increasingly sophisticated research approaches developed to map the rich interactive environments afforded by language learning environments in Web 2.0. Meskill and Quah highlight the range of CALL research approaches that have been used to understand the complex online, virtual and social environments that language learners now use. They argue that in researching these new social dimensions of CALL, new research approaches are being borrowed from other disciplines and developed in an applied linguistics context thus leading to an enrichment of CALL research and scholarship. The chapter focuses in particular on researching online language learning environments, the pedagogies being used and the 'online social/affective dimensions' to highlight a new set of methodological techniques to advance CALL research.

In Chapter 4 the focus turns to consider the important challenge of teacher education. Motteram, Slaouti and Onat-Stelma present a strong case for the need to have a broad realignment of teacher education related to CALL based on sociocultural theory rather than theory from second language acquisition (SLA). Indeed, sociocultural theory is an increasingly strong presence in work on CALL research and the chapter reflects this social turn among leading scholars, replacing the earlier cognitive approach with a more finely attuned understanding of the multifarious social and cultural contexts and dimensions in which learners study and learn languages. The chapter illustrates the argument with the aid of three vignettes developed from earlier research undertaken with Cambridge University Press on language teacher education and CALL (Motteram, 2011).

Developments in technology have been particularly evident in the internationally important area of language testing where significant developments have been made during the last three decades. In Chapter 5, 'Research on Computers in Language Testing: Past, Present and Future', James Dean Brown provides a thorough overview of research trends, examining the past, present and potential future of computer-based language testing (CBLT). Brown explains the practical research that dominated past engagement on the subject, particularly in the area of item banking and computer-adaptive language testing. Moving into the present, he demonstrates how a number of specialist areas have evolved and widened their approach in the process by incorporating foci on computer assessment of vocabulary items, as well as the four main skills, greater understanding of the test takers' characteristics and the training required of instructors who utilize new technologies.

In the final chapter in Part One, we turn to consider research on the important area of CALL materials design. In Chapter 6, 'Materials Design in CALL: Social Presence in Online Environments', two researchers from the UK Open University, Hauck and Warnecke, focus on Johnson's (1999) argument that understanding the sociocultural aspects of technology-enhanced learning could significantly enhance CALL course and materials design, thereby producing more effective language learning environments. They pursue these claims by examining the marginalized role of social presence (SP), a concept which derives from Garrison, Anderson and Archer's (2000) widely cited Community of Inquiry (CoI) model. Recent research from a study involving a tutor training course in teaching English for Academic Purposes (EAP) is presented in order to examine how materials design can be used to generate and enhance effective social presence in computer-mediated communication environments. By researching the asynchronous discussion board posts of the trainee tutors, they argue for the need to re-approach the community of inquiry model which has often been guilty of marginalizing social presence as opposed to cognitive and teaching presence. In their final recommendations, a new model is identified in which social presence plays a key role in informing the process of CALL materials design and development.

The concerns of these six chapters describe how CALL environments have changed and evolved over the last 30 years. They each reinforce the importance of new instructor-learner relationships and how new technologies have presented CALL materials designers and developers with opportunities to better realize interactive and collaborative pedagogies that have been imagined at earlier stages in the history of CALL but were previously impossible due to technical constraints.

References

Bax, S. (2003). CALL – Past, present and future. *System, 31*(1), 13–28.

— (2011). Normalisation revisited: The effective use of technology in language education. *International Journal of Computer-Assisted Language Learning and Teaching, 1*(2), 1–15.

Brown, J. D. (1997). Computers in language testing: Present research and some future directions. *Language Learning and Technology, 1*(1), 44–59.

Garrison, D. R., Anderson, T., & Archer, W. (2000). Critical inquiry in a text-based environment: Computer conferencing in higher education. *The Internet and Higher Education, 2*(2–3), 87–105.

Kehrwald, B. (2008). Understanding social presence in text-based online learning environments. *Distance Education, 29*(1), 89.

— (2010). Being online: Social presence and subjectivity in online learning. *London Review of Education, 8*(1), 39–50.

Levy, M., & Stockwell, G. (2006). *CALL dimensions: Options and issues in computer-assisted language learning.* Mahwah, NJ: Lawrence Erlbaum Associates.

Motteram, G. (2011). Developing language learning materials with technology. In B. Tomlinson (Ed.), *Materials development in language teaching* (pp. 303–27). Cambridge: Cambridge University Press.
Pegrum, M. (2009). *From blogs to bombs: The future of digital technologies in education.* Perth: University of Western Australia.
Tudini, V. (2010). *Online second language acquisition.* New York: Continuum.
Warschauer, M., & Healey, D. (1998). Computers and language learning: An overview, *Language Teaching, 31*, 57–71.

2

Historical perspectives on CALL

Graham Davies[1], Sue E. K. Otto and Bernd Rüschoff

Summary

Historically computer-assisted language learning (CALL) has been shaped not only by trends in language pedagogy and second language acquisition (SLA) theories, but also by the state of computer technology. While the evolution of computer technology can be described in a relatively linear and organized fashion, SLA and language pedagogy have developed as a disorganized, multipronged and often contradictory collection of notions and practices. As a result, viewing the growth of CALL through a theoretical and pedagogical lens reveals a complex and fascinating history that spans decades of technological advancement and reflects the multifaceted field of language pedagogy and SLA research from which it arose. This chapter traces the evolution of CALL from the last half of the twentieth century – when cognitive and psycholinguistic theories of SLA predominated – into the twenty-first century, when theories and pedagogies that emphasize the social dimensions of language learning have gained traction. Computer technology grew from primitive mainframes to powerful networked multimedia microcomputers with access to the internet and World Wide Web. Within this context, CALL has progressed from drill and practice exercises targeting grammar and vocabulary towards a wide array of sophisticated interactive programs for reading, writing, listening, pronunciation and culture.

Introduction

The history of CALL has been well documented. Sanders (1995) and Levy (1997) cover the period from its beginnings in the 1960s until the mid-1990s, and Delcloque (2000) provides a comprehensive account of CALL until the beginning of the new millennium. Davies (1997) covers the period 1976–96, reflecting on his personal experiences and reminding us that there are many lessons that we can learn from the past. Jung (2005) takes a bibliometric approach, focusing on the contents and nature of publications on CALL and how they have reflected its constantly changing manifestations. Butler-Pascoe (2011) takes us back to the early stages of the use of courseware in second language teaching in the 1960s, through the emergence of multimedia in the 1990s and up to new developments in the twenty-first century encompassing the use of Web 2.0 tools that provide new opportunities for computer-mediated communication (CMC). In light of these previous studies, the aim of this chapter is to provide a historical overview of the ways in which language learning technologies have been interpreted and to identify the antecedent conceptualizations, and relationships with other disciplines that have contributed to current usages.

Historically computer-assisted language learning has been shaped not only by trends in language pedagogy and SLA theories, but also by the state of computer technology. While the evolution of computer technology can be described in a relatively linear and organized fashion, SLA and language pedagogy have developed as a disorganized, multipronged and often contradictory collection of notions and practices. As a result, viewing the growth of CALL through a theoretical and pedagogical lens reveals a complex and fascinating history that spans decades of technological advancement and reflects the multifaceted field of language pedagogy and SLA research from which it arose. This chapter traces the evolution of CALL from the last half of the twentieth century, when cognitive and psycholinguistic theories predominated, through the first decade of the twenty-first century, during which rising interest in theories and pedagogy that emphasize the social dimensions of language learning has coincided with the explosion in social networking and mobile technologies.

Origin of the term CALL

It is not entirely clear when the term CALL first appeared. Computer-assisted instruction (CAI) and computer-assisted learning (CAL) predate CALL as generic terms, and CALI (computer-assisted language instruction) was incorporated into the name of the professional association CALICO (Computer-Assisted Language Instructed Consortium), which was founded in the United States in 1982. CALL appears to have originated in the United Kingdom, reflecting a student-centred focus on learning rather than instruction. The earliest documented use of the term CALL that we have found is in a conference paper by Davies and Steel (1981). By 1982 the term CALL was in widespread use in the United Kingdom, featuring in the title of the newsletter *CALLBOARD*, which was first published by Ealing College of Higher Education in 1982, and in Davies and Higgins (1982). TESOL also adopted the term CALL, setting up its CALL Interest Section (CALL-IS) in 1983 (Kenner, 1996; Stevens, 2003).

An alternative term to CALL emerged in the 1980s, namely technology-enhanced language learning (TELL), which was felt to provide a more accurate description of the activities which fall broadly within the range of CALL (Brown, 1988; Bush & Terry, 1997).

TELL was adopted by the TELL Consortium (now defunct), founded at the University of Hull in 1993, and it figured in the name of the journal of CALL-Austria, *TELL&CALL* (now defunct). The fact that the academic community that was involved in attempts to integrate computer technologies into language learning saw the need to rethink the original term and acronym is indicative of the fact that from very early on theoreticians and practitioners alike saw the potential for enhancing rather than simply assisting language learning and classroom practice when assessing emerging technological applications and tools.

Early CALL: 1960s to 1970s

Most of the activity in CALL in its early days took place in the United States. Programs were mainframe-based and primarily served the roles of tutor and drillmaster. These programs were touted as a means to relieve teachers of repetitive tasks in the classroom, allowing them to concentrate on communicative activities, give students immediate feedback on their errors and track student performance, providing remedial work when indicated. Pedagogically, language instruction was still guided by behaviourist models of cognitive theory, which emphasized learning through repetitive practice and negative and positive feedback. The audio-lingual method had emerged to place new emphasis on oral skills, but this method also emphasized drill-and-practice and reflected the continued belief in the importance of grammar, with roots in grammar-translation. Among the highest profile early mainframe projects were the PLATO project (Programmed Logic for Automated Teaching Operations) (Hart, 1995) at the University of Illinois and the TICCIT project (Time-shared Interactive Computer Controlled Information Television) (Anderson, 1976; Jones, 1995) at the University of Texas and Brigham Young University (BYU).

The PLATO project began in 1960 and hit its peak in the mid- to late 1970s with the PLATO IV project. Based on the computing power of a large mainframe computer, the PLATO IV system's most notable features were the plasma graphics terminals, which could display animation and smoothly rendered graphics, including complex foreign characters such as Chinese, its multimedia capability using a computer-controlled audio device, the touch-screen input option, centralized storage and delivery of large amounts of instructional material and an online community space where bulletin board exchanges and multiplayer gameplaying took place. PLATO's advanced technical features foreshadowed a number of key capacities we take for granted in our era of social networking, media-rich information and touch-screen hand-held technologies that increasingly rely on the Cloud for central storage of assets.

Using the TUTOR programming language, curricular materials were developed for many languages, including French, German, Hebrew, Chinese, Latin, Russian, ESL, Spanish, Hindi, Swahili and Swedish. Traditional grammar drill-and-practice lessons coexisted with lessons developed for Chinese tone recognition, German phonetics,

English literature and reading practice. Many PLATO terminals were installed at the University of Illinois, and by the late 1970s over 50,000 hours of language instruction per semester were typically logged (Hart, 1995). Part of the vision for PLATO was to have remote sites connected to the Illinois mainframe and services sold by subscription. PLATO terminals could be based anywhere there was a phone connection for distance time-sharing of the lesson development tools by teachers and of the instructional materials by students. In addition to the specific equipment involved and the cost of the subscription, the long-distance phone charges that accrued when users accessed the system were one of the biggest drawbacks of PLATO and constituted one factor for its lack of success as a viable distance learning option. Although PLATO did not ultimately succeed as a commercial distance education venture, it did succeed as a large-scale instructional platform during the years of its existence, delivering massive amounts of language instruction in multiple languages to an enormous number of students.

The TICCIT project began in 1972 as a joint project of the Mitre Corporation with the University of Texas and BYU that aimed to develop instructional materials for remedial English and mathematics combining computer and television technologies. The system used television to present information and examples. The student would select a desired video choice on the computer, which would send a message to an operator, who would load the appropriate tape and play the program, routing the signal to the television at the student's workstation (Anderson, 1976). Unlike some of the other instructional software of the time that carefully controlled the learner's pathway through lessons and prescribed the difficulty level and help based on performance, learner control was one of the basic tenets that guided TICCIT development (Jones, 1995). Students could move freely through the courseware, able to skip ahead, go back and repeat or ask for more explanation or help on a concept, as desired. Such developments, even when seen from a present-day perspective, can already be described as innovative from an educational perspective too. Developers already had in mind principles which are currently regarded as important ingredients of learning practice, such as self-determined and autonomous learning, flexibility of access or even student-orientation.

In 1977 the original grant funding expired and TICCIT moved to BYU, where it was expanded to include ESL, French, German, Italian and Spanish. (Although the TICCIT name persisted, the television technology disappeared from the system at this point.) Students could visually see what parts of the courseware they had completed and an advisor function made suggestions for what they should do next but, in keeping with the original TICCIT philosophy of learner control, it was up to the student to decide how to use the exercises (which ones and in what order) and which help mechanisms to access. The best-known foreign language work in TICCIT for languages was done at BYU by Randall Jones, who created a comprehensive course for German grammar, which combined tutorials and practice components and continued until 1992, when it was replaced by a microcomputer-based version known as CLIPS (Computerized Language Instruction and Practice Software). CLIPS still exists for English, ESL and

Spanish grammar, and it is available online by subscription offered by a commercial learning software company.

The 1970s saw the production of many other smaller software development projects on mainframes and minicomputers in the United States. These projects included development of authoring tools to create exercises such as *CALIS* (Hussein, Phelps & Bessent, 1980) and *Dasher* (Pusack & Otto, 1983–2010) – as well as packaged exercises and tutorials, such as *DECU/TUCO* (Taylor, 1987), and the *Course in Medical and Technical Terminology*, focusing on instruction in medical and scientific terms derived from Greek and Latin (Tebben, 1979). It is interesting to note that authoring tools were among the first developments in these early stages of CALL, as they were able to assist teachers in their efforts to provide their learners with more authentic, up-to-date as well as target-group-specific and learner-differentiated content.

In her article reporting the results of her 1978–9 survey on CAI in foreign languages in the United States, Olsen (1980) lists 62 language departments from 52 institutions in 24 of the 50 states as using computers for language instruction. Programs almost exclusively targeted first- and second-year language courses. Predictably, the top three languages for which CAI programs existed were French, Spanish and German, with Latin a close fourth. Many of the departments that responded to Olsen's survey had indicated that they did not use CAI, citing a number of common reasons, including: cost of equipment and program development; scepticism about the ability of a machine to teach languages; lack of peer recognition of CAI materials development efforts for tenure and promotion; lack of trained personnel; lack of ready-made programs; and the inability of local computing technology to handle diacritical marks or alternate fonts. Interestingly, these problems were to persist for decades, and one of the most frustrating and stubborn issues was to be typing and display of foreign characters.

In the early days of computing, foreign characters were always problematic. Regular terminals commonly used on campuses to connect to mainframes could not display the special characters required for foreign languages. (The PLATO system was an exception, as were a few other special graphics terminals available at the time.) Various conventions were typically used to indicate special characters – for example a vowel followed by a colon indicated an umlauted character or a vowel followed by an apostrophe indicated a character with an acute accent. Even when it became possible to display text that contained foreign characters, it was a long time before any real standardization existed for fonts containing characters beyond those used in common European languages. A multiplicity of foreign character fonts emerged for languages in non-Roman characters, such as Russian, Hebrew and Arabic; and there were even special boards that enabled typing and displaying languages such as Chinese. Solutions were often expensive and usually local – that is, dependent on locally installed hardware and software. With the creation of the Unicode consortium and their efforts over the last 20 years to establish a universal character encoding standard, these issues have slowly been resolved.

There was little significant activity in CALL in the United Kingdom until the early 1980s. Rex Last had been developing CALL materials on a mainframe ICL1904S computer at the University of Hull in the late 1970s, using an authoring package known simply as EXERCISE, which was Last's own creation, enabling him to produce large quantities of drill-and-practice activities for students of German. EXERCISE was also used to create materials for students of Dutch. Interesting though they were, Last's materials could not be used outside the environment in which they were created – one of the drawbacks of working on a university's mainframe computer (Last, 1984).

While most of the programs from the 1970s have long since disappeared, a few survived in one form or another into the early twenty-first century due to success in commercial distribution and sustained upgrading to new platforms, including *Dasher*, *CALIS* (later *WinCALIS*) and the *Course in Medical and Technical Terminology*, as mentioned above. Of course, despite their longevity, these older drill-and practice programs by no means represent current thinking about the best use of computer technology for language learning. Nevertheless, each generation of CALL has resulted in valuable lessons learned, which eventually filtered down to later adopters.

Each major advance in computing technology has triggered a temporary step backwards in the production and delivery of CALL materials. What had arduously been developed for one dominant technology had to be rethought and reprogrammed for the promising new technology. When microcomputers first appeared, they did not seem to pose a real threat to large mainframes that offered powerful data processing and centralized storage of lessons and record-keeping data. With their 48K of memory and no easily accessible storage for programs and data (floppy or hard disk), early microcomputers seemed more like toys than serious computers. Nevertheless, they quickly grew into the much cheaper platform of choice with graphics capabilities that allowed graphic, animation and foreign character entry and display not available from standard mainframe systems. When the internet and World Wide Web gained traction, developers had to shift gears again, facing problems such as a new generation of underdeveloped development tools and the loss of the ability to control and deliver media with the precision possible with older technologies such as videodisc. Of course, these issues now seem irrelevant, given the advances that produced the social Web that is defined by the mobile devices and creative tools and services that have emerged during the first part of the twenty-first century (O'Reilly, 2005).

This last transition to the Web has also signalled a significant shift in the use of technology for language learning. The exploitation of the technology as a tutor and drillmaster – that is, a replacement for the teacher – has faded into the background, overshadowed by an extensive array of Web-based tools to enable creative and communicative activities. Although there are still tutorial and practice programs, they are now produced as a matter of course by textbook publishers as part of the standard 'ancillary' package. At the same time, faculty developers no longer focus on programming or authoring exercise materials. Instead they have shifted their efforts to the design of activities that incorporate the powerful new communication tools at their disposal (Otto & Pusack, 2009).

CALL and the microcomputer: The 1980s

The impact of CALL and technology-enhanced applications for language learning changed dramatically with the advent of the first affordable microcomputers, which appeared in educational institutions in increasing numbers from the late 1970s onwards. This included primary and secondary schools, which up until this time had little or no access to computers. The first complete CALL packages for microcomputers emerged in the early 1980s, for example *Apfeldeutsch* (Williams, Davies & Williams, 1981), a substantial set of drill-and-practice exercises for beginners in German, which ran on the Apple II computer. Compatibility between different microcomputers was a major problem at this time. Each microcomputer manufacturer – and there were many of them – used its own operating system, with the result that programs could not easily be exchanged between institutions, and software publishers were unsure about which computer to target in order to achieve reasonable sales. The microcomputer boom period of the early 1980s saw a flurry of publications on CALL (Ahmad et al., 1985; Davies & Higgins, 1982; Davies & Higgins, 1985; Higgins & Johns, 1984; Hope, Taylor & Pusack, 1984; Kenning & Kenning, 1984; Last, 1984). The first professional CALL associations were also founded at this time: CALICO in the United States (1982) and EUROCALL in Europe (1986). EUROCALL was put on a firmer footing in 1993, when it received funding from the European Commission (EU) that enabled it to become a formal professional association.

Early microcomputers had limited graphic options and monochrome displays, but they offered considerable possibilities for text-based practice. In terms of language teaching pedagogy, however, the clock was turned back in the early 1980s, resulting in the production of an abundance of grammar and vocabulary practice programs – drill-and-practice or 'drill-and-kill' – in spite of the fact that the communicative approach was by now well established. But some programs were more imaginative, for example CLEF (1985) and TUCO II (Taylor, 1987), offering a semi-intelligent approach, making use of extensive tutorial sequences, discrete error analysis and feedback. Some CALL developers explored artificial intelligence (AI), utilizing semantic and syntactic parsers for processing students' natural language responses. Among the earliest attempts to produce microcomputer-based AI software for foreign language were the Spanish games for communicative practice, *Juegos Comunicativos* (Bassein & Underwood, 1985) and the German spy game *Spion* (Sanders & Sanders, 1995). These programs emphasized the communicative aspects of language, which resonated with current classroom methodologies that focused on proficiency and communicative competence.

Developers of CALL software began to find their feet using the new medium and discovered new pedagogical approaches, which led to the production of text-only simulations such as a *Granville: The Prize Holiday Package* (Cambridge University Press, 1986) and *London Adventure* (The British Council/Cambridge University Press, 1986). There were also computerized action mazes, based on printed works such as Berer and Rinvolucri (1981).

Apart from the simulations described above, there were few innovative pedagogical approaches in CALL that arose as a direct result of the use of information and communications technology (ICT). Respondents to Levy's survey of CALL conceptual frameworks, which he concluded in 1991, cited Data-Driven Learning (DDL) – the use of concordancers in the classroom – as the only approach that was 'conceived with the computer in mind' (Levy, 1997, p. 123). This approach was rooted in the idea that discovery-oriented, inductive or concept learning by or from examples might be more fruitful when addressing grammar or vocabulary (Johns & King, 1991). In addition, the tools developed, for example concordancing software or context-oriented learnware such as Johns's appropriately named *Contexts* program (Johns, 1997), are perfect examples of technology empowering classroom practice with new and additional options that would not have been possible without it.

It is interesting to note that the advent of technology-enhanced learning materials on microcomputers coincided with a rethinking of the methodological framework of language learning in general (Bax, 2003; Warschauer, 1996; Warschauer & Healey, 1998). Trends such as task-based learning (TBL) and cognitive-constructivist approaches gradually found their match in digital technologies, as it was recognized that computer tools might be one option to facilitate the implementation of a methodology for language learning focusing more on authenticity in contents, contexts and tasks. Digital technologies afforded more flexibility in application and exploitation, as these were not restricted, to name but one aspect, by the kinds of linearity in content presentation characteristic of analogue media, for example, audiotapes or videos. Consequently, new technologies started to be seen by some as having the potential to solve a number of practical problems, particularly in more flexibly exploiting authentic resources and exposing learners to 'thinking tasks', rather than pure exercises. This theoretical background did, in fact, stimulate both theoreticians and practitioners. DDL can be summarized as follows:

- a focus on the exploitation of authentic materials even when dealing with tasks such as the acquisition of grammatical structures and lexical items;
- a focus on real, exploratory tasks and activities rather than traditional 'drill-and-kill' exercises;
- a focus on learner-centred activities;
- a focus on the use of computer-assisted cognitive tools, for example text corpora and concordancing software, rather than ready-made or off-the-shelf learnware.

The ideas underlying DDL are, in fact, firmly rooted in some of the English as a Foreign Language paradigms emerging in the course of the 1980s. Most obviously, concepts described as TBL – an approach initially developed in the 1980s by the Indian language teaching specialist, N. S. Prabhu – form a relevant backbone to such developments in

CALL (Prabhu, 1987). There can be no doubt that TBL is relevant to the exploitation of new technologies for language teaching in general as well as DDL in particular. TBL is based on the idea that the acquisition of language and linguistic competence as well as language and language learning awareness can best be realized through tasks which encourage the learner not to focus explicitly on the structure and the rules of the new language. Learners will acquire the form of the foreign language because they are engaged in exploring aspects of the target language on the basis of authentic content. Task-oriented integration of CALL applications into language learning processes, based on constructivist principles, gradually became more common practice, and some of the following examples can be regarded as exemplary for that (Rüschoff, 2002a, 2002b).

Consequently, CALL developers started to consider options of facilitating the integration of genuine or authentic materials in the language classroom as well as to focus on more genuine and real activities in CALL-enhanced learning practice. Authentic or genuine materials, as Widdowson (1979, p. 80) pointed out, are language samples not constructed for the purpose of language learning. Authentic tasks would then be tasks and learning projects as well as activities of knowledge construction, which truly enable learners to explore the target language in its structure and functionality when working with such genuine 'texts'. Little (1989, p. 5) describes this approach to authenticity in language learning as creating opportunities for the learner to 'psychologically interact' with the target language, 'by which we mean the psychological processing of target language input in such a way that it interlocks with and modifies the learner's existing knowledge'.

Among the innovative uses of new technologies in language learning, tools for the creation of discovery-based and exploratory learning materials rank very highly within a typology of TELL software. One such tool is concordancing software, originally developed as a device to assist research in corpus linguistics. Concordancers can be used with any textual corpus consisting of a potentially unlimited number of texts compiled into a database. Their basic function is to extract lists with contexts of any word or structure entered into the search option, allowing the learner to research 'the company that words keep', as Johns (1986, p. 121) put it (based on Firth, 1957), and to try to discover how language works or what particular terms or vocabulary mean from sample contexts extracted from text corpora. Software such as Oxford University Press's *Micro-Concord* (Johns, 1986), Longman's *Mini-Concordancer* and later tools such as Athelstan's *MonoConc*, provided access to any electronic text and the possibility of conducting a search for the occurrence of particular words, structures or combination of words. These are then listed in contexts lists – so-called concordances. Learners are invited to deduce for themselves the exact difference in meaning, connotation and grammatical features with regard to the key word in context. Grammatical rules can be acquired as well when learners can discover, rather than to be taught, rules by examining many instances of targeted grammatical features. Options for developing learning tasks based on contexts and lists have been described in detail in publications by Johns (1986), Johns and King (1991), Tribble and Jones (1997) and Rézeau (2001).

'Total Cloze' programs such as Higgins's *Storyboard*, published by Wida Software in 1982, are another example of a pedagogical approach that necessitated the use of a computer, *Storyboard* was derived from Johns's *Textbag* program, in which a whole text is deleted, leaving only punctuation and markers representing the shape of words (Higgins & Johns 1984, pp. 54–7). In such programs the student's task was to complete the text using intelligent guesswork, trial and error and a variety of other strategies as documented, for example, by Trippen, Legenhausen and Wolff (1988). *Storyboard* spawned numerous imitations and spin-offs, including *Developing Tray*, *CopyWrite*, *Eclipse*, *Rhubarb*, *Quartext* and *Fun with Texts*.

At the same time as the development of CALL programs during the 1980s, there was a growth in generic applications such as word-processors, databases, desktop publishing software, spreadsheets and communications software (e.g., email). The increasing availability of these applications – dubbed 'office programs' by Hardisty and Windeatt (1989, pp. 29–46) – led to language teachers discovering innovative ways in which they could be exploited. The use of such generic programs could even be considered as a very early step towards the process of 'normalization' of the use of computers in the foreign languages classroom as described by Bax (2003). This can also be concluded from the fact that at this time the first add-ons and tools for word-processors for language learning were developed, which allowed for almost automatic processing of electronic text into worksheets and exercise materials. Such developments, which were started in the 1980s and could be defined as first-generation applications for language teachers, resulted in currently available tools such as *LingoFox*, an application that enables the production of electronic and printed exercises on lexis, orthography, syntax or reading comprehension from computer readable texts in many languages. After detailed parsing of a chosen text, the program provides information about the text, enabling the teacher to determine the difficulty level and to decide on its precise usage in learning. Exercise types range from a variety of gap-filling, cloze and scrambling to games and activities fostering reading and comprehension strategies, all generated from authentic texts.

A major drawback at this time was that microcomputers did not have the capability of recording and playing back sound, although various peripheral devices emerged to meet this need, including the TCCR 530 (Tandberg Computer Controlled Cassette Recorder). The Tandberg TCCR 530 was a modified audiocassette recorder that could be connected to a microcomputer, making it possible to integrate sound into learning materials in a controlled way. While this unit was initially used in more traditional exercise formats, such as listening comprehension tests, the option of integrating simple commands in learning software to play predefined clips quickly led to more interactive ways of integrating sound into CALL software. Learners were, for example, given the option of choosing and replaying alternative versions of a dialogue before dealing with comprehension questions. In addition, selected extracts from such dialogues could be made available as part of the help offered or integrated into the feedback provided by a learning package. This was, of course, a rather crude and – for the software developer – time-consuming way of creating such first-generation interactive audio-enhanced software, but ideas developed for such systems were quickly adapted to truly interactive digital sound-enhanced CALL software with the advent of sound cards, which began to appear in around 1988.

In the 1980s CALL programs in the United States took on new dimensions with advances in technology, particularly in the proliferation of microcomputers such as the Apple and the IBM PC. Many software packages of this period reflected a shift away from a grammar focus towards an emphasis on narrative contexts, listening, reading and intrinsic motivation through engagement with a game, story and/or an exploratory environment. During this decade interactive videodiscs represented the cutting-edge technology, one that provided easy and precise control over playback of content (video, text, audio and still images). A survey (Rubin et al., 1990) identified 72 interactive videodisc-based programs.

Among the highest profile CALL projects launched in the 1980s were the ambitious videodisc-based simulations that aimed to provide immersion experiences in the target language. The two best-known videodisc-based simulation projects were BYU's *Montevidisco,* for learners of Spanish, and MIT's *A la rencontre de Philippe,* for learners of French. In *Montevidisco* the learner is cast in the role of a tourist in a fictitious town in Mexico and must interact with salesmen, waitresses, policemen and other inhabitants (Schneider & Bennion, 1984). *A la rencontre de Philippe* wraps up language learning in a real-life simulation set in Paris. The learner must help Philippe, a freelance journalist living in Paris who has just broken up with his girlfriend, find an apartment and help him get a better job. *A la rencontre de Philippe* first appeared in the late 1980s, having been developed by the Athena Language Learning Project that ran from 1984 to 1989. It was later published by Yale University Press (Furstenberg, 1993), and a version on CD-ROM came out in 2006. EXPODISC (conceived in the late 1980s and published in 1990) simulated a business trip to Madrid in which the learner played the role of assistant to the export manager of a British company (Davies, 1991). The *Domesday* videodisc, which was published by the BBC in 1986 to commemorate the 900th anniversary of the creation of the original Domesday Book, was not intended primarily as a resource for language learning and teaching, but the rich collection of authentic texts that it contained, in combination with hundreds of photographs and maps, proved to be invaluable for teachers of English as a foreign language. The main drawback was that it required a cumbersome and unique hardware set-up, combining a BBC Master computer (an upgraded version of the BBC Micro), expanded with a SCSI controller and linked to a Philips VP415 videodisc player. The *Domesday* videodisc quickly became obsolete, but the BBC has now relaunched the project online (see www.bbc.co.uk/history/domesday).

However, there were only a modest number of videodiscs produced expressly for the foreign language market – in the range of 300 titles, not counting commercially distributed feature films, and the videodisc's failure to thrive in the commercial market led to its replacement in the educational market during the course of the 1990s by other technologies, particularly CD-ROMs, DVDs and, eventually, by streaming media servers.

Repositioning CALL: The 1990s

In the course of the 1990s the use of ICT in language learning and teaching became firmly established, and the use of the term CALL and its earlier associations with drills seemed inappropriate for newer approaches, for example Johns's concept of DDL as mentioned above. Levy, on the other hand, saw CALL in a much wider context, namely 'the search for and study of applications of the computer in language teaching and learning' (Levy, 1997, p. 1), and it is this definition that appears to have been accepted ever since.

When CALL began to reach a wider audience in the 1990s, a number of efforts were made to document its history and to identify its changing phases. Sanders (1995), Levy (1997) and Davies (1997) have already been mentioned. Warschauer (1996) and Warschauer and Healey (1998) identified three phases of CALL, classified according to their underlying pedagogical and methodological approaches:

> Behaviourist CALL: In this phase, which was conceived in the 1950s and implemented in the 1960s and 1970s, the computer played the role of tutor, serving mainly as a vehicle for delivering instructional materials to the learner. Drill-and-practice programs were a prominent feature of this phase.
>
> Communicative CALL: In this phase, which became prominent in the 1970s and 1980s, the computer continued to be used as a vehicle for practising language skills, but in a non-drill format and with a greater degree of student choice, control and interaction.
>
> Integrative CALL: This phase was marked by the introduction of two important innovations: multimedia and the Internet, both of which had become prominent by the mid-1990s.

The dates of these three phases can be called into question, however, as pointed out by Bax (2003). Bax offered a different critical examination and reassessment of the history of CALL, defining and describing three *approaches* to CALL as opposed to the three *phases* of CALL identified by Warschauer (1996) and Warschauer and Healey (1998). Bax saw the history of CALL in terms of (i) Restricted CALL, (ii) Open CALL and (iii) Integrated CALL, arguing that this allows a more detailed analysis of institutions and classrooms than earlier analyses. It was suggested that in 2003 we were using the second approach, Open CALL, but that the aim should be to attain a state of 'normalization' in which the technology is invisible and truly integrated into teachers' everyday practice.

The advent of the multimedia PC in the 1990s led to programs that were able to record and play back sound, a major breakthrough that language teachers had been waiting for since the first microcomputers appeared. This led to new pedagogical approaches, moving further away from the drill-and-practice programs of the 1980s and earlier. The Brøderbund series of 'Talking Books' CD-ROMs was launched, beginning with *Just Grandma and Me* (1992), which offered text and sound in three languages, US English, Latin American Spanish and Japanese. The learner could switch between the different languages, read and listen to the texts, and also click on objects on the screen, triggering a range of animations, sound effects and spoken language.

Simulations on videodisc, which had appeared in the 1980s (see previous section), soon began to give way to simulations on CD-ROM, such as *Nuevos Destinos*, companion software to a Spanish telenovela in which the student performs the role of a legal assistant to one of the main characters (Blake, McGraw-Hill College & WGBH/ Boston, 1993), and the multilingual mystery game, *Who is Oscar Lake*? (1995). Initially the quality of video on CD-ROMs was much inferior to that on interactive videodiscs, but it gradually caught up. The quality of audio recordings was, however, good and CD-ROMs offered new opportunities for students to engage in listen/respond/playback activities, for example, as in the *Encounters* series of CD-ROMs, published by Hodder and Stoughton and the TELL Consortium in 1997. CD-ROMs incorporating Automatic Speech Recognition (ASR) also appeared around this time, for example Syracuse's *Triple Play* series (later renamed *Smart Start*) and Auralog's *Talk to Me* and *Tell me More* series.

The appearance of the World Wide Web – now known simply as the Web – is probably the most significant development in ICT during the last 30 years. The Web was the brainchild of a British scientist, Tim Berners-Lee, who developed the idea while working at the Centre Européen pour la Recherche Nucleaire (CERN) in Switzerland. Initially a closed system, the Web went public with the launch of the first Web browser, *Mosaic* (1993), which was followed by *Netscape* in 1994. In its early days the Web was used mainly as a tool for locating resources. Most websites offered only texts, but some offered both texts and images. On the whole, however, Web interactivity was very limited, for example to discussion lists and forums. There was a growth of interactive possibilities on the Web when audio and video were introduced, but the quality of audio and video was initially inferior to that offered by interactive videodiscs and CD-ROMs.

The demand for interactive materials on the Web led in turn to a demand from teachers for authoring tools. *Hot Potatoes* (Arneil & Holmes, 1998–2009) is a typical example of a Web authoring tool. The *Hot Potatoes* templates enable the speedy creation of multiple choice, gap-filling, matching, jumbled sentences, crosswords and short text entry exercises. While it can be argued that such exercises are essentially drill-and-practice, this tool proved extremely popular with language teachers and it continues to be used extensively for the creation of interactive exercises and tests on the Web.

'E-learning' – usually interpreted as learning online – became the buzz word in the late 1990s, and there was an explosion of virtual learning environments (VLEs), such as *Blackboard*, to serve this need. VLEs proved to be useful in providing teachers with tools to create online courses, together with facilities for teacher-learner communication and peer-to-peer communication. However, they also attracted criticism insofar as the underlying pedagogy attempted to address a very wide range of subjects, and thus did not necessarily fit in with established practice in language learning and teaching. VLEs continue to be popular, however. The advent of *Moodle*, an open-source VLE, in the late 1990s has led to the wider adoption of VLEs. The UK Open University, for example, selected *Moodle* for the delivery of a wide range of its courses, including language courses, making it the largest user of *Moodle* in the world.

Faster and more efficient internet connectivity became available as the Web expanded, with the result that language teachers could exploit applications that went beyond offering sets of grammar exercises. Such applications included MUDs and MOOs – multi-user domains and multi-user-domains object oriented. MUDs were originally designed as text-based, role-playing adventure games to be engaged in across computer networks but they also offered opportunities for collaboration and education, including language learning. Players log into a MOO to communicate with other MOO users either synchronously or asynchronously. Von der Emde et al. (2001) and Shield (2003) describe how MOOs have been used as language learning tools.

MOOs were followed by MUVEs (Multi-User Virtual Environments), three-dimensional virtual environments, which are also known as virtual worlds. Examples of such virtual worlds, which appeared from the mid-1990s onwards, include *Active Worlds* (1995) and *Traveler* (1996). Svensson (2003) describes ways in which these 3D worlds could be exploited for language learning and teaching (see also Sadler & Dooly, this volume).

CALL and Web 2.0: The 2000s

By the early 2000s the quality of audio and video on the Web had improved considerably, and complete language courses began to appear, notably the range of courses offered by commercial entities, such as the BBC (www.bbc.co.uk/languages/) and by university and government projects, for example Chinese Online (East China Normal University, www.hanyu.com.cn/), LangNet (US Departments of Defense, Education and State, www.langnet.org/) and the CAMILLE Group's InGenio Project (Universidad Politécnica de Valencia, camilleweb.upv.es/camille/).

It should be noted though that the limitations of complete individualization by means of online self-study courses without guidance and integration had been recognized by this time. This resulted in the fact that 'e-learning' was redefined as 'blended learning' as it became clear that Web-based activities in a traditional self-study mode could not 'replace' classroom practice and social interaction on language learning but would support and extend it.

The term Web 2.0 gained popularity following the first of a series of Web 2.0 conferences initiated in 2004 (O'Reilly, 2005). Essentially, the term Web 2.0 was an attempt to redefine what the Web might potentially achieve or had become: a social platform for collaboration, knowledge sharing and networking. It was not a break with the past but more of a move towards the vision of the Web as originally conceived by its creator, Tim Berners-Lee, namely as a 'common information space in which we communicate by sharing information' and 'a realistic mirror (or in fact the primary embodiment) of the ways in which we work and play and socialize' (Berners-Lee, 1998, n.p.).

From the early 2000s there was a breath-taking increase in the number of Web-based communities that make use of typical Web 2.0 tools such as discussion lists, blogs, wikis and podcasts, as well as dedicated social networking websites and virtual worlds or MUVEs that promote sharing, collaboration and interaction (Thomas, 2009).

A host of Web applications now 'facilitate participatory information sharing, interoperability, user-centred design, and collaboration on the World Wide Web' – as the Wikipedia article on Web 2.0 puts it. The ever growing diversity and flexibility of digital media, together with the increased ease with which the communicative, interactive, multimedia and networking potential of computers and the internet can now be exploited, have also had a considerable influence on the way current principles and paradigms underlying foreign language learning methodology can now be put into practice. Current pedagogy advocates collaborative knowledge construction rather than simple instructivist learning, as well as authenticity and task orientation. Furthermore, new opportunities for research into language acquisition processes are opening up, as the tools and platforms available on the Web make traceable both the processes of creating and publishing meaningful output as well as the actual products themselves.

Digital media in their current realization have now become truly creative spaces which have become as naturalized in the real world as radio or television and telephones. In addition, access to personal or shared information has become so much easier than in the past, as tablet PCs, smartphones and other mobile devices have been developed into powerful appliances for daily use. In addition, data shared via social platforms, shared resources in the form of cloud computing and applications such as *Dropbox* have the potential to make collaborative creation, distribution and sharing of learning materials a regular part of teaching and learning languages. Looking at current trends in language education confirms this perception.

In addition, such platforms and Web 2.0 tools for the publication of text, for example *Wikispaces*, as well as media products in the form of podcasts or videocasts, such as YouTube, have become a realistic option to broaden the scope of output-oriented project work in language learning. This approach, very much rooted in current thinking in language teaching methodology, appears to be in line with current deliberations within the CALL and TELL community, and digital media are in the process of becoming part of the standard repertoire of language teaching and learning, making output-oriented language learning scenarios with a focus on stimulating meaning negotiation and output production more practical at the grassroots level. As Swain and Deters (2007, p. 831) put it, in language learning 'participation has found its place alongside acquisition'. Similar to the notion that language learning might benefit from contexts, in which language production results from processes of meaning negotiation, Web technologies and social software are rooted in the idea that knowledge can be accumulated more fruitfully when negotiated collaboratively by groups sharing a common goal. One of the remaining challenges that needs to be faced with regard to the full integration of digital media into language learning is to define appropriate frameworks for research into the actual processes that learners go through when participating in learning opportunities of the kind outlined in this chapter. Digital media offer new opportunities in this area, too, since participatory platforms and social software tools, such as wikis and podcasting, do offer the option of tracing processes of output-production, thereby making them observable. Consequently, all edits can be considered in terms of what they document and represent as far as acts and processes of language learning are concerned. Research of this kind will allow us to broaden the understanding of the effects and effectiveness of digital media in innovative, creative and participatory language learning.

In 2003 the 3D virtual world of Second Life (SL) was launched, following on from the earlier 3D virtual worlds of the 1990s mentioned above. Second Life soon began to attract the attention of language teachers. In 2005, Languagelab (www.languagelab.com), the first large-scale language school, was opened in Second Life, and since 2007 a series of in-world annual conferences known as *SLanguages* have taken place. Cooke-Plagwitz (2008) provides an introduction to Second Life and examines some of the advantages and disadvantages of its use as an instructional tool for foreign language students and educators. Molka-Danielsen and Deutschmann (2009) look at the wider context of learning in Second Life, focusing on instructional design, learner modelling and building simulations (see Sadler & Dooly, this volume).

Conclusions

There is no question that digital media are now having a significant impact on the way foreign languages are being taught and learned. It can now be argued that computer-assisted language learning has come of age, and that we are now entering a fully integrated and naturalized phase of CALL. Digital tools for learning have become integrated elements both in the real world and also in foreign language syllabuses. In view of the development of even more flexible tools for social networking and knowledge sharing, it can be said that CALL has reached the stage of normalization insofar as so-called Web 2.0 applications have become a common social phenomenon.

Nevertheless, the debate on normalization simmers on. In a Special Issue of *IJCALLT*, dedicated to this topic, Bax (2011) now questions the assumption that normalization is both inevitable and desirable, and he asks if normalization occurs to the same degree with each technology and if it follows the same steps for each technology.

Returning to the starting point of this chapter, namely our aim to match technological developments with pedagogical and methodological progress in language learning, one can say that in a number of cases the methodologies and paradigms discussed for quite some time seem to have found their match in recent phenomena observable in the way technologies are used in real life and language learning. One such example is the concept of process writing, where the focus is more on the *process* of creating written text rather than the end product, which is a principle underlying the use of and participation in wikis, writing blogs etc., as well as contributing to social networks (see Hegelheimer & Lee, this volume). In technological terms, simple use and consumption has been replaced by participation and contribution, principles which are now also seen as corner-stones of language learning, where 'participation has found its place alongside acquisition' (Swain & Deters, 2007, p. 831). As stated in an article on output-oriented language learning (Rüschoff, 2009), the challenge that needs to be faced, with regard to the full integration of digital media into language learning, is to define appropriate frameworks for research into the actual processes that learners go through when participating in learning opportunities of this kind. Such research would broaden our understanding of the effects and effectiveness of digital media in output-oriented, creative and participatory language learning.

Note

1 To the great sorrow of many friends and colleagues worldwide, Graham Davies passed away on June 20, 2012. Graham was a pioneer in the field of computer-assisted language learning—a smart, funny, creative, entrepreneurial, warm, and generous man, who will be fondly remembered as a dedicated teacher, prolific scholar, experienced software developer and publisher, and exceptional leader in our profession. Although he is gone, his voice can be heard one more time in the pages of this chapter.

References

Ahmad, K., Corbett, G., Rogers, M., & Sussex, R. (1985). *Computers, language learning and language teaching*. Cambridge: Cambridge University Press.

Anderson, S. J. (1976, October). *TICCIT Project*. Paper presented at the National Association of Educational Broadcasters, Chicago, Illinois. ERIC Document No. ED134226. Retrieved from www.eric.ed.gov/

Arneil, S., & Holmes, M. (1998–2009). *Hot Potatoes*. Victoria, British Columbia: University of Victoria and Half-Baked Software, Inc.

Bassein, R., & Underwood, J. (1985). *Juegos Comunicativos: Games for communicative practice in Spanish, based on Puntos de Partida*. New York: Random House, Inc.

Bax, S. (2003). CALL – past, present and future. *System, 31*(1), 13–28.

— (2011). Normalisation revisited: The effective use of technology in language education. *International Journal of Computer-Assisted Language Learning and Teaching, 1*(2), 1–15.

Berer, M., & Rinvolucri, M. (1981). *MAZES: A problem-solving reader*. London: Heinemann.

Berners-Lee, T. (1998). The World Wide Web: A very short personal history. Retrieved from www.w3.org/People/Berners-Lee/ShortHistory.html

Blake, R., McGraw-Hill College & WGBH/Boston (1993). *Nuevos Destinos CD-ROM.* Boston, MA: WGBH Educational Foundation and Washington, DC: Corporation for Public Broadcasting.
Brown, E. (Ed.) (1988). *Learning languages with technology.* Coventry: MESU.
Bush, M., & Terry, R. (Eds.) (1997). *Technology-enhanced language learning.* Lincolnwood, IL: National Textbook Company.
Butler-Pascoe, M. E. (2011). The history of CALL: The intertwining paths of technology and second/foreign language teaching. *International Journal of Computer-Assisted Language Learning and Teaching, 1*(1), 16–32.
CLEF Group (1985). (Including authors at the University of Western Ontario, the University of Guelph, the University of Calgary, and the London, Ontario, School Board.) *CLEF (Computer-assisted learning exercises for French).* Guelph, ON: University of Guelph.
Cooke-Plagwitz, J. (2008). New directions in CALL: An objective introduction to Second Life, *CALICO Journal, 25*(3), 547–57.
Davies, G. (1991). EXPODISC: An interactive videodisc package for learners of Spanish. In H. Savolainen & J. Telenius (Eds.), *EUROCALL 1991, International Conference on Computer-Assisted Language Learning* (pp. 133–9). Helsinki: Helsinki School of Economics.
— (1997). Lessons from the past, lessons for the future: 20 years of CALL. In A-K. Korsvold & B. Rüschoff (Eds.), *New technologies in language learning and teaching* (pp. 27–52). Strasbourg: Council of Europe.
Davies, G., & Higgins, J. (1982). *Computers, language and language learning.* London: CILT.
— (1985). *Using computers in language learning: A teacher's guide.* London: CILT.
Davies, G., & Steel, D. (1981, April). *First steps in computer-assisted language learning at Ealing College of Higher Education.* Paper presented at the CAL 81 Symposium, University of Leeds. Retrieved from www.ict4lt.org/en/Davies_Steel_1981.doc
Delcloque, P. (2000). *The history of computer-assisted language learning Web exhibition.* Retrieved from www.ict4lt.org/en/History_of_CALL.pdf
Firth, J. (1957). A synopsis of linguistic theory, 1930–1955. In J. R. Firth et al., *Studies in linguistic analysis.* Special Volume of the Philological Society (pp. 1–32). Oxford: Blackwell.
Furstenberg, G. (1993). *A la rencontre de Philippe.* New Haven, CT: Yale University Press. Retrieved from http://web.mit.edu/fll/www/projects/Philippe.html
Hardisty, D., & Windeatt, S. (1989). *CALL.* Oxford: Oxford University Press.
Harper, B. (1996). Using cognitive tools in interactive multimedia. Retrieved from www.auc.edu.au/conf/Conf96/Papers/Harper.html
Hart, R. S. (1995). The Illinois PLATO foreign languages project. In R. Sanders (Ed.) (1995), *Thirty years of computer-assisted language instruction: Festschrift for John R. Russell, CALICO Journal, 12*(4), 15–37.
Higgins, J., & Johns, T. (1984). *Computers in language learning.* London: Collins.
Hope, G. R., Taylor, H. F., & Pusack, J. P. (1984). *Using computers in teaching foreign languages.* Washington, DC: Center for Applied Linguistics and Harcourt Brace Jovanovich, Inc.
Hussein, K. O. F., Phelps, L., & Bessent, H. (1980). *CALIS.* Durham, NC: Duke University.
Johns, T. (1986). Micro-concord. In M. Lesbats, F. Frankel & M. Köchling (Eds.), *Triangle V: New technology and foreign language learning* (pp. 120–33). Paris: Didier Erudition, AUPELF, The British Council, Goethe-Institut.
— (1997). Contexts: The background, development and trialling of a concordance-based CALL program. In A. Wichmann, S. Fligelstone, T. McEnery & G. Knowles (Eds.), *Teaching and language corpora* (pp. 100–15). London: Longman.

Johns, T., & King, P. (Eds.) (1991). *Classroom Concordancing, English Language Research Journal, 4*, Special Issue. Birmingham: University of Birmingham.
Jones, R. L. (1995). TICCIT and CLIPS: The early years. In R. Sanders (Ed.), *Thirty years of computer-assisted language instruction: Festschrift for John R. Russell, CALICO Journal, 12*(4), 84–96.
Jung, U. (2005). CALL: Past, present and future – A bibliometric approach. *ReCALL, 17*(1), 4–17.
Kenner, R. (1996). A short history of the founding of the CALL-IS Interest Section, The CALL Interest Section: Community History, Montreal. Retrieved from http://rogerkenner.ca/Gallery/CALL_IS/founding.htm
Kenning, M., & Kenning, M.-M. (1984). *An introduction to computer-assisted language teaching.* Oxford: Oxford University Press.
Last, R. (1984). *Language teaching and the microcomputer.* Oxford: Blackwell.
Levy, M. (1997). *CALL: Context and conceptualisation.* Oxford: Oxford University Press.
Little, D. (Ed.) (1989). *Self-access systems for language learning.* Dublin: Authentik.
Molka-Danielsen, J., & Deutschmann, M. (2009). *Learning and teaching in the virtual world of Second Life.* Trondheim: Tapir Academic Press.
O'Reilly, T. (2005). What is Web 2.0? Design patterns and business models for the next generation of software. Retrieved from http://oreilly.com/web2/archive/what-is-web-20.html
Olsen, S. (1980). Foreign language departments and computer-assisted instruction: A survey, *The Modern Language Journal, 64*(3), 341–9.
Otto, S. E. K., & Pusack, J. P. (2009). Computer-assisted language learning authoring issues. *The Modern Language Journal, 93*, 784–801.
Prabhu, N. S. (1987). *Second language pedagogy.* Oxford: Oxford University Press.
Prensky, M. (2001). Digital natives, digital immigrants. *On the Horizon, 9*(5), 1–6.
Pusack, J., & Otto, S. (1983, 1992, 1996, 2000, 2010). *Dasher authoring system* and *WebDasher.* University of Iowa: CONDUIT and PICS.
Rézeau, J. (2001). Concordances in the classroom: The evidence of the data. In A. Chambers & G. Davies (Eds.), *Information and communications technology: A European perspective* (pp. 147–66). Lisse: Swets & Zeitlinger.
Roget's II: The New Thesaurus (1995). Boston, MA: Houghton Mifflin.
Rubin, J., Ediger, A., Coffin, E., Van Handle, D., & Whiskeyman, A. (1990). Survey of interactive videodiscs, *CALICO Journal, 7*(3), 31–56.
Rüschoff, B. (2002a). Authenticity and innovative learning scenarios in technology enriched environments for language learning. In T. Abbott et al. (Eds.), *Paradigms shift! Implications of emerging technologies for teaching languages & cultures.* Proceedings of Digital Stream 4. Monterey: California State University Monterey Bay.
— (2002b). Languages. In H. D. Adelsberger, B. Collins & J. M. Pawlowski (Eds.), *Handbook on information technologies for education and training* (pp. 523–43). Berlin: Springer Verlag.
— (2009). Output-oriented language learning with digital media. In M. Thomas (Ed.), *Handbook of research on Web 2.0 and second language learning* (pp. 42–59). Hershey, PA: Information Science Reference.
Sanders, R. (Ed.) (1995). Thirty years of computer-assisted language instruction: Festschrift for John R. Russell, *CALICO Journal, 12*(4).
Sanders, R., & Sanders, A. (1995). History of an AI spy game: Spion. In R. Sanders (Ed.), Thirty years of Computer-Assisted Language Instruction: Festschrift for John R. Russell, *CALICO Journal, 12*(4), 114–27.
Schneider, E. W., & Bennion, J. L. (1984). Veni, vidi, vici, via videodisc: A simulator for instructional courseware. In D. H. Wyatt (Ed.), *Computer-assisted language instruction* (pp. 41–6). Oxford: Pergamon.

Shield, L. (2003). MOO as a language learning tool. In U. Felix (Ed.), *Language learning online: Towards best practice* (pp. 97–122). Lisse: Swets and Zeitlinger.
Shield, L., & Kukulska-Hulme, A. (Eds.) (2008). *Mobile assisted language learning. ReCALL, 20*(3).
Stevens, V. (2003). How the TESOL CALL Interest Section began. Retrieved 15 November 2011, from www.vancestevens.com/papers/tesol/newsletter/callis_began.htm
Stockwell, G. (2007). Using mobile phones for vocabulary activities: Examining the effect of the platform. *Language Learning & Technology, 14*(2), 95–110.
Svensson, P. (2003). Virtual worlds as arenas for language learning. In U. Felix (Ed.), *Language learning online: Towards best practice* (pp. 123–46). Lisse: Swets and Zeitlinger.
Swain, M., & Deters, P. (2007). 'New' mainstream SLA theory: Expanded and enriched, *Modern Language Journal, 91*, 820–36.
Taylor, H. (1987). *TUCO II*. New York: Gessler Educational Software. Based on earlier programs developed by H. Taylor and W. Haas at Ohio State University in the 1970s: *DECU* (*Deutscher Computerunterricht*) and *TUCO* (*Tutorial Computer*).
Tebben, J. (1979). *A course in medical and technical terminology*. Minneapolis: Burgess Publishing and Pearson.
Thomas, M. (Ed.) (2009). *Handbook of research on Web 2.0 and second language learning*. Hershey, PA: Information Science Reference.
Tribble, C., & Jones, G. (1997). *Concordancing in the classroom: A resource guide for teachers*. Houston, TX: Athelstan Publications.
Trippen, G., Legenhausen, L., & Wolff, D. (1988). Lernerstrategien und Lernprozesse bei der Bearbeitung von CALL-Software. In W. Kühlwein & B. Spillner (Eds.), *Sprache und Individuum* (pp. 83–6). Tübingen: Gunter Narr Verlag.
Von der Emde, S., Schneider, J., & Kötter, M. (2001). Technically speaking: Transforming language learning through virtual learning environments (MOOs). *Modern Language Journal, 85*(2), 210–25.
Warschauer, M. (1996). Computer-assisted language learning: An introduction. In S. Fotos (Ed.), *Multimedia language teaching* (pp. 3–20). Tokyo: Logos International.
Warschauer, M., & Healey, D. (1998). Computers and language learning: An overview. *Language Teaching, 31*, 57–71.
Widdowson, H. (1979). Rules and procedures in discourse analysis. In T. Myers (Ed.), *The development of conversation and discourse*. Edinburgh: Edinburgh University Press.
Williams, A., Davies, G., & Williams, I. (1981). *Apfeldeutsch*. London: Wida Software.

3

Researching language learning in the age of social media

Carla Meskill and Joy Quah

Summary

Along with proliferate uses of the internet for teaching and learning languages has come a broadening and expansion of research approaches to these phenomena. The questions we ask and the ways in which we conceptualize, situate, observe, analyse and make sense of how language learners and instructors make use of social media now draw on a number of techniques and traditions that, until recently, lay outside of the field of applied linguistics and second language acquisition (SLA). Such varied perspectives and approaches serve to enrich our work as language educators in general, and as computer-assisted language learning (CALL) researchers in particular. It is in this spirit of expanding the horizons of possibilities and promises for research in the field that this chapter reviews approaches to examining language teaching and learning with online social media. We review the extant research and divide relevant studies into three categories: research that foregrounds (1) the online environment and its affordances; (2) online social/affective dimensions; or (3) pedagogical processes. Methodological approaches and techniques are highlighted and discussed with an emphasis on the researchers' foregrounding of the three foci.

Introduction

How language teachers and learners make use of new technologies has been the focus of a great deal of research over the past decade. This is in large part due to the advent and widespread availability of internet-based social media resources and implementations. Further, language teaching in formal, institutional contexts is swiftly moving to blended and online venues with educators seeing positive value in both asynchronous and synchronous forms of target language communication with their students. Online interaction with others – both native and non-native-speaking classmates and peers – is also widely viewed as authentic language practice with the greater freedoms social media venues afford for learners to observe and revise target language reading, writing and speaking (Meskill & Anthony, 2006, 2010; Tudini, 2010).

As the range and diversity of online communication practices continue to evolve, likewise the range and variety of foci and concerns for language education researchers are robustly developing. Along with increased interest in online language teaching and learning practices has come a rapid broadening of research epistemologies and methodological techniques and approaches fitted and retrofitted to new online language and literacy practices. In short, CALL researchers have moved to employing forms of inquiry that extend well beyond the traditions of SLA and applied linguistics drawing on methods traditionally associated with, for example, sociology, education, critical cultural studies, media literacy studies and communications. This expanding repertoire of inquiry perspectives and tools bears synthesis and it is the goal of this chapter on contemporary research practices in the digital age, particularly with social media, to provide this.

Technologies associated with social media are often discussed within the broader context of Web 2.0, a term which came into prominent use near the end of 2004. O'Reilly (2005) is generally credited for systematically describing some of the defining characteristics of the emerging phenomenon, a phenomenon that has enabled new forms of communication, participation, sharing and networking. Language educators have been quick to appropriate Web 2.0 technologies to facilitate participatory practices in language learning, guiding learners to individually or collaboratively generate content which can be posted, rapidly updated and continually revised. These potential means of collaboration provide opportunities to integrate language skills, while supporting the development of identity and critical literacy through ways that mirror authentic uses of social media in the general population (Warschauer, 2009). Research that examines such instructional activity of necessity calls for new ways of conceptualizing and in turn investigating how languages are being taught and learned with and within social media contexts.

Traditions

The formal study of language learning began as research strictly rooted in psychology. Research problems, questions, methods and interpretations were thus shaped by the belief that acquiring language is a matter of the architecture and functions of the individual human mind (Davis, 1995; Gass & Schacter, 1989). From this perspective, scientific experiments comprised the default methodological technique with mental modelling the goal of controlled experimentation. In addition to controlled laboratory-like approaches that involved such techniques as language testing and target language elicitation techniques, questions concerning how languages are learned were tackled via close study of language classes. Groups of learners were used as control and experimental subjects with methods and materials as interventions, metrics of learner characteristics as correlates and questions about minds in interaction with methods and materials posed. Measures of learner and teacher traits along with the influences of interventions were often the focus. It is from this positivist tradition that many concepts about language education widely held today had their genesis, and the psychological perspective continues to be employed in language and literacy studies currently. However, while the psychological perspective on second language learning research continues to hold sway, the explosive advent of online social media in both formal and informal language teaching and learning has, of necessity, led to new research perspectives and approaches. Online social media, after all, involve the messy, unpredictable use of human language for motivated, authentic purposes, a phenomenon that does not lend itself to laboratory controls. Social media involve evolving forms of human interaction, forms of interaction that require new approaches to understanding language learning and teaching along with research perspectives, approaches and techniques that serve in building such understanding.

Precedent for a similar extension of research perspectives was set in the early 1970s with the educational study of foreign and second language classrooms, a shift that broadened concepts of language learning to include the social/contextual processes of teaching and learning. The dynamics of teacher and student interactions in live, intact language classrooms became focal (see, for example, Chaudron, 1988). Indeed, one of the earliest studies on internet-based language learning activity through social interaction was shaped by these parallel concerns and, thereby, illustrates the potentially parallel perspectives and methods of classroom-based research in approaching questions about online language learning (Sauvignon & Roithmeier, 2004). As is demonstrated in this and many subsequent studies of social media for language education, research techniques such as observation and analysis of class and group activities using the written and aurally recorded utterances of teachers and students make good sense for inquiries that examine various perspectives and dimensions of online social/instructional interaction. Such approaches help to account for the complex social interactions that occur such as teacher talk, learner production, group interactions, question types, misunderstandings, clarification and the like as these unfold online. Moreover, sociolinguistic and ethnographic approaches that examine communication in action, including examination of how and why humans acquire new languages, have themselves evolved new techniques and approaches in the last decades (Nunan & Bailey, 2007). For example, classroom-based language research that has examined language teacher talk, learner–learner interactions, oral and written feedback types, learner products, etc. has brought new understandings and insights to both theory and practice in language education while establishing a solid base of empirical work on which those within the field can build. It is from these roots that current research practices in language education through social media are likewise developing. After all, both online social media practices and language classroom interactions share the same goals and are pre-eminently social in nature.

In the context of research, online interactions with others closely parallel interactions in F2F classrooms. It is therefore not surprising to find a number of studies whose theoretical frames, research questions, methods and analyses emulate to some degree second and foreign language classroom research. Combined methodological techniques of, for example, ethnography in combination with quantification used as a supporting tool to determine and track patterns in participant interaction are starting to be employed. On the other hand, practitioner reports are at the same time proliferating. Warschauer and Grimes (2007) have observed that although 'a number of educators are beginning to report on their experiences (in L2 education), publications to date mostly consist of lists of suggestions or summaries of experiences by practitioners' (p.12). Because social media tools are relatively new, language educators clearly need time to appropriate their use to effectively complement pedagogical practices (Meskill, Anthony, Hilliker, Tseng & You, 2006). As such, many reports of social media uses to date involve teacher-researchers attempting to integrate these tools into classroom pedagogy. This kind of teacher research has thereby emerged as a distinct and significant trend of inquiry among language practitioners (e.g., Von Der Ende et al., 2001).

Lankshear and Knobel (2005) point out that practitioner research and academic research both share systematic and methodical approaches to investigation because they are 'derived more or less directly from academic discipline areas' (p. 20). The main distinction between the two is perspective and guidance via theory. The emphases of practitioner research are issues of practice and therefore, the authors go on to observe that 'professional-practitioner researchers will spend less time dabbling with the niceties of theory and the theoretical and conceptual disputes in the discipline area and more time making a wise selection of systematic methods and tools for addressing the practical issue' (p. 20). However, they stressed that practitioner researchers are not exempt from maintaining 'appropriate standards for "being systematic" ' (p. 20).

Because the purpose of teacher research – to illuminate opportunities and means for local instructional change – are distinct, these are not included in the following discussion of trends in methodological approaches and techniques in researching social media in language education.

Environments, socio/affective dimensions and pedagogical processes

In the following sections we provide a synthesis of key techniques in the research of language learning in online social networks in the context of three research foci we see dominating the current literature: the online environment, the socio/affective dimension and pedagogical concerns. The aim behind this categorization is to make clear distinctions between the major purposes and perspectives that drive research in the field while outlining the methodological techniques employed by researchers within each of these categories. The rationale for doing so lies in the vast diversity of research problems, purposes and approaches that characterizes the current state of research and a concurrent need we see to sort through and name these diverse positions so as to further discussion and future directions.

The first category comprises research studies that foreground as their focus the design, tools and resources of a given online social media environment. In short, studies that fall into this category focus primarily on the online environment and its affordances. Such studies tend to view the environment as impacting communicative exchanges in ways that are unique and/or of direct relevance to language and culture learning. Therefore, research questions, data interpretations, implications and conclusions foreground the online environment and its characteristics. The second category of research concentrates on the socio/affective dimensions of online social media as these relate to language education. When socio/affective aspects are foregrounded, learners' reactions and reflections are elicited via a range of methodological techniques and form the core of such studies' chief observations. Finally, our third category, pedagogical concerns, comprises research that focuses on teaching practices with social media technologies. Included in this category are studies that centre on the pedagogical tasks, strategies and discourse of language educators as they design and orchestrate learning in online venues.

Criteria for including studies rest squarely with the *social aspect* of online social media. Included are empirical research studies that state clearly framed research questions, employ suitable approaches for gathering, analysing and interpreting data, and that contribute to understanding theory and practice of language learning. We discuss these three groups of studies in terms of the research approaches and techniques each applied. We then attempt a synthesis of the current state of research in language learning technologies as reflected in the body of work selected and, in turn, future directions of the same.

Research focus: The online environment

Specific research focus on online environments, be they course management systems (CMSs), wikis, blogs, friendship applications, virtual worlds, etc., and what their design and resources afford for language learning and teaching reflects the earliest of research concerns in the history of CALL, *what the machine does* (Meskill, 2005). It is inquiry that is concerned specifically with the visual, physical and functional characteristics of what appears and occurs on the computer screen as it relates to language learning. What distinguishes current online social spaces from what might be considered traditional CALL spaces is the presence of other people and, therefore, opportunities to communicate with them for authentic purposes. In this respect, social spaces afford any number of interactive possibilities that are inherently social and, therefore, complex. Many researchers have thus turned to more socially motivated theoretical perspectives and concomitant methodological techniques and approaches that aim to narrate these human interactions as they unfold in online social spaces with emphasis on the specific affordances that in some way influence online language learning activity.

The foregrounding of the online spaces and their resources shapes the development of the research questions, approaches to and techniques of data collection, and the interpretations and implications that emerge for such studies. Thorne's (2003) case study of three foreign language learners as they employed online interactional spaces to practise the target language with native speakers is an example of such foregrounding. As an outgrowth of both the theoretical positioning developed for the study and the resulting questions and data interpretations, the research outcomes highlight the semiotic realm in which learners interacted as integral to online activity. The study concludes that uses and outcomes of online tools and resources for language education are contingent upon individuals as social actors in dynamic and complex activity, an observation similar to that of Flewitt and Lamy (2011) in their study of French-English learner exchanges. Both inquiries employed analyses of transcripts of learners' online interactions with the goal of characterizing how language learners respond to opportunities afforded by social media environments. Both studies' analyses were accomplished through coding systems that coordinated verbal and non-verbal interactions in conjunction with environmental affordances relevant to learners' interactions, a research technique afforded by video recordings of students as they interacted online.

In an examination of learners employing corrective feedback with one another online, Sauro and Smith (2010) analysed chatscripts (transcripts of synchronous student–student conversations) to determine whether a key affordance of online communication – control over time for planning, review and editing – impacted learners' monitoring of target language production. The researchers examined and coded the study's chatscripts for syntactic complexity, productive use of grammatical gender and lexical diversity as a means of determining learners' production planning and monitoring behaviours. Using similar methodological techniques, Smith (2005) tracked learner uptake of new lexical items during synchronous chats and likewise concluded that time and the visual representation of the language in use contributed positively to acquisition. Neither study employed additional methodological techniques to confirm these observations.

In another study that examines what the authors term 'chat logs', Zheng, Young and Wagner (2009) undertook four case studies of English learners interacting in game-based virtual worlds. Employing an environmental perspective, the researchers used a range of methodological techniques and data sources to pursue understanding of online language learner interactions while students gamed online: participant observation, interviews and the analysis of QA-related communication artefacts. The research also contrasts learners' F2F and online avatar interactions with the aim of detecting contextual influences. The researchers found emerging patterns of online interactions around the accomplishment of the gaming tasks afforded by the online environment in which students interacted. These they have labelled 'negotiations for action', or language used to coordinate activity online, a construct that is potentially valuable as more language learning research is carried out in gaming environments.

Jepson's (2005) mixed-method study compared patterns of repair moves in synchronous text chatrooms and voice chatrooms on the internet. The study draws its theoretical base from the role of social interaction in language acquisition, with a specific focus on repair moves related to negotiation of meaning and negative feedback. Data on repair moves were collected through transcripts of 5-minute, synchronous text and voice chatroom sessions made by participants. Quantitative statistical analysis revealed that a higher number of repair moves were made in voice chats compared to text chats. Qualitative discourse analysis and interaction analysis indicate that repair work in voice chats was often pronunciation-related. The research highlighted that although text chat is the more widely used, voice chat offers an environment which is more conducive for authentic meaning making that resembles F2F interaction. The conclusion was supported by evidence from voice chats which yielded a comparatively higher number of repair moves specifically related to negotiation of meaning.

Beyond the use of coded transcripts of online learner interactions, additional methodological techniques have been employed in exploring characteristics of the online environment along with the tools and resources learners use and to what effect. Lam and Rosario-Ramos (2009), for example, first distributed a questionnaire to hundreds of bilingual, bi-literate social media devotees. From these responses they invited a group of approximately 30 people to participate in focus groups. The researchers elicited participants' stories, observations and reflections concerning their multilingual, multicultural online practices and employed transcripts of these focus groups in their analysis of bilinguals' multi-literate practices in online social media sites. They focused particularly on the use of digital media and representations that participants employed as part of the online interactions. From these data and their attendant research questions, the authors conclude that digital media are important tools for young people to both maintain their mother tongue and expand uses of the host language and culture.

In an effort to characterize language learner collaborations when developing wiki entries, Kost (2011) employed systematic tracking of the planning, composing and revising strategies of native English speakers learning German as a second language. Using a taxonomy of revision types, patterns of students' collaborative writing strategies in an environment that affords linking, cross-referencing and consensus building were identified. Results suggest that wiki-hosted collaborative writing processes reflect the non-linear nature of both collaborative writing and content production in a wiki environment. Using a similar approach, Kuteeva (2011) also tracked learners' revision patterns in a wiki environment. In this study with learners of English for specific purposes, the focus was on determining if and how learners' awareness of audience – the broad readership of the internet – influenced their composing processes. Along with tracking writing revisions, learners' questionnaire responses revealed that composing in the wiki led learners to consider their readership. They consequently used a greater variety of interactional resources including different kinds of engagement markers (personal pronouns, questions and commands), self-mentions, attitude markers, hedges, boosters and so forth.

Integrating layers of metadata into research involving EFL learners collaborating on wiki entries, Lund (2008) analysed video records of F2F learner collaborations, digital records of learner content development, along with open-ended questions for learners to address regarding their collaboration and composing processes. Based on the premise that we come to knowledge by taking part in activities where individuals relate to a greater collective that evolves over time and where language and material artefacts function as structural resources, the researcher probed the ways that oral discourse supports written discourse given the tools, resources and purposes of wiki content building. The study illustrates research techniques by which learners' voices and identities can be methodologically integrated into profiles of online language learner collaborations.

Section summary: Environment

While each of these studies foregrounds the affordances of online social media environments, each develops and approaches its dataset (transcriptions of online and offline instructional interactions, focus groups and interviews) differently according to its theoretical positioning, purpose and system of data coding. In order to identify how venue affordances steer and influence online discourse, the focus of coding becomes learner uses and interactions with and through such affordances (Flewitt & Lamy, 2011; Thorne, 2003), learner syntactic and lexical uptake (Sauro & Smith, 2010; Smith, 2005), different language repair strategies by venue (Jepson, 2005), language use specific to online tasks (Zheng et al., 2009), bilingual/bicultural identity constructions with digital media (Lam & Rosario-Ramos, 2009), the tracking of collaborative constructions (Kost, 2011), the development of collective group practices over time (Lund, 2008) and the specific features of the online venue that shape these.

By tracking language learner uses and perceptions of online social media with an eye on the characteristics of the venue, researchers are documenting particular practices in evolving discourse genres attendant to these spaces. In the following section where the focus of research shifts to socio-affective outcomes of online interactions, we see similar systems of data collection and analytic techniques applied through a different lens.

Research focus: Socio/affective dimensions

The social turn in second language studies has been well documented (Block, 2003). To some extent one could point to the advent of online social media as playing a catalytic role in this shift from focusing on the individual learning mind to focusing on minds learning in social contexts. Many among the most recent generations of language learners after all are native to these online social spaces and daily participate in their evolution (Turkle, 2011).

One of the earliest indicators of a social turn in CALL research was Warschauer's (1999) study of online, socially motivated language learning spaces (see Warschauer, 2000 for an article-length account). In this seminal two-year ethnography of culturally diverse learners interacting online to develop their language and literacy, a combined data collection approach and analysis including observations, interviews and transcripts of learner interactions resulted in narrative case studies. Key moments are highlighted and explicated by the researcher with socio/affective dimensions as the focal concern. In-depth analysis of cases reveals the importance of digital literacies as a form of social/affective empowerment, with online spaces providing opportunities for target language voice and language development.

In a more recent study of language learners interacting in social media sites using the target language, Clark and Gruba (2010) employed an auto-ethnographic (diary studies) research technique to track the practices and uses of English by Japanese students in LiveMocha. From their thematic analysis of longitudinal transcript and student diary data, the researchers observed learners gaining confidence in the target language thereby securing their places as members of an online community; members who alternatively took on the roles of language learners and language teachers. Using similar methodological techniques, Harrison and Thomas (2009) observed that language learners who would otherwise be reticent to seek out conversation opportunities with native speakers were comfortable and proficient in doing so in this same online social media site.

In a study of classroom community-building employing blogs, learners of Italian contributed posts to a class blog about Italian food (Miceli, Murray & Kennedy, 2010). Use of the shared space of a class blog, in lieu of individual student blogs, was a strategy to promote authentic interaction as a community. Data sources included transcripts of blog entries and end-of-semester questionnaires administered to determine if the blogging activity positively or negatively influenced participants' sense of belonging to the class-group. Blog transcripts were coded using Rovai's (2001) scheme of 'connected voice', indicating a higher sense of belonging, and 'independent voice', indicating a lower sense of belonging. Analyses suggested that the blogging activity successfully promoted learner interaction and engendered a strong sense of community among the students.

Employing a corpus of learner interactions with native speakers of the target language accompanied by participant interviews, Pasfield-Neofitou (2011) probed evolving L2 and target culture identity work on the part of language learners. Of particular importance in this study was the experience of *foreignness* as students negotiated new L2 identities in virtual worlds. The researcher employed online and F2F interviews, transcripts of participation in blogs, wikis, and other social media venues and focus group data collection techniques. The researcher undertook analyses using a social realism framework. Pasfield-Neofitu observed that virtual immersion has both benefits (motivation to use L2 authentically, access to authentic materials) and constraints (feeling of foreignness that results in reluctance to use the L2).

Arnold (2007) examined language learners' communication apprehension online. The investigation was situated within socio-affective areas of attitudes and motivation in language learning. Three communicative formats – face-to-face, synchronous and asynchronous – were included to compare affective dimensions of the environments. Students interacted through six group discussions where they discussed open-ended personal topics in stable groups of three to four learners.

The dataset consisted of pre- and post-questionnaire responses to items probing levels of nervousness and self-confidence while engaging in discussions along with an adaptation of Horwitz et al.'s (1986) Foreign Language Classroom Anxiety Scale (FLCAS). The post-questionnaire included an open-ended section which gave students opportunities to provide self-reports on their experiences of oral communication in the foreign language. Analyses of these data indicate no statistically significant differences between the asynchronous and the synchronous communication groups in terms of communication apprehension reduction. In fact, both forums for discussions seemed to provide positive communication experiences for students. However, they do suggest that practice in synchronous communication might be more beneficial for increasing students' confidence levels due to similarities with F2F communication.

Finally, a study of language learning utilizing Second Life, a popular 3D simulated world, Henderson, Huang, Grant and Henderson (2009) traced Chinese learners' degree of self-efficacy as they actively used the target language to socialize in this virtual environment. The researchers collected extensive pre- and post-questionnaire data regarding learners' beliefs about their abilities to use Mandarin effectively when communicating with others. Mixed results lead to a call for more research on 'possible connections between virtual worlds and perceived relevance of enactive mastery experiences' (Henderson et al., 2009, p. 471).

Section summary: Socio/affective dimensions

In order to discover and describe socio/affective trends and outcomes for language education with social media, a number of data strategies are being employed. Coded observations of both online and F2F learner interactions, learner self-reporting, interviews and questionnaires are being used to probe socio/affective dimensions of social media in terms of empowerment (Clark & Gruba, 2010; Harrison & Thomas, 2009; Warschauer, 1999), community building (Miceli, Murray & Kennedy, 2010), L2 user identity (Pasfield-Neofitou, 2011) and learner confidence (Arnold, 2007; Henderson et al., 2009). As uses of and research on social media for language education expand, so too will interest in affective dimensions of learning languages in social media environments.

Research focus: Pedagogical processes

How language educators can best capitalize on social media environments for extended activities as well as blended and fully online instructional practices are becoming central, critical concerns for language educator professional development across the novice-seasoned instructor spectrum. And, as more language education develops for online venues, research that focuses on pedagogical strategies, task design and teacher practices becomes particularly important (Meskill & Anthony, 2010). The practical and concomitant conceptual changes that come with moving some or all language instruction online are, after all, substantial (Meskill & Sadykova, 2011).

In a 2005 study of teacher-guided telecollaboration between learners of English and learners of Korean, Chung, Graves, Wesche and Barfurth examined transcripts of correspondence between the two groups. What marks this study as distinct from those with a focus on socio/affective outcomes is the researchers' foregrounding of the importance of task design, curricular coherence and teacher orchestration and guidance throughout these exchanges. With these instructional dimensions firmly in place, language learners in both groups demonstrated their ability to both complete tasks using the target language while coaching one another in the focal content and language in use. Similarly Müller-Hartmann's (2000) analysis of transcripts of online language learner interactions also foregrounds the importance of instructional tasks and task structures for successful learner exchanges online. In Dekinet's (2008) study focusing on instructional strategies, conversation analysis was used to determine whether and how peer-tutoring techniques would be responded to by learners of ESL. Native-speaker undergraduates were trained in online peer language assistance strategies that they employed with international students. Post-tutoring surveys indicate that NNS participants' language awareness was raised in response to trained tutor feedback on their target language output. Similarly, Wang (2009) examined the pedagogical context and procedures involved in preparing language learners to provide one another feedback on their blog posts. Learners were carefully instructed in effective ways to respond to one another. Transcripts of their blog interactions were subsequently analysed to determine if and how the feedback training was used and, if so, whether and how it was responded to.

Using F2F classroom recordings, transcripts of online interactions, and reflections of participating teachers, Lund (2006) conducted three case studies of EFL professionals' teaching practices in blended environments. The researcher tracked developing teaching practices that crossed and merged between online and F2F instructional contexts over the course of 18 months. Data reveal changes in what language got taught as well as the ways the target language was consequently used. Additionally, the research highlighted the specific pedagogical practices that must constantly accommodate new agencies and artefacts between and within instructional venues. Similarly, in a longitudinal classroom-based study Dooly (2011) examined the interplay of online telecollaborative discourse practices and those of the daily F2F classroom. From the emerging blended practices under observation, Dooly identified important consonances and dissonances between teacher plans and actual language learning, a critical consideration in the design, implementation and evaluation of pedagogical practices that integrate social media. Dooly employed discursive analysis of F2F and online interactions using close, line-by-line description and diachronic interpretation of the interactions in context.

Examining the impact of the online instructional language teaching strategy of highlighting text or 'textually enhanced feedback', Sachs and Suh (2007) found that this instructional strategy contributes to language learners' awareness of gaps in their target language development via student self-reports in conjunction with pre/

post-online conversation assessments. In this inquiry, verbal protocols were used to probe learner awareness of text enhancements during authentic online communication and their influence on learning.

In a series of studies that similarly focused on instructional conversation strategies in online venues, Meskill and Anthony (2005, 2007, 2008) found that learners of Russian responded both in terms of lexical and syntactic uptake and increased language awareness in response to a set of verbal strategies used by their instructors as they responded to teachable moments in blended and fully online courses. Each inquiry employed combined methodological techniques of archival transcript coding, pre- and post-student questionnaires and student interviews in determining learner responses to instructor-orchestrated online conversations. Iterative data analyses included tracking learner uptake throughout semester-long transcripts and interview protocols whereby learners commented directly on their contributions in course transcripts. Linkages between online discourse and evidence of language learning could thereby be drawn.

In a study of tandem learning, whereby learners with different mother tongues interact online to teach one another, Hauck and Youngs (2008) examined task design and participant interaction in asynchronous and synchronous modes. The collaborative task required learners to compare their immediate and wider physical environments. Multiple data sources included pre- and post-treatment questionnaires, recordings of online interactions between tutor and participants, student products in blogs, transcripts of discussions among learner and tutor participants and semi-structured interviews. The post-questionnaire elicited learners' perceptions of the two different learning environments, tasks, connectivity and interactivity. The multimodal affordances, especially the graphics tools, enabled learners to construct sophisticated visual representations of their physical surroundings, which was a central requirement in the task. In spite of these observations concerning online environments, the authors' main conclusion was that 'unless there are well-constructed tasks, simply participating in a synchronous oral/aural exchange does not necessarily lead to effective and motivated language and intercultural learning' (p. 102).

Using transcripts of intermediate EFL learners as they undertook collaborative tasks in Second Life, Peterson (2010) examined learners' participation structures by task and within task. Types of pedagogical tasks determined the amount and quality of learner interactions and also elicited synchronous participation strategies specific to tasks in virtual worlds, a promising direction for inquiry as virtual worlds become commonplace venues for language instruction.

Section summary: Pedagogical processes

The preceding studies foreground the pedagogical processes involved in the utilization of social media for language education. Each employs similar methodological strategies for doing so with coding by instructional task (Hauck & Youngs, 2008; Peterson, 2010) and by instructor pedagogical behaviours predominating (e.g., Chung et al., 2005; Dooly, 2011; Lund, 2006; Meskill & Anthony, 2005, 2007, 2008). Additional research strategies of examining the outcomes of explicitly training students to provide peer feedback via analysis of peer interaction transcripts are represented in Dekhinet (2008) and Sachs and Suh (2007). While the ways that language educators are integrating social media tools and practices continue to be reported as teacher research (see earlier discussion), and as language educators gain expertise and confidence in integrating social media into their instruction, additional research questions and approaches will consequently arise and be taken up through extended inquiry. For the moment, the methodological strategies of tracking instructional practices, tracking instructor language and its impact and tracking student perceptions of instructional events are represented.

Conclusion, future directions

In their book, *Internet Inquiry: Conversations about Method*, Markham and Baym (2008) ask

> Can we still draw on theories that were developed in an earlier epoch to frame our inquiry and explain our findings? How do we apply procedural models to a study when these models do not seem to fit anymore? How can we move beyond documenting the new to saying things of lasting value about phenomena that change so rapidly? (p. xiii)

At this point in the historical and conceptual evolution of online social media in language education, the bulk of research data is comprised of transcripts of online interactions with three foregrounded foci emerging: focus on the environment, focus on socio/affective outcomes and focus on pedagogy. The methodological techniques for probing these aspects of social media for language education are many, with the predominant dataset consisting of the convenient transcript of online interactions between and among learners, others and their instructors.

We have identified several notably more sophisticated methods of capturing data to help describe student interactions in social media spaces including focus groups, interviews, iterations of learner revisions, video records of face-to-face learner collaborations, digital records of learner content development, open-ended questionnaires, learner self-reports, questionnaires and transcripts of collaborative work. The third group of studies we reviewed highlights methodological strategies of tracking student perceptions of instructional events, tracking of instructional practices, instructor language and its impact. The datasets include transcripts of online language learner interactions, classroom video recordings, written teacher reflections, questionnaires, interviews, student self-reports, verbal protocols and samples of student products and samples of written student feedback. The studies and their methodologies point to an increasingly greater sophistication in using various tools to capture and describe student interactions in online environments, while also focusing on various pedagogies and online affordances that support student language acquisition.

Research questions fashioned to address online language teaching and learning, along with the theories and methods that animate these, have, like the phenomena themselves, expanded and diversified. And, as with second language acquisition studies more generally, this is in large part due to the limitations of positivist psychology-based inquiry. Strictly controlled comparison of, for example, teaching methods or materials becomes problematic both in terms of implementation and external validity. Likewise, the situation-dependent and anarchic nature of language learner interactions with others in social media venues does not lend itself to controlled experimentation. Instead, as we have seen, language education researchers have been actively exploring utilization of more robust research methods beyond restrictive psychology-based approaches.

New uses of new technologies inspire new inquiry. Learning languages in cyberspace is no exception. The challenge is to conceptualize, problematize and research the complex relationships that are organically arising between educators and students and the technologies they use in these spaces. Like internet practices generally, research design is always evolving. Examining complex phenomena such as language in these online venues can thereby never be static or prescriptive. Nor are research methods recipes for success. They are, rather, means, tools of argument and ways to narrate and illuminate what goes on in the world from well-established perspectives. We have surveyed the current range of research approaches and techniques employed for language education and social media as they fall into one of the prevailing three perspectives: the environment, socio/affective dimensions and pedagogy. Future directions for such work will be accommodating ever-evolving online discourse communities as well as exemplary online teaching practices as these develop. Consideration of these three areas of emphasis and their respective research techniques may assist researchers in being clear and consistently explicit about the purposes and perspectives of their studies.

References

Arnold, N. (2007). Reducing foreign language communication apprehension with computer-mediated communication: A preliminary study. *System, 35*(4), 469–86.

Block, D. (2003). *The social turn in second language acquisition.* Washington, DC: Georgetown University Press.

Chaudron, C. (1988). *Second language classrooms: Research on teaching and learning.* New York: Cambridge University Press.

Chung, Y., Graves, B., Wesche, M., & Barfurth, M. (2005). Computer-mediated communication in Korean-English chat rooms: Tandem learning in an international language program. *The Canadian Modern Language Review, 62*, 49–86.

Clark, C., & Gruba, P. (2010). The use of social media sites for foreign language learning: An autoethnographic study of *Livemocha.* In C. H. Steel, M. J. Keppell, P. Gerbic & S. Housego (Eds.), *Curriculum, technology & transformation for an unknown future.*

Proceedings ascilite Sydney. Retrieved from http://ascilite.org.au/conferences/sydney10/procs/Cclark-full.pdf

Davis, K. (1995). Qualitative theory and methods in applied linguistics research. *TESOL Quarterly, 29*(3), 427–53.

Dekhinet, R. (2008). Online enhanced corrective feedback for ESL learners in higher education. *Computer Assisted Language Learning, 21*(5), 409–25.

Dooly, M. (2011). Divergent perceptions of telecollaborative language learning tasks: Task-as-workplan vs. task-as-process. *Language Learning & Technology, 15*(2), 69–91.

Flewitt, R., & Lamy, M. (2011). Describing online conversations: Insights from a multimodal approach. In C. Devotte, M. Lamy & R. Kern (Eds.), *Décrire la conversation en ligne: Le face à face distanciel* (pp. 71–93). Lyon: Ens Éditions.

Gass, S., & Schacter, J. (1989). *Linguistic perspectives on second language acquisition.* New York: Cambridge University Press.

Harrison, R., & Thomas, M. (2009). Identity in online communities: Social media sites and language learning. *International Journal of Emerging Technologies and Society, 7*(2), 109–24.

Hauck, M., & Youngs, B. L. (2008). Telecollaboration in multimodal environments: The impact on task design and learner interaction. *Computer Assisted Language Learning, 21*(2), 87–124.

Henderson, M., Huang, H., Grant, S., & Henderson, L. (2009). Language acquisition in *Second Life*: Improving self-efficacy beliefs. In *Same places, different spaces. Proceedings ascilite Auckland 2009.* Retrieved from www.ascilite.org.au/conferences/auckland09/procs/henderson.pdf

Horwitz, E. K., Horwitz, M. B., & Cope, J. (1986). Foreign language classroom anxiety. *Modern Language Journal, 70*(2), 125–32.

Jepson, K. (2005). Conversations and negotiated interaction in text and voice chatrooms. *Language Learning & Technology, 9*(3), 79–98.

Kost, C. (2011). Investigating writing strategies and revision behavior in collaborative wiki projects. *CALICO Journal, 28*(3), 606–20.

Kuteeva, M. (2011). Wikis and academic writing: Changing the writer–reader relationship. *English for Specific Purposes, 30*(1), 44–57.

Lam, E., & Rosario-Ramos, E. (2009). Multilingual literacies in transnational digitally mediated contexts: An exploratory study of immigrant teens in the United States. *Language and Education, 23*(2), 171–90.

Lankshear, C., & Knobel, M. (2004). *A handbook for teacher research: From design to implementation.* Maidenhead, UK: Open University Press.

Lund, A. (2006). The multiple contexts of online language teaching. *Language Teaching Research, 10*(2), 181–204.

— (2008). Wikis: A collective approach to language production. *ReCALL, 20*(1), 35–54.

Markham, A., & Baym, N. (2008). *Internet inquiry: Conversations about method.* New York: Sage.

Meskill, C. (2005). Metaphors that shape and guide CALL research. In J. Egbert & G. Petrie (Eds.), *CALL research perspectives* (pp. 25–40). Mahwah, NJ: Erlbaum.

Meskill, C., & Anthony, N. (2005). Foreign language learning with CMC: Forms of online instructional discourse in a hybrid Russian class. *System, 33*(1), 89–105.

— (2007). Form-focused communicative practice via computer mediated communication: What language learners say. *CALICO Journal, 25*(1), 69–90.

— (2008). Computer mediated communication: Tools for instructing Russian heritage language learners. *Heritage Language Journal, 6*(1), 1–22.

— (2010). *Teaching languages online.* Bristol, UK: Multilingual Matters.

Meskill, C., & Sadykova, G. (2011). Introducing EFL faculty to online instructional conversations. *ReCALL Journal, 23*(3), 200–17.

Meskill, C., Anthony, N., Hilliker, S., Tseng, C., & You, J. (2006). Computer Assisted Language Learning: A survey of K-12 ESOL English to speakers of other languages teacher uses and preferences. *TESOL Quarterly, 40*(2), 439–51.
Miceli, T., Murray, S. V., & Kennedy, C. (2010). Using an L2 blog to enhance learners' participation and sense of community. *Computer Assisted Language Learning, 23*(4), 321–41.
Müller-Hartmann, A. (2000). The role of tasks in promoting intercultural learning in electronic learning networks. *Language Learning & Technology, 4*(2), 129–47.
Nunan, D., & Bailey, K. (2007). *Exploring second language classroom research.* Boston: Heinle.
O'Reilly, T. (2005). What is Web 2.0. Retrieved January 23, 2012, from http://oreilly.com/web2/archive/what-is-web-20.html
Pasfield-Neofitou, S. (2011). Second language learners' experiences of virtual community and foreignness. *Language Learning & Technology, 15*(2), 92–108.
Peterson, M. (2010). Learner participation patterns and strategy use in Second Life: An exploratory case study. *ReCALL Journal, 22*(3), 273–92.
Rovai, A. (2001). Building classroom community at a distance: A case study. *Educational Technology, Research and Development, 49*(4), 33–48.
Sachs, R., & Suh, B. (2007). Textually enhanced recasts, learner awareness, and L2 outcomes in synchronous computer-mediated interaction. In A. Mackey (Ed.), *Conversational interaction in second language acquisition* (pp. 196–227).
Sauro, S., & Smith, B. (2010). Investigating L2 performance in text chat. *Applied Linguistics, 31*(4), 554–77.
Savignon, S., & Roithmeier, W. (2004). Computer-mediated communication: Texts and strategies. *CALICO Journal, 21*(2), 265–90.
Smith, B. (2005). The relationship between negotiated interaction, learner uptake, and lexical acquisition in task-based computer-mediated communication. *TESOL Quarterly, 39*(1), 33–58.
Thorne, S. (2003). Artifacts and cultures-of-use in intercultural communication. *Language Learning & Technology, 7*(2), 38–67.
Tudini, V. (2010). *Online second language acquisition.* New York: Continuum.
Turkle, S. (2011). *Alone together: Why we expect more from technology and less from each other.* New York: Basic Books.
Von der Emde, S., Schneider, J., & Kötter, M. (2001). Technically speaking: Transforming language learning through virtual learning environments (MOOs). *The Modern Language Journal, 85*(2), 210–25.
Wang, H. (2009). Weblog-mediated peer editing and some pedagogical recommendations: *A case study. JALT CALL Journal, 5*(2), 29–44.
Warschauer, M. (1999). *Electronic literacies: Language, culture, and power in online education.* Mahwah, NJ: Lawrence Erlbaum.
— (2000). On-line learning in second language classrooms: An ethnographic study. In M. Warschauer & R. Kern (Eds.), *Network-based language teaching: Concepts and practice* (pp. 41–58). New York: Cambridge University Press.
— (2009). 'Foreword'. In M. Thomas (Ed.), *Handbook of research on Web 2.0 and second language learning.* Hershey, PA: Information Science Reference.
Warschauer, M., & Grimes, D. (2007). Audience, authorship, and artifact: The emergent semiotics of Web 2.0. *Annual Review of Applied Linguistics, 27,* 1–23.
Zheng, D., Young, M., & Wagner, M. (2009). Negotiation for action: English language learning in gamebased virtual worlds. *Modern Language Journal, 93,* 489–511.

4

Second language teacher education for CALL: An alignment of practice and theory

Gary Motteram, Diane Slaouti and Zeynep Onat-Stelma

Summary

This chapter presents a case for a greater alignment of teacher education for computer-assisted language learning (CALL) to sociocultural theory. It suggests that this is an appropriate alignment because the field of second language teacher education (SLTE) has increasingly taken this perspective and there is a good argument for moving teacher education for CALL more towards an educational perspective and away from its home roots of second language acquisition (SLA). This chapter presents the development of the growing field of teacher education for CALL, a brief overview of sociocultural theory and then shows how this can be applied via three illustrative vignettes arising from a recent project with Cambridge University Press. The 2-year project explored the practices of a large group of adult language teachers around the world utilizing technology and was captured in 17 case studies.

Introduction

Teacher education for CALL has been part of the teacher education landscape for at least twenty years, but has only started to have a separate identity as a subject for serious study and scholarship in the last ten. Over this period it has grown and developed from its roots in applied linguistics, but as this chapter will argue, it is time to accelerate this growth and ally CALL more closely with the educational mainstream and the developing trends in the fields of SLTE. These trends encompass what Johnson (1996) and others have termed the 'sociocultural turn' and we will argue and demonstrate through vignettes of teachers using technology why we believe that this is an appropriate development.

There is an ongoing debate in research into language learning which sees researchers in the cognitive tradition and those in the sociocultural not able to agree on how they view the field of language development, or the methods of investigation that they use. This debate is commonly agreed to have been brought into focus by an article by Firth and Wagner (1997) who argued:

> that SLA [Second Language Acquisition] research requires a significantly enhanced awareness of the contextual and interactional dimensions of language use, an increased 'emic' (i.e., participant-relevant) sensitivity towards fundamental concepts, and the broadening of the traditional SLA data base. (p. 285)

The cognitive tradition commonly referred to as SLA, views language development as a process that occurs in isolation in the mind of the individual and methods used to research language development are still generally experimental. Much of the research focuses on the acquisition of grammar and vocabulary and not much occurs in real classroom contexts. This tradition has developed out of the work of Chomsky (1965) and Krashen (1981).

The sociocultural tradition, which has its roots in Vygotsky (1978, 1986), views language development as a process that occurs in the social realm first and the meaning that is made in the social realm is then internalized. The research traditions are more holistic and look at what happens in the activity of language learning itself taking into account all of the elements in the environment and all of the actors. As a result we get a richer and broader understanding of how languages are acquired and what the practices are that facilitate the process.

There has been a tradition in CALL research that has followed the more cognitive SLA route, although we can see this slowly changing as the influences of the sociocultural turn begin to be felt more strongly. However, researchers like Warschauer and Kern (2000) have argued for some time that CALL came of age when it started to enable people to do the things they wanted to do with language through technology, enabling language activity to be social and also observable. In an edited collection published in 2000, they and others reported on activity that they termed network-based language learning (NBLT). Warschauer and Kern have suggested that we therefore need a broader theory set than that provided by cognitive SLA and Warschauer wrote one of the early articles in the CALL field that laid out a sociocultural viewpoint (1997). Others have also followed this tradition: Thorne, Black and Sykes (2009), for example, extended the use of these theories to other virtual spaces, for example, internet interest groups and online games. Gánem-Gutiérrez (2009) has explored classroom practice learning language with computers.

This chapter therefore will show how the 'sociocultural family of learning theories' (Roth & Lee, 2007, p. 189), which is already partially being used in the field of CALL research (Motteram, 2012), is applicable to teacher education for CALL and has the necessary explanatory power to promote its growth as a serious subject for academic study. It will further argue that the adoption of the broader theory set would enable us to build the field on a more solid foundation and more easily allow us to compare the work we do.

The broad domain

In order to know where to better position teacher education for CALL, we need to develop an understanding of how the field has developed. A good place to start is a recent book by Burns and Richards (2009), which has 30 chapters on different aspects of what they term SLTE. Alongside the other 28, there are 2 later chapters that look specifically at ways that educational technology has begun to impact on the field of SLTE. The fact that a recent general book on teacher education should consider it important to include at least two chapters on aspects of educational technology is in itself a good indication of the sub-domain's growing importance and that technology in education is now considered a part of the mainstream. This trend is found increasingly in general introductions to language teaching methodology, where technology features more and more (e.g., Tomlinson, 2011). In Burns and Richards (2009) there is a chapter on language teacher education at a distance by Hall and Knox (2009) and one on the what and the how of technology in teacher education for CALL by Reinders (2009).

The opening section of Burns and Richards (2009), called the 'Landscape of Second Language Teacher Education', has four chapters: Scope; Trends; Critical LTE; and Social and Cultural Perspectives. In the introduction to the book Burns and Richards argue that while English has become a global phenomenon and supports the developing global economy as a lingua franca, the ratio of learners to teacher educators in many parts of the world is very high leading to an explosion of teacher education courses and one might argue, although Burns and Richards do not, an increase in the move towards technology supported courses run at a distance to try to help solve this problem.

Internal debates within the field of language teaching in general have an impact on what people choose to focus on in teacher education courses, as do debates in the wider field of teacher education. Burns and Richards (2009) talk, for example, of reflective practice and teacher identity as being an internal debate within the SLTE field, whereas this has its origins in the broader world of teacher education, however, these perspectives have been taken on as a core activity within the world of SLTE, they are no longer considered as outliers. External pressures, including the global trends mentioned above, also include the development of independent standards that we adhere to, or work towards in different domains. We will consider external standards for CALL teacher education as part of the sociocultural domain later, but suffice it to say for the time being that institutions like the European Commission or national governments have an increasing view on the what and how of teacher development and the way that teachers practise in classrooms. The European Commission are very keen on making sure that ICT is used effectively in schools and have a set of competences that they are expecting all member states to work towards (www.ecompetences.eu/) and TESOL International have also developed their own set of standards (Healey et al., 2011).

Burns and Richards (2009) mention that within SLTE there is considerable diversity in the courses on offer and alongside the development of courses that include technology has been the development of courses specializing in working with teachers of business English, or young learners, for example. They go on to consider the knowledge base, the nature of teacher learning, the role of context, teacher cognition, teacher identity, teacher methods and strategies, accountability and critical language teacher education.

A key feature of the discussion in the Burns and Richards is the move towards a sociocultural perspective when it comes to considering both language development and language teacher education; this is further explored by Johnson in chapter 2 of their book. Johnson wrote an early and influential article on this development in 2006, and has since then produced her own book that explores the realm of the sociocultural in teacher education (2009), as well as a collection of articles with Golombek (Johnson & Golombek, 2011). Johnson (2009) argues we need to shift the focus in the knowledge base away from the parent disciplines of, for example, linguistics, course design and testing that have traditionally been the bedrock of language teacher education to exploring alongside this what Shulman (1986) has termed pedagogical content knowledge (PCK). This is the knowledge that teachers have about teaching their subject discipline, the theories about teaching that they have built out of their practice.

While it is important to change our understanding of the knowledge base, it is also important to explore how teachers might change their understandings of what they do and why and how this might be changed with the development of practice around reflection, action research and cooperative development. We will also be considering this in relation to SLTE for CALL.

A third aspect of the change that Johnson highlights is the move away from the narrow definition of SLA to the broader understanding of the field to include context and interaction, but which focus on the viewpoint of the learner. She cites the article by Firth and Wagner (1997) that we have already touched on.

Another important and related field that has developed in importance as SLTE has grown is that of teacher beliefs (Ertmer, 2005) or teacher cognition (Borg, 2006). Part of the process of encouraging teachers to make (more) use of technology in their teaching is to work with them to explore the beliefs they have about its efficacy and implementation when it comes to improving learner language development. Teacher belief and teacher cognition research have shown that for teachers to change their practices and to begin to effectively include technology in their teaching they have to have a belief that this is going to be of benefit to their learners and also a value for themselves. This is an important aspect of the sociocultural domain as has been argued by Alanen (2003), in a chapter which focuses on young language learners' beliefs about language learning.

We now turn to second language teacher education for CALL to see how far it measures up to these developments.

Second language teacher education for CALL

This chapter will not offer a comprehensive literature review in the traditional sense and will be mainly focused on materials published in and since the 2006 book by Hubbard and Levy, however, it will look briefly at important relevant contributions to the thesis presented here from earlier publications.

The first collection of articles on teacher education and CALL was a special issue of the journal *Language Learning & Technology* published in 2002. This was edited by Zhao and Tella (2002) and while all of the articles explore aspects of the world of teachers and technology only one focuses specifically on the area of teachers being trained to use technology in classrooms. In the article Egbert, Paulus and Nakamichi (2002), suggested, following Freeman (1996), that SLTE was 'an unstudied problem' (p. 108). They therefore chose to explore whether and how teachers transfer training into their classrooms and whether, in fact, the training course is particularly important in developing teachers' use of CALL. They considered four research areas: how teachers develop knowledge about CALL and the types of activities that are typically found in classrooms; what impact the coursework had on the teaching that they were doing; whether there were particular factors that made a difference to the teachers using technology in their classrooms; and whether and how teachers develop and master new ideas about CALL after finishing the course (p. 109).

Their study explored the practices of 20 recent graduates who had taken a graduate-level CALL course and looked at how they applied what they had learned on the course into their teaching. Their conclusions can be summarized as follows:

- Teachers who show some interest or skill in using technology in classes before they start the course are more likely to continue using it, but perhaps in different ways.
- Teachers also turn to the Web and other colleagues for help solving particular classroom issues and it is not a lack of interest on the part of the teachers, but time pressure, the curriculum and not having the right resources that influence whether they are successful.
- Egbert, Paulus and Nakamichi (2002) go on to argue that there is a need for 'more contextualised instruction' (p. 122) and begin to refer to the work of Lave and Wenger (1991) and ideas of situated practice.

The next key work in the field of teacher education for CALL is the Hubbard and Levy (2006) book where we find a mixture of chapters, some that approach the field of teacher education from the perspective of applied linguistics and some take an SLTE approach. Examples of chapters that follow the SLTE approach include: Slaouti and Motteram (2006) who engage with the theory of situated practice and Egbert (2006) in her exploration of how to engage teachers in the realities of classroom teaching while being on a course. Debski (2006), in exploring project-oriented learning on an MA programme at the University of Melbourne, supports his discussion with Papert's constructionism. Chin-chi Chao (2006) uses the cognitive apprenticeship model of Collins, Brown and Newman (1989) and both Meskill (2006) and Hanson-Smith (2006) make reference to communities of practice (COP).

The chapters listed above recognize the importance of the sociocultural turn in SLTE and suggest the beginnings of an alignment towards a more education-focused teacher education for CALL, which will be of benefit to the developing field.

This chapter will now go on to explore some of the origins of sociocultural turn and look at how it helps us understand what teachers do in their classrooms and how this can have impact on the teacher education process.

The sociocultural in SLTE for CALL

A situated perspective

In the same way that in order to understand language development from the perspective of the individual in a particular space at a particular time, teachers encountering teacher education for CALL either in pre- or in-service courses, or informally in a community of practice are governed in what they do by the context, the beliefs of the individual teacher, the teacher's knowledge base, the teacher's pedagogical content knowledge, other colleagues, the nature of the curriculum, the available technologies, the perspective of the home institution, the support of technical colleagues and so on.

Elliott (1993) refers to this as situational understanding. Others use the term 'situated' and this term comes to us primarily through the work of Schön (1987) and Lave and Wenger (1991). Lave and Wenger are concerned with how people learn, not with teachers and what they do. However, the underlying principles that we are interested in are similar and the distinction between learning and a term like 'coming to know' (Somekh, 2007, p. 148), often used to describe teacher learning through practice, are very close in meaning. Lave and Wenger argue for the social construction of knowledge, which takes place within frameworks for practice. Wenger (1999, p. 4) explains such knowledge acquisition as referring:

> . . . not just to local events of engagement in certain activities with certain people, but to a more encompassing process of being active participants in the

practices of social communities and constructing *identities* in relation to these communities.

Learning or 'coming to know' then comes out of engagement with other people and their ideas; the same is true with teachers and teacher education. Teachers on a training or development course 'come to know' about an aspect of teaching filtered through their background knowledge and experience as learners (pre-service) or teachers (in-service), the community that they engage with, the input that is part of the course, their reflection on their understanding of their practice and their willingness to entertain new ideas and put these into practice. As Schön (1987) argues practitioners reflect both 'in-action' and 'on-action'. 'In-action' reflection means reflection in a situation, while it is occurring. 'Reflection-on-action' occurs after the event, but is still about the particular context. This reflection may cause them to re-examine their knowledge and beliefs and this might lead to change according to Schön (1987). This can occur on a training or development course as well as in the throws of practice itself.

As we have argued, the view of teaching and learning has been constrained so far by a cognitive approach. We now turn to a more detailed overview of sociocultural theory to gain a broader picture and to understand why this picture is so relevant to teacher education for CALL.

Sociocultural theory

Sociocultural theory has a number of starting points, but is very often associated with Vygotsky and colleagues, Luria and Leont'ev. Vygotsky was concerned in his work with bringing back together two strands of psychology: the more experimental and psychometric approach that focuses on trying to reveal the cognitive landscape of the isolated mind; and a cultural approach that saw development as being a dialectic between humans and their environment, and which recognized the fundamental role that cultural artefacts and history play in human development (Cole, 1996).

Humans have two parts to their nature, their physical and biological attributes and their ability and desire to create cultural artefacts (agency) that are passed on to the next and later generations, and which become altered and augmented over time. These cultural artefacts enable humans to develop the unique skills and abilities that allow them to supersede their inherent physical and biological attributes and make us fundamentally different from other species:

> The internalization of socially rooted and historically developed activities is the distinguishing feature of human psychology, the basis of the qualitative leap from animal to human psychology. (Vygotsky, 1978, p. 57)

Vygotsky was interested in children's development and the role that the cultural artefact of language had on the development of higher psychological processes. As humans we have the biological capability to produce the sounds that make up spoken language and the cognitive capability to make meaning through words, we also relate these words together through morphology and syntax. In this way humans are enabled to make sense of the situations they encounter in the world and to engage in communicative acts with others. These acts in the world help to develop the processes that make up the human mind. However, it is only through engagement with the physical world and the cultural artefacts found there that the human mind can grow and develop.

The development of language (and other symbol systems like numbers) over time has had a profound impact on human development. Initially starting with spoken language, where stories and other information were passed down the generations by telling, the later developments of writing in its various forms has changed how humans can record their history and develop a broad knowledge base, accessible, potentially, to all. These developments in cultural artefacts have had and continue to have an impact on human mental processes. In our moves through different ages from the agricultural to the industrial and latterly information age, we have seen the impact that writing in different media and other types of recording (sound and video) have had on the ability of people to access and use information (Briggs & Burke, 2009).

We will now look more closely at sociocultural views of mediating tools and teacher action in the world.

First generation sociocultural theory, which is how Vygotskian theory is often characterized (Roth & Lee, 2007, p. 189), sees a subject focused on an object and using 'sign or semiotic mediation, especially in the form of speech' (ibid.) to engage in development. This first generation theory is often represented as a triangle where the base of the triangle is the stimulus and response of behavioural theory (Figure 4.1).

Vygotsky added to this the mediating cultural artefact that he proposed was always in evidence when learning occurred (Figure 4.2).

Vygotsky's research focused on children, because they were still in the process of developing, and such developments could be seen and monitored. We can see a child trying to reach for a toy that they are interested in playing with, perhaps initially pointing at it and then later beginning to imitate the sounds that the adult carer uses when the child reaches for the toy. After time, this sound becomes fully formed complex sentences that are later used by the child in a generalizable way to get what they want; they no longer need to point. Vygotsky's colleagues later looked at adults who suffered some form of neurological damage and their road to recovery in order to understand how they had recovered. Leont'ev extended Vygotsky's initial work to show how the broader community was involved in an activity. Leont'ev (1977) used a description of a hunt to show how different parts of an activity system work together (or against) the

FIGURE 4.1 *A behavioural view of learning challenged by Vygotsky.*

subject(s) to achieve their object. In a hunt you might have beaters who work to chase the birds from the woods towards the group who have guns and who shoot the birds. The shooters have to be careful that they only fire in a certain direction so as not to wound any of the beaters. Next to the shooters stand people who load the guns. At the end of the day the shooters keep most of the game, but each beater and loader also receives one bird as their pay. The Subjects use guns to kill animals, they observe certain rules of shooting in order not to kill other people; there is a community of people involved in the process: beaters, loaders and others who divide up the labour between them.

Leont'ev (1977) did not represent his work as triangles, this was Engeström's (1987) creation of a heuristic based on Leont'ev's ideas (see Figure 4.3). Engeström took Leont'ev's (1977) story of a primitive hunt and re-created it as a heuristic to show how human activity is made up of a number of elements which surround the core relationship between the Subject and Object.

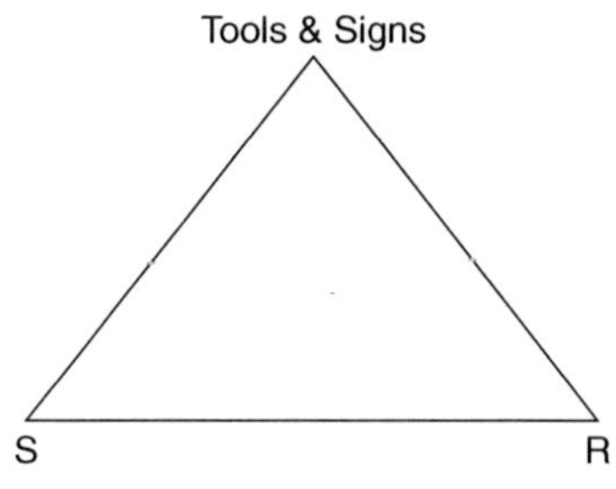

FIGURE 4.2 *Cultural mediation in development.*

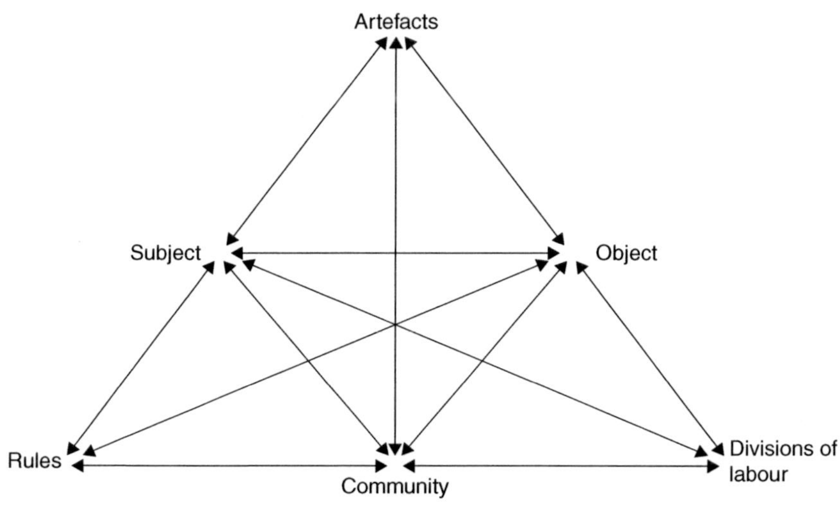

FIGURE 4.3 *Engestrom's (1987) representation of Leont'ev's (1977) description of a hunt.*

Any activity is thus a complex matrix; to gain an overall impression of sociocultural teacher education we need to consider all of the elements. We may not be able to focus on all of these at the same time, but they are always going to be there having an impact on what we do in the teacher education process and once teachers begin to work in classrooms. Egbert acknowledges this in both her 2002 article (with Paulus and Nakamichi), but extends this idea in her 2006 chapter. While Hubbard and Levy's book focused on the teacher in 2006, the domain that we need to explore now is rather broader and we are aware of this from the literature from SLTE, as we have shown. If we are to build up the field of teacher education for CALL, then we need to consider all of these different elements.

Activity theory

The activity theory heuristic of the triangle can be a useful way of representing all of the different elements of a situation that need to be taken into account when we consider what should be the domain of teacher education for CALL. It is one of the developments of sociocultural theory that has been used by a number of writers in the field of CALL (e.g., Blin, 2004) and it is argued here is the most useful for an understanding of teachers in their classroom settings.

Here is a representation of the issues that we believe to be relevant to the teacher education for CALL arguments that we have presented so far (see Figure 4.4).

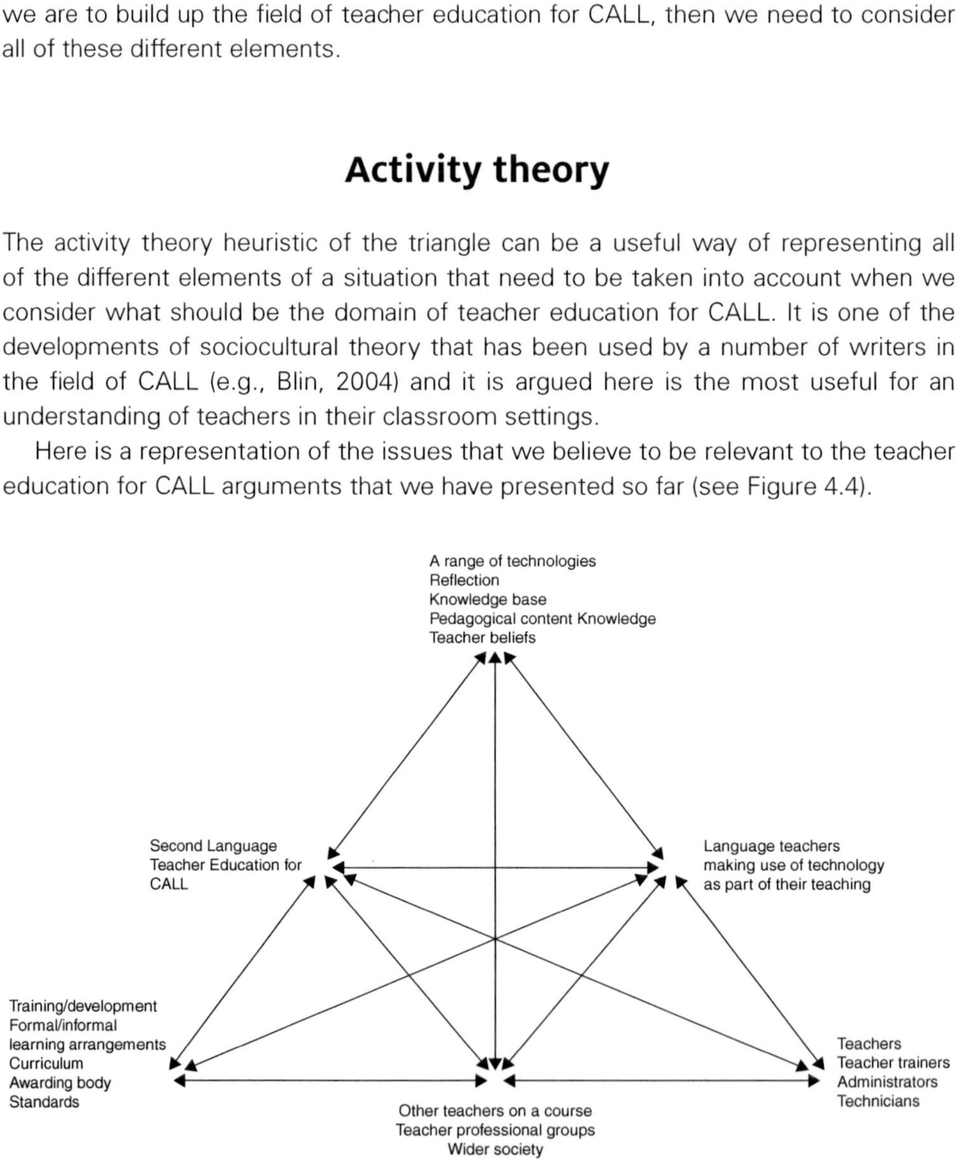

FIGURE 4.4 *The sociocultural domain of teacher education for CALL.*

All of the elements that have been discussed so far are included in the heuristic. We see the growing field of teacher education for CALL and the influences on the process of supporting language teachers who are trying, or some cases perhaps, being required to use technology in their classrooms. We can see at a glance what the different factors are and we can equally show others the complexity of what needs to be taken into account when starting to work with teachers and support them to make use of technology to support language teaching.

The Cambridge study

The chapter will now present data from teachers who were involved in a recent project conducted with Cambridge University Press exploring the practices of adult teachers of languages using technology. This project lasted for 2 years and as well as surveying a large number of teachers around the world, also developed 17 case studies showing the kind of detail of the practice that we have been discussing so far.

What follows is a vignette based on one of the detailed case studies. This gives a flavour of a teacher going through a process of 'coming to know' about his practice.

Simon[1]

Simon, originally from the US, works at a Japanese state university teaching general English and TOEFL and TOEIC exam classes to undergraduate students from a mix of disciplines. Class sizes vary from 10 up to 30 or 40. Learner motivation can be equally wide-ranging, Simon describing some who are forced to learn English as having had any interest, 'drilled out of them'. Like many universities in Japan, there is a lot of technology available. Students have access to a virtual private network, personalised desktops, and WiFi. The latter is not widely exploited by students, however, who do not usually have their own laptops, making greater use of mobile phones, to the extent that Simon believes that 'some have skipped a computer generation and just do not know how to use a PC or laptop'. Any ambitions to exploit their phones for learning activities have also thus far been fruitless, as despite Simon perceiving potential there, they cannot connect to the wireless network. There are, nevertheless, institutional aspirations for e-learning as a way to maintain currency in the student market. Simon attributes a university vision for the development of 'ready e-learning content' for any teacher to use with specific client groups to an ambition to cater for declining general student numbers (an outcome of falling birth rates) through larger staff-student ratios. His own use of technology does not chime with a 'ready solutions' vision; flexible responses to his learner needs such as production of listening content (MP3 files, iTunes) which he can manipulate as he wishes (slowing down rate of speech in Quicktime), tasks created with text manipulation software (Hot Potatoes) and embedded into the class VLE (Moodle),

> learners practising pronunciation with Audacity all bear witness to his description of his practice as tool-based, a practice enabled by his own technology-using confidence. Today he is teaching a conversation class in a recently installed 'state-of-the art' CALL lab. Equipped with computers, arranged in rows, with Internet connection for both teacher and students, Simon can control all machines in the room. A document camera allows him to display the textbook on a central screen. 'I didn't really "choose" the classroom technologies, as the room was actually assigned to me against my will,' he says. 'Although I'd planned on using the VLE (Moodle) for course support, I didn't think the physical layout of the room would be conducive to good conversation practice, but in the end everything worked out quite well.' A task for conversation practice, an interactive listening quiz produced using Hot Potatoes, and a link to an external vocabulary quiz, have all been added to Moodle before the lesson. Students have submitted an assignment and preparatory notes for the present lesson. Simon observes that a 90-minute lesson has involved him in two hours of checking of 30 submissions, and about one hour to create, upload, and embed the quiz. After checking Simon's comments on their work, Simon 'turns off' the monitors around the room, and students' attention is turned to the textbook displayed on the document camera. Focussing on the shared screen, pairs carry out a review task; their computers are then 'released' again for the listening task and quiz. Despite Simon observing wryly, 'our "advanced" system does not seem to allow for the playing of audio over the speakers in the room' his reflections are more positively coloured. 'When this is done in groupwork, problems don't stand out as much. This may have had negative effects on motivation for the weaker students, but it did allow me to step up and offer personal assistance'. Simon makes a point of noting that this has contributed to 'better bonds between lower level students and the teacher, fostering a better learning relationship'.

This vignette paints a brief picture of Simon in his contextual reality. Readers of this description may recognize some of the detail of their own institutional setting, or of Simon's technology use and thinking, though probably not all. We, therefore, start with a view that our understanding of what teachers do and how they do it relates to interpretations of contextual realities, filtered through the knowledge and beliefs they hold about themselves and about language teaching and learning and their students. We can understand some aspects of the situations that the teachers are in through observation or by gathering more objective data, as we did through a survey that was a part of the Cambridge study, however, we only really understand how the teacher views their situation by exploring both teachers' actions and their interpretation of those actions, as we did through the case studies in the project. The picture that emerges from this process not only provides exemplars of teachers' technology use in the real world, but also reflects the increasing acceptance, not only in our field but in many other areas of life, that in order to come close to genuine understanding of how and why people act, we must look beyond the individual alone. We *are* interested in the individual, which is why we focus on teacher cases, but in the individual as they act in their environment.

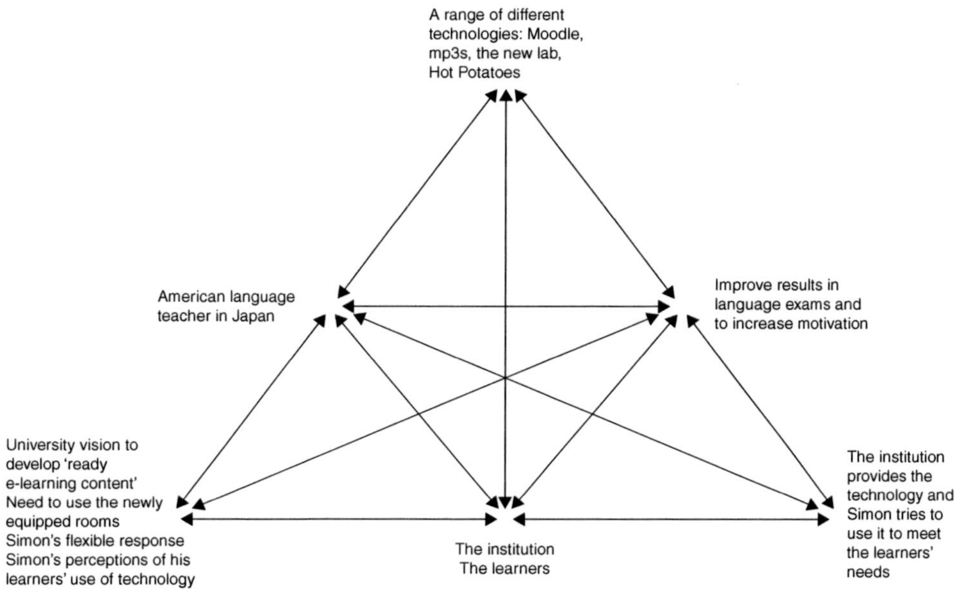

FIGURE 4.5 *A sociocultural perspective on Simon.*

We can represent Simon's context and our analysis of it in Figure 4.5.

The case study and its representation in this heuristic helps us to begin to build a stronger and more trustworthy picture of the realities of teaching using CALL and these understandings can feed into the teacher education process. We can show on our teacher education courses working with teachers to develop their skill using technology that there is a reason why we focus not simply on introducing teachers to technology, but also on considering learning theory, the context that they work in, the societal drivers, the nature of learners and whether they can get effective support from their institution.

We now turn to voices of two other teachers, who use technology with their adult learners. First, Ilya, working in Switzerland, talks about her ambitions to use wikis to encourage her advanced learners to see writing development as a social and situated practice. Next, Aaron reflects on perceptions of how the pedagogical opportunities that technology integration can bring may mean working in ways which are counter to his Colombian university learners' expectations.

Ilya

I've noticed that learners can improve quite a bit through guided correction of their work. I use a code to describe the mistakes they make, sometimes marking the mistake and sometimes not, letting them correct these themselves. I also use the comment function on digitally sent homework, explaining certain problems. This has worked well in making their work more correct, though many learners are unable to increase the vocabulary and use of structures in their writing. On the other hand there are a few learners who have reached a degree of complexity which is desirable and from which the other learners could profit. Up until now I haven't found a way to let learners work together on writing and correction for more than just a very few lessons because of the time involved. With the wiki learners work on a text they have written (further texts from the learners can be added) and profit from each other. They are sharing with each other, comparing language and making changes without fear of 'ruining' the text as the different versions can be compared and I'll monitor the process. Since this can take place outside the classroom, it frees up time for other things and gives them as much time as they need or want for looking up words and finding expressions.

Aaron

I try to integrate the CD-ROMs as much as possible because otherwise it's just going to be like an add-on and they're not going to be taken seriously. But even then they are not taken that seriously, and that relates to the teacher-learner relationships here. They're very traditional in the sense that students look at teachers and they think that we know everything. They will ask us instead of finding out for themselves – what's the term – it's a 'first answer' approach. They will find the first answer and that will be it, they don't need to know anything more and I think that Web activities contradict this idea of what students perceive the role of teachers to be. That's why it is very difficult here for distance learning courses to take off. They just think 'well the teacher's not doing anything here, I'm doing everything, what's going on. Why am I paying for a course where I have to do everything – I have to find the answers, that's not right'. That's all because of this traditional sort of teacher-student relationship.

These short extracts show us the insider, the 'emic' viewpoint and give us a clear sense of teacher perceptions of the attributes of specific technologies. They show teachers' starting points and the way their ideas develop based on the needs of their learners. This emphasizes the role of the beliefs that the teachers have about learning and teaching with technology and how these relate to the decision-making process connected with technology in the classroom. How this decision-making can provide different learning opportunities in relation to the beliefs of the different teachers about how language learning takes place and their understandings of how their learners like to learn. They also exemplify how decisions to use or not to use technology involve an interaction with the environment in which they work, the nature of the community, the community's rules and the divisions of labour between different participants in the community. As many of these teachers who are reporting the case studies are also involved in teacher education courses of various kinds, further work can be undertaken to show the link between such courses and what happens when they are back in their teaching posts as Egbert, Paulus and Nakamichi (2002) tried to show.

The broader understandings that we have of teachers' lives with technology from these case studies and the way that these show the importance of broader sociocultural domain can have a direct positive washback effect into teacher education for CALL and the work we do as trainers and educators on our courses. They also highlight practice for those working independently in informal communities of practice, who may be wondering whether their experiences chime with others in the domain.

Conclusions

The argument that has been made in this chapter is that while the origins of the field of teacher education for CALL were more closely connected to applied linguistics, we need to move away from this and more closely ally ourselves to the work currently being undertaken in SLTE. SLTE, as evidenced by recent publications by key researchers in this field, is focusing quite clearly on a sociocultural turn and this turn allows us to have a more significant understanding of what occurs in the real situations that our teachers find themselves in. By drawing on the kinds of case studies that were collected as part of the Cambridge study into adult language learning with technology and using in this case, an activity theory heuristic, we can show the connectedness of different studies and the realities of teachers' lives. This can be used to effectively focus on teachers' pedagogical content knowledge captured in the real world of activity, we can review the beliefs of teachers and the impact that they have on decision-making, we can consider what are likely to be the constraints that occur in teaching environments and how teachers have circumvented them. How a community of like-minded teachers can help to support each other in the development of their practice can be considered and we teachers can be involved in reporting their successes to the world. For us this is an important and significant step forward.

Acknowlegements

We would like to acknowledge the support of Cambridge University Press who funded this project and the Cambridge project team leaders Karen Momber and Daniel Stunell.

Note

1 Most of the teachers in this study wanted us to use their real names, although the contexts have not been identified directly.

References

Blin, F. (2004). CALL and the development of learner autonomy: Towards an activity-theoretical perspective. *ReCALL, 16*(2), 377–95.

Borg, S. (2006). *Teacher cognition and language education.* London: Continuum.

Briggs, A., & Burke, P. (2009). *Social history of the media: From Gutenberg to the Internet.* Cambridge: Polity Press.

Burns, A., & Richards, J. (Eds.) (2009). *The Cambridge guide to second language teacher education.* New York: Cambridge University Press.

Chao, C.-C. (2006). How WebQuests send technology to the background: Scaffolding EFL professional development in CALL. In P. Hubbard & M. Levy (Eds.), *Teacher education in CALL* (pp. 221–34). Amsterdam: John Benjamins.

Chomsky, N. (1965). *Aspects of the theory of syntax.* Massachusetts: MIT Press.

Cole, M. (1996). *Cultural psychology: A once and future discipline.* Harvard: Harvard University Press.

Collins, A., Brown, J., & Newman, S. (1989). Cognitive apprenticeship: Teaching the craft of reading, writing and mathematics. In L. B. Resnick (Ed.), *Knowing, learning and instruction: Essays in honor of Robert Glaser* (pp. 453–94). Hillsdale, NJ: Lawrence Erlbaum.

Debski, R. (2006). Theory and practice in teaching project-oriented CALL. In P. Hubbard & M. Levy (Eds.), *Teacher education in CALL* (pp. 99–114). Amsterdam: John Benjamins.

Egbert, J. (2006). Learning in context: Situating language learning in CALL. In P. Hubbard & M. Levy (Eds.), *Teacher education in CALL* (pp. 167–81). Amsterdam: John Benjamins.

Egbert, J., Paulus, T. M., & Nakamichi, Y. (2002). The impact of CALL instruction on classroom computer use: A foundation for rethinking technology in teacher education. *Language Learning and Technology, 6*(3), 108–26.

Elliot, J. (1993). Professional education and the idea of a practical educational science. In J. Elliott (Ed.), *Reconstructing teacher education.* London: Falmer Press.

Engeström, Y. (1987). *Learning by expanding: An activity-theoretical approach to developmental research.* Helsinki, Finland: Orienta-Konsultit Oy.

Ertmer, P. A. (2005). Teacher pedagogical beliefs: The final frontier in our quest for technology integration? *Educational Technology Research and Development, 53*(4), 25–39.

Firth, A., & Wagner, J. (1997). On discourse, communication, and (some) fundamental concepts in SLA research. *The Modern Language Journal, 81*(3), 285–300.

Freeman, D. (1996). The 'unstudied problem': Research on teacher learning in language teaching. In D. Freeman & J. Richards (Eds.), *Teacher learning in language teaching* (pp. 351–78). Cambridge: Cambridge University Press.

Gánem-Gutiérrez, G. A. (2009). Repetition, use of L1, and reading aloud as mediational mechanisms during collaborative activity at the computer. *Computer Assisted Language Learning, 22*(4), 323–48.

Hall, D. R., & Knox, J. S. (2009). Language teacher education by distance. In A. Burns & J. C. Richards (Eds.), *The Cambridge guide to second language teacher education* (pp. 218–29). Cambridge: Cambridge University Press.

Hanson-Smith, E. (2006). Communities of practice for pre- and in-service education. In P. Hubbard & M. Levy (Eds.), *Teacher education in CALL*, (pp. 301–15). Amsterdam: John Benjamins.

Healey, D., Hanson-Smith, E., Hubbard, P., Loannou-Georgiou, S., Kessler, G., & Ware, P. (2011). *TESOL technology standards: Description, integration, implementation.* Alexandria, VA: TESOL.

Hubbard, P., & Levy, M. (Eds.) (2006). *Teacher education in CALL*. Amsterdam: John Benjamins.
Johnson, K. E. (1996). The role of theory in L2 teacher education. *TESOL Quarterly 30*(4), 765–71.
— (2009). *Second language teacher education: A sociocultural perspective*. London: Routledge.
Johnson, K. E., & Golombek, P. R. (Eds.) (2011). *Research on second language teacher education: A sociocultural perspective on professional development*. New York: Routledge.
Krashen, S. D. (1981). *Second language acquisition and second language learning*. Oxford: Pergamon.
Lave, J., & Wenger, E. (1991). *Situated learning: Legitimate peripheral participation*. Cambridge: Cambridge University Press.
Leont'ev, A. N. (1977). *The development of mind*. Moscow: Progress Publishers.
Meskill, C., Anthony, N., Hilliker-VanStander, N. S., Tseng, C-H., & You, J. (2006). Expert-novice teaching mentoring in language learning technology. In P. Hubbard, & M. Levy (Eds.), *Teacher education in CALL* (pp. 283–98). Amsterdam: John Benjamins.
Motteram, G. (2012). Re-aligning research into teacher education for CALL and bringing it into the mainstream, *Language Teaching*. Available on CJO doi:10.1017/S0261444811000632.
Reinders, H. (2009). Technology and second language teacher education. In A. Burns & J. C. Richards (Eds.), *The Cambridge guide to second language teacher education* (pp. 230–7). Cambridge: Cambridge University Press.
Schön, D. (1987). *Educating the reflective practitioner*. San Francisco: Jossey-Bass
Shulman, L. S. (1986). Those who understand: Knowledge growth in teaching. *Educational Researcher, 15*(2), 4–14.
Slaouti, D., & Motteram, G. (2006). Reconstructing practice: Language teacher education and ICT. In P. Hubbard & M. Levy (Eds.), *Teacher education in CALL* (pp. 81–97). Amsterdam: John Benjamins.
Somekh, B. (2007). *Pedagogy and learning with ICT: Researching the art of innovation*. Oxford: Routledge.
Thorne, S. L., Black, R. W., & Sykes, J. (2009). Second language use, socialization, and learning in internet interest communities and online games. *Modern Language Journal, 93*, 802–21.
Tomlinson, B. (2011). *Materials development in language teaching*. Cambridge: Cambridge University Press.
Vygotsky, L. S. (1978). *Mind in society: The development of higher psychological processes*. Cambridge, MA: Harvard University Press.
— (1986). *Thought and language*. Massachusetts: Massachusetts Institute of Technology Press.
Warschauer, M. (1997). A sociocultural approach to literacy and its significance for CALL. In K. Murphy-Judy & R. Sanders (Eds.), *Nexus: The convergence of research & teaching through new information technologies* (pp. 88–97). Durham: University of North Carolina.
Warschauer, M., & Kern R. (Eds.) (2000). *Network-based language teaching: Concepts and practice*. Cambridge: Cambridge University Press.
Wenger, E. (1999). *Communities of practice: Learning, meaning and identity*. Cambridge: Cambridge University Press.
Zhao, Y., & Tella, S. (2002). From the special issue editors. *Language Learning & Technology*, 6(3), 2–5.

5

Research on computers in language testing: Past, present and future

James Dean Brown

Summary

The purpose of this chapter is to examine developments in computer-based language testing including what we have learned in the past, current trends and directions in future research. In the past, four sets of issues were addressed and fairly well resolved: item banking, using the new technologies, computer-adaptive language testing and the effectiveness of computers in language testing. Most of that research was practical in nature. More recently, much of the literature on computer-based language testing (CBLT) has focused on the following topics: overviews of the CBLT literature itself, CBLT delivery issues (including computer-adaptive language testing, computer vs traditional testing formats, Web-based language testing, interface architecture, the test takers' experience with CBLT and CBLT training for teachers), CBLT content (including computer assessment of vocabulary, speaking or oral skills, writing, listening and reading), example CBLTs and CBLT tools/resources. CBLT is not a new area of research, but it is clearly growing and generating a good deal of excitement within language testing.

Introduction

Roughly a decade and a half ago, Brown (1997) found that the CBLT literature was discussing: (a) how to use an item bank, (b) how to use new technologies, (c) how to build computer-adaptive tests and (d) how effective computers are in language testing. The purpose of the present chapter is to examine the CBLT literature that has appeared since that earlier article with the goal of summarizing how things have progressed and changed since then. To that end, this chapter will be organized under the following headings: overviews of CBLT, CBLT delivery, CBLT content, example CBLTs and CBLT tools and resources.

Since the literature on technology and testing, especially in language testing, is rife with acronyms that are used inconsistently across authors, I provide Table 5.1, which lists and spells out all of the general acronyms that I will use in this chapter. In the interest of clarity, I will limit myself to this list.

For similar reasons, I have provided Table 5.2, which lists and spells out various key acronyms for computer-based tests and testing systems and provides citations or URLs for getting more information about each.

Overviews of CBLT

Since Brown (1997, also reprinted in 2009), a number of other overview articles have appeared on the general topic of CBLT. For example, Gruba and Corbel (1997) focused almost entirely on CALT including discussions of the major contributions of CAT to CBLT; some specific test development projects; difficulties encountered in developing CALTs (including administrative, psychometric, test design and validity concerns); and future directions.

Alderson (2000a) briefly discussed how hardware and software had developed, how the TOEFL had arrived in a computer-based version, how the UCLES tests had become available in CD-ROM versions and how the internet was being used for language testing. In the process, he covered the advantages and disadvantages of CBLTs, the basics of CAT, the pedagogical advantages of CBLTs and advances in IBLTs, while focusing on examples from the TOEFL and DIALANG. He also proposed a research agenda.

Douglas (2000) provided an overview in the last chapter of his book of the roles of technology in assessment within LSP contexts (pp. 259–77). He included a section on internet resources for LSP testing (with a number of examples and URLs), as well as sections on CALTs and CBLTs for LSP.

Chapelle (2001) offered an excellent overview of CBLT to that date in her fourth chapter. She included a discussion of test method effects, an extensive examination of issues important for validation of CBLTs (validity arguments, validity criteria for evaluating tests and testing purposes, importance of construct validity, as well as empirical and logical analyses of validity), a section on CBLT usefulness criteria and detailed discussion of standards for empirically evaluating CBLTs.

In their overview of developments in CALL from 1900 to 2000, Liu, Moore, Graham and Lee (2003) included a section on CBLT (pp. 256–7) that summarized the major benefits of CBLT including the possibilities of: immediate feedback, individualized testing and randomization through test banks to increase testing security. This article also summarized the major criticisms of CBLT: the inability of technology to assess

TABLE 5.1 General acronyms used in this chapter

Acronym	Meaning	Notes
AES	Automated scoring systems	
AWE	Automated writing evaluation	
CALL	Computer-assisted language learning	
CALT	Computer-adaptive language test/testing	Specific to language testing
CAT	Computer-adaptive test/testing	General, in all fields
CBLT	Computer-based language test/testing	Synonym for computer-assisted language test/testing*
CBT	Computer-based testing	General, in all fields
CD-ROM	Compact disk read-only memory	
COPI	Computerized oral proficiency instrument	
IBLT	Internet-based language test/testing	Specific to language testing
IBT	Internet-based test/testing	General, in all fields
IRT	Item response theory	
IT	Information technology	
LSP	Language for specific purposes	
P&P	Paper-and-pencil	
PBLT	Paper-based language test/testing	Specific to language testing
SL/FL	Second language and foreign language	
SOPI	Simulated oral proficiency instrument	
UCLES	University of Cambridge Local Examinations Syndicate	
URL	Uniform resource locator	Commonly called an internet address
WBLT	Web-based language test/testing	Specific to language testing
WBT	Web-based test/testing	General, in all fields

* To avoid any possible confusion between computer-assisted language testing (shortened to CALT in some articles and computer-adaptive language testing (also shortened to CALT in some articles), I will consistently use the generic computer-based language testing abbreviated as CBLT when referring to all forms of computer-based or computer-assisted language testing. I will then reserve CALT for referring to computer-adaptive language testing.

TABLE 5.2 Acronyms used in this chapter for current computer-based tests and testing systems

Acronym	Test name	Where to find more information
ACT ESL	ACT English as a Second Language Placement Test	www.act.org/compass/tests/esl.html
BEST Plus	Basic English Skills Test	www.cal.org/aea/
BULATS	Business Language Testing Service	www.bulats.org/Bulats/The-Tests.html
CAPE	Computerized Adaptive Placement Exam	https://www.aetip.com/Products/CAPE/CAPE2.cfm
CB IELTS	Computer-Based International English Language Testing System	www.ielts.org/
CELSA	Combined English Language Skills Assessment	www.assessment-testing.com/celsa.htm
CEOTS	College English Oral Test System	Yu & Lowe (2007)
CLIPS	Computerized Language Instruction and Practice Software	Larson & Hendricks (2009)
DIALANG	A suite of diagnostics foreign language tests	Alderson & Huhta (2005)
French CAPT	French Computer-Adaptive Placement Test	Laurier (1999)
French CAT	French Computer-Adaptive Test	Burston & Monville-Burston (1995)
GPT/SPT	German Placement Test/Spanish Placement Test	Bernhardt, Rivera & Kamil (2004)
Hausa CAT	Hausa Computer-Adaptive Test	Dunkel (1999)
NEPTON	New English Placement Test Online	Papandima-Sophocleous (2008)
PAU	Prueba de Acceso a la Universidad (Spanish Internet-Based University Entrance Examination)	Garcia Laborda (2009)
PLEVALEX	Plataforma de Evaluación Valenciana de Lenguas Extranjeras	García Laborda (2007b, 2009)
R-CARPE	Russian Computer-Adaptive Reading Proficiency Examination	Larson (1999)
SPT	Spanish Placement Test	Zabaleta (2007)
SST	Spoken Spanish Test	Bernstein, Barbier, Rosenfeld & de Jong (2004)
TOEFL iBT	Internet-Based Test of English as a Foreign Language	www.ets.org/toefl/ibt/about

speaking and writing; the potential disadvantages that computer illiteracy could impose on novice computer users; and the decontextualized language presented in single screen formats.

Jamieson (2005) was organized around three steps in the evolution of CBLT. The first step was the use of traditional item types and language testing constructs that were simply put into computer formats. The second step involved the 'added value' (p. 230) of using IRT to develop CATs. She then turned to innovations that were likely to occur in the near term especially those related to designing language tasks and score reporting. In the more distant future, she saw computer scoring of productive language as a possibility as well as increasing use of new task types that include authentic video-taped language input.

Douglas and Hegelheimer (2007) followed up on Jamieson's (2005) article by surveying progress in constructing, delivering and scoring CBLTs. They did so with particular attention to the relationship between language constructs and Jamieson's three steps. In terms of constructing CBLTS, they covered computer-based options for authoring CBLTs. They also examined trends in scoring, feedback and reporting systems including specific scoring engines, automated writing evaluation, automated identification of off-topic essays and automated scoring of non-native speech. The authors ended by listing six major threats to validity posed by computer delivery systems.

Garcia Laborda (2007a) provided an introduction to the features of computer test design, some of the item types used in IBLTs and CBLTs (multiple-choice, writing and speaking) and a review of some of the high stakes tests used internationally. He also discussed the future of CBLT in the short-term (security, technical devices and capability, test features and design, as well as test interpretations and washback) and long-term (communities of language learners, language test preparation and test enjoyment).

Dooey (2008) discussed the importance of language testing and the effects of technology on reliability and validity. She went on to explore the research on construct validity with a focus on the computer-human interfaces in terms of the effects on scores of computer familiarity and anxiety. She also explored the practical advantages of computer delivery systems in terms of their flexibility with regard to when and where examinees can take the tests, item banking, instant feedback and data accumulation for research purposes. She ended with a section on the relative effects of technology on the testing of listening and reading on the CB IELTS and the testing of writing on the computer-based TOEFL and TOEFL iBT.

Ockey (2009) examined CBT as it applied to second language testing starting with Garret (1991), who described CBT as 'the computerized administration of conventional tests' (p. 88) and then explored the effects of CBLT on the way language abilities were characterized and tested. Ockey argued that the advantages of CBLT were that they: can deliver more authentic tests; allow relatively reliable, easy and quick scoring of speech and writing samples; and promote the use of authentic tasks in assessment. The disadvantages were that CBLTs still had security problems and that CALTs in particular had not yet lived up to their promise.

With a narrower focus, Prapphal (2008) reviewed new trends in language testing in Thailand including issues related to human resources development, professional certification, incorporation of IT into language testing, quality assurance, learner self-assessment and current innovations in language testing.

Chapelle and Douglas (2006) co-authored a book that covered a number of topics: (a) the place of CBLTs in language education including discussions of CBLTs and teachers, CBLTs and researchers and the future of CBLTs; (b) CBLT test method characteristics including temporal and physical circumstances, instructions and rubrics, inputs and expected responses, input/response interactions and assessment characteristics (construct definitions and scoring criteria/procedures); (c) problems with CBLTs including different types of test performance, novel task types, item selection limitations, erroneous automatic scoring, potential security problems and possible negative impacts; (d) CBLT implementation including a section on authoring tools and another that proposes a model for the system that underlies assessment (activity selection, presentation, processing of responses and summary scoring); (e) guidelines for evaluating CBLTs including points to consider before the test (planning the test purpose/function and test length, as well as writing items), during the test (examining the item response formats, giving feedback, thinking about the timing and recording the results) and after the test (evaluating the above score-based decisions and presenting the results to examinees); and (f) the impact of CBLTs including advances in language assessment and applied linguistics due to CBLT and future directions that need exploration. All of which, (a) to (f), serves the overall purpose of high-quality CBLT delivery, which is the topic in the next section.

CBLT delivery

A number of articles have concentrated on the issues involved in CBLT delivery including computer-adaptive language testing, computer versus traditional testing formats, Web-based language testing, interface architecture, test takers' experiences with CBLT and CBLT training for teachers.

Computer-Adaptive Language Testing

Brown (1997) examined the literature on CBLT and CBT and ended up focusing primarily on CAT, predicting that future research in language testing might tend towards addressing questions like the following about CALTs:

1. How should we pilot CALTS?
2. Should a CALT be standard length or vary across students?
3. How should we sample CALT items?

4 What are the effects of changing the difficulty of CALT items?

5 How can we deal with item sets on a CALT?

6 How should we score CALTS?

7 How should we deal with CALT item omissions?

8 How should we make decisions about cut-points on CALTs?

9 How can we avoid CALT item exposure?

10 Should we provide item review opportunities on a CALT?

11 How can we comply with legal disclosure laws when administering CALTs?

To some degree, Brown (1997) was correct. For example, Meunier (1994), Young, Shermis, Brutten and Perkins (1996), Dunkel (1999a) and Larson (1999) all began their discussions of CALT by listing the benefits to be derived from it: shorter tests; examinee self-pacing; test individualization to examinees' ability levels; enhanced test security; faster scoring and feedback; greater measurement precision; and use of multimedia. Meunier (1994) advocated using 'adaptive live-action simulations' to assess students' abilities to function in situations, which could in turn be adapted to the examinees' ability levels. Young et al. (1996) used CAT to develop a CALT for ESL reading comprehension using *HyperCAT*. In the process, they discussed three constraints on CAT development (i.e., the need for item unidimensionality, examinee homogeneity and neutral effects for test method). Dunkel (1999a) also focused on overcoming the challenges that face CALT developers in terms of: the basic language testing principles that govern all testing formats; psychometric and technical issues specific to CALT; basic software and hardware issues related specifically to CALT; and issues related to administering CALTs.

In contrast, Larson (1999) discussed the development of an L2 CALT Russian reading test that sequenced reading items much in the way many oral-proficiency interviews are sequenced – with a warm-up, level-check, ceiling-check and wind-down. In the same year, Laurier (1999) described the development of a CAT for French placement and the value of CAT for that purpose. He then turned to discussions of item banking, IRT models and software/hardware considerations.

Like many before them, Chalhoub-Deville and Deville (1999) began with the benefits and drawbacks of CBT and CAT, then went on to discuss the state of technology at that time, CAT item banking, test score comparability, item selection (in terms of deciding on the CAT entry point, determining the exit point and test length, as well as balancing content and item exposure) and a number of actual CALT development projects. Alderson (2007) also provided some quick definitions and a brief discussion of the advantages of CALT as well as a brief description of the DIALANG CALT project that he has been involved with (for more on the DIALANG project, see Alderson, 2005; Alderson & Huhta, 1995).

Other articles have addressed the more technical aspects of CAT in language testing. For example, McNamara (1999) discussed the fit of CAT with performance assessment applications, as well as method effects and the ideological/social implications of CAT. Eignor (1999) tackled a number of major issues in CAT, that is, dealing with complex test specifications; item exposure; and IRT modelling of testlets. Linacre (1999) described a measurement approach for simplifying complex constructs like reading comprehension in a way that balanced psychometric and psychological concerns. Luecht (1999) analysed two L1 reading CAT simulations differently using Rasch model in the first study and three-parameter item response theory (IRT) in the second; the author concluded that the three-parameter IRT did not do better than the Rasch model and that, practically speaking, the Rasch model is simpler and can be performed with smaller samples. Zumbo and MacMillan (1999) discussed the Eignor, Linacre and Leucht papers mentioned above with the goal of linking the views of researchers from different disciplines on CAT. In addition, Mislevy, Chapelle, Chung and Xu (2008) took the idea of adaptivity beyond Rasch statistical techniques by broadening the dimensions of adaptability (after Levy, Behrens & Mislevy, 2006) to include what they discussed as claim status, observation status and locus of control. In the process, they described specific examples of tests that exhibited various combinations of these three dimensions.

For more information on general trends in CAT see *C.A.T. Central: A Global Resource for Computerized Adaptive Testing Research and Applications* at: www.psych.umn.edu/psylabs/catcentral/

Computer versus traditional testing formats

A number of authors have also continued comparing CBLTs with traditional testing formats. Choi, Kim and Boo (2003) compared the validity of PBLT and CBLT by examining content and construct validity using corpus linguistic techniques (correlation, ANOVA and confirmatory factor analysis) finding that the CBLT and PBLT versions of their proficiency test were comparable. Coniam (2006) compared the efficacy and reliability of CBLT and PBLT for testing listening, finding that the CBLT version was somewhat easier than the P&P version and that the overall correlation of .76 between the two versions was high enough to support the value of the CBLT for low-stakes decisions. Sawaki (2001) compared PBLT with CBLT for reading ability by exploring the relationships between mode of presentation and reading ability, in the process, identifying a wide variety of factors that should be considered in future research on this topic.

In a different vein, Kenyon and Malabonga (2001) compared examinees' attitudes towards what they called computerized oral proficiency instruments (COPIs) and more traditional simulated oral proficiency instruments (SOPIs). Fifty-five examinees took both a COPI and a SOPI and several Likert scale attitudes/perceptions questionnaires. The results indicated that some examinees felt the COPI was easier than the SOPI, while others felt that the SOPI was a better measure of 'real-life conversation' (p. 80), but overall, the COPI and SOPI were rated similarly. (Also see comments on this article in Norris, 2001 and the response in Kenyon, Malabonga & Carpenter, 2001).

Web-based language testing

At least four papers have focused on WBLTs or IBLTs. Fulcher (1999) described an effort to lighten the placement testing burden on teachers by having students take the multiple-choice grammar subtest online. This pilot study focused on format bias against those who lack computer familiarity, and, similar to the studies in the previous section, Fulcher compared the WBLT with a P&P version, especially in terms of technology effects on test validity.

Roever (2001) began by defining WBLT and how it differed from CBT and describing the many possible types of WBLTs ranging from low-tech to high-tech. He then focused on low-tech WBLTs (because they are more practical) in terms of item types, validation concerns and the special issues involved in online CATs. He also discussed the advantages of WBLTs (time and place flexibility, empowerment of anyone with a computer and affordability) and their limitations (cheating, item exposure, the presence of the answers in the JavaScript, data storage requirements, getting data into spreadsheet format, server failure and browser incompatibility). He ended by advocating what he called stakes-driven decisions (pp. 90–1) and briefly described some potential areas for future WBLT research.

Bernhardt, Rivera and Kamil (2004) investigated the practicality of a Web-based approach for college-level placement testing in German and Spanish with a specific focus on the benefits for articulation between secondary and tertiary studies. Their conclusions were positive: the WBLT provided reliable and valid decisions, easy access to the test for students, fewer scheduling bottlenecks and effective individualized placement decisions.

Alderson's (2009) review of the TOEFL iBT briefly discussed the history of this test and described the reading, listening, speaking and writing sections in some detail. He then turned to discussion of the existing reliability and validity studies, and concluded that the test developers had made serious efforts to create positive washback on the website and in the accompanying materials. Along the way, he was critical of the fact that the test is linear (i.e., everyone completes the items in order) and not computer-adaptive. However, he concluded that the TOEFL iBT is a 'major step forward in testing language proficiency for academic purposes' (p. 630).

Interface architecture

A number of authors have addressed the issue of *interface design* or *architecture*, by which they typically mean the ways CBLTs fit with human capacities and needs. Fulcher (2003) described three phases of CBLT development in detail: (a) planning and initial design, (b) usability testing and (c) field testing and fine tuning. Chapelle and Douglas (2006) briefly described a different framework for designing CBLTs that included: an activity selection process, presentation process, response processing and summary scoring process (pp. 75–7).

In a cluster of studies, building on Fulcher's (2003) work, Garcia Laborda (2007b) evaluated the PLEVALEX platform for CBLT against Fulcher's model, while considering three sets of issues: designing prototypes (hardware and software issues), designing interfaces (navigation, page layout, toolbars, controls, text, text colour, icons, graphics and multimedia) and other design considerations (delivery systems, score retrieval, data storage and distribution, test rubrics, computer familiarity, piloting, reliability and internal and external validity). These factors also figured into the interface validation investigation presented in Garcia Laborda and Magal-Royo (2007). Garcia Laborda (2009) briefly considered issues of navigation, page layout, toolbars and controls, text, text color, icons and graphics in the PREVALEX and PAU platforms in comparison to the CB IELTS and TOEFL iBT. Garcia Laborda, Magal-Royo, Macario de Siqueira Rocha and Fernandez Alvarez (2010) set out to design an ergonomic interface for testing both oral and written English; they described the trialing, the experiment and the design process of the PLEVALEX, as well as a questionnaire, which led them to conclude that the 'PLEVALEX design was potentially valid for language testing' (p. 390), that even students with limited computer experience could use the system, and that the combination of piloting and consulting with computer specialists was beneficial.

Test takers' experience with CBLT

Interface architecture has to do with how examinees experience a CBLT. Perhaps that is why the examinee experience has also come under investigation. Brown and Iwashita (1996) examined the effects of language background on item difficulty in a CALT for Japanese. Based on item data from 1,400 English and Chinese speakers learning Japanese, the results showed that the item difficulties were quite different for these two groups of examinees, which illustrated and reinforced what language testers have long known: a test, CAT or otherwise, is not valid in-an-of-itself, but rather the scores on a test may be more-or-less valid for a specific purpose in a particular context with specific examinees (p. 205).

Kirsch, Jamieson, Taylor and Eignor (1998) investigated the effects of computer familiarity among TOEFL examinees. The results of a computer-familiarity scale developed by the researchers were compared with various background variables and examinees' P&P TOEFL scores. The authors concluded that examinees from Japan and Africa were more likely to need computer familiarization training than other examinees, that word processing skills seemed generally to be adequate for writing courses in the United States and that the computer familiarity questionnaire usefully helped in identifying students who needed help with computers.

Taylor, Jamieson, Eignor and Kirsch (1998) further analysed subsets of the same data from 613 computer-familiar examinees and 556, who were computer-unfamiliar. A series of elaborate ANCOVAs were performed with the scores on the CBT TOEFL items (after a CBT tutorial) as the dependent variable, TOEFL P&P as a covariate, computer familiarity as the independent variable and gender and reason for testing as moderator variables. The researchers found no meaningful relationship between computer familiarity and performance on CBT TOEFL items when language ability was controlled and examinees were provided with a CBT tutorial.

Gorsuch (2004) used retrospective interviews, post-test questionnaires and observation log data from six students to investigate the effects of various sources of error variance on the reliability of a CBLT for listening. Drawing on the literature, Gorsuch constructed a model containing a large number of systematic and random sources of error including test method, testing conditions and examinee-attribute factors. Her list of error sources was comprehensive and interesting in its own right.

Three other papers were related tangentially to the topic of experience with CBLTs. Jones (2004) reported on two studies that investigated the effects of written or picture annotations, or both on vocabulary learning, finding beneficial effects on vocabulary scores for these annotations and attributing the effects to the possibility of reviewing information repeatedly in different modalities. Among other things, Yu and Lowe (2007) conducted interviews and questionnaires with students and English teachers to study the attitudes of these stakeholders to the CEOTs test and how their attitudes affected their language learning (more on this study below). Macario de Siqueira, Martínez-Sáez, Sevilla-Pavón and Gimeno-Sanz (2011) described the current computer testing situation in Spain as well as the PAU/PLEVALEX testing system and reflected on an analysis of quantitative data from more than 200 students and their teachers, which indicated that students and teachers generally had 'very positive attitude toward this mode of learner assessment' (p. 665).

CBLT training for teachers

Garcia Laborda and Magal-Royo (2009) observed that many teachers may not be adequately equipped to deal with issues like the computer familiarity discussed in the previous section. In response, they surveyed the attitudes of 26 teacher trainees at the end of a 20-hour in-service training course in computer technology that included familiarizing them with computer testing tools as well as with the process of creating an online test and administering the test itself. The results indicated that most of the trainees had positive reactions to the training, but still lacked the confidence to use computers for testing in their own classrooms.

Garcia Laborda and Litzler (2011) described the training of a group of 24 English teachers to determine the feasibility of implementing an online university entrance examination in Spain, specifically with regard to whether the teachers ultimately changed their routines, teaching methods and attitudes towards computer assessment technology. They concluded that teachers should be helped to understand: how computers can be useful assessment tools, their own limitations with regard to these tools, the need to stay up-to-date with these tools and the existence of internet sites where they can draw on other teachers' experiences.

CBLT content

Chalhoub-Deville (2001) pointed out that actual implementations of CBTs and CATs in the real world had come up short. Citing Christensen (1997), she focused on the idea of *disruptive* technology, which was technology that changes how we conceptualize and apply our (testing) procedures. She finished by arguing for more innovative testing procedures which she calls 'disruptive applications'.

Garcia Laborda, Bakieva, Gonzalez-Such and Sevilla Pavon (2010) briefly considered the content of the internet-based Spanish University Entrance Examination (PAU). Their goal was to diminish the effects of the computerized test delivery system. To that end, they described and analysed the characteristics of a new test item taxonomy (including reading, writing, listening and speaking items/tasks).

By far the most common approach to CBLT content has been to consider the separate issues of computer assessment of vocabulary, speaking or oral skills, writing, listening and reading.

Computer assessment of vocabulary

The last chapter of Reed (2000), which considered 'the potential of computers to contribute to vocabulary analysis and assessment' (p. 223), was much more about vocabulary analysis than assessment, though the various forms of analysis that Reed discussed may prove important for the development of vocabulary CBLTs. Laufer and Goldstein (2004) developed bilingual (English-Hebrew and English-Arabic) CBLTs of English vocabulary size and strength; piloted the test in a P&P version on 435 EFL learners; demonstrated (using Guttman scaling) that a hierarchy exists in vocabulary strength; in the process, provided clear descriptions of the four different item types in their vocabulary CBLT. Jones (2004) primarily explaind two studies of the effects of written and picture annotations on vocabulary learning, but in the process, he described four different CBLT vocabulary tests that he developed. Other articles discussed elsewhere in this chapter included vocabulary subtests tangentially: Meunier (1995), Choi, et al. (2003) and Bernstein, Barbier, Rosenfeld and de Jong (2004).

Computer assessment of speaking or oral skills

Yu and Lowe (2007) evaluated the validity of a spoken English CBLT in China. Based on questionnaire and interview data from students and teachers, they examined reactions to the test and how it affected language learning, ways that construct and consequential validities were sometimes at odds and how CBLTs offer a solution to problems of negative backwash. Larson (2000) argued for using CBLTs for oral skills by discussing the benefits of such testing, arguing for their feasibility and describing Brigham Young University's Testing software for oral language tests. Garcia Laborda (2010) examined the effects of audiovisual clues on semi-direct interviews in CALT for speaking with the goal of furnishing a theoretical approach for using computers to provide audiovisual clues that supply context in semi-direct interviews in a Spanish University entrance examination and thereby improve examinee's scores. Blake, Wilson, Cetto and Pardo-Ballester (2008) explained how they administered the 20-minute *Versant for Spanish* oral test (including phone delivery and automatic scoring) to both classroom and distance-learning students. Bernstein et al. (2004) described how they developed and validated an Automatic Spoken Spanish Test (ASST). Chapelle and Chung (2010) also addressed issues important to CBLT speaking by exploring progress that had been made in natural language processing and automatic speech recognition/processing. Other articles that contributed secondarily to the discussion of oral skills assessment included Kenyon and Malabonga (2001), Norris (2001), Kenyon, Malabonga and Carpenter (2001), Bernstein, et al. (2004), Garcia Laborda (2007a), Alderson (2009) and Garcia Laborda, Magal-Royo, et al. (2010).

Computer assessment of writing

Dikli (2006a) defined *automated essay scoring* (AES) 'as the computer technology that evaluates and scores . . . written prose' (p. 4). She discussed the advantages of AES systems in terms of cost, time, reliability and generalizability of scores, and provided an overview of available approaches to AES. She also described *Project Essay Grader, Intelligent Essay Assessor, E-rater, CriterionSM, IntelliMetric, MY Access!* and the *Bayesian Essay Test Scoring System* in terms of who developed each, the scoring techniques involved, the main foci, instructional applications and the number of training essays required. Dikli (2006b) also described automated essay scoring systems, but only covered four of the six included in the 2006a article.

Chodorow and Burstein (2004) evaluated the relationships between several versions of the *E-rater* automated scoring system for TOEFL essays and holistic scores assigned by human raters. They found that an early version called *E-rater99* accounted for little variance in the holistic human scores beyond that predicted by essay length. However, the later *E-rater01* version performed much better because it included topical content measures as well as vocabulary complexity and diversity measures. Attali and Burstein (2006) described *E-rater* (version 2) and how it was different from previous versions, especially in terms of alternative forms reliability and validity (i.e., correlations with human raters). Chodorow, Gamon and Tetreault (2010) examined the use of *Criterion* and *ESL Assistant.* Warschauer and Ware (2006) described *My Access!, Criterion* and *Holt Online Essay Scoring* in terms of the companies that produced these programs, the software engines, the evaluation mechanisms and the types of scoring/feedback.

In addition, Weigle (2002) devoted a few pages in her book's last chapter (pp. 231–7) to the issues of writing assessment and technology including coverage of how technology affects writing, automatic computer scoring of writing and the gap in technology. Chapelle (2001) also devoted a few pages to CBLT for writing (pp. 109–11).

Finally, for readers interested in L2 writing, the L1 literature on computer-based writing assessment may prove interesting (see e.g., the *Computers and Composition* journal archived at http://computersandcomposition.candcblog.org/html/archives.htm).

Computer assessment of listening and reading

With regard to CBLTs for listening and reading, three sources included both listening and reading, while others focused on one or the other. Dooey (2008) explored the relative effects of technology on the testing of listening and reading on the CB IELTS. Choi et al. (2003) included reading and listening subtests in their study, but it was focused on comparing the effectiveness of PBLT versus CBLT. Chapelle (2001) devoted a few pages to CBLTs for listening (pp. 108–9) and reading (pp. 105–08, pp. 111–13).

With regard to listening alone, Dunkel (1999b) detailed the process of developing a listening CALT for Hausa. Gorsuch (2004) focused on the effects of a variety of sources of error variance on the reliability of a CBLT for listening. Coniam (2006) reported research that compared the efficacy and reliability of CBLT and PBLT for testing listening. And finally, Alderson (2009) described the listening subtests of the TOEFL iBT in his review of that test.

With regard to reading alone, Young, et al. (1996) described the development of a CALT for ESL reading comprehension based on a program called *HyperCAT*. Sawaki (2001) used a reading test to compare the effectiveness of PBLT with CBLT. In the process, she effectively reviewed and compared a number of research studies on the testing of reading. And finally, Alderson (2000b) briefly addressed various aspects of CBLT for reading in his book (pp. 351–4).

Perhaps the single largest concentration of articles on CBLTs for reading is the Calhoub-Deville (1999) edited collection. In that book, Grabe (1999) briefly discussed CAT in his extensive literature review centred on the reading proficiency construct. Alderson (1999) additionally connected reading constructs and reading assessment with special attention to the reading construct/assessment problems raised by Bernhardt (1999) and Grabe (1999) and a particular focus on addressing the 15 dilemmas posed by Grabe (1999). Larson (1999) discussed the pros and cons of CAT with specific reference to developing an L2 reading CAT for Russian. Chapelle (1999) argued that reading theory and testing issues must both be considered in developing CALTs for reading comprehension. She posited *inference* as the place where the two sets of concerns converge, arguing that theory needs to be applied to test design and that contextual factors must also be accounted for in the process of developing CAT reading tests. Eignor (1999), Linacre (1999), Luecht (1999) and Zumbo and MacMillan

(1999) provided technical discussions of CAT issues and were tangentially related to reading comprehension in some places.

Example CBLTs

One very noticeable change in the literature on CBLT since Brown (1997) is that a relatively large number of papers have described actual CBLT development projects. Among those, I include the 12 example CBLT projects in Table 5.3. Some of these papers have been cited above because they covered areas discussed elsewhere, but they all share the fact that they describe actual CBLT development projects.

Notice in Table 5.3 that the examples are organized alphabetically by language and author. Note also that there are three papers for English (two EFL and one ESL), two for French, one each for Hausa and Russian, three for Spanish, one for Spanish and German, and the last for fourteen different European languages. These tests were clearly developed for university level students, though they did cover a wide variety of testing purposes (including achievement, diagnostic, placement and proficiency testing as well as articulation/admissions), skill areas (including grammar, listening, reading, speaking, vocabulary, writing, pragmatics and appropriacy, abbreviated as G, L, R, S, V, W, P and A, respectively, in Table 5.3) and computer testing types (including CBLT, CALT, IBLT, IBLT and automatic scoring). All of this indicates that a good deal of CBLT development is occurring around the world primarily at the university level.

In the process of reviewing this literature, I came across a number of commercially available tests. Though these tests have not all appeared in academic papers, I feel obliged to list some of these and point to where more information can be obtained: (a) ALTA Language Testing Services (including tests for English, Spanish and 90 other languages, as well as for Medical English, translation, interpretation) available at www.altalang.com/language-testing/, (b) Versant (including tests for English, Spanish, Arabic and aviation English) available at www.versanttest.com/ and (c) Language Testing International (apparently including commercial tests in 64 languages, government tests in 73 languages and academic tests in 64 languages all available with varying options from telephone and computerized versions of ACTFL and ILR OPI to a variety formats of writing, reading and speaking formats) available at www.languagetesting.com/home.cfm.

CBLT tools and resources

Finally, a number of articles have appeared that have examined tools and resources useful for developers of CBLTs. The most general of these is Godwin-Jones (2001) which explored computerized testing tools, internet applications, test authoring tools, the outlook for CBLTs and useful resources (including testing resources on the internet;

TABLE 5.3 Papers describing actual CBLTs and their development

Citation	Language	Test name	Level	Purpose of test	Skills	Test type
Papandima-Sophocleous (2008)	English (EFL)	NEPTON	University	Placement	GRVW	IBLT/CBLT/ CALT hybrid
Young, Shermis, Brutten & Perkins (1996)	English (ESL)	Reading Comp Test	University	Not clear	R	CALT
Yu & Lowe (2007)	English (EFL)	CEOTS	University	Achievement	Oral	CBLT
Burston & Monville-Burston (1995)	French	French CAT	University	Placement	G	CALT
Laurier (1999)	French	French CAPT	University	Placement	GLRVA	CALT
Dunkel (1999b)	Hausa	Hausa CAT	University	Proficiency	L	CALT
Larson (1999)	Russian	R-CARPE	University	Proficiency	R	CALT
Larson & Hendricks (2009)	Spanish	Part of CLIPS	University	Diagnostic	GW	IBLT
Zabaleta (2007)	Spanish	SPT	University	Placement	GLPRV	CBLT
Bernstein, Barbier, Rosenfeld & de Jong (2004)	Spanish	SST	University	Proficiency	LS	CBLT with automatic scoring
Bernhardt, Rivera & Kamil (2004)	Spanish/ German	GPT/SPT	University	Articulation/ Admission	GV	IBLT
Alderson & Huhta (2005)	14 European	DIALANG	Mostly university	Diagnostic	GLRVW	IBLT

related institutions and organizations; existing CBLTs; available online practice tests; online CBLTs; as well as CBLT development tools and templates).

Polio (2001) provided a review of an online trial version of *Test Pilot*, which is a system for authoring and administering tests or surveys online server (currently available at www.clearlearning.com/). Winke and MacGregor (2001) provided a review of *Hot Potatoes* (currently available at http://hotpot.uvic.ca/index.php), which is a program that helps teachers create online exercises (or assessment activities) by using templates supplied by the program. Franco, Bratt, Rossier, Gadde, Shriberg, Abrash and Percoda (2010) briefly reviewed the literature on speech recognition and then provided good exposure for their product by describing features of Stanford Research Institute (SRI) International's *EduSpeak®* system (www.speechatsri.com/products/eduspeak.shtml) speech recognition and pronunciation scoring software development tool in terms of their strategy for scoring pronunciation at the phrase level or higher. Burstein, Chodorow and Leacock (2003) also provided excellent exposure for an Educational Testing Service product called *CriterionSM*. They described *CriterionSM* as an online essay evaluation system (for general information: www.ets.org/criterion) and evaluated the degree to which *CriterionSM* was sufficiently accurate to provide useful feedback (see also Chodorow & Burstein, 2004; Chodorow, et al., 2010).

Conclusions

As the reference list below will attest, the CBLT literature since Brown (1997) has been spread out over many journals and books. In addition, it has grown considerably in volume: only 29 of the 96 references in Brown (1997) were focused directly on CBLT, while 87 of the 89 references in the present chapter are directly related to CBLT.

As mentioned above, Brown (1997) found that the CBLT literature had covered: (a) how to use an item bank, (b) how to use new technologies, (c) how to build computer-adaptive tests and (d) how effective computers are in language testing. In the interceding years the literature seems to have moved well beyond the *How to . . .* topics covered earlier to new topics. First, a number of papers, chapters and books have periodically provided overviews of the CBLT literature. That was not previously common. While CBLT delivery issues like CALT were discussed at the *how- to* level, today, the discussion of CALT appears to be considerably more sophisticated and in-depth. In addition, while the computer vs traditional testing formats studies continue to be conducted, topics like WBLT, interface architecture, the test takers' experience with CBLT and CBLT training for teachers are entirely new. As for CBLT content issues, much of the literature appears to now focus on the issues involved in testing the various components of language like vocabulary, speaking or oral skills, writing, listening and/or reading with a particular concern for automatic scoring of spoken and written responses. Moreover, a fairly large number of example CBLTs are actually being developed and described in the literature along with the variety of tools and resources that have increasingly become available for CBLT development.

Brown (1997) examined the education literature on CBT for clues about the future directions that research on CBLT might take. Since CBT was focusing primarily on computer-adaptive testing (CAT), I predicted that future research in language testing might tend towards addressing ten questions about computer-adaptive language tests (CALTs). To some degree I was correct. However, I was also wrong. I fear that my assumption was that the general educational testing research was always ahead of language testing research and that CBLT research would therefore follow in the footsteps of CBT/CAT research. Instead, what has happened is that, while there was some work on CALT, CBLT also moved into practical and useful directions, perhaps relying on the general CBT literature to sort out the more technical issues of CALT.

However, in all fairness, Brown (1997) also predicted a number of other areas that CBLT might usefully pursue including (a) testing in intelligent teaching systems, (b) testing on the internet, (c) using speech and handwriting recognition, (d) scoring and analysing speech and writing samples and (e) developing alternative psychometric models that take advantage of the power of computers to analyse more complex information (p. 53). Three out of five of those earlier predictions appear to have come true: (b), (c) and (d) are areas that have burgeoned in the intervening years. The other two, (a) and (e) are areas in which research and development would still benefit the field. Clearly, the CBLT literature has pretty much gone its own way which makes sense given that the language part of language testing would naturally lead to a certain expertise and interest in topics like speech recognition and automatic scoring of writing.

In sum, CBLT is not a new area of research, but in recent years, it has clearly been growing and generating a good deal of excitement – perhaps because it allows language testers to respond to changes in the language teaching field, especially in teaching methodologies, using strategies never before available, and to do so much faster, more practically and in ways that are more closely aligned to what and how students are learning in their language classrooms.

References

Alderson, J. C. (1999). Reading constructs and reading assessment. In M. Chalhoub-Deville (Ed.), *Issues in computer-adaptive testing of reading proficiency* (pp. 49–70). Cambridge: Cambridge University Press.

— (2000a). Technology in testing: The present and the future. *System, 28*, 593–603.

— (2000b). *Assessing reading*. Cambridge: Cambridge University Press.

— (2005). *Diagnosing foreign language proficiency*. London: Continuum.

— (2007). Computer-adaptive language testing. In S. Granger (Ed.), *Optimizing the role of language in technology-enhanced learning* (pp. 1–3). Louvain-la-Neuve, Belgium: Integrated Digital Language Learning.

— (2009). Test review: Test of English as a Foreign Language: Internet-based Test (TOEFL iBT®). *Language Testing, 26*(4), 621–31.

Alderson, J. C., & Huhta, A. (2005). The development of a suite of computer-based diagnostic tests based on the Common European Framework. *Language Testing, 22*(3), 301–20.

Attali, Y., & Burstein, J. (2006). Automated essay scoring with e-rater® V.2. *Journal of Technology, Learning, and Assessment, 4*(3), 1–30.
Bernhardt, E. (1999). If reading is reader-based, can there be a computer-adaptive test of reading? In M. Chalhoub-Deville (Ed.), *Issues in computer-adaptive testing of reading proficiency* (pp. 1–10). Cambridge: Cambridge University Press.
Bernhardt, E. B., Rivera, R. J., & Kamil, M. L. (2004). The practicality and efficiency of Web-based placement testing for college-level language programs. *Foreign Language Annals, 37*, 356–66.
Bernstein, J., Barbier, I., Rosenfeld, E., & de Jong, J. (2004). Development and validation of an automatic spoken Spanish test. In *InSTIL/ICALL 2004 symposium on computer assisted learning, NLP and speech technologies in advanced language learning systems*, Venice, Italy, 17–19 June 2004, ISCA Archive.
Blake, R., Wilson, N. L., Cetto, M., & Pardo-Ballester, C. (2008). Measuring oral proficiency in distance, face-to-face and blended classrooms. *Language Learning & Technology, 12*(3), 114–27.
Brown, A., & Iwashita, N. (1996). Language background and item difficulty: The development of a computer-adaptive test of Japanese. *System, 24*(2), 199–206.
Brown, J. D. (1997). Computers in language testing: Present research and some future directions. *Language Learning and Technology, 1*(1), 44–59.
— (2009). Computers in language testing: Present research and some future directions. In P. Hubbard (Ed.), *Computer assisted language learning: Critical concepts in linguistics, Volume IV: Present trends and future directions in CALL* (pp. 115–37). New York: Routledge.
Burstein, J., Chodorow, M., & Leacock, C. (2003). *CriterionSM* online essay evaluation: An application for automated evaluation of student essays. *Proceedings of the fifteenth annual conference on innovative applications of Artificial Intelligence.* Acapulco, Mexico.
Burston, J., & Monville-Burston, M. (1995). Practical design and implementation considerations of a computer adaptive foreign language test: TIIE Monash/Melbourne French CAT. *CALICO Journal, 13*(1), 26–46.
Chalhoub-Deville, M. (Ed.) (1999). *Issues in computer-adaptive testing of reading proficiency.* Cambridge: Cambridge University Press.
— (2001). Language testing and technology: Past and future. *Language Learning & Technology, 5*(2), 95–8.
Chalhoub-Deville, M., & Deville, C. (1999). Computer adaptive testing in second language contexts. *Annual Review of Applied Linguistics, 19*, 273–99.
Chapelle, C. (1999). From reading theory to testing practice. In M. Chalhoub-Deville (Ed.), *Issues in computer-adaptive testing of reading proficiency* (pp. 150–66). Cambridge: Cambridge University Press.
Chapelle, C. A. (2001). *Computer applications in second language acquisition.* Cambridge: Cambridge University Press.
Chapelle, C. A., & Chung, Y.-R. (2010). The promise of NLP and speech processing technologies in language assessment. *Language Testing, 27*(3), 301–15.
Chapelle, C. A., & Douglas, D. (2006). *Assessing language through computer technology.* Cambridge: Cambridge University Press.
Chodorow, M., & Burstein, J. (2004). *Beyond essay length: Evaluating e-rater®'s performance on TOEFL® essays. TOEFL Research Reports #73.* Princeton, NJ: Educational Testing Service.
Chodorow, M., Gamon, M., & Tetreault, J. (2010). The utility of article and preposition error correction systems for English language learners: Feedback and assessment. *Language Testing, 27*(3), 419–36.
Choi, I.-C., Kim, K. S., & Boo, J. (2003). Comparability of a paper-based language test and a computer-based language test. *Language Testing, 20*(3), 295–320.

Christensen, C. (1997). *The innovator's dilemma: When new technologies cause great firms to fail.* Boston, MA: Harvard Business School.
Coniam, D. (2006). Evaluating computer-based and paper-based versions of an English-language listening test. *ReCALL, 18*(2), 193–211.
Dikli, S. (2006a). An overview of automated scoring of essays. *Journal of Technology, Learning, and Assessment, 5*(1).
— (2006b). Automated essay scoring. *Turkish Online Journal of Distance Education, 7*(1), article 5 (no page numbers).
Dooey, P. (2008). Language testing and technology: Problems of transition to a new era. *ReCALL, 20*(1), 21–34.
Douglas, D. (2000). *Assessing languages for specific purposes.* Cambridge: Cambridge University Press.
Douglas, D., & Hegelheimer, V. (2007). Assessing language using computer technology. *Annual Review of Applied Linguistics, 27*, 115–32.
Dunkel, P. (1999a). Considerations in developing or using second/foreign language proficiency computer-adaptive tests. *Language Learning & Technology, 2*(2), 77–93.
— (1999b). Research and development of a computer-adaptive test of listening comprehension in the less-commonly taught language Hausa. In M. Chalhoub-Deville (Ed.), *Issues in computer-adaptive testing of reading proficiency* (pp. 91–121). Cambridge: Cambridge University Press.
Eignor, D. (1999). Selected technical issues in the creation of computer-adaptive tests of second language reading proficiency. In M. Chalhoub-Deville (Ed.), *Issues in computer-adaptive testing of reading proficiency* (pp. 167–81). Cambridge: Cambridge University Press.
Franco, H., Bratt, H., Rossier, R., Gadde, V. R., Shriberg, E., Abrash, V., & Percoda, K. (2010). EduSpeak[R]: A speech recognition and pronunciation scoring toolkit for computer-aided language learning applications. *Language Testing, 27*(3), 401–18.
Fulcher, G. (1999). Computerising an English language placement test. *English Language Teaching Journal, 53*, 289–99.
— (2003). Interface design in computer-based language testing. *Language Testing, 20*(4), 384–408.
Garcia Laborda, J. (2007a). ON THE NET: Introducing standardized EFL/ESL exams. *Language Learning & Technology, 11*(2), 3–9.
— (2007b). From Fulcher to PLEVALEX: Issues in interface design, validity and reliability in internet based language testing. *CALL-EJ Online, 9*(1).
— (2009). Interface architecture for testing in foreign language education. *Procedia Social and Behavioral Sciences, 1*, 2754–7.
— (2010). Contextual clues in semi-direct interviews for computer assisted language testing. *Procedia Social and Behavioral Sciences, 2*, 3592–5.
Garcia Laborda, J., & Litzler, M. F. (2011). Constraints in teacher training for computer assisted language testing implementation. *International Education Studies, 4*(2), 13–17.
García Laborda, J., & Magal-Royo, T. (2007). Diseño y validación de la plataforma PLEVALEX como respuesta a los retos de diseño de examines de lenguas para fines específicos. *Journal of the European Association of Languages for Specific Purposes, 14*, 79–97.
— (2009). Training senior teachers in compulsory computer based language tests. *Procedia Social and Behavioral Sciences, 1*, 141–4.
Garcia Laborda, J., Bakieva, M., Gonzalez-Such, J., & Sevilla Pavon, A. (2010). Item transformation for computer assisted language testing: The adaptation of the Spanish University Entrance Examination. *Procedia Social and Behavioral Sciences, 2*, 3586–90.

Garcia Laborda, J., Magal-Royo, T., Macario de Siqueira Rocha, J., & Fernández Álvarez, M. (2010). Ergonomics factors in English as a foreign language testing: The case of PLEVALEX. *Computers & Education, 54*, 384–91.
Garrett, N. (1991). Technology in the service of language learning: Trends and issues. *Modern Language Journal, 75*, 74–101.
Godwin-Jones, B. (2001). Emerging technologies: Language testing tool and technologies. *Language Learning & Technology, 5*(2), 8–13.
Gorsuch, G. (2004). Test takers' experiences with computer-administered listening comprehension tests: Interviewing for qualitative explorations of test validity. *CALICO Journal, 21*(2), 339–71.
Grabe, W. (1999). Developments in reading research and their implications. In M. Chalhoub-Deville (Ed.), *Issues in computer-adaptive testing of reading proficiency* (pp. 11–47). Cambridge: Cambridge University Press.
Gruba, P., & Corbel, C. (1997). Computer-based testing. In C. Clapham & D. Corson (Eds.), *Language testing and assessment* (pp. 141–9). Dordrecht: Kluwer Academic.
Jamieson, J. (2005). Trends in computer-based second language assessment. *Annual Review of Applied Linguistics, 25*, 228–42.
Jones, L. (2004). Testing L2 vocabulary recognition and recall using pictorial and written test items. *Language Learning & Technology, 8*(3), 122–43.
Kenyon, D. M., & Malabonga, V. (2001). Comparing examinee attitudes toward computer-assisted and other oral proficiency assessments. *Language Learning & Technology, 5*(2), 60–83.
Kenyon, D. M., Malabonga, V., & Carpenter, H. (2001). Response to Norris commentary. *Language Learning & Technology, 5*(2), 106–8.
Kirsch, I., Jamieson, J., Taylor, C., & Eignor, D. (1998). *Familiarity among TOEFL examinees. TOEFL Research Report 59*. Educational Testing Service, Princeton, NJ.
Larson, J. W. (1999). Considerations for testing reading proficiency via computer-adaptive testing. In M. Chalhoub-Deville (Ed.), *Issues in computer-adaptive testing of reading proficiency* (pp. 71–90). Cambridge: Cambridge University Press.
— (2000). Testing oral language skills via the computer. *CALICO Journal, 18*(1), 53–66.
Larson, J. W., & Hendricks, H. H. (2009). *A context-based online diagnostic test of Spanish. CALICO Journal, 26*(2), 309–23.
Laufer, B., & Goldstein, Z. (2004). Testing vocabulary knowledge: Size, strength, and computer adaptiveness. *Language Learning, 54*(3), 399–436.
Laurier, M. (1999). The development of an adaptive test for placement in French. In M. Chalhoub-Deville (Ed.), *Issues in computer-adaptive testing of reading proficiency* (pp. 122–35). Cambridge: Cambridge University Press.
Levy, R., Behrens, J. T., & Mislevy, R. J. (2006). Variations in adaptive testing and their online leverage points. In D. D. Williams, S. L. Howell & M. Hricko (Eds.), *Online assessment, measurement, and evaluation* (pp. 180–202). Hershey, PA: Information Science.
Linacre, J. M. (1999). A measurement approach to computer-adaptive testing of reading comprehension. In M. Chalhoub-Deville (Ed.), *Issues in computer-adaptive testing of reading proficiency* (pp. 182–95). Cambridge: Cambridge University Press.
Liu, M. L., Moore, Z., Graham, L., & Lee, S. (2003). A look at the research on computer-based technology use in second language learning: A review of the literature from 1990–2000. *Journal of Research on Technology in Education, 34*(3), 250–73.
Luecht, R. (1999). The practical utility of Rasch measurement models. In M. Chalhoub-Deville (Ed.), *Issues in computer-adaptive testing of reading proficiency* (pp. 196–215). Cambridge: Cambridge University Press.

Macario de Siqueira, J., Martínez-Sáez, A., Sevilla-Pavón, A., & Gimeno-Sanz, A. (2011). Developing a Web-based system to create, deliver and assess language proficiency within the PAULEX Universitas Project. *Procedia Social and Behavioral Sciences, 15*, 662–66.
McNamara, T. F. (1999). Computer-adaptive testing: A view from outside. In M. Chalhoub-Deville (Ed.), *Issues in computer-adaptive testing of reading proficiency* (pp. 136–49). Cambridge: Cambridge University Press.
Meunier, L. E. (1994). Computer adaptive language tests (CALT) offer a great potential for functional testing. Yet, why don't they? *CALICO Journal, 11*(4), 23–40.
— (1995). Human factors in a computer assisted foreign language environment: The effects of gender, personality and keyboard control. *CALICO Journal, 13*(2&3), 47–72.
Mislevy, R., Chapelle, C. A., Chung, Y.-R., & Xu, J. (2008). Options for adaptivity in computer-assisted language learning and assessment. In C. A. Chapelle, Y.-R. Chung & J. Xu (Eds.), *Towards adaptive CALL: Natural language processing for diagnostic language assessment* (pp. 9–24). Ames, IA: Iowa State University.
Norris, J. M. (2001). Concerns with computerized adaptive oral proficiency assessment. *Language Learning & Technology, 5*(2), 99–105.
Ockey, G. J. (2009). Developments and challenges in the use of computer-based testing for assessing second language ability. *Modern Language Journal, 93*, 836–47.
Papadima-Sophocleous, S. (2008). A Hybrid of a CBT- and a CAT-based New English Placement Test Online (NEPTON). *CALICO Journal, 25*(2), 276–304.
Polio, C. (2001). Review of *Test Pilot*. *Language Learning & Technology, 5*(2), 34–7.
Prapphal, K. (2008). Issues and trends in language testing and assessment in Thailand. *Language Testing, 25*, 127–43.
Reed, J. (2000). *Assessing vocabulary*. Cambridge: Cambridge University Press.
Roever, C. (2001). Web-based language testing. *Language Learning & Technology, 5*(2), 84–94.
Sawaki, Y. (2001). Comparability of conventional and computerized tests of reading in a second language. *Language Learning & Technology, 5*(2), 38–59.
Taylor, C., Jamieson, J., Eignor, D., & Kirsch, I. (1998). *The relationship between computer familiarity and performance on computer-based TOEFL test tasks. TOEFL Research Report 61.* Princeton, NJ: Educational Testing Service.
Warschauer, M., & Ware, P. (2006). Automated writing evaluation: Defining the classroom research agenda. *Language Teaching Research, 10*(2), 1–24.
Weigle, S. C. (2002). *Assessing writing.* Cambridge: Cambridge University Press.
Winke, P., & MacGregor, D. (2001). Review of *Hot Potatoes. Language Learning & Technology, 5*(2), 28–33.
Young, Y., Shermis, M. D., Brutten, S. R., & Perkins, K. (1996). From conventional to computer-adaptive testing of ESL reading comprehension. *System, 24*, 23–40.
Yu, X., & Lowe, J. (2007). Computer assisted testing of spoken English: A study to evaluate the SFLEP college English oral test in China. In F. Khandia (Ed.), *11th CAA international computer assisted assessment conference: Proceedings of the conference on 10th and 11th July 2007 at Loughborough University* (pp. 489–502). Loughborough Leicestershire, UK: Loughborough University.
Zabaleta, F. (2007). Developing a multimedia, computer-based Spanish placement test. *CALICO Journal, 24*(3), 675–92.
Zumbo, B., & MacMillan, P. D. (1999). An overview and some observations on the psychometric models used in computer-adaptive language testing. In M. Chalhoub-Deville (Ed.), *Issues in computer-adaptive testing of reading proficiency* (pp. 216–28). Cambridge: Cambridge University Press.

6

Materials design in CALL: Social presence in online environments

Mirjam Hauck and Sylvia Warnecke

Summary

Over a decade ago Johnson (1999) pointed out that the potential of technology to transform language teaching was the main assumption underlying CALL course and material design and that conceptual frameworks which emphasize the social, cultural and discursive implications of using computers in teaching could actually provide far more appropriate guidance. One such framework highlighting the importance of social presence (SP) in text-based computer conferencing is Garrison, Anderson and Archer's (2000) Community of Inquiry (CoI) model which forms the backdrop to this chapter. We present and evaluate materials developed for a training program preparing tutors for teaching English for Academic Purposes (EAP) online. As the materials are specific to the environment rather than the subject, they are readily transferable to the learning and teaching of any language as well as other content in technology-assisted contexts. Our aim is to illustrate the impact of material design on generating SP. To that effect we explore the dynamics among participants as a result of their task performances during the training. Our analysis is based on postings to the tutor training forum and the tutor group fora (groups of learners and their respective tutors). It suggests that SP as defined by Kehrwald (2008), namely the ability of the individual to demonstrate his/her availability for and willingness to participate in interaction, is the central driving force for a successful CoI such as the trainees and the student groups with whom they subsequently embarked on the EAP online journey. However, drawing on Morgan's (2011) critique of Garrison et al. (2000) we argue for a fundamental re-consideration of the CoI's tripartite approach which separates SP from cognitive and teaching presence. We propose Galley, Conole and Alevizou's (2011) 'community indicators' as an alternative framework for online education in general and CALL in particular with SP as the guiding principle for material and task design for both (language) teaching and learning and teacher education purposes.

Introduction

In Levy and Stockwell's (2006) seminal volume *CALL Dimensions*, the term *CALL materials* encompasses tasks, software, courseware, websites, online courses, programs and learning environments to create 'a sense of continuity between CALL and language teaching more generally . . . especially in relation to language-learning materials design and development' (p. 3). This approach allows the authors to subsume everything from tasks as the starting point for materials development to online learning environments in which tasks are carried out under the 'materials umbrella'. They see this as the logical continuation of Breen, Candlin and Waters' (1979) distinction between *content* and *process* materials in relation to communicative language teaching highlighting the need to develop both. While the former centre on data and information, the latter provide 'guidelines or frameworks for the learners' use of communicative knowledge and abilities' (Breen et al., 1979; cited in Levy & Stockwell, 2006, p. 3). Online learning environments are perceived as such a framework within which learners can use and practise their communicative skills.

We see tasks and materials designed to foster the development of SP as sitting on the interface of the content and process dichotomy: on the one hand they deal with reflective content such as what motivates us to engage and participate online; on the other they draw on the affordances of the environment to help shape and guide online communication and interaction and thus SP as defined by Kehrwald (2008).

In CALL SP tends to be perceived as a secondary element, mainly relevant in terms of meeting the learners' social and affective needs, and as a facilitator of cognitive processes or deep learning. This understanding is informed by the CoI model developed by Garrison et al. (2000) in the context of the 'Study of the Characteristics and Qualities of Text-Based Computer Conferencing for Educational Purposes' project (http://communitiesofinquiry.com). The model distinguishes between cognitive, social and teaching presence – as relatively unvarying entities – and remains to date one of the most commonly referenced frameworks for investigations of formal higher-level online education.

Donaldson and Kötter (1999), for example, see the significance of SP in creating a 'far more effective and enjoyable' environment (p. 543). Lomicka and Lord (2007) propose that SP 'may facilitate the success of cognitive presence' and that it 'engages groups in interaction and communication and thus sustains and furthers critical skills' (p. 211). And Arnold and Ducate (2006) conclude that social activity might even outweigh cognitive density, especially if tutor presence is missing.

The study presented here questions such isolating and hierarchical views of the social and cognitive dimensions of computer-mediated collaborative (language) learning in a CoI and moves SP right into the centre of the learning and teaching process. Our findings assert the role of SP as the *conditio sine qua non* for learning in CMC contexts and thus as a core e-literacy skill rather than a facilitating element. The chapter further explores aspects of task design that promote the development of SP skills such as sending, reading and interpreting SP clues. We start with a brief introduction to SP with a focus on asynchronous teaching and learning contexts as this also applies to the present study. This is followed by an outline of the project which informs this contribution – set-up, methodology, participants, task design and content – as well as the approach to data collection and evaluation. Next we present and discuss our findings and argue for an alternative framework for CoIs in general and CALL and CMC-based language learning and teaching in particular. In this framework SP is at the centre of material and task design for both tutor training and language learning and teaching purposes.

Social presence

As early as 1995, Harasim et al. drew our attention to the fact that students are more engaged in the learning process when working in discussion boards. Lamy and Goodfellow (1999) found that such discussion boards encourage 'reflective conversation' and Mason and Weller (2000) stress their importance in terms of the social aspects of learning. These observations are reinforced by Davis and Thiede (2000) who found that discussion forums support the development of discourse-related awareness and the ability to abide by social norms. Bacon (1995) suggests that the key to success of asynchronous interaction is 'sustained interaction between participants' (Bacon 1995; cited in Lomicka & Lord, 2007, p. 210) thus shifting the focus slightly away from the qualities of interaction to the need for participation per se as a first step towards interaction. These studies emphasize the significance of the social dimension of CMC.

Yet, the actual concept of SP was motivated by the attempt to distinguish between mediated (e.g., telephone) and non-mediated (face-to-face) interactions and defined by Short, Williams and Christie (1976, p. 65) as 'the degree of salience of the other person in a mediated interaction and the consequent salience of the interpersonal interaction'. It was seen as a characteristic of the medium and its affordances where the 'capacity to transmit information about facial expression, direction of looking, posture, dress and non-verbal vocal cues, all contribute to the Social Presence of a communications medium' (Short et al., 1976, p. 65). Subsequently, SP was used to theorize communications media and became closely related to media richness theory (Daft & Lengel, 1986). Unsurprisingly, from this perspective text-based CMC was conceived of as a 'lean' medium in comparison to face-to-face interaction (Spears, Lea & Postmes, 2001, p. 605) Humans' capacity to adapt to lean media and to develop strategies to compensate for reduced cues was foregrounded by later theories of communications media (Walther, 1992, 1994). Along these lines Gunawardena (1995) argued that although text-based CMC afforded only low social contextual cues, participants' perception of the medium would primarily be based on their sense of community and that relationships could be social, active and interactive. Thus SP began to be increasingly viewed in terms of the quality of the communication rather than as an inherent quality of the media (for a more detailed overview, see Satar, 2010).

However, to this day a shared definition of SP remains a *desideratum*. In line with SP studies that explore the skills of those engaged in interaction we define SP as the ability of the individual to demonstrate his/her availability for and willingness to participate in interaction (Kehrwald, 2008).

Kehrwald's (2008, 2010) case study of SP – drawing on text-based and mainly asynchronous interactions – belongs to a minority of investigations that approach SP from the learner's perspective. The majority of definitions and research to date reflect researchers' understanding of SP and the ways in which it is established and manifests itself. Kehrwald explores SP in four online postgraduate education courses using dialogic interviews and focus groups. He concludes that SP is 'subjective projections of self . . . into technology mediated environments, subjective assessments of others' presence and assessments of the subject's relations with others' (Kehrwald, 2010, p. 41). This explains the importance he attaches to the learners' ability to send and read SP cues and the way in which these skills are learned collaboratively 'through seeing and experiencing how others project themselves into the environment, how others interact with one another and how others react to their personal efforts to cultivate a social presence' (p. 47). Kehrwald's understanding of SP is in line with that of Rourke, Garrison, Anderson and Archer (1999), namely 'the ability of learners to project themselves socially and affectively into a community of inquiry' (p. 50). Their framework for analysing SP comprises of three dimensions – affective, interactive and cohesive – and is briefly presented next.

Social presence within a Community of Inquiry

The CoI framework developed by Garrison et al. (2000) distinguishes between cognitive presence, social presence and teaching presence (see Figure 6.1).

Cognitive presence is described as 'the extent to which the participants in any particular configuration of a community of inquiry are able to construct meaning through sustained communication' (Garrison et al., 2000, p. 89). Social presence is understood as the projection of learners' personal characteristics into a CoI through use of emotional expression, open communication and various means to establish group cohesion. Cognitive presence is perceived as the core element of successful learning while SP supports critical thinking through meeting the learners' social and affective needs, thus providing indirect support for cognitive presence. It is accepted as a direct facilitator when sustaining interaction throughout a course is of significant importance, as, for example, in the case of distance education. Teaching presence is reflected in appropriate design of learning materials, facilitation of online discussions, and subject area ('directed') instruction, and seen as supporting and directing cognitive and social procedures.

Morgan (2011) confirms that 'much of current research that adopts the community of inquiry framework has largely focused on the social presence dimension' (p. 1). Rourke et al. (1999) developed a content analysis framework for the interpretation of learner group interactions via online discussion boards in order to support their theory with empirical data. This framework has been the basis for most content analysis work carried out in SP research to date including language learning and language teacher education studies. Others like, for example, Swan (2002) and Lomicka and Lord (2007) have built on and expanded the original framework of 15 equally weighted SP indicators grouped under the three aforementioned categories. The version proposed by Swan (2002) is shown in Table 6.1:

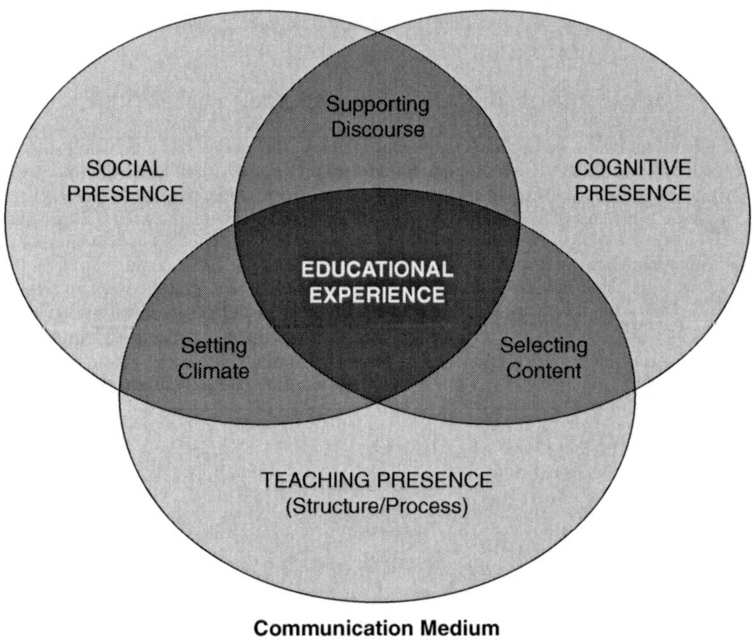

FIGURE 6.1 *Community of Inquiry by Garrison et al. (2000).*

TABLE 6.1 Swan's (2002) social presence indicators

Affective	Interactive	Cohesive
Paralanguage	Greetings and salutations	Acknowledgement
Emotion	Vocatives	Agreement/disagreement
Value	Group reference	Approval
Humour	Social sharing	Invitation
Self-disclosure	Course reflection	Personal advice

CALL studies based on the SP indicators framework

In a small-scale study at the UK Open University (OU), Satar (2007) used the original template to analyse text-based synchronous CMC discussions between English language teachers and native speakers of English and found that some indicators such as self-disclosure, emotions and continuing a thread, were challenging to apply. Furthermore, in her qualitative analysis of the interactions, Satar comments on the significance of other factors such as peer status, empathy, discourse markers and politeness, some of which also came to the fore in our study.

Arnold and Ducate (2006) analysed asynchronous CMC interactions in English of overall 23 FL teacher trainees subdivided into groups of four or five members. The trainees' reflection on teaching materials and their practical applications in the classroom indicated that they felt a sense of community, albeit to varying degrees across groups. Content analysis of a total of 27 discussion threads revealed that social activity outweighed cognitive density which the authors tentatively attribute to the intentional lack of tutor/trainer presence. Participant postings were graded along a cognitively oriented continuum ranging from mere theoretical knowledge, via connecting theory to individual experiences, to interactivity and – at the most advanced stage – to active contribution. Emotional SP indicators were hardly present in the exchanges, which the authors explain by the fact that the grading scheme discouraged any non-task-related exchanges. Yet, they registered a high volume of interactive and cohesive SP indicators contributing to a sense of community within the groups which – in turn – was conducive to cognitive activity.

Lomicka and Lord (2007) investigated the use of asynchronous interaction tools – reflective journals kept either individually, in email pairs or on a group discussion board – by a total of 14 FL teacher trainees in three groups documenting their classroom experiences during a four-month academic term. The main aim of the project was to design a methodology course for future FL teaching assistants. They examined how SP was co-constructed in different media and found that 'the expression of feeling, vulnerability, self-constructive comments, complements, encouragement, asking questions, advice/opinion, agreement, salutations, and the use of names' (pp. 223–4) were used more often in all groups than any other SP indicators. Lomicka and Lord surmise that SP 'may facilitate the success of cognitive presence' and that it 'engages groups in interaction and communication and thus sustains and furthers critical skills' (p. 211). They conclude that future research needs to explore how social presence is developed, under what conditions and through what media and to establish which indicators are particularly prominent in a 'socially present online community'.

Batstone, Stickler, Duensing and Heins (2007) compared face-to-face and distance FL tutorials conducted via audio-graphic conferencing in terms of the quality of interaction. They observed interactive and cohesive SP indicators across all tutorials, but significant variations in relation to affective indicators which they see as a consequence of task type, tutoring style and learner behaviour. Although part of their study does – strictly speaking – not fall into the category of mediated interactions discussed here, that is, those of an asynchronous nature, we have included it as they highlight the interrelation between instances of affective SP and task design. Our study confirms the influence of materials and tasks on SP (see below, 'Some Findings').

All of these investigations come to the conclusion that SP has an impact on both form and content of CMC-based learning. Yet, at the same time, they continue to rank SP as secondary to cognitive density or cognitive presence as defined by Garrison et al. (2000) in the CoI framework. One reason might be that most published research deals with the SP construct from the researchers' or teacher-as-researchers' perspective. Although the latter applies to the present chapter too, our study differs in that it focuses at the same time on the learners' perspective – tutors as learners on a training program.

The project: Set-up, participants, methodology and task design

Set-up, participants and methodological approach

The training followed an iterative process with participants working on a series of activities before transferring the insights gained to their individual EAP tutor groups. This was followed by feedback and joint reflection on their experiences in the tutor training forum. Table 6.2 provides an overview of the project.

Apart from experiential modelling which aims at immersing future tutors 'in the use of the technologies, while at the same time providing them with the freedom and framework within which to experience the practical application of the theory in their own learning' (Hoven 2007, n.p.), the program was also influenced by Allwright and Hanks' (2009) understanding of 'exploratory practice':

> Third-party research in general cannot meet our purposes, and practitioner research, the form of AR [action research], has not yet taken us far enough away from the third-party model to overcome these limitations. . . . The first two parties for research on education are the teachers and the learners. (Allwright & Hanks, 2009, p. 145)

Exploratory research originated in the 1990s in an attempt to bridge the teacher-researcher gap. Allwright (2003) focuses on the social nature of teaching and the need for all participants to be aware of the processes involved. Similarly Allwright and Hanks (2009) stress that language learning and teaching and research are social processes and thus call for learners as 'key practitioners' without excluding teachers. Instead, both should be considered 'practitioner colleagues' with the teacher playing a collegial role in helping learners develop as researchers of their own practices and as

TABLE 6.2 Project overview of Swan's (2002) adaptation of the SP template developed by Rourke et al. (1999)

Aims	Tutor familiarization with their peer group, the teaching materials, the learning and teaching environment (a bespoke version of Moodle) and forms of moderation in asynchronous settings (forum and wiki).
Duration	Six weeks in total whereby four weeks overlapped with the tutors starting to teach the module.
Design approach (methodology)	The program was inspired by a. Hoven's (2006) 'experiential modelling approach' where the tools and processes the tutors were expected to use in their teaching were experienced beforehand from a learner's point of view; b. Allwright's (2003) and Allwright and Hanks' (2009) understanding of 'exploratory practice' or inclusive practitioner research which allowed us to foreground the learners' (tutors as learners) perspective.
Participants	Nine tutors representing a multifaceted CoI with many being new to the British Open University, new to teaching in an online only context, but with some experience of using email for teaching and learning purposes, yet also new to the unique blend of students (native speakers of English and speakers of English as an additional language). Seven participants were new to tutoring via a forum.
Students	A similarly mixed cohort of adult learners in terms of academic histories, linguistic backgrounds, range of e-literacy skills and objectives for studying beyond EAP online.

'practitioners of learning' (p. 146). This collegial role was taken on by one of the two authors of this chapter who endeavoured throughout the training to ask questions to trigger participants' reflection on the processes they were involved in rather than providing ready-made answers. The way in which the tasks were introduced reflects this approach.

Task design and execution

In Lomicka and Lord's (2007) study variations in the manifestation of SP are attributed to different task types, structured versus unstructured tasks in particular. They propose that 'further research might . . . examine results from different types of tasks (other than journaling) that are prevalent in FL teacher training' (p. 212). This study picks up the baton and introduces a different task design. While Lomicka and Lord's (2007, p. 213) tasks were 'weekly journal entries [without any] particular topic that students were required to discuss, though they were instructed to reflect on their experiences in their classrooms each week', the activities in this training program all followed the same structure. Each week the participants carried out three tasks (see Figure 6.2 for week 3, task 1).

Week 3 Task 1 - Patterns of participation: Forum

Dear all,

This week we will consider two key issues with regard to the tutor role in asynchronous communication: motivation and participation. We want to find out to what extent our work can tip the balance either in favour or against participation and whether what [participant] calls 'let students get on with it' is something we need to take on board and to communicate to our learners.

Now:

- Think about your own patterns of participation (either as a moderator or as a student). How often, when, why, how intensively do you participate?
- Then have a look at the attached document which is a collation of common patterns of online participation as categorized by Salmon (2002).
- Which one applies to you? Is there anything you have learned that you want to practise in order to help your group become / be / stay (inter)active?

FIGURE 6.2 *Task on patterns of participation.*

Here the trainees were asked to consider Salmon's (2002) patterns of online participation (see Figure 6.3).

The following posting is an example response to week 3, task 1:

> As a student, I am definitely a rabbit: I live online and I check forums and emails as soon as I come home and again several times a day. I like participating and I especially love receiving mail . . .
>
> As a tutor, I tend to be very active at the beginning to greet the students, value their contributions and also to try to stimulate the interaction. Later, I try to post something at least every week to show that it is worth checking the forum regularly . . .
>
> The list [of animals] is very useful because it suggests possible solutions to every kind of problem. However, it is based on the idea that students' patterns of participation are linked to their attitude towards forums/the Internet or their personality. While these attitudes certainly play a part, students often say that they don't participate because they are very busy, they have technical problems, they cannot see the relevance or usefulness of the forum activities or because participation is not compulsory. (Discussion Thread (DT)7, Contribution (C)2, Trainee (T)4, 01/02/2010)

It is a representative contribution insofar as the trainees soon realized that Salmon's recipe-type approach to participation ignores many of the factors at play in online (language) learning and teaching contexts.

Type	Behaviours	E-moderator response
The wolf	Visits once a week, lots of activity, then disappears again until next week, or even the week after!	Nudge wolf by e-mail to encourage to visit again and see responses that s/he has sparked off.
The elephant	Steady – visits most days for a short time.	Congratulate. Ask elephant to encourage and support others – especially mouse and squirrel.
The squirrel	Always catching up: completes two weeks in one session then disappears again for some time.	Nudge squirrel by e-mail to suggest life is easier with more regular access. Check on other commitments. Provide regular summaries and archiving to enable squirrel to catch up easily and contribute.
The mouse	Visits once a week, reads and contributes little.	Check that mouse can access all messages. Check language difficulties. May need boost of confidence. Give specific role.
The mole	Inclined to post disembodied comments in a random way.	Try to include relevant comments from mole in summaries and invite resp onses. Needs support and e-stroking.
The rabbit	Lives online, prolific message writer, responds very rapidly.	Rabbit may need counselling to hold back and let others shine through. Give structured roles such as summarizing after a plenary.
The stag	Tendency to dominate discussion at certain times.	Invite stag back frequently. Offer a structured and specific role.
The magpie	Steals ideas without acknowledging.	Foster a spirit of acknowledgement and reinforcement of individual ideas. Warn magpie directly if necessary.
The dolphin	Intelligent, good communicator and playful online.	Ensure dolphin acknowledges and works well with others. May annoy participants who think it's all very serious.

FIGURE 6.3 *Patterns of participation (© G. Salmon (2002).* Etivities: The key to active online learning. *Kogan Page, p. 171).*

Week 3 Task 2 - Motivation: forum

Dear all,

searching the web for information on 'motivation techniques' for online forum groups you come across statements like this one:

'*However, motivating students to use the online discussion groups is one of the main challenges. It is often the case that the better performing students engage in the debates, whilst the remainder of the class either offer limited debate or fail to engage at all. This lack of engagement could be due to poor motivation, confidence or fear of embarrassment at posting a message that the student perceives will be interpreted as being stupid by their peers. It is therefore important that the tutor manages the online discussion and its progression to ensure that viewpoints are constructively received and further debate can be instigated.*'

(http://www.heacademy.ac.uk/assets/hlst/documents/case_studies/using_online_discussion_forums_as_a_learning_tool.pdf)

I guess you would all agree. However, the question remains: **HOW** can this be done?

1. I also discovered a slide show about what motivates people to be active on the Social Web. it gives some clues as to the range of motivational aspects we will come across in our work: http://www.slideshare.net/trebor/motivating-people-to-participate?from=share_email.
2. Have you found anything you were not aware of? What are you conclusions in respect to your work on EAP online?
3. And a bit more input... ☺ The University of Newcastle put together a website with information, tips and tricks regarding online distance learning including motivation: http://www.newcastle.edu.au/ctl-resources/Teaching-in-the-online-environment/Facilitating/Motivating_students.htm
4. Select two points you would include in a short guideline for forum moderators. Please post these points here and explain your choice.

FIGURE 6.4 *Task on motivation.*

Closely related to reflections on patterns of participation was the task that instigated exchanges about learner motivation (see Figure 6.4 for week 3, task 2).

The first section of each task related to the participants' previous teaching experience, in face-to-face, online only or blended contexts. The second part asked them to engage with research findings or practitioner recommendations and their underlying rationale. In part three they reflected on their current experiences both in the EAP online classroom with their students and as part of the tutor trainee group, and tried to relate these to the scholarly input as well as their own teaching background.

Throughout the training the moderator-colleague linked all tasks and the resulting exchanges with each other referring back to participant contributions to earlier discussion threads and explaining how these relate to the new topic at hand. This can be described as a 'storyline approach', where participants are continuously made aware of the interrelationship between the activities they carry out, the training program as a whole, their past and current teaching practice and their own and others' understanding of the processes and dynamics they are engaged in. Interweaving the trainees' activities during the training, their past experiences and joint conclusions reflects Appel and Lantolf's (1994, p. 437) observation that 'performance [in a task] depends crucially on the interaction between individual and task'. It also shows 'how tasks – or rather the activities that comprise participants' task performances – serve as a form of mediation that can bring about learning' (Ellis, 2003, p. 185). The way in which the teacher trainees interpreted the task in their task performances, also highlights Coughlan and Duff's (1994) point that researchers as well as teachers should not conceptualize task as an absolute term or constant in research since 'the activity it generates will be unique' (p. 191).

The topics covered during the training ranged from getting to know the module website, sharing icebreaker ideas and challenges associated with motivation and participation (see Figures 6.2 and 6.4) to error correction and assessment of forum contributions. Next, we explain our approach to analysing the interactions that took place.

Data collection and evaluation

Similar to Arnold and Ducate (2006) we carried out a content analysis of the trainees' asynchronous interactions – in our case postings to the training and tutor group for a – through the lens of the CoI framework (Garrison et al., 2000), more specifically by applying Swan's (2002) adaptation of the original coding template for SP indicators (see Table 6.1). We soon realized though that a categorization of the forum contributions according to SP indicators was unhelpful for our purpose as most postings not only presented us with a dense mix of indicators it also led us away from their actual content. The following example illustrates this:

> . . . I think . . . these kinds of classifications [Figure 6.3] have to be used with caution . . . I guess our forum identity is as multifaceted as any other (what is a multilingual forum identity like???) which I think T8 (sorry if misattributing but need names in front of me if I'm to remember them – should have taken notes when reading forum) alluded to in discussions about whether our behaviour on a forum is similar to our behaviour elsewhere. (DT7, C12, T6, 2/02/2010)

The extract reflects a number of obvious SP indicators such as the use of affective 'conventional expressions of emotion, or unconventional expressions of emotion, includes repetitious punctuation' (Lomicka & Lord 2007, p. 212). At the same time this trainee shows 'self-disclosure' when talking about patterns of behaviour outside the class and expressing a degree of vulnerability. Cohesive 'addressing or referring to participants by name' (Lomicka & Lord 2007, p. 212) is also present. According to Swan's (2002) template and Lomicka and Lord's (2007) additions the use of expressions such as 'I guess' or the use of punctuation as in'. . . I think . . .' cannot be appropriately classified. In our view this extract shows a strong 'interactive' message, for example through the link it makes with Salmon's table – the 'course reflection' (see Table 6.1). However, according to established SP indicators the highly personal way in which other participants are invited to follow T6's unfinished thought process, cannot be identified nor labelled with existing SP indicators. Yet, on the basis of our observations we would claim that this is one of the core features of SP and explains its potential impact on text-based online interactions.

The diversity in task performance due to a wide range of academic, cultural and personal backgrounds is evident in the participants' individual approaches. Thus the focus of our study was not task completion but what was happening while the trainees were carrying out the tasks, that is, how the affordances of the environment helped shape communication and interaction and thus SP to gradually emerge in their exchanges (see introduction). We therefore decided to look at the contributions to the training forum from a broader perspective to explore how the trainees were developing awareness of the interactions they were involved in and thus of their own and others' SP and its impact. In what follows we summarize and comment on some of our findings based on postings to the training forum only.

Some findings

The many variables that define the context of this study (see above) illustrate Morgan's (2011) exhortation of what we need to keep in mind if we want to understand what happens in CoIs. Morgan finds it surprising that although the CoI framework was developed with distance education in mind, it does not take account of a community's various contexts (global and local) and their impact on issues such as power relations, agency and identity.

The fact that Rourke et al.'s (1999) original SP template was not deemed sufficient, and that several attempts have been made to distinguish new and different aspects of SP which acknowledge the influence of variables such as the affordances of the media, group dynamics and number of participants (Lomicka & Lord, 2007), peer status and discourse markers (Satar, 2007) and task type (Batstone et al., 2007) is – in our view – indicative of this dilemma.

Morgan also stresses that the CoI framework does not take full account of the sociocultural dimensions of CMC. In the same way as Morgan asserts that within a 'sociocultural theoretical approach to understanding online course interactions on the COI framework . . . teaching presence needs to be redefined' (p. 2), we suggest that the SP construct needs to be fundamentally reconsidered. Much CMC-based learning happens in multi-faceted sociocultural contexts, even within one institution, a reality that is as of yet not acknowledged in the framework and existing attempts to categorize the many aspects of SP with catalogues of indicators.

Similarly we have found that the CoI does not provide sufficient scope for the constant shifting of roles, identities and participation patterns characteristic for computer mediated interactions.

Shifting roles and identities and varying patterns of participation

To illustrate our observations we have selected data from three participants reflecting the diversity in the group of trainees that formed the CoI in this study and thus also the complexity highlighted by Morgan (2011). The chosen extracts are related to tasks 1 and 2 in week 3 (see Figures 6.2 and 6.4). Unsurprisingly, these contain the highest volume of reflective comments on the very topic of participation.

T1 was new to teaching her subject online as well as to working at the OU, although she had been an OU student. She was one of the most active and creative contributors to the discussions. T2 had some experience with teaching in discussion forums from tutoring a different OU English language course. T2 infrequently contributed lengthy yet constructive postings but did not engage in the exchanges as such. T3 had extensive experience in English language teaching both at a distance and in face-to-face settings. He was part of the production team of the EAP module and had also experienced distance learning as an OU student on other modules. T3 joined the discussion infrequently with encouraging, very informative yet short contributions. The following is a representative posting from T3:

> I find my patterns vary quite a lot so cannot find one animal that fits perfectly. I think my messages tend to be short compared to many. . . . (DT7, C6, T3, 02/02/2010)

The activity outlined in Figure 6.2 triggered a lively exchange about motivation including reflections about the changing nature of participation according to assigned roles, personal circumstances and/or institutional settings. Here is an extract from T1:

> Hi All,
>
> . . . Some students have posted lots of comments and seem really keen (rabbits?), whereas others have not yet been seen.
>
> 1. In terms of my own participation I think as a student I was probably a bit of a squirrel. I would look at the forum when I needed help and found it hard to fit it in to my busy life . . .
>
> 2. As a tutor I think I am far more engaged with the forum as I really enjoy the interaction with the students, even better is when you can read the conversations they have had with each other without your involvement. I seem to visit quite frequently (elephant?) . . .
>
> I have made an effort to reply to each student's introductory message as I wanted to make sure I had some contact with each of them early on. In my reply I asked further questions to try to stimulate more participation. I noticed [moderator-colleague] did this when we started using the [training] and found it very welcoming.

> 3. I will be looking out for ways to help the [students] to participate. I wonder, is it worth showing the list [Figure 6.3] to stimulate discussion about forum use? . . . (DT7, C19, T1, 03/02/2010)

The following comments are by T2:

> . . . making online activities part of the assessment helps motivate those students and places those activities at the top rather than the end of the list of priorities . . .
>
> Beyond the assessed activities, the TGF [Tutor Group Forum] is a resource that tutors can encourage students to use. For example, by creating a constant 'presence' in the TGF (posting something new each week) and replying to students' posts if no one else is doing so. However, if your students just don't want to use the TGF I don't see the point in needlessly worrying about it. It's vital to keep up the online presence and even in quiet TGFs you'll see most students are at least reading your messages.
>
> You can compare low TGF participation rates with a handful of students bothering to attend tutorials – some people sign up to distance learning because they just want to get the course materials, read them and get on with the assignments – they don't want to be 'step locked' into following the course week by week or having to interact unnecessarily with other students. As an OU student I fall into this category – I have never attended a tutorial, e-tutorial or posted anything to a course forum or TGF beyond what is compulsory to pass a TMA [Tutor Marked Assignment]. (DT7, C4, T2, 02/02/2010)

T3 also commented:

> A quote I find interesting is:
>
> 'Students are like themselves, only more so, when online. The chatty ones write long responses, the worriers modify their messages, the dutiful ones do what is required reliably but without brilliance, and the irresponsible are conspicuous by their absence.' (Hiltz & Meinke, 1989, p. 441). I suspect I am like myself and perhaps more so online. Decide for yourself how well I do. (DT7, C9, T3, 02/02/2010)

In view of such contributions Salmon's categorizations of online behaviours and moderator responses seem rather rigid as they do not take account of the transient nature of online participation.

Their task performances move the participants well beyond the self as a 'static entity' in online interactions. The examples reflect the on-going process of identity formation depending on ever changing contextual circumstances on the one hand and insights gained from newly acquired or pre-existing theoretical knowledge on the other.

The three extracts also highlight the need to distinguish between participatory literacy as a prerequisite for SP and SP as such, and suggest that what we can actually train for in CALL teacher education is participatory literacy as defined by Pegrum (2009, p. 42), that is, 'digital communicative literacy, which provides a foundation for online interactions . . . and which facilitates the collaborative processes at the core of participatory literacy'. Task-based training can achieve this by systematically raising awareness for SP cues such as the cohesive SP indicator 'invitation' in 'Decide for yourself how well I do'. Such an approach corroborates Kehrwald's (2010) understanding of SP as the ability to send and read SP cues and his assertion that these skills are best acquired collaboratively 'through seeing and experiencing how others project themselves into the environment, how others interact with one another and how others react to their personal efforts to cultivate a social presence' (p. 47).

Experiential modelling and exploratory practice

The extracts also hint at the added value of experiential modelling and exploratory practice in terms of cultivating a SP (see D7, C19, T1, 03/02/2010, in particular).

Moreover they emphasize the central role of task design and performance as an opportunity to experience the aforementioned processes, become aware of them through joint reflection and finally apply them to one's own practice:

> The training we had at the start of the course was just excellent, not just for the focus on different aspects of VLE and forums and the needs of the online/distance learner, but also for the model it provided of how to respond to posts. It created a 'safe' environment on the forums; for example, the trainer never made me feel 'put down', regardless of the stupidity of my comment or question; I have pinched phrases she used in her replies in my own responses to students. (End-of-course survey, question 3, C4, anonymous, 02/10/2010)

This remark suggests a direct link between experiential modelling and SP as the ways in which others position and reposition themselves in a CoI presents a model which can be adopted and followed and thus learned. To that effect the moderator-colleague who ran the training intentionally positioned herself in a variety of ways which – in turn – allowed her to make shifting of roles and identities the topic of the exchanges. Other ways in which participants benefited from experiential modelling are apparent in D7, C19, 03/02/2010, second point (see above).

How then, can we capture SP as a phenomenon that emerges through task performance in CMC-based CoIs? As a potential answer we propose the Community Indicators Framework by Galley et al. (2011).

The Community Indicators Framework

In order to understand types of user behaviour in online sites such as fora Galley et al. (2010) reviewed the literature on different frameworks for describing communities including the CoI model. They suggest that the notion of communities in social and participatory sites is different as 'participatory web processes and practices have . . . opened up new spaces for, and styles of interaction – social spaces which enable transient, collaborative, knowledge building communities, and the development of shared . . . interests, goals, content and ideas' (n.p.).

Based on their review they developed the Community Indicators Framework which consists of four broad aspects associated with behaviour and attributes of participants, situational factors and how participants feel. 'Each of these aspects' they underline 'is interrelated and the whole reflects the multifaceted complexity of what we experience as community' (see Figure 6.5).

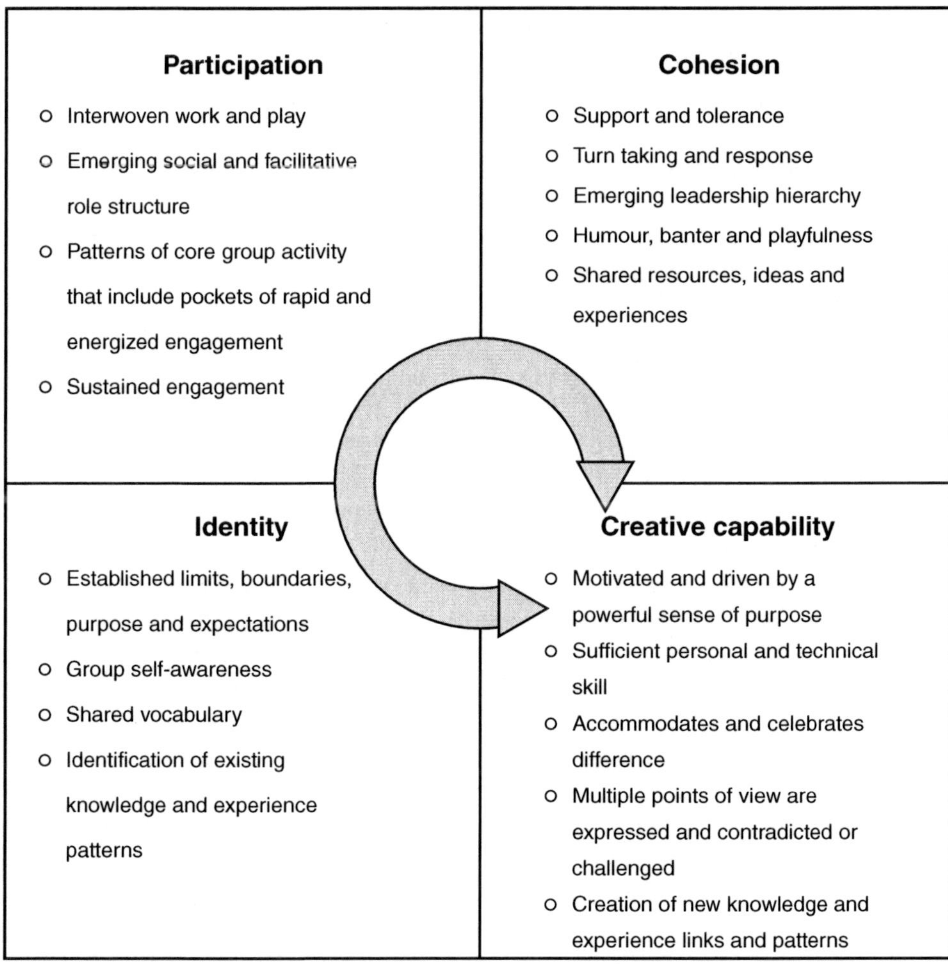

FIGURE 6.5 *Community Indicators Framework by Galley et al. (2011).*

Galley et al. try to reflect the organic nature of communities by taking account of the constant movement and dynamics that link all aspects of the framework. Significantly, the category of identity found its way into the understanding of online communities and the distinction between teacher and learner has been removed.

We suggest a re-consideration of the SP construct in the light of this framework as an overarching concept that is both the means *and* the end of online communication and interaction and the result of participatory literacy as understood by Pegrum (2009).

Conclusions

Morgan (2011, p. 1) observes 'that a shift to understanding teaching presence within a sociocultural perspective has important implications for teaching and design'. In our view, the same holds true for SP. On the basis of our study we would argue that tasks designed to spark collaborative reflection on issues related to participation, motivation and thus SP, seem particularly well suited to foster SP itself and should therefore be more systematically trialled and integrated into CALL and CMC-based teacher education and learner preparation for online interaction. However, as they operate on a meta-cognitive level and try to raise awareness for the very phenomenon that is at stake while trainees engage in task performance, such tasks constitute a particular challenge for all involved. Still, we can claim with some certainty that it was the participants' interpretation of tasks designed to trigger exchanges on motivation and participation that led to reflection, discussion and thus learning about the relevance of SP in online communities and – at the same time – helped SP emerge among the trainees. By witnessing how others 'project themselves into the environment, how others interact with one another and how others react to their personal efforts to cultivate a social presence' (Kehrwald, 2010, p. 47) participants gradually acquired the skill to send, receive and interpret SP cues. They found out about the shifting of roles and identities which are typical for online learning communities and which – in turn – allowed them to continually re-conceptualize their position in the online interactions and to accept the transient nature of their role.

Most of SP research to date is based on text-based and asynchronous CMC interactions and has largely ignored the influence of multimodal elements on and skills needed for the projection of the self via emerging CMC technologies. A significant exception in terms of investigations of SP and emerging CMC technologies is Satar's (2010) work which explores SP in online multimodal communication.

The SP literature also largely reflects the teacher-researchers' perspective rather than the learners' view. The present study has attempted to bridge the second gap by applying Allwright and Hank's (2009) concept of 'exploratory practice' where teacher trainees become researchers of their own learning. A joint way forward for SP training and research in both asynchronous and synchronous online contexts and echoing the spirit of open source instructional materials, might be the use of teacher and learner ethnographies building on and expanding the 'storyline approach' of the study presented here. Once captured in the shape of an online journal, then repurposed, customized and integrated into open textbooks or journals for subsequent cohorts of teacher trainees and/or learners, the exchanges resulting from tasks such as the ones used in this study could provide the basis for further and new reflections, interactions and evaluations.

References

Allwright, D. (2003). Exploratory practice: Rethinking practitioner research in language teaching. *Language Teaching Research*, *7*(2), 113–41.

Allwright, D., & Hanks, J. (2009). *The developing language learner: An introduction to exploratory practice.* Basingstoke: Palgrave Macmillan.

Appel, G., & Lantolf, J. P. (1994). Speaking as mediation: A study of L1 and L2 text recall tasks. *The Modern Language Journal*, *78*(4), 437–52.

Arnold, N., & Ducate, L. (2006). Future foreign language teachers' social and cognitive collaboration in an online environment. *Language Learning & Technology*, *10*(1), 42–66.

Bacon, S. (1995). Coming to grips with the culture: Another use of dialogue journals in teacher education. *Foreign Language Annals*, *28*, 193–207.

Batstone, C., Stickler, U., Duensing, A., & Heins, B. (2007). Social presence in face-to-face and online language tutorials. Presented at the BAAL-CUP Seminar: Spoken online learning events: The need for a new paradigm in languages research and practice, Milton Keynes.

Breen, M. P., Candlin, C., & Waters, A. (1979). Communicative materials design: Some basic principles. *RELC Journal*, *10*(2), 1–13.

Coughlan, P., & Duff, P. (1994). Same task, different activities: Analysis of SLA from an activity theory perspective. In J. P. Lantolf & G. Appel (Eds.), *Vygotskian approaches to second language research* (pp. 173–94). Norwood, NJ: Ablex.

Daft, R. L., & Lengel, R. H. (1986). Organizational information requirements, media richness and structural design. *Management Science*, *32*(5), 554–71.

Davis, B., & Theide, R. (2000). Writing into change: Style shifting in asynchronous electronic discourse. In M. Warschauer and R. Kern (Eds.), *Networked-based language teaching: Concepts and practice* (pp. 87–120). Cambridge: Cambridge University Press.

Donaldson, R. P., & Kötter, M. (1999). Language learning in cyberspace: Teleporting the classroom into the target culture. *CALICO Journal*, *16*(4), 531–57.

Donato, R. (2000). Sociocultural contributions to understanding the foreign second language classroom. In J. P. Lantolf (Ed.), *Sociocultural theory and second language learning* (pp. 27–50). Oxford: Oxford University Press.

Ellis, R. (2003). *Task-based language learning and teaching.* Oxford: Oxford University Press.

Galley, R., Conole, G., & Alevizou, P. (2010). Indicators of community – A framework for evaluating relational and transient communities on Cloudworks. OULDI workshop paper, 19 March. Milton Keynes: The Open University.

— (2011). Indicators of community table – Presentation transcript. Retrieved from www.slideshare.net/OULDI/indicators-of-community-table

Garrison, D. R., & Cleveland-Innes, M. (2005). Facilitating cognitive presence in online learning: Interaction is not enough. *American Journal of Distance Education*, *19*(3), 133–48.

Garrison, D. R., Anderson, T., & Archer, W. (2000). Critical inquiry in a text-based environment: Computer conferencing in higher education. *The Internet and Higher Education, 2*(2–3), 87–105.

—(2010). The first decade of the community of inquiry framework: A retrospective. *The Internet and Higher Education, 13*(1–2), 5–9.

Gunawardena, C. N., & Zittle, F. J. (1997). Social presence as a predictor of satisfaction within a computer-mediated conferencing environment. *American Journal of Distance Education, 11*(3), 8–26.

Harasim, L. Hiltz, S. R., Teles, L., & Turoff, M. (1995). *Learning networks: A field guide to teaching and learning online*. Cambridge, MA: MIT Press.

Hoven, D. (2006). Designing for disruption: Remodelling a blended course in technology in (language) teacher education. Proceedings of the 23rd Annual Ascilite conference: *Who's learning? Whose technology?* 3–6 December (pp. 339–49). Sydney: University of Sydney.

— (2007). The affordances of technology for student teachers to shape their teacher education experience. In M. A. Kassen, R. Z., Lavine, K. Murphy-Judy and M. Peter (Eds.), *Preparing and developing technology-proficient L2 Teachers* (pp. 133–62). CALICO Monograph Series, *6*. Texas: CALICO.

Johnson, M. (1999). CALL and teacher education: Issues in course design. *CALL-EJ ONLINE, 1*(2).

Kehrwald, B. (2008). Understanding social presence in text-based online learning environments. *Distance Education, 29*(1), 89.

— (2010). Being online: Social presence and subjectivity in online learning. *London Review of Education, 8*(1), 39–50.

Kim, E. (2007). Students' perception of social presence and its influence on their learning in an online environment: A case study. In E. Simonson (Ed.), *2007 annual proceedings* (Vol. 1). Presented at the annual convention of the association for educational communications and technology (pp. 118–24). Anaheim, CA: Nova Southeastern University.

Lamy, M. N., & Goodfellow, R. (1999). Reflective conversation in the virtual language classroom. *Language Learning & Technology 2*(2), 43–61.

Levy, M., & Stockwell, G. (2006). *CALL dimensions: Options and issues in computer-assisted language learning*. Mahweh, NJ & London: Lawrence Erlbaum Associates.

Lomicka, L., & Lord, G. (2007). Social presence in virtual communities of foreign language (FL) teachers. *System* 35, 208–28.

Mason, R., & Weller, M. (2000). Factors affecting students' satisfaction on a Web course. *Australian Journal of Educational Technology 16* (2), 173–200.

Morgan, T. (2008). *The negotiation of teaching presence in international online contexts.* Unpublished dissertation, University of British Columbia.

— (2011). Online classroom or community-in-the-making? Instructor conceptualizations and teaching presence in international online contexts. *Journal of Distance Education, 25*(1), 1–15.

Pegrum, M. (2009). *From blogs to bombs: The future of digital technologies in education.* Perth: University of Western Australia Press.

Richardson, J. C., & Swan, K. (2003). Examining social presence in online courses in relation to students' perceived learning and satisfaction. *Journal of Asynchronous learning networks, 7*(1), 68–88.

Rourke, L., Anderson, T., Garrison, R., & Archer, W. (1999). Assessing social presence in asynchronous text-based computer conferencing. *Journal of Distance Education, 14*(2), 50–71.
Salmon, G. (2002). *E-tivities: The key to active online learning.* Sterling, VA: Stylus Publishing.
Satar, H. M. (2007). *The effects of computer mediated communication on oral language development.* Unpublished MRes dissertation. Milton Keynes: The Open University.
— (2010). *Social presence in online multimodal communication: A framework to analyse online interactions between language learners.* Unpublished PhD thesis. Milton Keynes: The Open University.
Short, J., Williams, E., & Christie, B. (1976). *The social psychology of telecommunications.* London: Wiley & Sons.
Spears, R., Lea, M., & Postmes, T. (2001). Social psychological theories of computer-mediated communication: Social pain or social gain. In W. P. Robinson & H. Giles (Eds.), *The new handbook of language and social psychology.* London: John Wiley & Sons.
Swan, K. (2002). Building communities in online courses: The importance of interaction. *Education, Communication and Information, 2*(1), 23–49.
van Langenhove, L., & Harré, R. (1999). Introducing positioning theory. In R. Harré & L. van Langenhove (Eds.), *Positioning theory: Moral contexts of intentional action* (pp. 14–31). Oxford: Blackwell.
Walther, J. B. (1992). Interpersonal effects in computer-mediated interaction: A relational perspective. *Communication Research, 19*(1), 52–90.
— (1994). Anticipated ongoing interaction versus channel effects on relational communication in computer-mediated interaction. *Human Communication Research, 20*(4), 473–501.
Wang, J. (1996). *Same task: Different activities.* Unpublished research report. Pittsburgh, PA: University of Pittsburgh.
Weir, C. (1988). *Communicative language testing.* Exeter Linguistic Studies, Vol. 11. Exeter: University of Exeter.
White, C. (2003). *Language learning in distance education.* Cambridge: Cambridge University Press.

PART TWO

CALL learning environments

Section introduction

Hayo Reinders, Michael Thomas and Mark Warschauer

Recent years have seen a shift of attention away from the teacher and onto the learner and the ways in which the learning process, both inside and outside the classroom, can best be supported. The use of virtual learning environments (VLEs), blended learning, self-access centres and work-based learning initiatives, are only some of the manifestations of the desire to broaden language development beyond traditional settings and into learners' lives. Technology has played an important role in facilitating a reconceptualization of the ways in which information can be delivered and shared, not just from teacher to learner, but also between learners themselves. Technology has also increased our understanding of the importance of informal learning processes in education and has led to a recognition of the key role of the wider environment, including the classroom, the school, the community and informal networks, in the language learning process (Allford & Pachler, 2007; Conacher & Kelly-Holmes, 2007). Related to this, in recent years there has been a growing recognition of the importance of developing in learners the ability to draw on this wider environment, and in this way to support their lifelong learning.

At the same time, it is clear that both teachers and learners are not always ready to develop this capacity. More research is needed to establish how learning can best be supported and how learners can best be prepared for taking responsibility for their own learning. Similarly, more research is needed that investigates what happens outside formal education, or in developing low-tech contexts. It is unclear how learners manage their own learning before and after taking courses, in their workplace, and their daily lives, and what the role of technology is in these. New, innovative methodologies need to be developed to better understand the specific needs of learners, their learning preferences and the ways their learning can be enhanced.

The chapters in Part Two address some of these concerns by looking at areas of CALL that go beyond the classroom in isolation and by reviewing technologies that can help to broaden students' access to learning opportunities. Distance CALL, as covered by Marie-Noëlle Lamy, is an example of the range of methods, means and environments this can occur in. As Lamy argues, distance CALL is diverse in nature;

it can be delivered entirely online or in a blended form, it can be entirely or only partly mediated by technology, it can offer flexible as well as structured, open or traditional, informal as well as formal education (White, 2006). Lamy offers an integrated model of distance language learning, built around a learning design approach, the presence of an institutional strategy for distance learning and the development of a distributed learning environment. Distance CALL is a good example of the ways in which technology can help to create new contexts for learning and teaching, that require their own methods and research.

Another example of the way technology creates new contexts for learning is through telecollaboration. Robert O'Dowd reviews current models and practice of the use of online communication tools for the development of language and intercultural skills. He also reviews emerging practice in the application of Web 2.0 tools and environments, which have led to greater opportunities for multimodal exchange and the development of new task types (see also, Peterson, 2010). O'Dowd shows how the integration of telecollaboration into formal education may require a rethinking of teaching practices and the implications this may have for language learning.

An entirely new environment is offered in many of the virtual words, discussed by Randall Sadler and Melinda Dooly. In their chapter, they review current research and practice, showing their potential as well as the various barriers to their use in either formal of informal education (see for the latter also Schwienhorst, 2007). In the second part of their chapter they report on a case-study project involving young (6–12 years) learners building a virtual art gallery. Sadler and Dooly show how the immersive and collaborative features of the virtual world helped with the children's development of a range of literacies. They warn, however, that there is as yet too little understanding of how learning (and teaching) in virtual worlds works. A great deal more research into the affordances of these types of learning environments is needed.

Digital games have received a great deal of interest in recent years (Reinders, 2012; Thorne, Black & Sykes, 2009) for their purported potential to motivate students, increase time on task and encourage collaboration and situated communication. Chun Lai, Ruhui Ni and Yong Zhao review the use of digital games in language learning and discuss the potential for adapting or drawing on existing commercial language games. One of the main challenges in this type of learning environment is to find the right balance between instruction and gameplay and to draw as much as possible on the affordances inherent in this type of environment.

Similar challenges exist in the area of mobile learning. Glenn Stockwell looks at the potential for mobile technologies to deliver materials and support the learning process relatively cheaply, and increasingly powerfully (Chinnery, 2006; Kukulska-Hulme & Traxler, 2005). Stockwell describes the ways in which mobile technologies have been researched and used in language education so far. He highlights their role in situated and distributed learning and their ability to provide learners with instant access to materials in small units, at times and in places convenient to them. He also cautions, however, against overly optimistic expectations and reviews the various limitations, such as limited screen size and students' reticence in having formal education move into the informal sphere. He goes on to argue for the need for thorough preparation and ongoing support when mobile technologies are used. Stockwell concludes by reviewing a number of emerging trends, such as ubiqitous, location-based and pervasive learning.

An entirely different perspective is offered by Dafne Gonzalez and Rubena St. Louis, who remind us of the many cases where technology is not widely available. The 'digital divide' remains in place in parts of the world (Warschauer, 2003). The authors report on the results of a survey sent out to teachers in low-tech contexts on their use of technology and the impediments to its implementation. From this they distil a number of recommendations for the use of CALL in low-tech environments that should be of benefit to educators around the world.

Each of these chapters describes how technology can help to support learning in new contexts and in new ways. As a result, we see the emergence of ecologies of learning that, although related to traditional education in myriad ways, are, also distinct and that offer new opportunities for learning and teaching. 'New language learning environments' is a term that has recently started to be used to encapsulate all of these developments (White, 2007). It refers to both the practical environments for learning and teaching as well as to the (changes in) pedagogy needed to sustain them. The chapters in this section chart the course for future developments in this area and give insight into their affordances as well as their constraints on language teaching and research.

References

Allford, D., & Pachler, N. (2007). *Language, autonomy and the new learning environments.* Frankfurt am Main: Peter Lang.

Chinnery, G. (2006). Going to the MALL: Mobile assisted language learning. *Language Learning and Technology, 10*(1), 9–16.

Conacher, J. E., & Kelly-Holmes, H. (Eds.) (2007). *New learning environments for language learning: Moving beyond the classroom?* Frankfurt am Main: Peter Lang.

Kukulska-Hulme, A., & Traxler, J. (Eds.) (2005). *Mobile learning: A handbook for educators and trainers.* London: Routledge.

Peterson, M. (2010). Task-based language teaching in networked-based CALL: An analysis of research on learner interaction in synchronous CMC. In M. Thomas & H. Reinders (Eds.), *Task-based language learning and teaching with technology* (pp. 41–62). London & New York: Continuum.

Reinders, H. (Ed.) (2012). *Digital games in language learning and teaching.* Basingstoke: Palgrave Macmillan.

Schwienhorst, K. (2007). *Learner autonomy and virtual environments in CALL.* London: Routledge.

Thorne, S., Black, R., & Sykes, J. (2009). Second language use, socialization, and learning in internet interest communities and online gaming. *Modern Language Journal, 93,* 802–21.

Warschauer, M. (2003). *Technology and social inclusion: Rethinking the digital divide.* Cambridge: MIT Press.

White, C. (2006). State-of-the-art review article: The distance learning of foreign languages. *Language Teaching, 39*, 247–64.

— (2007). Innovation and identity in distance language learning and teaching. *Innovation in Language Learning and Teaching, 1*(1), 97–110.

7

Telecollaboration and CALL

Robert O'Dowd

Summary

In the context of foreign language education, 'telecollaboration' refers to the application of online communication tools to bring together classes of language learners in geographically distant locations to develop their foreign language skills and intercultural competence through collaborative tasks and project work. The interaction has traditionally been text-based and asynchronous, however, the recent advances of Web 2.0 online communication have meant that synchronous oral communication as well as multimodal exchanges involving combinations of different media are becoming increasingly popular. This chapter reviews the different models or configurations of online intercultural exchange which have been employed in the foreign language classroom to date and also explores the new options and opportunities which are emerging from Web 2.0 contexts. We outline the main research findings related to this activity as well as its key contributions to foreign language learning. Finally, the challenges involving the integration of telecollaboration into formal education will be discussed.

Introduction

One of the major contributions of the internet to foreign language (FL) education has been its potential to bring language learners into virtual contact with members of other cultures and speakers of other languages. For example, a class of learners studying Spanish in the United States can now interact with relative ease with learners of English in Spain or Mexico using tools such as Skype and email. Exchanges can also be organized using a lingua franca. For example, classes of English language learners in Germany, Poland and China can now work together on projects on a daily basis using a shared workspace such as a wiki or social networking site like Ning. This application of online communication technologies to bring together language learners in geographically distant locations to develop their FL skills and intercultural competence through collaborative tasks and project work is known as telecollaboration and has been a popular area of CALL activity and research over the past three decades.

Although the term was originally used in the context of online FL education by Warschauer in his publication *Telecollaboration and the Foreign Language Learner* (1996), the definition of the activity was not fully delineated until the special edition of *Language Learning & Technology* (2003) in which Belz identified the main characteristics of FL telecollaboration to be 'institutionalized, electronically mediated intercultural communication under the guidance of a languacultural expert (i.e., teacher) for the purposes of foreign language learning and the development of intercultural competence' (2003, p. 2). However, since the emergence of the internet in the mid-1990s, telecollaborative activity has gone under many different names and it is perhaps useful to identify them and review their different connotations.

Warschauer's first collection of telecollaborative activities came under the title of *Virtual Connections* (1995), while primary and secondary school exchanges have been referred to as *e-pals* or *key-pals*. In more academic contexts, apart from 'telecollaboration', terms such as 'e-tandem' (O'Rourke, 2007), 'online intercultural exchange' (O'Dowd, 2007; Thorne, 2010) and 'Internet-mediated Intercultural Foreign Language Education' (Belz & Thorne, 2006) have all been used. In France the term EIEGL (Échanges Interculturels Exolingues en Groupe en Lingue) has been widely employed (Audras & Chanier, 2008), while in Brazil there is a growing body of work in this area under the umbrella term of 'teletandem' (Telles, 2009). Evidently, each of these terms tends to carry its own connotations and implications, depending on the educational context in which it is used. For example, the terminology *e-pal* or *key-pal* stems from the traditional activity of *pen pals* which linked together young learners in different countries through letter exchanges. As a result, these terms are generally used in primary and secondary school contexts and on websites which aim to link pre-university classes of learners in different countries (see, for example, www.epals.com/). Meanwhile, Belz and Thorne's term 'Internet-mediated intercultural foreign language education' was an attempt to highlight the focus on both FL learning and intercultural exchange, aspects which, they argued, were missing from other terms such as 'telecollaboration' and 'e-tandem' (Thorne, 2006, p. 3).

Over the past two decades, telecollaboration has begun to receive a great deal of attention in the academic literature and in research circles. There have been several book publications exclusively on the theme (Belz & Thorne, 2006; Dooly, 2008; Guth & Helm, 2010; O'Dowd, 2006, 2007; Warschauer, 1994) as well as two special editions of the journal *Language Learning & Technology* (volumes 7/2 and 15/1). There has also been important funding made available for research projects dedicated to the area including the European Commission's projects *Moderating Intercultural Collaboration and Language Learning* (Dooly, 2008), *Intercultural Communication in Europe* (Kohn & Warth, 2011) and *Integrating Telecollaborative Networks in Higher Education* (www.intent-project.eu/). In the United States significant funding has also contributed to many projects in this area, including *the Penn State Foreign Language Telecollaboration Project* (Belz, 2003).

Today, telecollaboration has come to be seen as one of the main pillars of the intercultural turn in FL education (Thorne, 2006) as it allows educators to engage their learners in regular, (semi-) authentic communication with members of other cultures in distant locations and also gives learners the opportunity to reflect on and learn from the outcomes of this intercultural exchange within the supportive and informed context of their FL classroom. In the words of Kern, Ware and Warschauer (2004), telecollaboration offers educators the opportunity to 'use the internet not so much to teach the same thing in a different way, but rather to help students enter into a new realm of collaborative enquiry and construction of knowledge, viewing their expanding repertoire of identities and communication strategies as resources in the process' (2004, p. 21). However, it is important to be aware that telecollaboration, in the words of Hauck and Lewis, 'takes many forms' (2007, p. 250) and is characterized today by its many different configurations, aims and task-designs. With this in mind, this chapter will examine the origins of this activity and will then go on to examine different telecollaborative configurations and the significant research findings which have been reported in the literature. Finally, the chapter will explore how the activity is being influenced by Web 2.0 tools and applications and will discuss the practical and organizational challenges facing educators who wish to integrate this activity into their teaching contexts.

The origins of telecollaboration

The origins of online intercultural exchanges in FL education can be traced to the learning networks pioneered by Célestin Freinet in 1920s France and later by Mario Lodi in 1960s Italy, decades before the internet was to become a tool for classroom learning (Cummins & Sayers, 1995, pp. 119–36). Freinet made use of the technologies and modes of communication available to him at the time to enable his classes in the north of France to make class newspapers with a printing press and to exchange these newspapers along with 'cultural packages' of flowers, fossils and photos of their local area with schools in other parts of France. Similarly, Lodi motivated his learners and helped to develop their critical literacy by encouraging them to create student newspapers in collaboration with distant partner classes. The link between the principles and activities of these educators and the online work being carried out today is discussed in detail by Cummins and Sayers (1995) and by Müller-Hartmann (2007).

With the emergence of the internet and local area networks (LANs) in the early and mid-1990s there was relatively little telecollaborative interaction between classrooms in different geographical locations as educators did not yet have wide access to partner classes in other locations and students found it difficult to access the internet outside of the classroom. In this context, online interaction was limited to learners in one class using synchronous text-based communication, such as chats, MOOs and LANs, to interact together in the target language. The text-based nature of the communication was seen at the time as being a manner of allowing FL learners to create a 'conversation in slow motion' (Beauvois, 1997, p. 93) which allowed students time to reflect on and plan their utterances in the FL before committing them to the online interaction with their classmates.

Nevertheless, some isolated examples of online intercultural exchange in the early 1990s can indeed be found in the literature. Early reports include the work of the Orillas Network (Cummins & Sayers, 1995), the AT&T Learning Circles (Riel, 1997), as well as more in-depth research studies into tandem exchanges (Brammerts, 1996; Eck, Legenhausen & Wolff, 1995). Warschauer's publication, *Virtual Connections: Online Activities for Networking Language Learners* (1995) included a collection of 'cross-cultural communication' projects which reported on students creating personal profiles, carrying out surveys and examining cultural stereotypes with distant partners. At this stage a number of webpages, including Intercultural E-mail Classroom Connections (IECC) and E-Tandem, also became available online in order to link up classrooms across the globe and to provide practitioners with activities and guidelines for their projects, while practitioners such as Ruth Vilmi in Finland (1994) and Reinhard Donath (1997) in Germany helped to make the activity better known by publishing practical reports of their students' work online. Vilmi's work focused on online collaboration between technical students at universities across Europe, while Donath provided German secondary school teachers with a wide range of resources and information about how projects could be integrated into the curriculum.

The IECC website also contained a very active discussion forum between 1994 and 1995 where practitioners were often asked by the moderator and IECC co-founder Bruce Roberts to react to questions related to how online intercultural exchanges could be integrated into the classroom and what type of tasks were successful in online exchanges. The responses to these questions reveal not only many of the challenges which pioneering telecollaborators were facing during the infancy of the internet, but also demonstrate that many of the key pedagogical principles of the time are still very relevant for 'modern-day' telecollaborating teachers. Practitioners wrote about the need for adequate time for students to reflect on their email interactions as well as for adequate access to resources to ensure fluid communication between classes. They also mention the importance of pedagogical leadership on behalf of the teachers in organizing and exploiting the exchange. Roberts summed up what he considered to be the key to success in email classroom connections as being the pedagogical integration of the activity into the class and the learning process: 'when the email classroom connection processes are truly integrated into the ongoing structure of homework and student classroom interaction, then the results can be educationally transforming' (1994, n.p.).

Since this initial period, telecollaboration has gone on to become one of the main pillars of computer-assisted language learning or network-based language teaching (NBLT) and the contribution of online contact and exchange to the development of intercultural awareness and intercultural communicative competence (ICC) has been one of the main areas of research in this area (Müller-Hartmann, 2000; O'Dowd, 2003;

Ware, 2005). Initially however, the intercultural learning outcomes of such contact tended to be at times exaggerated or oversimplified. For example, it was common to read that intercultural learning could be 'easily achieved through [email] tandem learning' (Brammerts, 1996, p. 122).

Soon however, a more critical and in-depth body of research was producing findings which demonstrated the difference between intercultural contact and intercultural learning. Kern suggested that in the context of online learning 'exposure and awareness of difference seem to reinforce, rather than bridge, feelings of difference' (Kern, 2000, p. 256). Similarly, Meagher and Castaños (1996) found in their exchange between classes in the United States and Mexico that bringing the students to compare their different attitudes and values leads to a form of culture shock and a more negative attitude towards the target culture. Furthermore, Fischer (1998), in his work on German-American electronic exchanges, warned that very often students, instead of reflecting and learning from the messages of their distant partners, simply reject the foreign way of thinking, dismissing it as strange or 'typical' of that particular culture.

By the arrival of the new millennium, two main models or approaches to organizing online intercultural exchange had established themselves in FL classrooms. These will be outlined in more detail in the following section.

Models of telecollaborative exchange

During the first decade of the new millennium, two broad models of telecollaborative exchange were dominant in FL education. The first of these, *e-tandem*, emerged from the tradition of *tandem language learning* which has been widely practised in many European universities. Tandem learning is essentially a language learning activity which involves language exchange and collaboration between two partners who are native speakers of their partners' target language. Its online equivalent, e-tandem, thus involves two native speakers of different languages communicating together and providing feedback to each other through online communication tools with the aim of learning the other's language. E-tandem exchanges are based on the principles of autonomy and reciprocity and the responsibility for a successful exchange generally rests with the learners, who are expected to provide feedback on their partners' messages and on their FL performance. In this sense, tandem partners take on the role of peer-tutors who correct their partners' errors and propose alternative formulations in the target language. The role of the class teacher in the e-tandem model is usually quite limited and learners are encouraged to take on responsibility for finding their own themes for discussion, correcting their partners' errors and keeping a learner diary or portfolio to reflect on their own learning progress. E-tandem began to gain popularity throughout European universities in the early 1990s and a centralized internet site with resources, bibliography and guidelines was financed by European project funding during this time (O'Rourke, 2007).

However, in the mid-1990s, the growing interest in online interaction as a tool for FL education in the United States and Asia and the increased importance attributed to the social and intercultural aspects of FL learning, led to the emergence of more complex forms of exchange, which were referred to under the umbrella terms of *telecollaboration* (Belz, 2003) and *Internet mediated Intercultural Foreign Language Education* (Belz & Thorne, 2006). These terms referred to the different formats and structures of online intercultural exchange being carried out in classrooms around the globe which had the dual aims of developing both linguistic competence and intercultural communicative competence. While the emphasis of e-tandem learning had often been on supporting student interaction outside of the classroom and to encourage the development of strategies for learner independence, intercultural telecollaboration strove to make more fluid connections between students' online interaction with their partners and what was being studied and discussed in the local classrooms. In this sense, students often began project work in class and then completed it by interacting with their distant partners, or read or viewed the same cultural materials as their partner class and then engaged in online interaction to compare reactions and findings.

Some of the better-known tasks involved requiring students to work together with their international partners to produce websites or presentations based on comparisons of their cultures. Belz (2002), for example, reports on a USA-German exchange which involved developing a website which contained bilingual essays and a bilingual discussion of a cultural theme such as racism or family. Another popular intercultural task for telecollaborative exchanges has been the analysis of parallel texts. Belz defines parallel texts as 'linguistically different renditions of a particular story or topic in which culturally-conditioned varying representations of that story or topic are presented' (2005, n.p.). Popular examples of parallel texts which have been used in telecollaborative exchanges include the American film *Three Men and a Baby* and the French original *Trois homes et un couffin*. In German, telecollaborative projects have engaged learners in the comparison of the German fairy tale *Aschenputtel* by the Brothers Grimm and the animated Disney movie *Cinderella.*

A further intercultural task adapted to telecollaboration was the application of ethnographic interviewing in synchronous online sessions. O'Dowd (2005) trained a group of German EFL students in the basic techniques of ethnographic interviewing and the students then carried out interviews with American informants in the United States using group-to-group videoconferencing sessions and one-to-one email exchanges before writing up reflective essays on their findings. The combination of synchronous and asynchronous tools allowed the students to develop different aspects of their intercultural competence. Videoconferencing was seen to develop students' ability to interact with members of the target culture under the constraints of real-time communication and also to elicit, through a face-to-face dialogue, the concepts and values which underlie their partners' behaviour and their opinions. However, email was employed to both send and receive much more detailed information on the two cultures' products and practices as seen from the partners' perspectives. In other words, email was suited to foster cultural knowledge, while videoconferencing supported the development of students' intercultural negotiating skills.

Another telecollaborative practice which has become very popular in recent years is the *Cultura* exchange (Furstenberg, Levet, English & Maillet, 2001; O'Dowd, 2005). This intercultural exchange used the possibility of juxtaposing materials from the two different cultures together on webpages in order to offer a comparative approach to investigating cultural difference. When using *Cultura*, language learners from two cultures (e.g., Spanish learners of English and American learners of Spanish) complete online questionnaires related to their cultural values and associations. These questionnaires can be based on word associations (e.g., What three words do you associate with the word 'Spain?), sentence completions (e.g., A good citizen is someone who . . .), or reactions to situations (e.g., Your friend in 22 and is still living with his parents. What do you say to him/her?). Each group fills out the questionnaire in their native language. Following this, the results from both sets of students are then compiled and presented online. Under the guidance of their teachers in contact classes, students then analyse the juxtaposed lists in order to find differences and similarities between the two groups' responses. Following this analysis, students from both countries meet in online message boards to discuss their findings and to explore the cultural values and beliefs which may lie behind the differences in the lists. In addition to the questionnaires, learners are also supplied with online resources such as opinion polls and press articles from the two cultures which can support them in their investigation and understanding of their partner class's responses. The developers of this model (Furstenberg, Levet, English & Maillet, 2001) report that this contrastive approach helps learners to become more aware of the complex relationship between culture and language and enables them to develop a method for understanding a foreign culture. It is also important to point out that in this model, as in most telecollaborative projects, while the data for cultural analysis and learning are produced online, the roles of contact classes and the teacher are considered vital in helping learners to identify cultural similarities and differences and also in bringing about reflection on the outcomes of the students' investigations on the *Cultura* platform.

Areas of telecollaborative research

An important corpus of research on telecollaborative exchange emerged during the first decade of the new millennium. The growing importance attributed in academia to online learning scenarios, the ample possibilities of collecting data from online text-based interaction and the new importance of sociocultural approaches to research and education meant that telecollaborative projects were of particular interest to researchers during this period. Much of this research was qualitative and ethnographic in nature, reflecting the arguments of Bax (2003) and Levy and Stockwell (2006) that it was necessary to provide rich, descriptive accounts of how CALL activities were being organized and how the local contexts were affecting learning outcomes. This research also reflected a growing understanding that CMC was not a genre in itself (Kern, 2006), and that the outcomes of each online intercultural exchange would inevitably be influenced by the different contextual factors involved. Warschauer (2003) described this as the 'social embeddedness of technology' and explained the concept in the following way: 'technology does not exist outside a social structure, exerting an independent force on it, but rather the technological and social realms are highly intertwined and continuously co-constitute each other in myriad ways' (2003, p. 26).

Researchers of telecollaborative exchange focused on how telecollaborative exchanges can contribute to different aspects of FL education including the development of linguistic proficiency, learner autonomy and intercultural learning. However, there has also been an important amount of qualitative research dedicated to how telecollaborative exchanges and tasks should be designed and structured. Each of these areas will now be looked at briefly.

Researchers working with e-tandem models have produced an important body of research focusing on its contribution to the development of learner autonomy (Schwienhorst, 2000) and how linguistic proficiency can be developed in this type of exchange. Many studies in this area take an interactionist perspective and look at online exchange through the lens of Long and Robinson's interaction hypothesis (1998) which proposes that negotiation of meaning can support the development of learners' interlanguage. Koetter (2003), for example, looked at the quantity and the quality of negotiation of meaning which took place in synchronous e-tandem exchanges and also explored how learners negotiated the use of the two languages in their MOO exchanges and managed to benefit from the expertise of their partners in their respective first languages. Vinagre and Muñoz (2011) examined the different strategies and correction techniques used by German and Spanish learners to foster attention to linguistic form in asynchronous e-tandem exchanges, while Bower and Kawaguchi (2011) compared the use of corrective feedback and negotiation of meaning in Japanese and Australian e-tandems. There are far fewer examples of e-tandem studies focusing on the development of intercultural competence (see Stickler & Emke, 2011 for a notable exception), and research in this area usually comes from the telecollaborative model of exchange.

Researchers have found telecollaboration to be a potentially powerful tool for intercultural development for various reasons. First, telecollaborative exchanges have been found to contribute to culture learning by providing learners with a different type of knowledge to that which they usually find in textbooks and in other traditional Cultural Studies resources (O'Dowd, 2006). As opposed to objective factual information, the accounts which students receive from their partners tend to be of a subjective and personalized nature. For this reason, exchanges can be particularly useful for making students aware of certain aspects of cultural knowledge (Byram, 1997), such as how institutions are perceived in the target culture and what significant events and people are in the target culture's 'national memory'.

Second, it has been found that telecollaboration can also contribute to the development of critical cultural awareness, as learners have opportunities in their online interaction to engage in intense periods of negotiation of meaning in which they can discuss cultural 'rich points' and illicit meanings of cultural behaviour from 'real' informants in the target culture. Learners are also led to become more aware of the relativity of their own cultural beliefs and values as they try to make them explicit for their partners. However, researchers emphasize that this is only the case when online exchange involves explicit comparison of the two cultures and the expression of direct opinions and reactions to the submissions of others (O'Dowd, 2003). Such dialogue between partners contrasts with interaction which involves an unreflective exchange of information between partners.

Third, Belz and Kinginger (2002, 2003) highlighted the potential of telecollaborative exchange for making learners aware of cultural differences in communicative practices. Their work has demonstrated how online exchange can contribute to the development of L2 pragmatic competence in FL learning. The authors found this to be the case because interaction with native-speaker peers can lead to the exposure of the learner to a broad range of FL discourse and also because learners consider their partners to be 'people who matter' and therefore are more motivated to establish successful working relationships with them in the FL.

Apart from studying the contribution of online exchange to linguistic and intercultural development in FL learners, many studies have also focused on the pedagogical structure and design of online exchange projects and their tasks (Meskill & Ranglova, 2000; Müller-Hartmann, 2000; O'Dowd & Ware, 2009), and on the influence of differing sociocultural and institutional factors on the development of exchanges.

Belz (2001, 2002) and Belz and Müller-Hartmann (2002, 2003) examined how social and institutional factors such as different levels of language proficiency, the misalignment of academic calendars, differences in societal norms with respect to technological access, divergent forms of assessment in the respective cultures and the different physical layout of the universities shaped the outcome of telecollaborative exchanges between university-level foreign-language students in Germany and the United States. Similarly, Ware (2005), in her qualitative study of an exchange between students of English and German in the United States and Germany identified the link between the different uses of linguistic features by both groups in their online interaction, socio-institutional factors and low group functionality. Ware found that Americans asked far fewer questions than their partners and also made fewer attempts to establish personal rapport. This type of to-the-point, task-oriented interaction led to what she describes as 'missed communication' between the students and left much of the German group dissatisfied with the exchange. Looking at an exchange between Spanish and North American students, O'Dowd (2005) examined the socio-institutional factors which affected the development of an exchange based on the Cultura model of telecollaboration. O'Dowd showed how the stereotypical images which each group had brought to the exchange about the target culture influenced the levels of motivation and participation of the students involved. The author found that the on-going war in

Iraq and the complex political relationship between Spain and the United States led many of the Spanish students to react negatively to the idea of an exchange with American students and a focus on American materials during class time.

Telecollaboration 2.0: Current approaches and research

In recent years some researchers and practitioners have expressed their disapproval of the class-to-class configurations which are still quite prominent in networked classrooms. First, there has been criticism of the underlying belief in the research on online intercultural exchange that members of different cultures use different genres and cultural communication styles in their online intercultural interactions and that it is this 'clash of genres' which often leads to breakdowns in online intercultural interaction. Kramsch and Thorne, for example, describe the breakdown in communication which occurred between classes of French and American students as 'two local genres engaged in global confrontation' (2002, p. 99). However, Goodfellow and Lamy warn that 'the assumption that a coherent "genre" or "style" is characteristic of national cohorts is rarely interrogated' (2009, p. 6). The authors question whether it is possible to speak about a 'French communicative style' and whether it is not an over-simplification to describe one monolithic cultural communicative style clashing or causing misunderstandings with another. Inevitably, the truth may lie somewhere half-way between the position that culture determines how people communicate and the other that suggests it is incorrect to say that members of a particular nationality exhibit a common communicative genre or style in online communication. Cultural differences in online communicative style have been clearly demonstrated by Belz (2002) and elsewhere, but research by O'Dowd and Ritter suggests that this should be seen as just one of an interconnected number of reasons why online intercultural communication can break down.

A second criticism of class-to-class exchanges comes from Hanna and de Nooy (2009), who lamented what they viewed as the limited authenticity of simply engaging L2 learners with other classrooms. They proposed as an alternative the activity of requiring learners to participate in the online asynchronous discussion forums which are provided by the websites of international newspapers such as *Le Monde* and the *Guardian*. The authors suggested that getting learners to take part in such forums would take them beyond the limitations of learner-to-learner communication and provide them with opportunities to join with native speakers in authentic interaction which required an awareness of the cultural rules and register of this genre of communication.

Against this background, recent years have seen the emergence of a third 'generation' or model of telecollaborative exchanges which reflects in many ways a more flexible and adaptable interpretation of how online intercultural interaction and exchange can contribute to FL learning. Described by Guth and Helm as *Telecollaboration*

2.0 (2010), this model focuses not only on the development of learners' linguistic and intercultural competence, but also on developing the online literacies necessary to socialize, learn and work in today's information society. The model is based on the 'social Web' that has emerged with the rise of Web 2.0 tools such as blogging, wikis and social networking sites, and is characterized by a less text-based and more multimodal form of communication (see Guth & Helm, 2010; Hauck, 2010). Certain variations of this model also involve a type of intercultural exchange that is more classroom independent than previous models and therefore allows for a much greater spectrum of possible partners, language set-ups and forms of interaction. For example, the Massachusetts Institute of Technology – Universidad Politécnica de Valencia Project (MITUPV project) brought together Spanish and North American students in a Web 2.0-based exchange which allowed students to share, annotate, restructure and analyse thousands of different multimedia objects (usually photos and videos) which they themselves had created using their own digital video recording devices (Morgenstern, 2009). However, in an interesting twist change from 'traditional' telecollaborative exchanges, this project platform was open to the general public as well as to classes at both institutions and this meant that the intercultural exchange benefited during its ten-year existence from the participation of students in other universities as well as of non-university-based participants.

Examples are also emerging of new-style telecollaborative exchanges which move completely away from the 'traditional' class-to-class set-ups and which engage learners in specialized interest communities or environments that focus on specific hobbies or interests. Thorne et al. (2009), for example, describe the potential for intercultural contact and learning in online fan communities, where learners can establish relationships with like-minded fans of music groups or authors and can even use Web 2.0 technologies to remix and create new artistic creations based on existing books, films and music. Learners also have increasing opportunities to use their FL skills and hone their intercultural communicative competence through participating in online multicultural communities such as multiplayer online games and public discussion forums, such as those described by Hanna and de Nooy (2009). Researchers working in this area are finding a complex range of data sources emerging from telecollaborative exchange taking place completely outside the context of formal education. Pasfield-Neofitou (2011), for example, analysed a corpus of blogs, emails, SNS interactions, chat conversations, game profiles and mobile phone communications between 12 Australian learners of Japanese with Japanese partners they had contacted outside of their formal learning environment, in order to explore issues of language choice, identity construction and feelings of national identity and 'foreignness' online.

Inevitably, this emerging model of telecollaboration requires learners to assume greater responsibility for how their linguistic and intercultural learning progress online as they are given greater freedom in their choice of potential intercultural learning partners and learning environments – many of which, as has been shown, may be completely independent of organized classroom activity. Thorne describes this form of telecollaborative learning as 'intercultural communication in the wild' (2010, p. 144) and speculates that this learning may be 'situated in arenas of social activity that are less controllable than classroom or organized online intercultural exchanges might be, but which present interesting, and perhaps even compelling, opportunities for intercultural exchange, agentive action and meaning making' (Thorne, 2010, p. 144).

Although this is undoubtedly true, increased attention to informal and independent telecollaborative activity may inevitably clash with attempts by educators and educational institutions to integrate and 'normalize' CALL activity within FL programmes (Bax, 2003; O'Dowd, 2011). Stephen Bax defines the normalization of computer-assisted learning activity in the following way:

> when computers . . . are used every day by language students and teachers as an integral part of every lesson, like a pen or a book . . . without fear or inhibition, and equally without an exaggerated respect for what they can do. They will not be the centre of any lesson, but they will play a part in almost all . . . They will go almost unnoticed. (2003, p. 23)

To achieve the integration of telecollaborative exchanges in formal education contexts, it is likely that educators will need access to regular and dependable virtual partnerships, easily observable and assessable student activity, tasks which are easily integrated into normal classroom interaction, and exchange structures which can be understood and adapted even by educators who have relatively low levels of electronic literacy. These requirements are likely to be difficult to meet in telecollaboration 2.0 activities involving the remixing of multimedia objects and participation in public-access 'fan sites' and public internet discussion forums. Finding models to accommodate both these trends is undoubtedly a challenge for future research in the area.

Conclusions

After almost two decades of practice and research, it is still difficult to assess the impact which telecollaboration has had on FL education. While research has demonstrated the contributions that online intercultural exchange can make to the language learning process, it appears that many FL educators are unwilling or unable to integrate such exchanges into their classrooms for various reasons. Many educators, for example, have highlighted the organizational complexity of these exchanges and the difficulties which they encounter when trying to dedicate time to the organization of an exchange while attending to their other duties and obligations. Warschauer and Ware, for example, suggest that the type of learning which telecollaboration involves can often be at odds with the institutional demands within which teachers are working:

> classroom teachers . . . are under pressure to raise test scores, and most thus shy away from creative project-based instruction in order to concentrate on more narrowly focused interventions related to state examination material. (2008, p. 231)

A survey of practitioners reported by O'Dowd (2011) also revealed other obstacles to the long-term 'normalization' of telecollaboration. These included a lack of stability in project partners, the limited interest of colleagues and the difficulties in integrating online exchanges into course syllabi and into course evaluation schemes. These findings would seem to suggest that unless action is taken from a top-down policy level, telecollaboration is destined to remain on the periphery of FL teaching and that its potential will only be exploited by teachers and students who are willing to take it as an addition to traditional skills-based language activities.

Nevertheless, examples do exist of initiatives which are providing telecollaborative projects with the curricular time, space and recognition they deserve. An example of an initiative that can facilitate the normalization of telecollaborative exchange into curricula is the Connect Programme run by the NGO Soliya (http://soliya.net/?q=connect_program). The organization brings together students from universities all around the world in a highly structured exchange set-up for which participating students can receive credit from their own universities.

Furthermore, the integration of telecollaborative projects with physical student mobility programmes such as the European Union's *Erasmus* programme may also facilitate the development of more stable partnerships among European classrooms. A European Commission Green Paper on promoting the learning mobility of young people refers to online exchange as a tool for preparing physical mobility and as a viable alternative for those students and young people who are unable to engage in traditional mobility programmes (Commission of the European Communities, 2009, p. 18). The report of the High Level Expert Forum on mobility also suggests the following: 'Virtual mobility is widely available, quick and cheap. Nevertheless, physical mobility provides a more intensive and deeper experience and is, therefore, irreplaceable. Developing the synergies between virtual and physical mobility is a central art of a new way of life' (2008, p. 11). Various projects and initiatives are currently exploring how telecollaboration can be integrated with physical mobility (see Zeiss & Isabelli-García, 2005; and the Mobi-blog project (http://mobi-blog.eu/) for two examples of these initiatives). In relation to this area, Kinginger suggests the following:

> A particularly intriguing application of this approach, as yet undocumented in the literature, would be to establish telecollaborative courses linking students at home to their in-country peers in the precise locations where they will study abroad and thereby to establish contacts through prior, institutionally sanctioned interaction. (2009, p. 111)

Undoubtedly, the greater integration of online technologies in students' social lives and study activities should also contribute to the consideration of online intercultural exchange as being a normal part of educational practices. Nevertheless, there is still a need for a virtual platform (similar to the ePals and eTwinning sites available for primary and secondary school educators) where university FL teachers can easily find potential partner classes as well as tools and resources for integrating and evaluating telecollaboration. There is also a need for greater awareness-raising among the FL teaching community of the advantages of telecollaborative activity and for a greater focus on training teachers in the pedagogical applications of new technologies rather than in their technical aspects. With this in mind, there is a growing body of research which aims to introduce future FL educators to telecollaboration by engaging them in online exchanges during their own training programmes (Dooly, 2011; Grosbois, 2011; Müller-Hartmann, 2007). With effective training practices such as those outlined in these studies, and a realistic awareness of its potential and limitations, telecollaboration stands to become an important part of CALL practice in the decades to come.

References

Audras, I., & Chanier, T. (2008). Observation de la construction d'une competénce interculturelle dans des groupes exolingues en ligne. *Revue Apprentissage des Langues et Systeme d'Information et de Communication (ALSIC), 11*, 175–204.

Bax, S. (2003). CALL – past, present and future. *System, 31*(1), 13–28.

Beauvois, M. (1997). Computer-mediated communication (CMC): Technology for improving speaking and writing. In M. Bush & R. Terry (Eds.), *Technology enhanced language learning* (pp. 165–83). Illinois: National Textbook Company.

Belz, J. (2001). Institutional and individual dimensions of transatlantic group work in network-based language teaching. *ReCALL, 13*(2), 213–31.

— (2002). Social dimensions of telecollaborative foreign language study. *Language Learning & Technology, 6*(1), 60–81.

— (2003). Linguistic perspectives on the development of intercultural competence in telecollaboration. *Language Learning & Technology, 7*(2), 68–99.

— (2005). Telecollaborative language study: A personal overview of praxis and research. *Selected Papers from the 2004 NFLRC Symposium.* Retrieved from http://nflrc.hawaii.edu/networks/nw44/belz.htm

Belz, J., & Kinginger, C. (2002). The cross-linguistic development of address form use in telecollaborative language learning: Two case studies. *Canadian Modern Language Review, 59*(2), 189–214.

— (2003). Discourse options and the development of pragmatic competence by classroom learners of German. The case of address forms. *Language Learning, 53*, 591–647.

Belz, J., & Müller-Hartmann, A. (2003). Teachers negotiating German-American telecollaboration: Between a rock and an institutional hard place. *Modern Language Journal, 87*(1), 71–89.

Belz, J., & Thorne, S. (Eds.) (2006). *Internet-mediated intercultural foreign language education.* Boston, MA: Heinle & Heinle.

Brammerts, H. (1996). Language learning in tandem using the internet. In M. Warschauer (Ed.), *Telecollaboration in foreign language learning* (pp. 121–30). University of Hawaai'i: Second Language Teaching and Curriculum Centre.

Byram, M. (1997). *Teaching and assessing intercultural communicative competence.* Clevedon: Multilingual Matters.

Commission of the European Communities (2009). Green paper: Promoting the learning mobility of young people. Retrieved from http://eur-lex.europa.eu/LexUriServ/LexUriServ.do?uri=COM:2009:0329:FIN:EN:PDF

Cummins, J., & Sayers, D. (1995). *Brave new schools: Challenging cultural literacy through global learning networks.* New York: St. Martin's Press.
Donath, R., & Volkmer, I. (Eds.) (1997). *Das Transatlantische Klassenzimmer.* Hamburg: Koerber-Stiftung.
Dooly, M. (Ed.) (2008). *Telecollaborative language learning: A guidebook to moderating intercultural collaboration online.* Bern: Peter Lang.
— (2011). Divergent perceptions of telecollaborative language learning tasks: Tasks-as-workplan vs. task-as-process. *Language Learning & Technology, 15*(2), 69–91.
Eck, A., Legenhausen, L., & Wolff, D. (1995). *Telekommunikation und Fremdsprachenunterricht: Informationen, Projekte, Ergebnisse.* Bochum: AKS-Verlag.
Fischer, G. (1998). *E-mail in foreign language teaching: Towards the creation of virtual classrooms.* Tuebingen: Stauffenburg Medien.
Furstenberg, G., Levet, S., English, K., & Maillet, K. (2001). Giving a virtual voice to the silent language of culture: The culture project. *Language Learning & Technology, 5*(1), 55–102.
Goodfellow, R., & Lamy, M.-N. (2009). Introduction: A frame for the discussion of learning cultures. In R. Goodfellow & M-N. Lamy (Eds.), *Learning cultures in online education* (pp. 1–14). London: Continuum.
Grosbois, M. (2011). CMC-based projects and L2 learning: Confirming the importance of nativisation. *ReCALL, 23*(3), 294–310.
Guth, S., & Helm, F. (Eds.) (2010). *Telecollaboration 2.0: Language, literacies and intercultural learning in the 21st Century.* Bern: Peter Lang.
Hanna, B., & de Nooy, J. (2009). *Learning language and culture via public internet discussion forums.* New York: Palgrave Macmillan.
Hauck, M. (2010). Telecollaboration: At the interface between multimodal and intercultural communicative competence. In S. Guth & F. Helm (Eds.), *Telecollaboration 2.0: Language and intercultural learning in the 21st century* (pp. 219–48). Bern: Peter Lang.
Hauck, M., & Lewis, T. (2007). The tridem project. In R. O'Dowd (Ed.), *Online intercultural exchange* (pp. 250–9). Clevedon, UK: Multilingual Matters.
High Level Expert Forum On Mobility (2008). *Making learning mobility an opportunity for all.* Retrieved from http://ec.europa.eu/education/doc/2008/mobilityreport_en.pdf
Kern, R. (2000). *Literacy and language teaching.* Oxford: Oxford University Press.
Kern, R., Ware, P., & Warschauer, M. (2004). Crossing frontiers: New directions in online pedagogy and research. *Annual Review of Applied Linguistics, 24,* 243–60.
Kinginger, C. (2009). *Language learning and study abroad: A critical reading of research.* Basingstoke, UK: Palgrave Macmillan.
Kohn, K., & Warth, C. (2011). *Web collaboration for intercultural language learning.* Münster: MV-Wissenschaft.
Kötter, M. (2003). Negotiation of meaning and codeswitching in online tandems. *Language Learning and Technology, 7*(2), 145–72.
Kramsch, C., & Thorne, S. (2002). Foreign language learning as global communicative practice. In D. Block & D. Cameron (Eds.), *Globalization and language teaching* (pp. 83–100). London: Routledge.
Levy, M., & Stockwell, G. (2006). *CALL dimensions: Options and issues in computer-assisted language learning.* New Jersey: Lawrence Erlbaum & Associates.
Long, M., & Robinson, P. (1998). Focus on form: Theory, research, and practice. In C. Doughty & J. Williams (Eds.), *Focus on form in classroom second language acquisition* (pp. 15–63). Cambridge: Cambridge University Press.
Meagher, M., & Castaños, F. (1996). Perceptions of American culture: The impact of an electronically-mediated cultural exchange program on Mexican high school students.

In S. Herring (Ed.), *Computer-mediated communication. Linguistic, social and cross-cultural perspectives* (pp. 187–201). Amsterdam: John Benjamins.
Meskill, C., & Ranglova, K. (2000). Sociocollaborative language learning in Bulgaria. In M. Warschauer & R. Kern (Eds.), *Network-based language teaching: Concepts and practice* (pp. 20–40). Cambridge: Cambridge University Press.
Morgenstern, D. (2009). ITUPV: Language, media, and distance in an online community. In I. Lancashire (Ed.), *Teaching literature and language online* (pp. 190–202). New York: Modern Language Association of America.
Müller-Hartmann, A. (2000). The role of tasks in promoting intercultural learning in electronic learning networks. *Language Learning & Technology, 4*(2), 129–47. Retrieved from http://llt.msu.edu/vol4num2/ muller/default.html
— (2007). Teacher role in telecollaboration: Setting up and managing exchanges. In R. O'Dowd (Ed.), *Online intercultural exchange* (pp. 167–93). Clevedon, UK: Multilingual Matters.
O'Dowd, R. (2003). Understanding 'the other side': Intercultural learning in a Spanish-English e-mail exchange. *Language Learning and Technology,* 7(2), 118–44.
— (2005). Combining networked communication tools for students' ethnographic research. In J. Belz, & S. L. Thorne (Eds.), *Computer-mediated intercultural foreign language education* (pp. 86–120). Boston, MA: Heinle & Heinle.
— (2006). *Telecollaboration and the development of intercultural communicative competence.* Berlin: Langenscheidt.
— (Ed.) (2007). *Online intercultural exchange: An introduction for foreign language teachers.* Clevedon: Multilingual Matters.
— (2011). Online foreign language interaction: Moving from the periphery to the core of foreign language education? *Language Teaching, 44*(3), 368–80.
O'Dowd, R., & Ritter, M. (2006). Understanding and working with 'Failed Communication' in telecollaborative exchanges. *CALICO Journal, 23*, 623–42.
O'Dowd, R., & Ware, P. (2009). Critical issues in telecollaborative task design. *Computer Assisted Language Learning*, 22(2), 173–88.
O'Rourke, B. (2007). Models of telecollaboration (1): eTandem. In R. O'Dowd (Ed.), *Online intercultural exchange* (pp. 41–61). Clevedon, UK: Multilingual Matters.
Pasfield-Neofitou, S. (2011). Second language learners' experiences of virtual community and foreignness. *Language Learning and Technology, 15*(2), 92–108. Retrieved from http://llt.msu.edu/issues/june2011/pasfieldneofitou.pdf
Riel, M. (1997). Learning circles make global connections. In R. Donath & I. Volkmer (Eds.), *Das Transatlantische Klassenzimmer* (pp. 329–57). Hamburg: Koerber-Stiftung.
Roberts, B. (1994). *What works?* Retrieved from www.iecc.org/discussion/what-works.html
Schwienhorst, K. (2000). *Virtual reality and learner autonomy in second language acquisition.* Unpublished PhD thesis, Trinity College Dublin.
Stickler, U., & Emke, M. (2011). Literalia: Towards developing intercultural maturity online. *Language Learning & Technology, 15*(1), 147–68.
Telles, J. A. (Ed.) (2009). *Teletandem: Um contexto virtual, autônomo e colaborativo para aprendizagem de línguas estrangeiras no século XXI.* Campinas: Pontes Editores.
Thorne, S. (2006). Pedagogical and praxiological lessons from internet-mediated intercultural foreign language education research. In J. Belz & S. L. Thorne (Eds.), *Internet-mediated intercultural foreign language education* (pp. 2–30). Boston, MA: Heinle & Heinle.
— (2010). The intercultural turn and language learning in the crucible of new media. In S. Guth & F. Helm (Eds.), *Telecollaboration 2.0: Language and intercultural learning in the 21st century* (pp. 139–65). Bern: Peter Lang.

Thorne, S. L., Black, R. W., & Sykes, J. (2009). Second language use, socialization, and learning in internet interest communities and online games. *Modern Language Journal, 93*, 802–41.
Vilmi, R. (1994). Global communication through e-mail: An ongoing experiment at Helsinki University of Technology. Paper presented at TESOL 94 Conference, Paris. Retrieved from: www.hut.fi/~rvilmi/Publication/global.html
Vinagre, M., & Muñoz, B. (2011). Computer-mediated corrective feedback and language accuracy in telecollaborative exchange. *Language Learning & Technology, 15*(1), 72–103.
Ware, P. (2005). Missed communication in online communication: Tensions in fostering successful online interactions. *Language Learning & Technology, 9*(2), 64–89.
Warschauer, M. (Ed.) (1995). *Virtual connections: Online activities and projects for networking language learners*. Honolulu, HI: University of Hawai'i Second Language Teaching and Curriculum Center.
— (Ed.) (1996). *Telecollaboration in foreign language learning*. Honolulu, HI: University of Hawai'i Second Language Teaching and Curriculum Center.
— (2003). Technology and equity: A comparative study. Paper presented at the Annual Meeting of the American Educational Research Association, 24 April 2003. Chicago, Illinois.
Warschauer, M., & Ware, P. (2008). Learning, change, and power: Competing discourses of technology and literacy. In J. Coiro, M. Knobel, C. Lankshear & D. J. Leu (Eds.), *Handbook of research on new literacies* (pp. 215–40). New York: Lawrence Erlbaum.
Zeiss, E., & Isabelli-García, C. (2005). The role of asynchronous computer-mediated communication on enhancing cultural awareness. *Computer Assisted Language Learning, 18*(3), 151–69.

8

Distance CALL online

Marie-Noëlle Lamy

Summary

In this chapter a distinction is made between CALL and distance CALL (henceforth DCALL), two fields of activity often assumed to be overlapping. Two factors, one political and the other conceptual, contribute to the enduring nature of such an assumption. They relate, respectively, to the pressures that researchers in DCALL encounter when facing the politics of dissemination and publication, and to the conceptual confusion that is manifest in the terminology used to refer to distance learning. The first factor leads to under-articulation by DCALL researchers and practitioners of the unique features of their work, leaving space for misconceptions fed by the second. In order to dispel these misconceptions and to arrive at a definition of DCALL that accurately reflects the field and its neighbour, CALL, a brief discussion of the political background is offered in the rest of this Introduction. This is followed by a section in which the terminology of distance learning (henceforth DL) is clarified and the uniqueness of DL defined. Two further sections then address the implications that derive from this definition, introduce an integrated model of teaching and learning in DL and apply it to selected examples from the distance language learning literature. The chapter closes with considerations on current and future research directions.

Introduction

Blake (2009) concludes his review of DCALL as a body of publications by saying that DCALL 'draws heavily on previous research done in computer-assisted language learning (CALL)' (p. 822), a claim in need of qualification as will be argued in this chapter. DCALL is part of an academic dissemination and publishing pursuit, competing with other fields for exposure, and it is in that context that Blake's observation can best be understood. Borrowing from the approach that Coleman (2005) took when examining the status of CALL, this chapter is based on a review of specialized books, journals and conferences to determine the visibility of DCALL as a field. While Coleman's conclusion shows a marginalization of CALL at the hands of the 'traditional' language research community, in the case of DCALL, the marginalization is perhaps more of a self-inflicted injury: indeed as pointed out by Degache and Depover (2010) the DCALL community in its emerging state two decades ago made some questionable choices. It chose to publish in already established CALL journals and conferences – for example in special issues such as *Language Learning & Technology* (2003), or in journals with a wider focus, for example, *Language Teaching Research* (2006), rather than to create its own instruments of dissemination, which would have required a deal of political and economic leverage, or to use the established vehicles of the DL research industry, which would have afforded insufficient exposure in language specialist circles. In the past decade, few DCALL submissions have found their way into DL publications or conferences.

In preparing this chapter, the outputs of 13 major DL journals published between 2006 and 2011 were analysed, a period chosen because it started with the appearance of White's (2006) state- of-the-art article on distance language learning research. It was found that only 42 papers from that corpus pertained to DCALL, out of over 2,000 articles. So, distance language writers are under-published in the literature of DL, while in order to be widely relevant to readers of the CALL literature, they have to minimize their distance specificities and maximize the aspects of their work that are transferable across both distance and presence settings. The launch of a dedicated DCALL journal is still a long way off, as is the establishment of a regular DCALL conference – with the exception, still without a sequel today, of the 2003 *Independent Language Learning Conference* at the UK Open University. Most writers in DCALL continue to submit to CALL conferences and publications. As for books, the only available monograph on our topic is White (2003), which deals with distance-language learning and includes coverage of technological mediation but encompasses other foci, as does the volume by Holmberg et al. (2005). The reluctance of DCALL researchers to publish in DL outlets and their tendency to minimize the specificities of DL when publishing in CALL outlets, to appeal to a less niche readership, do nothing to illuminate the identity of DCALL or to show how it has rooted itself in pedagogical concerns. This chapter elaborates on those areas.

What is distance CALL?

Terminological confusion

The confusion surrounding distance learning terminology has been noted by generic distance education writers (Guri-Rosenblit & Gro, 2011) and by language writers (Blake, 2009): what are the differences between *computer-assisted, flexible, open, supported, blended* and *e-learning*? A good source of disambiguation is Glikman (2002), who inspired the following terminological clarification.

First, there is no necessary association between DL and *computer-assisted* learning, since distance learners can be (and before the mid-1990s always were) served by other technologies such as print, sometimes enriched by analogue recording or broadcast technologies and the telephone. However, contemporary DL is delivered through digital technology, which may explain its popular image as futuristic education through virtual worlds and other 'advanced' gadgets. Second, there is no necessary association between DL and *online* learning either, since DL universities may not teach 100% online, but through a blend of digital, postal and face-to-face contact, for example, the UK Open University, the TÉLUQ in Québec or Queensland University of Technology. Third DL and *flexible* learning are also frequently confused but again, there is no necessary connection between the two. Flexible learning requires a set of conditions under which the learner's own time and place constraints play a major and explicit role in the institution's way of organizing teaching and learning. Yet in some regulated contexts such as corporate training or preparing students for national examinations with immovable schedules, such as at the Centre National d'Enseignement à Distance in France for example, DL may be practised with very little time flexibility. Another confusion is between the terms *distance* and *open*. They too sit in a complementary but non-necessary relationship. Open learning requires no academic qualifications of any sort as prerequisites for entry. Some institutions specify prerequisites (e.g., the FernUniversität in Germany or the Universidad Nacional de Educación a Distancia in Spain), so they cannot be said to offer open learning although they are distance-teaching universities.

A further cause for confusion comes from the use of the term *supported*. Supported learning refers to settings where the activities are supported by teachers who accompany learners for a greater or lesser part of their study time, guiding those aspects of self-study that may offer unexpected problems and providing evaluation and feedback as well as affective support. Face-to-face education, with its physical presence of teachers in classrooms is always 'supported', and has no need of the term. But distance models are varied and those providing no support are not rare, making it important for the more learner-oriented institutions to stress the supported dimension of the services they offer. The notion of support also helps us understand what can be meant by 'courses taught entirely online'. For instance Blake (2008) argues that one reason for the paucity of DCALL research is that 'isolating the experimental treatment so as to focus on the medium alone (DL vs. Classroom instruction), to the exclusion of all other factors, remains a daunting, if not insurmountable, challenge' (p.113). This chapter suggests that it would be helpful if a distinction were not made between 'DL' and 'classroom instruction', but instead between supported fully online courses (which may offer online classroom instruction) and DL courses that are unsupported or minimally supported. Last in this catalogue, *e-learning* is often used interchangeably with distance learning, and covers so many different meanings – including all the above – as to be unusable as a descriptor, which is why it will not be used in this chapter.

A definition of distance learning

Given the plethora of DL models – from fully-distance-based, in specialist distance institutions, to partially-distance-based, in conventional institutions running distance projects – Glikman (2002) suggests that a program counts as DL if 'the *bulk* of knowledge transmission, or of learning, is undertaken outside of a direct, face-to-face, relationship between co-present teachers and learners' (p. 19, original italics, my translation). Contrary to rival definitions based on lack of co-presence (Schulte & Krämer, 2008) or lack of classroom contact (Blake, 2009), Glikman's formulation is invulnerable to the counterargument that co-presence can happen online and classroom contact too, thanks to synchronous learning environments. Instead she draws attention to an institutional dimension of DL: once it is understood that in DL the *bulk* of the learning takes place in non-co-presence, then it can be seen that consequences follow for the DL institution, learner and teacher. In a DL setting defined in this way, the bulk of the contact is mediated by digital or older technologies. For language schools in such settings it follows that face-to-face interaction – traditionally a main ingredient of language programs – can only be a supplementary activity, in some cases a non-compulsory one. Alternative ways therefore have to be found of providing learners with the learning advantages afforded by face-to-face interaction. In language learning programs they comprise: synchronous interactive-speaking opportunities for fluency development, listening opportunities under synchronous conditions for listening strategy development, quasi-immediate progress monitoring and feedback by the teacher in written and spoken forms. Lastly but very importantly for distance learners who may never meet their peers physically, ways need to be found to integrate the students into a community of language learners. In early distance learning of languages (1880s to mid-1990s) all these experiences were necessarily absent, but as early as the mid-1990s, DCALL was mobilized to address such difficulties (Jegede & Gooley, 1994) and it has been most successful where it has been used within systemic educational designs that have the specific needs of distance learners built into their core, as will be elaborated shortly.

In a perspective that sees bulk of non-co-presence as the distinguishing criterion between DL and other formats, what then is the position of *blended* learning? According to Nicolson, Southgate and Murphy (2011) blended learning refers to 'a combination of forms of instructional technology, including traditional forms of learning used in conjunction with web-based, online approaches' (p. 6). Because 'blends may cover a wide spectrum ranging from those at the simpler end, combining a couple of delivery options, print materials and telephone conferencing, for example, to more complex combinations' (ibid.), it is difficult to see blended learning as a mix of particular technologies. A more helpful way of looking at it is by focusing on the teaching and learning dimension of blends:

> For example, in some cases, conventional classroom teaching of new material is complemented by opportunities for practice through online activity. In others,

> particularly in distance and open settings, new material may be presented in self-study resources, while language practice and reinforcement are offered via teacher-facilitated sessions either online or in a face-to-face classroom. (Nicolson et al., 2011, p. 7)

In this perspective the notion of bulk retains definitional usefulness: the balance between self-study and co-present as well as non-co-present supported time is what determines whether a blend is part of a DL model or a traditional one.

In sum, although *distance* learning should be clearly distinguished from *flexible* and from *open* learning, research has long confirmed that best practice in DL does involve degrees of flexibility and openness even though there are DL organizations across the world where these criteria are not meshed harmoniously or not met at all. Indeed in the history of distance pedagogies evidence of vastly variable quality can be found (Jonassen et al., 1995). When later in this chapter practices and issues that are specific to distance CALL are identified, the distance element will be understood to include a degree of flexible and open learning within a supported model.

A disciplinary identity for DCALL

Some of the tenets of DL for languages simply reflect sound educational thinking. They overlap with those which guide practice in co-present formats; others apply to all distance learning whether in languages or other disciplines; others still are specific to distance *language* learning. These disciplinary overlaps may be visualized in Figure 8.1.

Figure 8.1 displays a central area with single hatchings (representing the overlap between generic DL and DCALL) and one with cross-hatchings (representing the overlap between DCALL and CALL). Typical of the single-hatched area are universal

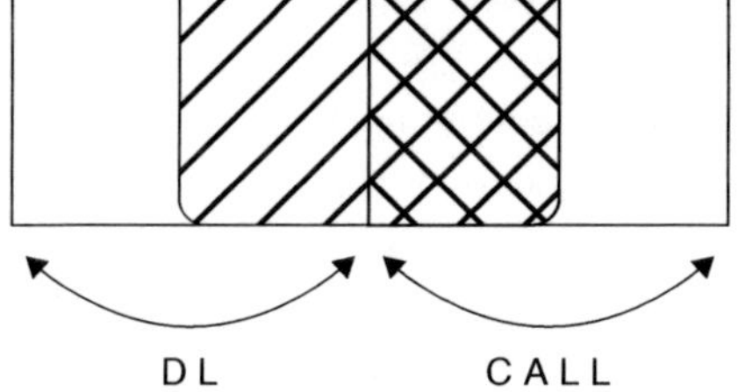

FIGURE 8.1 *The relationship of DL with DCALL and CALL.*

DL issues, such as diagnostic self-testing on entry or expectation management, which have a relevance for language learning but are not unique to it, as against other distance issues applicable only to other disciplines, for example equipment-loaning policies in the sciences (which therefore belongs to the clear area to the left of the figure).

This chapter is concerned with issues in the cross-hatched section of the figure. In order to better understand what they are, that is which elements of DCALL differ from CALL, it is useful to first consider the role of integration in the design of distance learning, both in general and for languages.

An integrated model of distance language learning

In distance organizations education is delivered on an industrial scale (Glikman, 2005) but with a concern to ensure individual support, because DL institutions know from retention figures that individualization is a factor in the successful completion of studies. This tension between 'one-size-fits-all' economics and personal attention is mitigated through the development of student autonomy and is embodied in the two features that pervade DL systems: batteries of tools for students to self-train in the use of language school services, for greater economies of scale; and, more relevantly for our discussion in this chapter, the integration into the materials and processes of detailed and *explicit* rationales for everything that students are invited to do – from the macro level of curriculum choices down to the micro level of individual language exercises and tests. Furthermore, integrated with this is the *flexible* provision of alternative forms of learning for a range of student circumstances. *Explicit* and *flexible* are thus two keywords that will be developed shortly. *Integrated,* as Murphy and Hurd (2011) rightly insist, is the third keyword here, since catering for different needs and circumstances involves 'not simply a collection of different ways of reaching the same goals for learners to choose between, but rather the *integration* of different modes' (p. 49, original emphasis).

White (2003) is right to draw attention to 'the need for complementary perspectives in conceptualizing distance learning' (p. 86). Those who have articulated these perspectives have shown how important systemicity is in DL. Whether it be White's 'learner-context interface', a construct which sees 'the establishment of an effective interface between each learner and his or her learning context [as] the crucible for distance language learning' (ibid.) or whether it be Blake's (2008) encouragement to the DCALL profession 'to tailor the curriculum to individual student readiness and potential, to make learning goals and paths clear, to link inquiries to genuine problems to enhance motivation, and to provide prompt constructive feedback' (p.126), clearly best-practice in DL involves struggling to counter isolation and separateness. There is therefore, according to these experts, a recognition that distance CALL should be a highly integrated activity. A representation of how distance systems can offer integration and balance is offered in Figure 8.2 and is followed by a commentary.

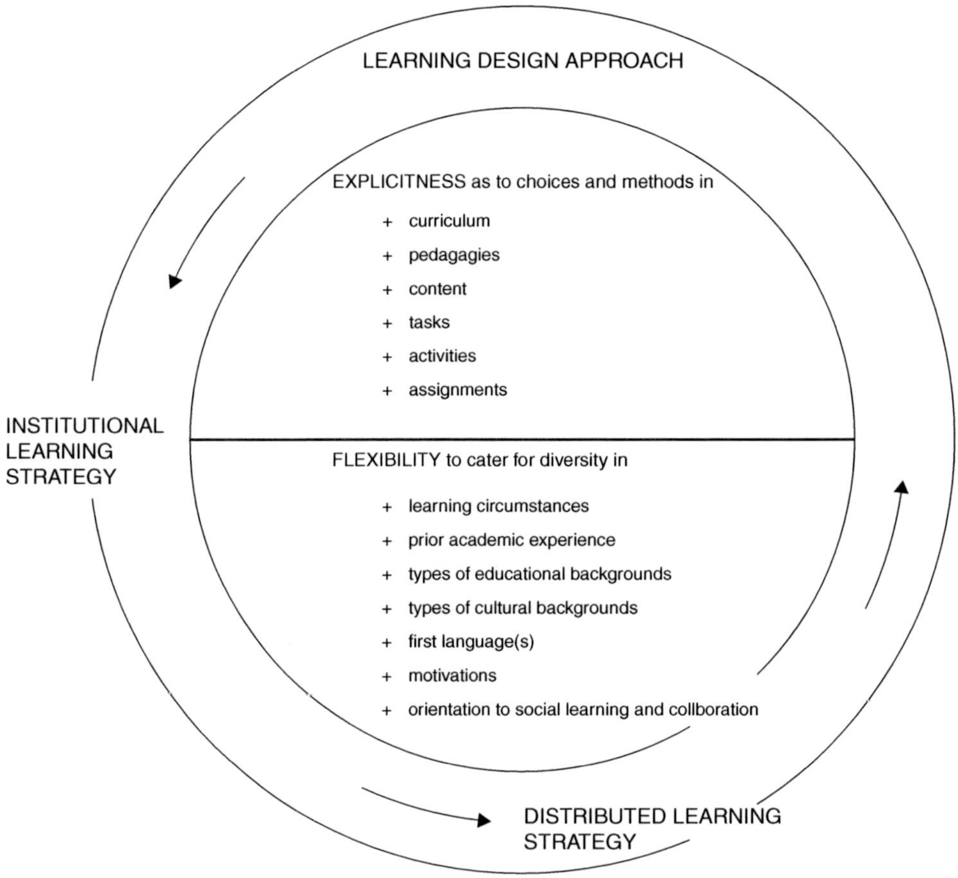

FIGURE 8.2 *A system for supported distance language learning.*

The leading concerns of a distance educator are to be as *explicit* and as *flexible* as possible. When studying at a distance and in isolation, learners need most of all for the learning processes to be totally transparent: there is no-one to ask for help if they stumble on an obstacle. Consequently, running through all aspects of the learning experience is the criterion of explicitness (top semi-circle in Figure 8.2). The other key characteristic of the distance learning public is its heterogeneity: it is made up of learners from all age groups and all walks of life, hence the importance of building in flexibility (bottom semi-circle) into all aspects of the program so that the learner's experience is optimal whatever her or his circumstances. In order to ensure that both explicitness and flexibility are built into the DL model and maintained throughout the phases of the creation of courses, from design through to delivery, three types of resource must be available, represented in the outer ring of Figure 8.2: a learning design approach, an institutional learning strategy and a distributed learning environment.

A learning design approach is defined by Conole (2009) as 'a means of formally representing (and thus reusing) learning sequences' (p. 580). By formally representing them in detail, course designers clarify them and make it easier for materials authors and tutors to be explicit with students about the purpose and manner of study. Further, by designing them for reuse, designers respond to the requirements inherent in DL as a mass education mode. A learning design approach involves networking within teams, which – in well-resourced cases – may include not only materials authors, tutors and developmental-tester learners, but also educational technologists, Web editors and audio-visual Web-asset producers.

Second, a teaching and learning strategy, which informs decision-making across the DL institution, will if well-disseminated to staff and backed up by management in a facilitative (rather than micro-managing fashion), allow a languages school to frame its curriculum, study materials, communications resources, assessment instruments and learner support mechanisms in ways compatible with institutional resources and cultures.

Finally, a distributed learning environment, that is, one which can support learning wherever and on whatever machine the learner's needs determine, should be provided. This may involve well-resourced arrays of tools or humbler arrangements combining postal delivery with telephone support. Whatever the educational technology choices, Sclater (2011) observes that 'we only see significant adoption of technologies for teaching and learning when they are already commoditised' (n.p.). By the time that commoditized stage is reached (e.g., when ownership of a Smartphone is no longer an eccentricity but is widespread) the learning and teaching can be designed so as to be applied to Smartphones in addition to those machines already used by students. The commoditized technology is not leading the learning, but it is added to the panoply at the point where it has become a sufficiently important part of the distributed environment and can accompany students flexibly through their social and academic lives. In contrast, in less well-served countries, the distributed environment may exclude personal machines but include cybercafés (45.2% of students at a Nigerian university obtain access that way, according to Jagboro, 2003). The learning design then also needs to take into account the cultures of those locales for example, the cultural taboos on women using them (Gunawardena et al., 2009).

These three resources, learning design approach, institutional strategy and distributed learning environment, each has a role to play in the maintenance of an ethos of explicitness and flexibility. To illustrate this, it may help to imagine that the inner and outer rings of Figure 8.2 rotate so that certain points can be lined up with each other, somewhat like an orienteering compass: for example, a distributed learning environment is a relevant resource to cope with the required flexibility (e.g., students with different needs may need to study using different devices) but if the outer rings rotate 180 degrees, it can also be seen as a resource in the learning design. Similarly, an institutional learning and teaching strategy must be in place to ensure support for the activities going on in learning design. Equally, the institutional strategy should support the flexibility required by the diversity of student profiles (such as providing materials equally suitable for learners with no disabilities as for those with sight-impairment or dyslexia, or again varying the presentation of materials so that they enable equal achievement of learning goals by less proficient as by more proficient language learners registered together on a given module). Together, the three resources form an integrated system that should perhaps structure most forms of teaching, but is an indispensible ingredient in modes where the bulk of the learning is carried out without co-presence.

DCALL research seen through the integrated model

Ironically, investigations of language learners and DL systems have not been systematic. Rather, it is once again in generic DL research that systemic views are articulated. However, some examples can be found that relate to distance language learning. The following selection will give an insight into these practices and their relationship to the integrated model, thus providing an answer to the question that arose from the discussion of Figure 8.1, about which elements of DCALL are different from CALL.

Learning design issues

Open-source VLEs allow developers to customize or create modules and features. Some DCALL research has highlighted the relationship between this technology, pedagogy and learner needs, and has been able to inform the planning of distance courses. For example, Shield and Kukulska-Hulme (2006) studied pedagogical and external websites that were recommended to learners in their DCALL studies and identified two components of website usability: pedagogical usability (Is the practice of multimodal communication on websites a facilitator or inhibitor of progress in L2 communication?) and intercultural usability (How do members of Culture A interpret the Web interface and icon styles of Culture B?). Another example is Stickler and Hampel (2010) and their case study on the use of a Moodle-based virtual learning environment including wikis for collaboration and blogs for reflective learning. Distance learners were registered on an online language course with a design combining different approaches. Findings showed a link between students' choice of tools and their learning preferences (e.g., focus on form or communication; preference for written or spoken language) thus contributing to decisions that would shape the distributed environment for future iterations of the course.

In DCALL the penalty for faulty design can be heavy: remote, isolated learners whose learning is impeded or halted by design issues cannot obtain immediate help, nor can designers intervene swiftly to recast pedagogical orientations that have been explicitly described for the learners in the self-study materials already released to them. Both the above studies exemplify the extent of the scrutiny under which the learning and technological designs must come in order to ensure that the environmental and pedagogical resources in the integrated model actually mesh. Both studies also show how to frame this scrutiny within the context of our particular discipline.

Flexibility as to study circumstances

The following three studies of mobile devices create a three-way link between the study circumstances, the learner's experiences and the technology. While podcast-based teaching can be studied in the context of general CALL for the benefits it may bring to skills development (Ducate & Lomicka, 2009), the DCALL researcher looks for additional dimensions, such as the technology's potential for maximizing isolated learners' learning opportunities. Thus Edirisingha et al. (2007) derived a model of learner support through podcast use which afforded both formal and informal learning, the latter being accessed through peer knowledge, which is a plentiful resource among the adult audiences typical of DL. Some less successful projects were reviewed by Rosell-Aguilar (2009), who studied literature on the use of podcasts for language learning. Many students in these studies choose to work with podcasts through their institution's VLE rather than subscribe to RSS feeds, which 'would appear to contradict some of the potential benefits of podcasting . . . (e.g., portability, attractiveness, learning on the move, informality' (p. 27). The author wondered whether the explanation lay in the lack of integration between course design and the different environments involved:

> [m]any of the files were embedded within a VLE where students had to complete activities based on the media resources. If students have to listen to a piece of audio to prepare for an activity or lecture or complete activities based on it, why would they de-contextualize that audio and transfer it to a portable device? (ibid.)

He also reminded the reader that podcasts have a characteristic which differentiates them from ordinary audio files: they form regularly updated series, encouraging extended listening over time. He found that this feature was not exploited either. In these cases, flexibility of environment had been considered, but the learning design failed to exploit the affordances of this environment. In contrast, an intervention study by Demouy and Kukulska-Hulme (2010) specifically focused on such affordances. They set up an experiment comparing two groups of 35 distance learners. Group 1 was asked to carry out listening and speaking activities on mobile phones; Group 2 carried out listening activities on MP3 player and iPods and could then practise the speaking closely related to those listening tracks on their computer with the course DVD-Rom. The researchers found that Group 1

> engaged with the project activities in a variety of settings. 'Other' locations included at work, in the streets or public spaces, in hotel rooms, at the beach or at a supermarket. The majority of participants indicated that they were doing something else whilst listening to the clips. This usually meant travelling (with public transport scoring an average of 36% and driving 12% over the six-week period) or exercising (walking 45%, jogging 15%) ranking higher in the choices available. By comparison, Group 2 responses show a marked preference for working with the project's activities at home. (Demouy et al., 2010, p. 222)

The authors concluded that 'interactive speaking activities are not done easily in public places, in front of others or while doing something else. Participants generally chose to do them at home. They rarely managed to find a "quiet" spot or time to try out an activity outside their home' (p. 228). With a local institutional policy that encourages mobile learning, and a distributed environment that includes all the above devices, it is particularly important, as the research shows, that the learning design should be constructed in full consideration of the learners' real experiences with, and preferred uses of, the technological environment.

In the integrated model discussed earlier, the institution also plays a role in supporting students in their particular study circumstances. There is only one report to date on the effect of an institutional learning strategy on DCALL: Hopkins' (2010) work on assessment at the Universidat Oberta de Catalunya (UOC). Whereas from its inception in 1994 the all-online UOC excluded synchronous activity because its busy students could not be expected to attend online events at set times, the English department fought to show that real-time interactivity based on collaborative tasks was important to language learning. Having demonstrated through research the willingness of UOC students to engage with synchronous online learning, Hopkins and colleagues were able to modify the direction of the institutional strategy and the UOC now offers synchronous activities. Their innovative approach to oral assessment exemplifies DCALL research, in that while CALL inspired the principles that underpinned the construction of the assessment, the particular DCALL contribution is to have embedded those in a scheme that took full notice both of the institutional constraints and of the students' circumstances. Specifically, the tests involved discussions in which students worked in small groups towards a negotiated consensus through oral interactions triggered by a scenario. No tutors or assessors were present at the test itself, which was student-led and recorded for later marking. Hopkins explains the dual rationale that determined this choice:

> The autonomous, student-led nature of the tasks responded in part to practical issues of timetabling and the impossibility of instructors attending the sessions of all of their students. In addition, in light of previous research findings regarding the general teacher centeredness of the interaction in [Synchronous Audiographic Conferencing] environments discussed previously, a further aim was to explore a situation in which the teacher's role was not that of session leader, but rather post-session observer and provider of feedback. (p. 238)

Additionally the research discovered a further reason why the method fitted well with DL and its focus on student self-management: some students had found listening to the recording of the assessed speaking activity useful. According to one of them 'The fact that you can listen to yourself afterwards is very positive and you become aware of your errors, your pronunciation, etc' (ibid., p. 249). While the assessment designers can be credited with bringing about the educational benefits and student satisfaction levels reported by Hopkins, it is clear that the UOC's willingness to change its policy in favour of an innovation such as a non-staffed synchronous summative test has also been key, underlining again the need for systemic approaches if DL practices are to flourish.

Previous academic experience

The following study is a good example of DCALL research and development, in that the authors understand DL's preoccupation with the diversity of academic experience which is characteristic of open learning cohorts. Although this is a generic distance learner characteristic, the authors' proposals for addressing it are specifically contextualized to language learning and technology. Ros I Solé and Mardomingo (2004) designed a multiple-pathways Web-based project for cultural learning for L2 learners of Spanish. The design offered distance students varying degrees of scaffolding through the pathways (or 'trajectories') depending on how confident they felt with both the medium and the language. Having self-selected a 'trajectory', students were then automatically guided through the tasks with the degree of scaffolding that matched their proficiency, based on self-assessment. Findings were encouraging but suggested that further support was needed to help students select realistically (which in most cases meant not underestimating their own strengths).

Previous educational cultures

Doherty (2009) proves by counterexample that a DCALL learning design that pays scant attention to prior learning cultures will fail, particularly if it coincides with a similarly monocultural strategy on the part of the institution. She presents a study of what she calls 'assessment trouble' on a distance MBA administered by an Australian university through the medium of English, with an enrolment of advanced L2 speakers of English (Malaysian and Chinese) studying alongside L1 Australian peers. The L2 cohort soon starts expressing a high degree of anxiety on the course forum about the nature of the course assessment. The Australian cohort, less vocal in the forum discussions (41% of all such queries for two thirds of the enrolments), seems to implicitly understand the tutor's account of the institution's assessment requirements. He posts to the forum that students are expected to produce an assignment that is 'professionally presented with appropriate use of headings and sub-headings [for which the] precise format is up to the individual student' (p. 141). As a result, the L2 cohort's questions intensify, ranging from word limits and document formatting to interpretation of the wording in the advice offered: 'Is it possible for you to clarify in more specifics' or, again, 'I've a few problems trying to understand what I'm supposed to touch on' (ibid., p. 141). Finally, the tutor offers to post an example 'on the understanding that it is not a "model" but only an example' (ibid., p. 142). Analysing the fresh 'stream of trouble' (ibid., p. 143) that greets this initiative, Doherty observes that the L2 cohort has 'limited experience of the norms in the Australian university sector [where they were] positioned as guests' (ibid., p. 141), in contradiction to the University's marketing discourse that promoted the course as one international online community. Australian students faced with the same instructions, on the other hand were able to decode the tutor's guidelines.

In terms of the integrated model discussed earlier, then, the troubles in this case can be mapped to weaknesses in the learning design. There was insufficient explicitness about the assessment procedures, and insufficient (or even nil) account was taken of the prior educational cultures of the L2 speakers. Arguably, further weaknesses lay in the distributed learning environment (e.g., reducing communication to an asynchronous forum when synchronous teleconferencing might have been more useful in helping with linguistic disambiguation) and in the institutional strategy (which legitimized only one assessment model).

Motivation and anxiety

The identification of linguistic activities and contents suitable for study times when full attention is engaged, and others when attention or motivation are lower, is arguably something that generic CALL should encourage. Language studies, with their mix of skills-based and content-based work, times of lone reflection and times of communication with others, can be seen as particularly well suited to variations in learning routines. Yet no CALL research on this topic has come to light in the preparation of this chapter. In DCALL, in contrast, motivation is an increasingly researched field. The design of DL materials plays a role in motivation maintenance. For example Murphy and Hurd (2011) have specific recommendations for pacing the material so as to minimize moments of low motivation. They also illustrate the need to provide learners with the content and technological resources that allow them to exercise motivation monitoring themselves 'and become aware of the decisions [about their learning that] they can and should be making' (p. 56).

Concerning anxiety, a few studies of emotions around language performance are now also available (Bown & White 2010; Pichette, 2009) . Yet papers with a specific focus on these affective issues as they play out within a digitally mediated DL format are harder to find, although two examples are Ozdener and Satar's (2008) study on affect in the use of text and voice chat, and de los Arcos et al. (2009) reporting on emotions in audiographic conferencing. These authors identified ways in which the medium respectively heightened and diminished certain types of emotion in learners attending regular online tutorials with peers and tutors whom they have never met.

Current and future directions

In her state-of-the-art review of ten years of distance language learning White (2006) found that by that point in the new century, three broad topics had emerged as priorities for distance language researchers: 'the process of choosing technology in particular sociocultural contexts, the contribution of "low-end" technologies, and the potential and contribution of new learning environments' (pp. 254–5).

In light of the priorities that she saw emerging in 2006, this chapter concludes with a look at the issues that occupy DCALL researchers today. To that effect, a corpus of research and theses from the UK Open University published in 2010 and 2011 or in press at the time of writing was examined. 54 studies were found to belong to DCALL, covering the following topics (in descending order of number of publications): multimodality (8); knowing more about learners, their characteristics and contexts (8); online teaching and teacher training (7); autonomy (4); motivation (4); emotions and anxiety (4); intercultural issues (4); mobile learning (4); task design (3); beginners (3); the speaking skill (1); collaboration (1); feedback (1); assessment (1); and Open Educational Resources for teachers (1). The top seven items on the list may be seen as priority activities for DCALL, as follows.

The first one is multimodality, a field which has become important to DCALL in the last ten years, as the mediation of distance learning has been able to take place via ever more sophisticated digital platforms. Understanding interaction in these environments (Hampel, in press; Hampel & Stickler, 2012; Mirza & Lamy, 2010), learner competence (Hauck, 2010) and methodologies for researching multimodal interactions (Lamy, 2012; Lamy & Flewitt, 2011) make up three productive strands of multimodality research.

The joint top-ranking category (knowing more about learners) is driven by a key feature of DCALL mentioned earlier on in the chapter, that is, being flexibly responsive to the wide variety of DL audiences, for example to learner diversity (Adams & Nicolson, 2011), to learner characteristics and how they link to attainment (Coleman & Furnborough, 2010) or to learner preferences (Stickler & Hampel, 2010).

The training of online distance teachers of languages has been an object of research for nearly two decades and is likely to continue so, as teachers have to cyclically adapt their teaching to evolving technology settings, and institutions need to better understand the implications for teacher workloads and rewards. New issues for DCALL teachers in blended formats are discussed in Nicolson et al. (2011), Beaven et al. (2010), Comas-Quinn (2011), Gallardo et al. (2011), and in Guichon and Hauck's (2011) special issue of *ReCALL*.

Research on motivation has been mentioned earlier. Together with research on autonomy (Murphy & Hurd, 2011) and on emotions (Kukulska-Hulme & de los Arcos, 2011) it is key to retention of distance learners and can be predicted to be a continuing priority in the future.

In DCALL, intercultural research has placed less emphasis on telecollaboration than has been the case in CALL more generally. This may be due to the demographic profile of distance learners (generally older, with more accumulated life experiences including travel, and therefore in need of a different approach to 'developing intercultural awareness' than younger audiences). There may also be some reluctance on the part of distance course designers to involve their learners in periods of contact with a second remote community, given the time that learners already devote to connecting with their primary remote community, that is, their tutors and peers. However, specific approaches to intercultural learning for distance audiences are a live research topic, including, recently, intercultural development in adult European beginners learning Chinese at a distance (Álvarez, 2011; Álvarez & Kan, in press).

Finally, research into mobile language learning in distance contexts (Kukulska-Hulme, 2010) has two different rationales, as seen earlier. One is the need, in DL, for as close a fit as possible with the adult learner's personal technologies of choice, the other predominantly relates to teachers of English in the compulsory school sector in under-served countries, and has more of an inclusion agenda (Power & Shrestha, 2010). The research aims within the former can be so varied, the needs of the two sectors so different and the technology itself so ubiquitous and versatile that the time may have come when the label 'mobile learning' is no longer an accurate descriptor, whether in distance or co-present formats, while the practice itself continues to follow the technology and to provide new objects for research.

However, to remain true to the avoidance of technological determinism which has guided the writing of this chapter, a more cultural note should be sounded in conclusion: DCALL overlaps but is not co-terminous with CALL and instead has specific concerns related to distance, openness, flexibility and support for learners. Distance teaching and learning of languages is now a mature field, albeit as mentioned earlier, still facing the task of establishing its own dissemination territories. Through their continuing endeavour to scrutinize, document and address the challenges of remote language learning and teaching, DCALL practitioners bring valuable pedagogical and design insights into the thinking of the CALL community at large.

References

Adams, H., & Nicolson, M. (2011). Learner diversity. In M. Nicolson, L. Murphy & M. Southgate (Eds.), *Language teaching in blended contexts* (pp. 24–43). Edinburgh: Dunedin Academic Press.

Álvarez, I. (2011). Learning about Chinese-speaking cultures at a distance. In J. Fenoulhet, & C. Ros i Solé (Eds.), *Mobility and localisation in language learning: A view from languages of the wider world* (pp. 145–72). Oxford: Peter Lang.

Álvarez, I., & Kan, Q. (in press). Supporting intercultural learning for beginners' Chinese language learners at the Open University in the United Kingdom. In M. Cortazzi & L. Jin (Eds.), *Researching intercultural learning*. Basingstoke: Palgrave Macmillan.

Beaven, T., Emke, M., Ernest, P., Germain-Rutherford, A., Hampel, R., Hopkins, J., Stanojevic, M. M., & Stickler, U. (2010). *Needs and challenges for online language teachers – the ECML project DOTS. Teaching English with Technology: A Journal for Teachers of English, 10*(2), 5–20.

Blake, R. (2008). *Brave new digital classroom: Technology and foreign language learning.* Washington, DC: Georgetown University Press.

— (2009). The use of technology for second language distance learning. *The Modern Language Journal, Focus Issue, 93*, 822–35.

Bown, J., & White, C. (2010). Affect in a self-regulatory framework for language learning. *System, 38*(3), 432–43.

Coleman, J. (2005). CALL from the margins: Effective dissemination of CALL research and good practices. *ReCALL 17*(1), 18–31.

Coleman, J. A., & Furnborough, C. (2010). Learner characteristics and learning outcomes on a distance Spanish course for beginners. *System, 38*(1), 14–29.

Comas-Quinn, A. (2011). Learning to teach online or learning to become an online teacher: An exploration of teachers' experiences in a blended learning course. *ReCALL, 23*(3), 218–32.

Conole, G. (2009). Capturing practice and scaffolding learning design. In U. Bernath, A. Szücs, A. Tait & M. Vidal (Eds.), *Distance and e-Learning in transition: Learning innovation, technology and social challenges* (pp. 579–94). Hoboken, NJ: John Wiley.

Degache, C., & Depover, C. (Eds.) (2010). *La distance dans l'enseignement des langues, frein ou levier? Distances et Savoirs, Special issue, 3*(9), 319–24.

de Los Arcos, B., Coleman, J. A., & Hampel, R. (2009). Learners' anxiety in audiographic conferences: A discursive psychology approach to emotion talk. *ReCALL, 21*(1), 3–17.

Demouy, V., & Kukulska-Hulme, A. (2010). On the spot: Using mobile devices for listening and speaking practice on a French language programme. *Open Learning: The Journal of Open and Distance Learning, 25*(3), 217–32.

Doherty, C. (2009). Trouble and auto-ethnography in assessment genre: A case for postnational design in online internationalised pedagogy. In R. Goodfellow & M-N Lamy (Eds.), *Learning cultures in online education* (pp. 131–50). London: Continuum Books.

Ducate, L., & Lomicka, L. (2009). Podcasting, an effective tool for honing students' language pronunciation? *Language Learning and Technology, 13*(3), 66–86.

Edirisingha, P., Rizzi, C., Nie, M., & Rothwell, L. (2007) Podcasting to provide teaching and learning support for an undergraduate module on English language and communication. *Turkish Online Journal of Distance Education, 8*(3), 87–107.

Gallardo, M., Heiser, S., & Nicolson, M. (2011). Teacher development for blended contexts. In M. Nicolson, L. Murphy & M. Southgate (Eds.), *Language teaching in blended contexts* (pp. 219–31). Edinburgh: Dunedin Academic Press.

Glikman, V. (2002). *Des cours par correspondance au 'e-Learning'*. Paris: Presses Universitaires de France.

— (Ed.) (2005). *Tutorat à distance et logiques industrielles. Distances et Savoirs, 3*(2), 127–31.

Guichon, N., & Hauck, M. (Eds.) (2011). Teacher education research in CALL and CMC: More in demand than ever. Special issue of *ReCALL, 23*(3), 187–99.

Gunawardena, C., Alami, A., Jayatilleke, G., & Bouachrine, F. (2009). Identity, gender and language in synchronous cyber-cultures: A cross-cultural study. In R. Goodfellow & M-N. Lamy (Eds.), *Learning cultures in online education* (pp. 30–51). London: Continuum Books.

Guri-Rosenblit, S., & Gro, B. (2011). e-Learning: Confusing terminology, research gaps and inherent challenges. *The Journal of Distance Education/Revue de l'Éducation à Distance, 25*(1), (n.p.). Retrieved from www.jofde.ca/index.php/jde/article/viewArticle/729/1206

Hampel, R. (in press). Multimodal computer-mediated communication and distance. In C. A. Chapelle (Ed.), *Encyclopedia of applied linguistics*. Oxford: Wiley-Blackwell.

Hampel, R., & Stickler, U. (2012). The use of videoconferencing to support multimodal interaction in an online language classroom. *ReCALL 24*(2).

Hauck, M. (2010). Telecollaboration: At the interface between multimodal and intercultural communicative competence. In S. Guth & F. Helm. (Eds.), *Telecollaboration 2.0:*

Language, literacies and intercultural learning in the 21st century (pp. 219–48). Bern: Peter Lang.

Holmberg, B., Shelley, M., & White, C. (Eds.) (2005). *Distance education and languages: Evolution and change.* Clevedon, UK: Multilingual Matters.

Hopkins, J. E. (2010). Distance language learners' perceptions of assessed, student-led speaking tasks via a synchronous audiographic conferencing tool. *Innovation in Language Learning and Teaching, 4*(3), 235–58.

Jagboro, K. O. (2003). A study of internet usage in Nigerian universities: A case study of Obafemi Awolowo University, Ife-Ife, Nigeria. *First Monday,* 8(2). (n.p.) Retrieved from http://firstmonday.org/htbin/cgiwrap/bin/ojs/index.php/fm/article/view/1785/1665

Jegede, O. J., & Gooley, A. (1994). A front-end evaluation of audiographic conferencing system in open and distance learning in Queensland. In proceedings from *The First International Conference on Open Learning, 9–11 November* (pp. 175–80). Brisbane: University of Southern Queensland.

Jonassen, D., Davidson, M., Collins, M., Cambell, J., & Haag, B. B. (1995). Constructivism and computer-mediated communication in distance education. *The American Journal of Distance Education, 9*(2), 7–26.

Kukulska-Hulme, A. (2010). Charting unknown territory: Models of participation in mobile language learning. *International Journal of Mobile Learning and Organisation, 4*(2), 116–29.

Kukulska-Hulme, A., & de los Arcos, B. (2011). Triumphs and frustrations of self-motivated language learners using mobile devices. In *The CAL Conference 2011 – Learning Futures: Education, Technology and Sustainability,* 13–15 April 2011, Manchester.

Lamy, M N. (2012). Click if you want to speak: Reframing CA for research into multimodal conversations in online learning. *International Journal of Virtual and Personal Learning Environments, 3*(1), 1–18.

Lamy, M-N., & Flewitt, R. (2011). Describing online conversations: Insights from a multimodal approach. In C. Develotte, R. Kern & M-N. Lamy (Eds.), *Décrire la communication en ligne: Le face-à-face distanciel* (pp. 71–94). Lyon: ENS Editions.

Mirza, C., & Lamy, M-N. (2010). Quel est le rôle des environnements audio-graphiques synchrones dans les interactions d'un cours de langue en ligne? *Revue Internationale des Technologies en Pédagogie Universitaire, 7*(1), 47–67.

Murphy, L., & Hurd, S. (2011). Fostering learner motivation and autonomy in blended teaching. In M. Nicolson, L. Murphy & M. Southgate (Eds.), *Language teaching in blended context* (pp. 43–58). Edinburgh: Dunedin Academic Press.

Nicolson, M., Murphy, L., & Southgate, M. (Eds.) (2011). *Language teaching in blended contexts.* Edinburgh: Dunedin Academic Press.

Ozdener, N., & Satar, M. (2008). Computer-mediated communication in foreign language education: Use of target language and learner perceptions. *The Turkish Online Journal of Distance Education, 9*(2), (n.p.).

Pichette, F. (2009). Second language anxiety and distance language learning. *Foreign Language Annals, 42*(1), 77–93.

Power, T., & Shrestha, P. (2010). Mobile technologies for (English) language learning: An exploration in the context of Bangladesh. In *IADIS International Conference: Mobile Learning 2010,* 19–21 March 2010 (n.p.). Porto, Portugal: IADIS Press.

Rosell-Aguilar, F. (2009). Podcasting for language learning: Re-examining the potential. In L. Lomicka & G. Lord (Eds.), *The next generation: Social networking and online collaboration in foreign language learning.* (pp. 13–34). San Marco: Calico, Texas, USA.

Ros I Solé, C., & Mardomingo, R. (2004). Trayectorias: A new model for online task-based learning. *ReCALL, 16,* 145–57.

Schulte, D., & Krämer (2008). The impact of new technologies on distance learning students. In proceedings from *The 2008 Conference of the European Association of Distance Teaching Universities, 18–19 September*. Online document. Retrieved from http://bit.ly/qhA4q2

Sclater, N. (2011, 18 March). Can technology significantly impact learning before it has been commoditised? [Web log comment]. Retrieved from http://sclater.com/blog/?p=566

Shield, L., & Kukulska-Hulme, A. (2006). Are language learning websites special? Towards a research agenda for discipline-specific usability. *Journal of Educational Multimedia and Hypermedia, 15*(3), 349–69.

Southgate, M., & Murphy, L. (2011). The nature of the 'blend': Interaction of teaching modes, tools and resources. In M. Nicolson, L. Murphy & M. Southgate (Eds.), *Language teaching in blended contexts* (pp. 13–27). Edinburgh: Dunedin Academic Press Ltd.

Stickler, U., & Hampel, R. (2010). CyberDeutsch: Language production and user preferences in a Moodle VLE. *CALICO Journal, 28*(1), 49–73.

White, C. (2003). *Language learning in distance education*. Cambridge: Cambridge University Press.

— (2006). State-of-the-art review article: The distance learning of foreign languages. *Language Teaching, 39*, 247–64.

9

Language learning in virtual worlds: Research and practice

Randall Sadler and Melinda Dooly

Summary

Virtual Worlds (VWs) are online 3D environments populated by individuals in the form of their avatars. These worlds provide sustained persistent social environments that may be accessed by their users 24 hours a day. For language learners, VWs can provide opportunities to have immediate, visual and affective access to speakers of the language(s) they are learning in a way that is not possible in other online communication formats. This chapter will include two sections. Part one will provide a brief overview of the development of VWs, from their early text-based forms, to the more graphically oriented environments of today such as Second Life™ and a review of the research being performed in this area. The second part of this chapter will examine the use of VWs for language and content learning, based on several research projects by the authors.

Introduction

For many of the readers of this book, their introduction to environments like VWs may have been through television or movies. This might have been via the *holodeck* on *Star Trek: The Next Generation* (1987), where characters from the show could enter a room that was able to display almost any 3D setting with which they could interact, or in movies like the original *Tron* (1982), where Jeff Bridge's character was pulled into a 3D Virtual World against his will. However, the fictional exploration of VWs may be traced back much further in books, beginning with Weinbaum's *Pygmalion's*

Spectacles where a character discusses his creation of a technology that would go beyond a traditional movie to 'add taste, smell, even touch' creating an environment where 'instead of being on a screen, the story is all about you, and you are in it' (1935, section 1).

The VWs that exist today do not share all the wonders of their fictional counterparts (i.e., we are not yet able to step physically into a holodeck of the sort portrayed in Star Trek), but all VWs do share certain characteristics, as discussed in Sadler (2011):

- Modern VWs are online 3D environments;
- Players are represented by avatars;
- They are primarily synchronous, focusing on real-time interactivity;
- They are accessible 24 hours a day;
- They are persistent, with the world continuing to exist after an avatar logs out;
- They are social spaces;
- Numbers are important. In most VWs there are many players online in the world at the same time.

The 3D environments provided by VWs are used for a large variety of functions. These include the battles and strategic teamwork common to Massively Multiplayer Online Roleplay Games (MMORGs) like *World of Warcraft*, with the functions in VWs ranging from virtual dancing, socializing, virtual building, buying and selling, holding business or club meetings and, of course, gathering for educational purposes. While almost no modern VWs were created solely for use in education, the flexibility of these spaces means that educators can easily adapt them for language learning in general and language learning in particular, as discussed later in this section.

In order to explore these issues in more detail, this chapter includes two sections. Part one will provide a brief overview of the development of VWs, from their early text-based forms, to the more graphically oriented environments of today such as *Second Life*, followed by a review of language learning practices and research being performed in this area. The second part of this chapter will examine the use of VWs for language and content learning from a perspective that has so far been rarely explored – the use of a VW for language learning with young children (e.g., from 6–12 years old). The chapter will conclude with a discussion of the future of VWs for language learning for all ages, and suggestions for future research.

While some educators might not yet see the potential of VWs for their students, it is increasingly clear that many individuals (ranging from toddlers to senior citizens) are making heavy use of those environments (see Figure 9.1). Over the last three years

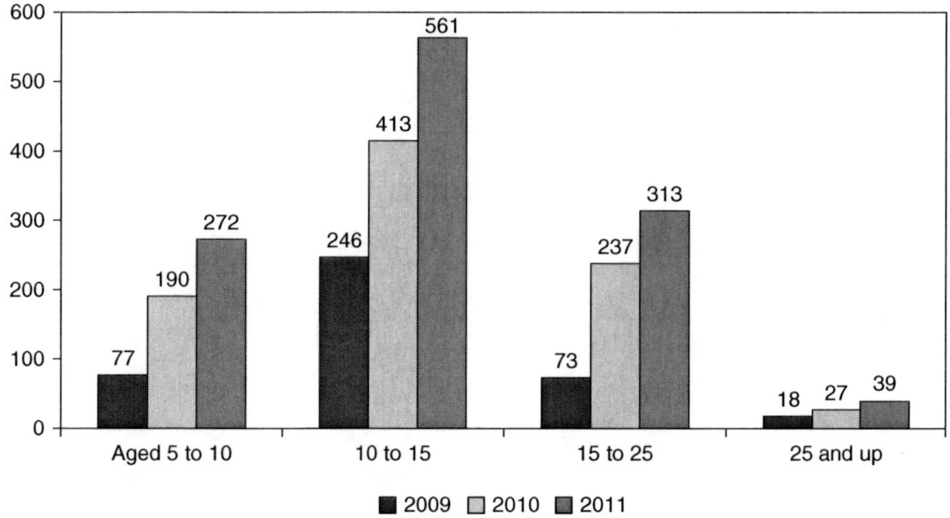

FIGURE 9.1 *VW users (in millions Q1 2009–Q1 2011) by age level (KZERO, 2011).*

the number of users of VWs has increased at every age level. In 2009, there were over 414 million users of VWs worldwide – a truly staggering number – and yet by 2011 this number had increased to 1.185 billion (almost 3 times the number of participants of just 3 years ago). Just as other forms of computer-mediated communication (CMC) discussed in this book have become ubiquitous, VWs have become integrated into everyday life for many people across the globe as a means of communication and socialization. This is especially apparent among younger users, where the most rapid growth in usage has taken place.

Even among the smallest group shown in Figure 9.1, those aged 25 and above, the number of users is impressive but it should also be noted that the numbers discussed above refer to environments considered to be VWs rather than MMORPGs. Although those more purely game-focused platforms are not the focus of this chapter, the addition of that latter group would push these user numbers far higher. Some of the popularity of VWs has to do with the wide variety of choices now available, and the increasing aiming of VWs at specific audiences. The site mmorpg.com, which tracks a range of MMORPG environments ranging from 'real life' (e.g., Second Life), to 'fantasy' (e.g., World of Warcraft), historical, science fiction and sports, currently lists 497 environments.

There has been little research performed that specifically examines the issue of how and to what extent language learning is accomplished in virtual worlds (Panichi & Deutschmann, 2012) but the sheer number of VW users worldwide, and the increasing use of individual VWs by users from many different countries, has created a situation where the potential for both language learning and teaching is great (Sadler, 2011).

A history and overview of VWs

The 'ancestors' of the VWs of today can be traced back to the earliest days of networked computers (for an in-depth overview of this history see Sadler, 2011). In the early 1960s, PLATO (Programmed Logic for Automated Teaching Operations) was developed at the University of Illinois at Urbana-Champaign. While PLATO is often thought of as a system designed to provide behaviourist learning activities (more than 15,000 hours of such activities were developed), it was also the birthplace of many tools that we now take for granted, including 'email, newsgroups, real-time chat, multiplayer games, distance learning, audio, high-resolution graphics, and touch-screen interfaces, a quarter-century before the birth of the Web' (Silberman, 1997, para. 1).

As computer networks began to develop in the 1970s, some programmers saw the potential for this technology to engage in gaming, resulting in the creation of new game environments like *Colossal Cave Adventure* (1975) and *Zork* (1977). This was followed by the creation of a new environment by Roy Trubshaw (1978) called a Multi-User Dungeon (MUD). This environment included responses by the computer program in reaction to actions taken by the player (all text-based), but added a new element – interaction with other human players in the setting. Over time, these environments continued to develop, evolving into MOOs (MUD, Object-Oriented) that allowed the owner of the space (or people designated by the owner) to make changes in the space itself – they could add new rooms or objects into those rooms. Although these were all, once again, text-based environments, this change brought many teachers into the field, with many education-oriented MOOs created for chat and collaboration. What we now call VWs began to take on a more familiar form in 1986, with the introduction of Habitat, created by Lucasfilm. This was a two-dimensional environment, but it included a graphical interface in which users moved about via their avatars on the screen, with the avatars able to communicate via text chat.

Although virtual environments focused entirely on role play (e.g., World of Warcraft) are not the focus of this chapter, they do have possible applications for language learners (see Thorne, 2008 for more discussion on this; also Lai, Ni & Zhao, this volume).

The design and set-up of many VWs today – though not always specifically stated in the program literature – are aimed at a particular age range as shown in Figure 9.2. As might be expected, the VWs that are aimed at a younger audience (e.g., Poptropica, Club Penguin) have more restrictions and safeguards for their users than those aimed at adults. In Club Penguin, for example, parents may choose from two options regarding how their children can communicate with other avatars in the world: ultimate safe chat or standard safe chat. In addition, Club Penguin also has on-site moderators who monitor both chat and the activities of players. This is a feature shared by a number of VWs aimed at younger users, such as Panfu (see Figure 9.3) where players can communicate via open chat, but (as with Club Penguin) chat communication is filtered so that inappropriate words cannot enter the environment and chat is only allowed when moderators are present.

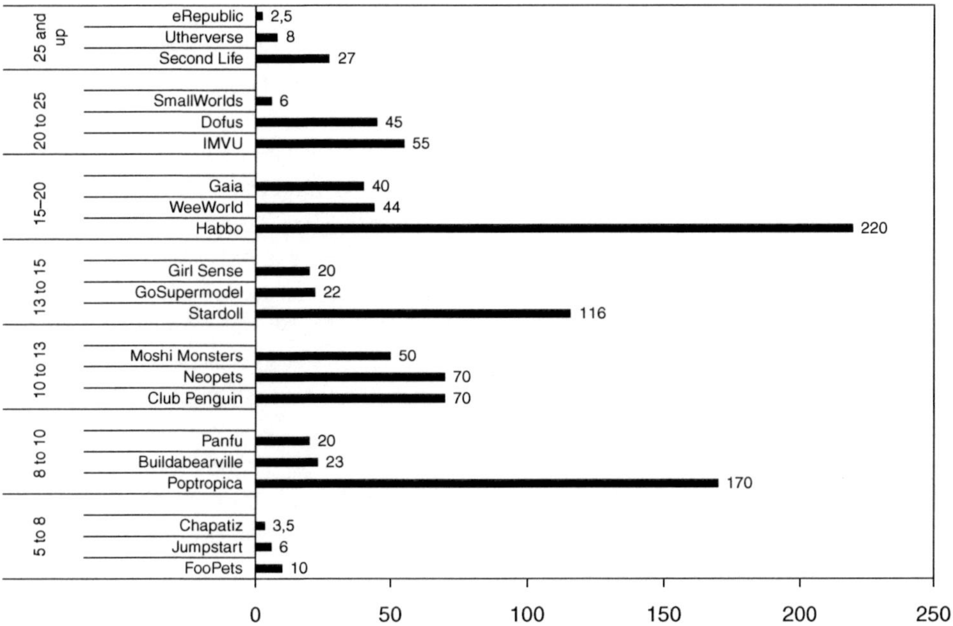

FIGURE 9.2 *Most popular VWs by age level in Q2 2011 (KZERO, 2011).*

FIGURE 9.3 *Castle courtyard in Panfu.*

Some VWs, such as the popular Poptropica (or Club Penguin, with Ultimate Safe Chat) only allow their users to communicate via the scripted chat options in order to ensure that their young users remain safe. From an educational standpoint, this has the benefit of adding a strong safety factor, as well as providing language for the students in the form of the pre-set language options. However, for language learners beyond the elementary level the restrictions on language in the ultimate safe chat from Club Penguin or the scripted chat options in Poptropica may have the effect of limiting the variety of language practice that may take place. While this is potentially detrimental for communicative language learning, many of the VWs aimed at younger learners also include game and/or learning elements, though some of these are only available to paid members. For example, Panfu members (even free ones) have access to a number of fun learning games (CALL rather than CMC-based) at their underwater school, including basic lessons in Spanish.

Until recently, very few of the popular VWs were aimed at girls. Nevertheless, as competition among these environments has grown, and as the number of users – both male and female – has exploded a variety of VWs specifically aimed at girls have been created. As was shown in Figure 9.2, the three most popular VWs at this time in the 13 to 15 age range are all aimed at that audience: Girl Sense, GoSupermodel and Stardoll. While most VWs still have a majority of male users, it is the case now that some of the most popular ones, such as Habbo, have a majority of female users (Chappell, 2011) and the number of female users in VWs is increasing overall, a pattern that should not be surprising given the similar history in internet usage over the last two decades.

Research on virtual worlds

Just as modern VWs are relatively new phenomena, the research taking place on them is still developing. For an overview of the field, there are three books which may provide a deeper understanding of how VWs may aid in the learning process. *Higher Education in Virtual Worlds: Teaching and Learning in Second Life* (Molka-Danielsen & Deutschmann, 2009) and *Learning and Teaching in the Virtual World of Second Life* (Wankel & Kingsley, 2009) are both excellent edited volumes with a number of studies on the topic. *Virtual Worlds and Language Learning: From Theory to Practice* (Sadler, 2011) also provides an in-depth examination of the role of VWs in language learning.

As discussed earlier, VWs are primarily social environments, and share some of the same characteristics as other forms of computer-mediated communication. It is not unexpected, then, that researchers have documented some of the same benefits for language learners in VWs as have been discussed for both asynchronous and synchronous CMC tools such as email, message boards, texting, instant messaging, voice chats and video chat. As might be expected given their nature, a number of researchers have discussed the potential for VWs for encouraging collaboration (e.g., Ball & Pearce, 2009; Bani et al., 2009; Brown & Bell, 2004; Churchill & Snowdon, 1998;

Dillenbourg, Schneider & Syntenta, 2002; Price & Rogers, 2004; Roussou, 2004; Sadler, 2009a, 2009b; Shaffer, Squire, Halverson & Gee, 2004; Skiba, 2007). This focus on the collaborative nature of VWs should not come as a surprise since they are designed to be social and collaborative environments. From a theoretical perspective this is in keeping with Vygotsky's Zone of Proximal Development (ZPD) (1978), which maintains that 'human learning presupposes a specific social nature and a process by which children grow into the intellectual life of those around them' (p. 88). This social nature of learning (and VWs) means that in real-life interaction (or in VW interaction) 'children are [therefore] capable of doing much more in collective activity' (p. 88). This issue was confirmed by Bystrom and Barfield (1999), who found that their students were able to complete tasks much better when working with a partner. Steinkuehler (2004) had a similar finding in her research on cooperation in MMOGs.

Researchers have also found that VWs can lessen learner anxiety, most often attributed to two factors: the potential for delayed communication and the influence of the avatar. Since VWs (and many forms of CMC in general) allow time for students 'to more completely formulate their thoughts as they respond to the class discussion', they may feel less pressure in the environment (Childress & Braswell, 2006, p. 188). This is particularly true since most VWs that allow for oral communication (e.g., Second Life) also have text-based chat, which permits the user more time to read the incoming communication and to compose outgoing messages. An additional factor in explaining this decrease in pressure is the play component that is integral to a VW (whether that *play* is in the form of chat, role play, or VW-based computer games within the environment). As mentioned by Brown and Bell (2004), VWs may also aid in helping 'communities of players to form who exchange new activities and forms of play with each other' (p. 357).

The lessening of anxiety and the play aspect of VWs also seem to be supported by one of the key component of a VW – the avatar. Because players in VWs are represented by avatars (the type and appearance often partially determined by the VW), they are able, in essence, to be whoever (or whatever) they would like to be. This has the effect of helping the individuals controlling those avatars to 'loosen . . . up a bit' (Love, Ross & Wilhelm, 2009, p. 68), while also allowing them 'to experiment with new and powerful identities' (Shaffer et al., 2004, p. 6). A language learner who might be shy in a traditional classroom can hide behind a mask (avatar) of his own choosing in a VW, resulting in the confidence to communicate more than he would otherwise. The 'personality' of the avatar with which a language learner is interacting may also influence the motivation and participation of the learner, especially for very young learners (as will be discussed in the case study).

As mentioned earlier in this chapter, there has been relatively little research accomplished at this point which investigates how, exactly, VWs are being used for language learning and teaching. Thorne (2008) looked at how language was used by two gamers in the MMORPG World of Warcraft (WoW). One of the gamers was from the United States while the other was based in the Ukraine. In his case study he found that the game environment provided abundant opportunities for natural language production that – enhanced by the game environment – resulted in complex interactions and a variety of complex usages of language. Faivre (2009) implemented a semester-length project which utilized Second Life in a business class designed for non-native speakers of English, requiring her students to work with business owners in Second Life to design business models for them. She found that this work required a wide variety of English usage for her students that went well beyond that which would normally be used in a traditional classroom environment. Finally, Sadler (2011) conducted a survey examining language use and learning in SL. This survey (with 237 respondents from SL) found that over 50% of the participants either sometimes or usually used some other language than their first while communicating in SL, and even 78% used another language at least rarely. In addition, the survey takers used a wide variety of strategies for improving their second language skills in SL, ranging from SL classrooms, to listening to audio chat and joining groups. While research specifically examining language learning in VWs is still in the early stages, these projects seem to indicate great potential for the technology.

Potential barriers to language learning in VWs

The fact that virtual worlds are largely a synchronous environment may create additional problems in the time management (time zones, academic calendars) of any language learning project that involves more than one partner. While these are restraints that are common to any CMC medium, it is especially relevant for interaction in VWs. Similarly, technical aspects and potential problems that are common to CALL or CMC language learning projects may be exacerbated by the amount of storage and capacity of images needed for VWs along with the fact that educational institutions (from primary onward) often have high security measures in their internet management that render some VWs inaccessible.

Moreover, the learning curve for VWs is higher than other CMC tools. For instance, learners must not only know how to manipulate their avatar's mobility, they must know how to control the communicative settings that are audio, textual and gestural and fully understand 'geographical' markings – and this is only for handling the avatar. If the language learning project also includes building, the amount of time needed to assimilate these skills is even higher.

At the level of primary education, much of the current work in virtual worlds and primary education focuses on allowing children opportunities to design and create spaces and virtual characters themselves, which may then become part of a wider educational project (cf. Vertex Project, Fathom Project). This implies a need for funding – which may come from the school or other public funding – or else will probably rely on individual practices of teachers who try to take advantage of already existent virtual environments or who are willing to finance VW language learning projects themselves. Funded projects (which necessarily include a period of time for planning and building the environment) risk being a one-time effort which ends once the money has run out. There does not appear to be any systematic endeavours to make VWs an easily accessible foreign language teaching tool, especially at the level of primary education for this level. Further restrictions when working with young learners will be discussed in the next section.

Primary education in virtual worlds: To Rez or not to Rez?

According to a recent report for the Office of Policy Analysis and Research, Georgia Tech Research Institute, there were over 150 virtual worlds for children and youth in 2008 (Pechar, 2008). The most common aim of virtual worlds for educational purposes with children from kindergarten through the final year of compulsory education is 'to expand the classroom and allow students to experience what they would normally learn only out of a textbook' (Pechar, 2008, p. 2). Common examples in language learning include experiences that allow the students to receive and give input in near-authentic situations that also represent cultural features of the language use (e.g., a Spanish-guide for a tour down the Amazon river (Pechar, 2008). The underlying principle is that the motivating learning environments foment learner engagement (Dede, Clarke, Ketelhut, Nelson & Bowman, 2006; Squires, 2002).

There are, however, caveats continuously brought to the fore in most literature on 'virtual education' for young people, principally the threat of 'cyber predators' (Bugeja, 2007) and the easy access and potential exposure to mature, adult-only virtual content as well as concerns about pupil interaction – bullying, verbal abuse and inappropriate behaviour, facilitated through the very technologies being used to create the environment (e.g., audio or text chats). Other impediments are the costs in time, effort and money (educators must 'buy' virtual land and spend time and effort 'building' the environment or else use 'public' land, where they can no longer control the environment or the visitors to the virtual location).

Finally, it seems that for many primary education teachers there is a question of relevance. The complexity of foreign language use, while trying to induct young children into virtual worlds, may seem too daunting for many foreign or second language teachers (Dooly, 2009; Schwartz, 2008). Other problems for self-created virtual materials fall within the specificities of the young language learner: materials should be of short duration, fall within their range of interests and topics, require minimal technological skills (e.g., typing) and should not be primarily text-based – or for very young learners, should have little or no written input. Additionally, young learners tend to be beginners in foreign language learning, while

> collaborative use of the Internet usually requires communication at quite a sophisticated level. An application for use by young beginners must somehow contrive a situation where young learners can use what language they have in a realistic, meaningful and communicative way. (Milton & Garbi, 2000, p. 287)

Still, as Merchant (2007) has pointed out, many educators are coming to the conclusion that new technology – in particular virtual worlds (see Milton & Garbi, 2000) might help motivate reluctant young language learners, and to help ensure meaningful contexts for multiple literacy/ies – especially since these environments are very text, audio, digital and visually oriented (Dooly & Hauck, 2012). Taking an educational ethnographic approach, this case study aims to outline one such endeavour.

Project outline

The applied linguistics research project, funded by the Spanish Ministry of Education (Project Title: PADS, EDU2010–17859), aimed to design, experiment and evaluate telecollaborative Project-Based Language Learning (PBLL) approaches in primary education. The project was first piloted in the academic year 2010–11, based on an internet-mediated exchange between a school in Catalonia, Spain and a school in Ontario, Canada. The pedagogical design and subsequent research was triangulated and coordinated by two teacher educators from the Universitat Autònoma de Barcelona. The students from Catalonia were 6-year-old beginners in English as a Foreign Language (EFL) and the students from Canada were 8-year-old students, working from a focus of language arts (in English). In order to break away from a 'language-only' focus, the project was deliberately designed to be cross-disciplinary so that multiple competences would come into play. The research aimed to see what, if any, development took place in various literacies – linguistic (e.g., communicative competences), digital competences, artistic competences and intercultural competences.

The main online activities were divided into three phases. The first (introductory) phase consisted of video introductions by the students (recorded and edited by the students themselves; a Q&A forum based on the introductory videos to work on language production and comprehension as well as helping to contextualize learning about the 'other' and information exchange concerning their shared topic (described in phase 2).

Phase 2 was based on the building up of shared knowledge. Two local artists (one from Catalonia, Joan Abelló, and one from Ontario, Rob Gonsalves) were chosen as the focus of study for both groups.[1] After studying their chosen artist's techniques, lives and selected paintings, the students exchanged information about the artist with their online partners. The information was used to build a virtual art gallery in Second Life where paintings by both artists (and a few others for added complexity) were displayed (see Figure 9.4). Although Second Life is not a VW that is designed for use for children, this environment was chosen for several reasons. First, it is very easy to build custom environments in Second Life, especially given the wide range of items available either for free or to buy in that VW. Second, one of the authors of this paper was able to set up the gallery used for this project high above an island in Second Life so that there was a secure space for the interaction. Finally, the children participating in the project were not 'in-world' themselves, so there was no potential for them to go to other areas in Second Life that might have been inappropriate for them.

In the final phase students created an e-book together, based on the fictional idea that the artists had become friends. The artists' adventures were inspired by the

FIGURE 9.4 *Virtual art gallery in Second Life.*

paintings they had studied (e.g., depictions of a beach, Le Moulin Rouge) in the virtual gallery.

For this chapter, we will focus on the activities in the virtual art gallery which were designed to promote students' construction of knowledge in several areas. The students in this project gathered in the classroom in front of their teachers and a projection screen which showed the virtual art gallery in SL. An avatar in the form of *Snoopy* was in the art gallery (controlled by one of the authors unseen in the back of the classroom), and the students first had to greet their 'guide', then give Snoopy directions to walk around the art gallery. This technique was extremely effective in the sense that in the first half of the sessions the students were quite unaware that Snoopy was being controlled by the researcher. Instead, they seemed convinced that their oral commands given to Snoopy on the screen were having an immediate effect on the actions taken by the avatar (see transcript and analysis of session 1 below).

The first session consisted of a tour to have a look around the gallery. In the next session the students helped Snoopy find a particular painting (from their local artist) described by the teacher (e.g., 'in this painting there is a large statue'). The following sessions consisted of teams giving descriptions to their classmates so that they could then 'help' Snoopy find the painting (Figure 9.5), at times belonging to their local artist and at other times belonging to the Canadian artist. Thus, the students were slowly introduced to and became familiar with the work of both artists.

In other sessions, students were read descriptions from their exchange partners about the other artist's paintings and, once more, they gave instructions to Snoopy to walk around the virtual gallery to find the right painting according to the description given. By the end of the session sequences, students had taken over the role of

FIGURE 9.5 *Students take over control of Snoopy.*

giving descriptions, giving instructions and eventually, 'manipulating' the Snoopy avatar.

During this phase, the learners assimilated language competences such as giving greetings, giving and understanding directions and commands as well as particular lexicon associated with the paintings in the art gallery (e.g., rocks, windmill, beach, street, tower, descriptions of people, etc.). Both local artists were chosen in part because they depicted the local geography as well as places they had visited (e.g., Moulin Rouge in Paris, Easter Island, Trafalgar Square), thus promoting world knowledge and allowing the introduction of map-reading to the 6-year-olds. The students also came to recognize the two artists' main works of art and to distinguish between their techniques and other artists (decoys in the virtual art gallery) as well as learning about cities associated with the two artists.

Data and analysis

As mentioned above, this case study takes an educational ethnography perspective. The compiled data consisted of: video and audio recordings of all the sessions (transcribed), collection of specific output from the students, evaluative feedback from the teachers (all the disciplines), student self-evaluation of learning and post-PBLL recall activities. It is not possible to enter into a detailed description and analysis of all the transcription extracts, however, departing from a perspective that 'cognition is as much a socially situated activity as it is an individual phenomenon' (Markee, 2011, p. 604), a sequential analysis of language learning behaviours, enacted in the language learners' different speech events during the PBLL exchange, shows language skills evolving during the whole process.

Taking recurrency as a factor, the examples given here illustrate excerpts of data that are being analysed according to an adaptation of Markee's 'learning behavior tracking (LBT)' methodology (2008, 2011). As Markee (2011) points out, while most conversation analysis studies take a 'micro-longitudinal time frame' (p. 605), studies have been carried out that focus on 'realtime language learning behaviors that occur in different speech events . . . over more extended periods of time' (p. 605). LBT proposes not only focusing on extended time periods of language learning behaviours but also 'tracking' demonstrations of the language learner's orientation to details of talk through different speech events. However, considering the difficulties of this type of tracking in young language learners (limited proficiency in the target language and limited resources for demonstrating orientation of their own cognitive processes), the tracking here focuses on recurrent patterns of language use that are clearly situated in response to the social context (in this case a VW), versus what might be called 'teacher prompting' in the format of initiation response feedback (IRF, see Sinclair & Coulthard, 1992). Recurrent patterns of learning behaviour have been found and there is ample evidence of what Barab, Hay and Yagamata-Lynch (2001) call 'episodes of action' defined as the 'minimal meaningful ontology for capturing cognition *in situ*' (p. 64).

Session 1: Introduction to virtual art gallery

Teacher: Marc, could you tell Snoopy (.) Snoopy go left.[2]

Marc: Snoopy go left.

(Avatar moves)

Teacher: Ahh_ look. Stop! And Snoopy stops.

(students gasp)

[. . .]

Teacher: Snoopy speaks in English. Alright. Listen to me. If you want Snoopy to walk (imitates walking) you need to say (writes on board the word 'straight') go_

Students (several, unidentified): strit (mispronunciation of straight)

Students in chorus: Go straight on.

Teacher: Repeat!

Students in chorus: Go straight on. Go straight on. Go straight on. (begin to take on chanting rhythm).

The initial reaction of these young learners (a loud gasp of pleased surprise, in unison), when introduced to 'Snoopy' support Love, et al.'s assertion that the influence of the avatar in VWs can lessen learner anxiety (2009), even if the students themselves did not create the avatar to represent themselves. The students' reaction (throughout all the sessions as will be demonstrated further on) also supports previous literature that highlights the role VWs have in reducing student anxiety through 'play' (Brown & Bell, 2004; Roussou, 2004). The young learners were eager to 'communicate' with 'Snoopy' and unlike in previous sessions of more teacher-fronted classroom interaction where some of the students were more unwilling to answer, in this case the students were not reluctant to 'demonstrate' their language knowledge.

Inevitably, in session 1, the students need substantial 'scaffolding' by the teacher in order to give the Snoopy avatar simple directions. By session 3 (which took place the following week), however, the students are better able to 'help' Snoopy get around the gallery and peer collaboration replaces teacher intervention.

Session 3: Student scaffolding of interaction

Pau: Snoopy go left. (Snoopy moves left and stops). Left. (Snoopy moves left again and keeps walking) Stop. Snoopy go str-str_ straight on. (Snoopy goes straight on and then stops at the wall).

Teacher: continue Joan.

Joan: Snoopy go left.

Several students: no no no (shouting)

Joan: Snoopy go right

Other students: NO go straight on

In the previous sessions, the young language learners had spent considerable time *listening* to descriptions of the paintings, read out to them by the teacher or the researchers in order to 'guide' Snoopy around the gallery until they found the described painting. (The descriptions were adaptations of texts written by the students in Spain and Canada to help their exchange partners learn about their artists' work.)

Following the questions and descriptions given (extract session 5), the students were easily able to identify the painting in the virtual art gallery and give Snoopy directions to the painting without any prompting from the teacher. As Childress and Braswell (2006) have argued, the virtual gallery provided the young language learners with an opportunity to observe how others interacted with the avatar (exposure to contextualized communicative events) as well as the possibility of exploring new elements (e.g., a virtual art gallery with famous paintings and the possibility of interaction with a fantasy figure – Snoopy) which are not easily available in real life.

Session 5: Students give description

Teacher: you have to describe this painting [. . .] top secret OK don't copy you (.) come Lara (.) come here (shows students the picture they have to describe). [. . .] you have to describe this painting (.) is it Rob Gonsalvez or Joan Abelló

Student: Rob Gonsalves

Teacher: Rob Gonsalves yes

(teacher helps the students formulate the description by showing them objects that they could name, e.g. rocks, beach, boys swimming. Students from the other team listen to the description and then have to ask questions for more information. Only one question was asked.)

[. ..]

Student from other team: What's the weather like?

Lara: It's cloudy

The use of the virtual art gallery also provided an excellent means of lexical repetition that did not become tiresome and repetitive for the learners and yet allowed them opportunities for 'incidental learning' of contextualized vocabulary, combined with the possibility of rehearsing the target language through oral comprehension and 'mini' sessions of social interaction – all suitable to their age and language level.

In the final session (in the third week), students took turns controlling the avatar (Figure 9.5), which meant that they were not only able to give instructions; they were able to comprehend instructions given to them.

Final session: Students control Snoopy

Teacher: Ethan (indicating Ethan's turn to give instructions to Snoopy)

Ethan: (whispers)

Teacher (repeating Ethan's answer for the rest of the class): Go left Snoopy

(Paula, manipulating the avatar, mouths 'left' as she moves Snoopy with the keyboard)

The researchers asked the teachers to keep an online diary during the whole process. The input was generally positive (see Figure 9.6).

However, to triangulate these data, these were then followed by interviews from which a general consensus emerged that student knowledge had been assimilated, not only in the specific subjects of each teacher but also in connection with other fields. This was correlated by questionnaires that the students had filled in at the end

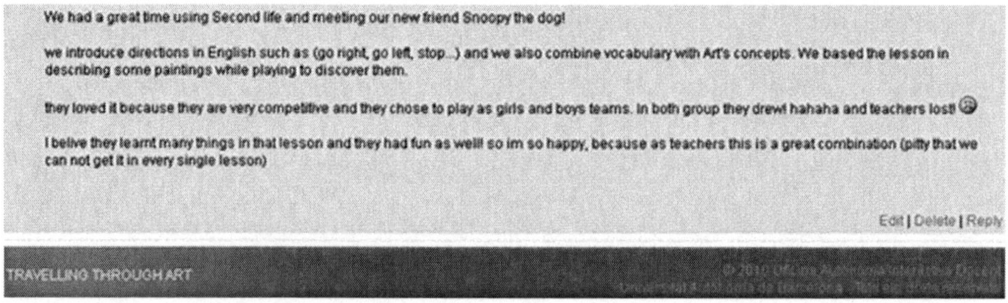

We had a great time using Second life and meeting our new friend Snoopy the dog!

we introduce directions in English such as (go right, go left, stop...) and we also combine vocabulary with Art's concepts. We based the lesson in describing some paintings while playing to discover them.

they loved it because they are very competitive and they chose to play as girls and boys teams. In both group they drew! hahaha and teachers lost!

I belive they learnt many things in that lesson and they had fun as well! so im so happy, because as teachers this is a great combination (pitty that we can not get it in every single lesson)

Edit | Delete | Reply

TRAVELLING THROUGH ART

FIGURE 9.6 *Extract from teacher's online diary.*

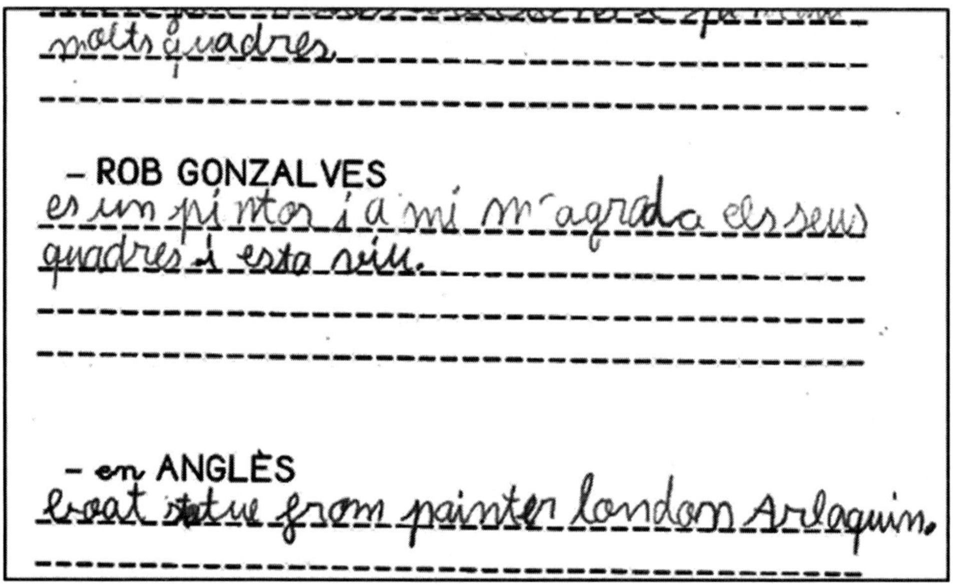

FIGURE 9.7 *Student self-evaluation sheet.*

of the telecollaborative exchange in which they had to answer the question: What did I learn? (see Figure 9.7).

Students were able to enumerate concepts, notions and specific knowledge related to both content and language (see transcriptions from compiled examples in Figure 9.8).

It is relevant to note the students' burgeoning intercultural competence as they are evidently beginning to recognize and situate 'the other' who lives at a great distance from them; a cognitively demanding task for children of 6. The development of social awareness can be complemented by language learning, as young children move away from a main interest in self to more social awareness of the other (McKay, 2006). For a young child, learning a foreign language implies venturing beyond their experiences in their first (or second) language towards new possibilities of identity and subjectivity

He conegut els nens de Canadà. Hi ha un pintor. Parlen en anglès i francès i es pot XXXXX[1] que hem fet un quadre per els nens de Canadà i és i maig i juny.

[I have met children from Canada. There is a painter. They speak English and French and you can XXXXX. We have made a painting for the children from Canada and it is May and June.]

Que són de molts països. Que parlen different i que hem treballat amb ells de Canadà. Que són de Toronto i de Canadà.

[They are from many countries. They speak differently and we have worked with them from Canada. They are from Toronto and from Canada.]

Que hi ha nens i nenes. Trabaja su pintor i van a una escola i juga al pati i dissabte i diumenge que no van.

[There are boys and girls. They work on their painter and go to a school and play on the playground and Saturday and Sunday they do not go.]

Parlen en angles molt rapid.

[They speak English very quickly.]

Ells jugan a futbòl.

[They play soccer.]

[1] XXXX: writing was illegible and exact word could not be deciphered.

FIGURE 9.8 *Example from compiled student evaluations.*

(Carr, 2003), as demonstrated by their use of English with the monolingual Snoopy and their understanding of the language varieties of their Canadian counterparts.

Still, language learning and introduction of intercultural competences in very young learners is not often interrogated and there is a need to delve more into what it means to young children to discover that there are other ways of speaking and communicating and that these ways are often linked to cultures with other values and symbols different from their own (Doyé & Hurrell, 1997). Given that VWs can be considered as yet another 'culture' when working with students to develop Intercultural Competences (Dooly, 2011), the ways in which VWs can contribute to this is also a venue for further exploration.

A month after the project had ended, the researchers returned to the classroom to see if the students could recall and apply some of the knowledge in contexts different from the ones where it was originally learned. One of the activities the students were asked to do was related to the learning associated with the Second Life virtual gallery. Students were given a map and asked to give the Harlequin[3] instructions on how to arrive to the local museum (Figure 9.9). The students were able to tell the researcher who was holding the pen and marking the trajectory on the map (see Figure 9.9) how to get to the museum, using contextualized language first learned and employed in the virtual gallery.

FIGURE 9.9 *Tracking of verbal directions on maps.*

As illustrated, some students were more successful with this task than others with the first student drawing a fairly direct route between the two points on the map while the second student took a more 'scenic' trip.

Session: Giving directions on a map

Researcher: First of all, can you take a red pen, a red pen

(Pau takes a red pen from box of coloured pens and looks at the researcher)

Researcher: perfect (.) write your name here (indicates place on the map)

(9 seconds pass while student writes name)

Researcher: now can I have the pen please (holds out hand; Pau hands her the pen)

Researcher: thank you (.) now look (.) here we have the harlequin (indicates the position of the harlequin in the map) here we have the museum (indicates museum on map)

[Researcher repeats instructions until certain of comprehension]

Researcher: so the harlequin is here what does he do?

Pau: uh Snoopy (.) go straight on

Researcher (repeats while tracing the map) go straight on

Pau: go straight on go straight on stop

Researcher: stop (draws a large dot where the 'harlequin' stops then turns map to help student maintain orientation) now let's look here what do we have? NOW we're here and we want to go where?

Pau: Snoopy go (.) ehm (looks at researcher) ehm (.) snoopy go left

(sequence continues in similar pattern until the harlequin 'reaches' the museum)

Pau shows comprehension of specific vocabulary related to concepts studied during the interaction with Snoopy in the virtual gallery (colours, giving directions, basic pedagogical instructions or classroom language) and is able to reiterate the contextualized language learned during the previous sessions. He even 'slips' into character and addresses the harlequin as Snoopy. Arguably, the telecollaborative PBLL exchange facilitated cognition within a larger social context as the young learner engaged with different online tools and virtual environments in order to construct new knowledge (see Figure 9.10).

Conclusions

Several researchers in language acquisition propose that cognition and learning processes must be understood within a paradigm that includes the individual, the

FIGURE 9.10 *Pau applies previously learned knowledge in new context.*

environment and the ways in which participants use tools/artefacts in the environment to assimilate new knowledge (Rüschoff & Ritter, 2001; Schwartz, 2008). This case study of young language learners (with beginners' knowledge of the target language) demonstrates the way in which the use of a VW environment helped create a complex interdependency between the young learners and various new technologies (as artefacts) in long-term and shared knowledge-building activities. The design of the interaction provided opportunities for the '5 Cs', as outlined by the American Council on Teaching of Foreign Languages for efficient language learning processes to take place: *communication* (i.e., students were able to practise oral production of the foreign language), *cultures* (i.e., students were given glimpses into new cultures – both virtual and real since the VW gallery provided insight into the Canadian artist's perspectives), *connections* (i.e., students were required to connect new language knowledge with other content such as art, geography, topography and technology), *comparisons* (i.e., students took first steps towards developing new insight into ways language can be used in online situations) and *communities* (i.e., the young language learners were 'safely' introduced into a new online community, which as described in the outline above is vastly multilingual and multicultural, as part of their classroom experience).

As demonstrated in this chapter, using a VW – even in a limited manner – has the potential to enrich the educational process in a number of important ways that are not possible in a traditional classroom. VWs also make it possible to create a single virtual space (in this case an art gallery) that has the potential to be used by partners in locations around the world. For very young language learning beginners, VWs can provide a highly engaging means to 'contrive a situation where young learners can use what language they have in a realistic, meaningful and communicative way' (Milton & Garbi, 2000, p. 287).

This chapter also demonstrates that this type of collaboration can be accomplished with relatively little money (the art gallery was set up using materials already in the possession of one of the researchers, with the only cost being the uploading of images of art materials (approximately US$1.50 total) and without the need for extensive technology. While this sort of collaboration has great potential when each student has access to a computer and an avatar (especially for more advanced participants), in this case only a single computer with an internet connection was required and a projector was used to 'bring' the students into the art gallery. If necessary, the students could have simply looked at the interaction on a regular computer monitor, though the larger screen was very effective.

As discussed earlier in this chapter, there has been relatively little research performed examining how language learners (whether young or older) use VWs in that process. Further research is necessary in order to help overcome the barriers mentioned previously. This means that this environment is wide open for future research, in both qualitative and quantitative methodologies. A quick glance at the numbers illustrates this point – VWs are increasingly more popular and are engaging for a wide range of ages and profiles – billions of users testify to that. The potential for language learning (informally, as highlighted by several researchers) as well as formally (as described here) is exponential and requires further research in the language learning and teaching processes. There are many areas and sub-areas of possible study: young language learners, adult language learners, communicative and intercultural competences, the influence of gender on interaction and language learning (real life and avatar gender), the use of VWs in blended learning environments, VWs and cross-disciplinary language learning and academic language learning in VWs, to name a few. Precisely because it is such a relatively new field and has had little exposure in more formal settings implies that much research has to be done. Inside VWs there are promising and innovating horizons for future researchers willing to explore this exciting new environment for language learning.

Notes

1 It is important to highlight that the project took place in a blended-learning environment and combined several activities that were not language-oriented: a field excursion to an art museum, a 'mini' unit on transportation and experiments with different artistic techniques.

2 Participants' names have been changed to protect their identity. Broad transcription has been used. (.) signifies approximately 1 second pause; _ indicates elongation of the last sound.

3 A well-known sculpture by the local artist.

References

Ball, S., & Pearce, R. (2009). Inclusion benefits and barriers of 'once removed' participation.

Bani, M., Genovesi, F., Ciregia, E., Piscioneri, F., Rapisarda, B., & Salvatori, E. (2009). Learning by creating historical buildings. In J. Molka-Danielsen & M. Deutschmann (Eds.), *Learning and teaching in the virtual world of Second Life* (pp. 125–44). Trondheim: Tapir Academic Press.

Barab, S. A., Hay, K. E., & Yamagata-Lynch, L. C. (2001). Constructing networks of action-relevant episode: An in situ research methodology. *The Journal of Learning Sciences, 10* (1/2), 36–112.

Brown, B., & Bell, M. (2004, November). *CSCW at play: 'There' as a collaborative virtual environment*. Paper presented at the 2004 ACM Conference on Computer Supported Cooperative Work, Chicago, Illinois.

Bugeja, M. (2007, 14 September). Second thoughts about Second Life. *The Chronicle of Higher Education*. Retrieved from http://chronicle.com/article/Second-Thoughts-About-Second/46636/

Bystrom, K. E., & Barfield, W. (1999). Collaborative task performance for learning using a virtual world. *Presence, 8*(4), 435–48.

Carr, J. (2003). Culture through the looking class: An intercultural experiment in sociolinguistics. In A. J. Liddicoat, S. Eisenchlas & S. Trevaskis (Eds.), *Australian perspectives on internationalising education* (pp. 75–86). Melbourne: Language Australia.

Chappell, B. (2011, April). 2011 social network analysis report – geographic – demographic and traffic data revealed. [Web log post]. Retrieved from www.ignitesocialmedia.com/social-media-stats/2011-social-network-analysis-report/#Habbo

Childress, M. D., & Braswell, R. (2006). Using massively multiplayer online role-playing games for online learning. *Distance Education,* 27(2), 187–96.

Churchill, E. F., & Snowdon, D. (1998). Collaborative virtual environments: An introductory review of issues and systems. *Virtual Reality, 3*, 3–15.

Dede, C., Clarke, J., Ketelhut, D., Nelson, B., & Bowman, C. (2006, April). *Fostering motivation, learning and transfer in multi-user virtual environments*. Paper presented at the 2006 AERA conference: San Francisco, CA.

Dillenbourg, P., Schneider, D., & Synteta, P. (2002, October). *Virtual learning environments*. Paper presented at the 3rd Hellenic Conference information & communication technologies in education. Rhodes: Greece.

Dooly, M. (2009). New competencies in a new era? Examining the impact of a teacher training project. *Recall, 21*(3), 352–69.

— (2011). Crossing the intercultural borders into 3rd space culture(s): Implications for teacher education in the twenty-first century. *Language and Intercultural Communication, 11*(4), 319–37.

Dooly, M., & Hauck, M. (2012). Researching multimodal communicative competence in video and audio telecollaborative encounters. In M. Dooly & R. O'Dowd (Eds.),

Researching online interaction and exchange in foreign language education: Methods and issues (pp. 134–60). Bern: Peter Lang.

Doyé, P., & Hurrell, A. (Eds.) (1997). *Foreign language education in primary schools (age 5/6 to 10/11). Language policies.* Council for Cultural Co-operation of the Council of Europe. Strasbourg: Council of Europe Press.

Faivre, S. (2009). *ESL online, a curriculum project: How to wire students to today's educational grid using Second Life and other internet resources* (Unpublished MA Thesis). The University of Illinois at Urbana-Champaign.

KZERO. (2011). KZERO Worldwide. Retrieved 15 November 2011, from www.kzero.co.uk/#

Love, E., Ross, S. C., & Wilhelm, W. (2009). Opportunities and challenges for business education in Second Life. In C. Wankel, & J. Kingsley (Eds.), *Higher education in virtual worlds: Teaching and learning in Second Life* (pp. 65–82). Bingley: Emerald.

Markee, N. (2008). Toward a learning behavior tracking methodology for CA-for-SLA. *Applied Linguistics, 29*, 404–27.

— (2011). Doing, and justifying doing, avoidance. *Journal of Pragmatics, 43*, 602–15.

McKay, P. (2006). *Assessing young language learners.* Cambridge: Cambridge University Press.

Merchant, G. (2007). Writing the future. *Literacy, 41*(3), 1–19.

Milton, J., & Garbi, A. (2000). VIRLAN: Collaborative foreign language learning on the internet for primary age children: Problems and a solution. *Educational Technology & Society, 3*(3), 286–92. mmorpg.com. (2010, 20 November 2011). MMORPG. Retrieved 20 January 2011, from www.mmorpg.com/

Molka-Danielsen, J., & Deutschmann, M. (Eds.) (2009). *Learning and teaching in the virtual* world of Second Life. Trondheim: Tapir Academic Press.

Panichi, L., & Deutschmann, M. (2012). Language learning in Virtual Worlds – Research issues and methods. In M. Dooly & R. O'Dowd (Eds.), *Researching online interaction and exchange in FL education* (pp. 206–33). Telecollaboration in Education Series. Bern: Peter Lang.

Pechar, E. (2008). *Virtual worlds and education.* Office of Policy Analysis and Research, Georgia Tech Research Institute.

Price, S., & Rogers, Y. (2004). Let's get physical: The learning benefits of interacting in digitally augmented physical spaces. *Computers and Education, 43*, 137–51.

Roussou, M. (2004). Learning by doing and learning through play: An exploration of interactivity in virtual environments for children. *AMC Computers in Entertainment, 2* (1), 1–23.

Rüschoff, B., & Ritter, M. (2001). Technology-enhanced language learning: Construction of knowledge and template-based learning in the foreign language classroom. *Computer Assisted Language Learning, 14*, 219–32.

Sadler, R. (May, 2009a). *Strange new worlds: Opportunities and cautions in virtual world research.* Keynote Address at Illinois Language and Linguistics Society 1: Language Online, University of Illinois at Urbana-Champaign, Urbana, IL.

— (2009b). Can you build this? Virtual construction for language learning in Second Life. In L. Stone & C. Wilson-Duff (Eds.), *Task-based III: Expanding the range of tasks with online resources* (pp. 212–26). IALT.

— (2011). *Virtual worlds and language learning: From theory to practice.* Volume 2. Telecollaboration in education. Bern: Peter Lang.

Schwartz, N. (2008). Exploiting the use of technology to teach: The value of distributed cognition. *Journal of Research on Technology in Education, 40*(3), 389–404.

Shaffer, D. W., Squire, K. R., Halverson, R., & Gee, J. P. (2004). *Video games and the future of learning.* Madison: University of Wisconsin-Madison and Academic Advanced Distributed Learning Co-Laboratory.

Silberman, S. (1997, March). Physics in the 1960s: PLATOFest. Retrieved from http://physics.illinois.edu/history/PLATOfest.asp

Sinclair, J., & Coulthard, M. (1992). Towards an analysis of discourse. In M. Coulthard (Ed.), *Advances in spoken discourse analysis* (pp. 1–34). London: Routledge.

Skiba, D. J. (2007). Nursing education 2.0: Second Life. *Nursing Education Perspectives, 28*(3), 156–7.

Squires, K. (2002). 'Cultural Framing of Computer/Video Games' Game Studies available at http://gamestudies.org/0102/squire/ last accessed 12th May, 2007.

Steinkuehler, C. A. (2004). *Learning in massively multiplayer online games.* Paper presented at the International Conference on Learning Sciences, Santa Monica, California.

Thorne, S. L. (2008). Transcultural communication in open internet environments and massively multiplayer online games. In S. Sieloff Magnan (Ed.), *Mediating discourse online* (pp. 305–27). Amsterdam: John Benjamins.

Vygotsky, L. (1978). *Mind in society: The development of higher mental processes.* Cambridge: Harvard.

Wankel, C., & Kingsley, J. (Eds.) (2009). *Higher education in virtual worlds: Teaching and learning in Second Life* (pp. 47–63). Bingley: Emerald Group Publishing Limited.

Weinbaum, S. (1935). Pygmalion's Spectacles. *Wonder stories:* Project Gutenberg. Retrieved 15 July 2010, from www.gutenberg.org/etext/22893

10

Digital games and language learning

Chun Lai, Ruhui Ni and Yong Zhao

Summary

The emergence of digital games has elevated game-based language learning to a new level. In this chapter we first review innovative uses of stand-alone video games, commercial massive multi-player role playing-games (MMORPGs) and 3D collaborative virtual environments in language learning. We examine issues of pedagogical adaptation of these three types of commerical off the shelf game (COTS), and highlight the importance of aligning the selection of the COTS with the intended instructional purposes. We also note the importance of providing appropriate pedagogical support to maximize learning in gaming environments. We assess design issues for serious educational language learning games and simulations, such as balancing entertaining and learning and fitting the game into educational contexts. We conclude the chapter with a discussion on the future development of digital game-based language learning and potential research directions.

Introduction

Games and simulations have been considered valuable in language teaching for their potential to enable experiential and discovery learning, transform drill-based learning to context-based acquisition and lower affective filters (Crookall, 2007; Sorensen & Meyer, 2007; Tomlinson & Masuhara, 2009; Wright, Betteridge & Buckby, 2006). The emergence of digital games, especially recent developments in MMORPGs and social virtual spaces, has elevated game-based language learning to a new level by extending games from the physical arena to the virtual context. The claimed benefits of games have been further expanded: that goal-directed tasks/quests in digital games enable task-based language teaching (Peterson, 2010a; Purushotma, Thorne & Wheatley, 2009); that increased needs for collaboration encourage the development of collaborative social relationships and collaborative learning (Dalgarno & Lee, 2010; Peterson, 2010a); that masking of identity of the learners reduces anxiety and encourages greater risk-taking and creative use of language (Rankin, McNeal, Shute & Gooch, 2008; Shih & Yang, 2008); and that cohesive and meaningful contexts create situated and immersive learning experience (Chen & Huang, 2010; Gee, 2008).

The language education field has been quick to seize the various benefits of digital games for language learning. Recent years have seen a great number of initiatives and the innovative use of various genres of digital games, as well as the creative use of gaming for language learning. These initiatives are based either on the adaption of COTS or on specifically designed educational language learning games and simulations. In this chapter, we will first review examples of innovative digital game-based learning, then examine issues around the pedagogical adaption of COTS and the design of educational language learning games and simulations, and conclude with a discussion on the future development of digital game-based language learning and research directions.

Emerging initiatives on digital game-based learning

Traditional stand-alone video games, such as PS2 music games, adventure games and interactive fiction games, have continued to be used to enhance language development (Chen & Huang, 2010; Chen & Yang, 2011; deHaan, Reed & Kuwada, 2010; Lu, Lou, Papa & Chung, 2011; Ranalli, 2008). Innovative uses of digital gaming techniques are also emerging. For instance, Wii technology has been used for Chinese character learning (Hao et al., 2010), and video-capture virtual reality techniques have been used to enable physical interactions with virtual objects in English learning games (Yang, Chen & Jeng, 2010). There are also innovative pedagogical uses of extant games and gaming concepts for language learning. For instance, Catel (2008) imported characters from a French novel into the simulation game, the Sims, and engaged students in acting out the everyday life of these characters in the gaming environment. A European Commission Comenius Project entitled, *ARGuing for Multilingual Motivation in Web 2.0*, borrowed the concept of Alternate Reality Game, a game genre originally used as a marketing tool, and used Moodle as the multilingual gaming platform to engage 14–16-year-old students from 6 European countries in solving quests or puzzles collaboratively. In the process of co-questing, students searched information online, engaged in cross-cultural and multilingual communications, and updated narratives, videos, blogs that represent themselves and their respective cultures (Connolly, Stansfield & Hainey, 2011).

In addition to stand-alone digital games, commercial MMORPGs, such as *World of Warcraft* and *Ever Quest II* (Oliver & Carr, 2009; Rankin, Gold & Gooch, 2006; Rankin, McNeal et al., 2008 ; Thorne, 2008) and extant 3D collaborative virtual environments, such as *Second Life* and *Active Worlds* (Deutschmann, Panichi & Molka-Danielsen, 2009; Koenraad, 2008), have been increasingly adapted to create immersive language and culture learning experience. For instance, *World of Warcraft* (WoW) has been used for a distance-learning project that connected middle school EFL learners in China and US English-speaking graduate students to enhance the learners' English communicative abilities (Waters, 2007). Tasks or cross-cultural quests have been designed in 3D collaborative virtual environments, such as *Active Worlds* and *Quest Atlantis*, to engage monolingual or tandem language learners in collaborative language and culture learning (Peterson, 2006; Zheng, Young, Wagner & Brewer, 2009). In addition, various approaches have been initiated to integrate the use of commercial social virtual spaces into classroom language teaching. Examples include supplementing in-class grammar instruction and communicative activities with out-of-class co-questing on *Second Life* (Clark, 2008), using open-source 3D virtual environment development software such as *OpenSim* to create interesting scenario-based tasks that align with the language curriculum (Chen & Su, 2011), and engaging students to co-create a virtual space within *Second Life* based on a novel they are studying (Balkun, Zedeck & Trotta, 2009).

Adapting extant games and gaming environments is one approach to capitalize on the potentials of digital games for language learning. Educators are also developing 3D serious gaming environments to foster various aspects of language development. For example, a 3D multi-user virtual environment, *Croquelandia*, has been developed to facilitate Spanish interlanguage pragmatic development and to enhance metapragmatic strategies (Sykes, 2009; Sykes & Cohen, 2009). A Web-based MMORPG, *Zon*, creates an immersive learning experience for Chinese-as-Second-Language learners (Zhao & Lai, 2009). Moreover, the use of intelligent tutoring systems to construct immersive learning environments for cross-cultural learning has also been developing quickly. Often cited examples are *Tactical Language and Culture Training System* (Johnson, 2007; Johnson & Wu, 2008) and *ELECT BiLAT*, where learners are confronted with embodied pedagogical agents to negotiate culture-embedded tasks. Educators are not only developing online serious language learning gaming environments, but also combining these virtual environments with Web 2.0 tools to capitalize on the affordances of various interaction formats for language learning. For instance, the *International NIAFLAR Project* (Network Interaction in Foreign Language Acquisition and Research Project) blended a video Web conferencing environment and a 3D virtual environment for better communication purposes. The *VEC3D* project connected a researcher-constructed virtual world and webpage as an in-group interaction platform with open virtual worlds, *Active Worlds* and *Second Life*, for access to the target language and community (Shih, 2010).

Thus, the burgeoning field of digital games and language education yields a rich repertoire of innovative use of digital games for language learning. How to make the most out of such environments then becomes the focal attention. In the section below, we will examine current research findings on the adaption of COTS.

Adaption of commercial off the shelf (COTS) games

Language educators have been adapting three types of commercial digital platforms for language learning: video games, MMORPGs and collaborative virtual environments. These three types of commercial digital platforms have proven to possess different affordances for language learning.

Learning from COTS

Commercial stand-alone video games have been used for language learning for decades (Coleman, 1990; Taylor, 1990). Studies have found that playing commercial video games are beneficial to vocabulary learning and for improving listening and reading ability, but not for enhancing speaking and writing skills due to the fact that stand-alone video games do not offer communication opportunities and usually demand physical responses, rather than spoken and written output, for game procession (Chen & Huang, 2010; Chen & Yang, 2011; Lu et al., 2011). The benefits on vocabulary learning are most agreed-upon and have been consistently found across different types of games, including the Sims (Ranalli, 2008), PS2 music games (deHaan et al., 2010), adventure games (Chen & Yang, 2011), interactive fiction games (Neville, Shelton & McInnis, 2009), and the benefits come from the strong contextual and visual cues found in the games (Purushotma, 2005; Schaffer, Squire, Halverson & Gee, 2005). In terms of the relative advantage of different game genres, adventure games have been recommended highly for language learning due to their rich oral and written input, repeated use of vocabulary and sentences and the centrality of textual understanding to the gameplay (Chen & Huang, 2010; Lu et al., 2011). For instance, Lu et al. (2011) found that playing an adventure game, *Alice is Dead*, helped improve university EFL students' reading skills and enhance their reading efficacy. Chen and Yang (2011) provided an adventure game, *Bone*, to their EFL university students to play outside the class and students reported playing the game increased their listening, reading and vocabulary skills.

MMORPGs provide immersive language and cultural learning experience with rich embodiment of actions and concepts (Thorne, Black & Sykes, 2009) and bring human–human interaction into the game (Sykes, Reinhardt & Thorne, 2010). Its challenge/adventure structure naturally provides an organic context for task-based language learning (Rankin et al., 2006), and the theme-based gameplay provides abundant opportunities for recycling vocabulary and grammatical structure. Gaming together with native speakers and learners from different countries increases the opportunities to develop communicative competence and cross-cultural knowledge (Peterson, 2010b). The most researched MMORPGs for language learning are *World of Warcraft* and *Ever Quest II*. Similar to stand-alone video games, MMORPGs are reported to benefit vocabulary learning, reading and writing (Bytheway, 2011; Rankin, Morrison, McNeal, Gooch & Shute, 2009; Roy, 2007). Suh, Kim and Kim (2010) carried out a large-scale two-month experimental study on the effects of MMORPGs. 118 elementary EFL learners were taught with an English online RPG, *Nori School*, in two 40-minute class sessions per week, whereas the 102 counterparts were taught in regular face-to-face classrooms. The MMORPG group was found to outperform the traditional group in listening, writing and reading. In contrast to stand-alone video games, the affordances of human–human interactions in MMOPRGs lend themselves to fostering communicative competence and pragmatic socialization (Palmer, 2010; Thorne, 2008): MMORPG elicits extensive target language outputs and beneficial forms of interaction (Rankin et al., 2009; Thorne, 2008) and induces a variety of speech acts (Rankins et al., 2009) and socioemotional talk (Peña & Hancock, 2006). MMORPGs are also found to foster collaborative trans-cultural and multilingual relationships (Sykes et al., 2010; Thorne, 2008) and encourage a long-term commitment to language learning (Roy, 2007).

With the virtual embodiment of human agents and the support of human–human interaction, 3D collaborative virtual environments share some common advantages for language learning with MMORPGs in fostering communicative competence and pragmatic socialization. At the same time, they also differ from MMORPGs in that they provide a configurable universe with no embedded gameplay, which grants teachers and students the freedom to customize their own learning environments and experience as well as the objectives and goals of play in such environments. This freedom makes it easier to align learning in such environments with existent language curriculum, and the lack of embedded gameplay lends itself well to support deep levels of communication, collaboration and relationship building (Dalgarno & Lee, 2010; Lee & Hoadley, 2007; Yee & Bailenson, 2007). The collaborative learning experience in virtual environments has also been found to enhance language learners' self-efficacy (Henderson, Huang, Grant & Henderson, 2009; Zheng et al., 2009).

Therefore, current experimentation with the three types of COTS has suggested that different COTS hold different affordances for language learning and could be used to serve different purposes of language education. At the same time, researchers have cautioned that careful pedagogical considerations and instructional strategies are key to harnessing their potential since these commercial digital platforms were not originally designed for language learning (Kim, Park & Baek, 2009).

Pedagogical considerations in adapting COTS

To ensure successful integration of commercial digital gaming platforms into language learning and teaching, educators must take into account how to get learners ready for gameplay and for learning, how to build seamless connections between the games and the language curriculum, and how to configure optimal gameplaying conditions. In the case of 3D collaborative virtual environments, task design is also a crucial pedagogical consideration.

Playing digital games requires sophisticated technical and metacognitive skills that are often found lacking among students (Chen, 2010), and thus scaffolding of both gameplay and language learning is crucial. Scaffolding of gameplay includes:

1. discussing tips for gameplay and providing lists of objectives at different stages to keep students from getting overwhelmed or lost as a result of the freedom of action found in most digital gaming platforms (Neville et al., 2009);
2. familiarizing students with the chaotic turn-takings in MMORPGs and collaborative virtual worlds and discussing strategies to deal with the unique conversational patterns and discourse feature in such environments (Örngren Berglund, 2006);
3. familiarizing students with the unique culture and conventions of social behaviour and interactions in the multi-user gaming environments and helping them build a repertoire of communication strategies to ensure successful interactions both during the gameplay and in offline contexts (Sykes et al., 2010); and
4. giving students meta-cognitive training to raise their awareness of the affordances of a particular virtual environment (Deutschmann et al., 2009; Neville et al., 2009) and equip them with gaming and learning strategies. For instance, Kim, Park and Baek (2009) trained 117 ninth-graders on three meta-cognitive strategies specific to gameplaying (self-recording; modelling and thinking aloud) to support their interaction with a MMORPG, *Gersang*, and found that training of the three meta-cognitive strategies contributed to both students' achievement in learning and game performance.

Scaffolding gameplay gives learners a smooth and enjoyable gaming experience, but a fun gaming experience does not necessarily guarantee language learning. Since commercial digital platforms were designed originally for entertainment and not for language learning in specific, students, when immersed in play, are very likely to overlook important information such as potential language learning opportunities (Rankin et al., 2008). Thus pedagogical scaffolding is essential and can be provided at the pre-, during- and post-play stages. A pre-play orientation session both on the gameplay and the difficult words that appear in the game is recommended, especially for lower-proficiency learners (Bryant, 2007; Chen & Huang, 2010; Rankin et al., 2006). For learners with relatively limited language proficiency, encouraging active participation and training on compensation strategies are also needed since those learners usually lack the confidence and motivation to actively use the target language to communicate with others (Shih & Yang, 2008). The during-play scaffolding could take the form of easy access to emergent language support (Rankin et al., 2006) and of teachers' supportive linguistic behaviour to increase learner engagement (Deutschmann et al., 2009). For instance, Bryant (2007) supported his German 101 students' co-questing in *WoW* by leading them to work together to interpret the narrative text of each quest prior to the gameplay and then providing unobtrusive corrections and explanations when necessary during the gameplay.

In addition to pre- and during-play scaffolding, a post-play collaborative debriefing session on learning out of the gaming experience is extremely important (Bryant, 2007; Chen & Huang, 2010). Thorne and Reinhardt (2008) proposed the 'bridging activities' model where the digital texts and practices generated during the gaming experience are brought to class discussions to raise critical awareness of the social practices and language used in a particular digital context and encourage the application of the critical awareness vis-à-vis language socialization in different communication contexts.

Another important element in enhancing learning with gaming is to strengthen the connection between the game and the curriculum so as to make gaming part of a holistic learning experience. Such integration could be achieved by including the game as part of a graded assignment and/or through in-class guided reflections on the gaming experience, and the strategies students used during play (Chen & Huang, 2010; Neville et al., 2009). Integration also could be achieved by aligning the gaming elements with the curricular topics and targeted communicative functions (Chen & Su, 2011; Oliver & Carr, 2009). A deeper reaching measure is to build a task-based curriculum around the game, and use quests or lines of quests as 'orthogonal units' in the curriculum where pre-tasks can be centred around the narrative of a particular quest, the task stage would be the in-game questing, and the post-task stage would involve students in reporting on the quests and their questing experience (Sykes et al., 2010).

Optimizing gameplaying conditions is yet another way to enhance learning in gaming environments. Collaborative play with stand-alone video games and co-questing in online gaming environments are important since playing a game collaboratively creates heightened attention to language and the opportunities for co-construction of knowledge about the language. Piirainen-Marsh and Tainio (2009) observed two 13-year-old boys playing an action adventure game, *Final Fantasy X*, and found that the boys used frequent lexical and prosodic repetition to co-construct their understanding, enjoyment and experience of the game. Interaction with native speakers in MMORPGs or virtual worlds proves beneficial to learning and helps sustain players' interest in the game. Rankin et al.s' (2008) study on advanced ESL learners' experience in *Ever Quest II* found that playing together with native speakers produced significantly greater learning than playing the game alone. Furthermore, students were found to benefit both from interacting directly with and in the game and from watching the gameplay. Interacting with the game directly fosters embodied learning whereas watching gameplay induces heightened attention to language. DeHann, Reed and Kuwada (2010) did an interesting comparative study on the effect of game interactivity on vocabulary learning and found that students who watched peers playing the game actually gained more than those who only played the game. Thus, alternating different formats of the game, from participation to watching, is a sound and helpful approach.

Since 3D collaborative virtual environments leave the construction of learning experience to the users, task or quest design must be considered when adapting such environments for language learning (Chen, 2010; Deutschmann et al., 2009). To make the gaming experience in 3D collaborative virtual environments interesting, researchers have advocated combining and balancing different types of tasks/quests. Sykes, Reinhardt and Thorne (2010) suggested combining tasks that provide improvised and open-ended play, tasks that provide rule-bound play and tasks that engage competition. Deutschmann et al. (2009) recommended the use of a repertoire of tasks that target the social-communicative dimension, the creative-cultural dimension and the physical dimension respectively. Some tasks they recommended are: conversation tasks on personal issues as well as more complex issues; tasks in which learners build or create a joint piece of work or an object; tasks that engage students in the exploration of cultural identity and cross-cultural sensitive issues; and tasks that involve physical movements such as scavenger hunts, tours around a place, asking or giving directions. Tasks that are authentic, challenging and relevant to learners' life are found to be more effective (Deutschmann et al., 2009). Thus, designing some open-ended tasks that leave room for the incorporation of student-contributed ideas, problems and texts may make the learning experience more meaningful to the learners. Researchers have further pointed out that tasks/quests of looser rather than tighter structure might work better and that tasks/quests that encourage learner community are central to the learning experience (Deutschmann et al., 2009).

The key issues related to the adaption of COTS for language learning involve striking a balance between the selection of COTS and the intended instructional purposes and making appropriate pedagogical arrangements that provide the support required to maximize the learning arising of the gaming experience. The design of serious educational language learning games involves considering quite different issues such as balancing entertaining and learning in the game and fitting the game to the educational contexts.

Design of serious educational language learning games

Designing games for educational purposes remains challenging; the games must maintain a strong and playful character while at the same time integrating a clear pedagogical rationale. Thus striking the right balance between entertaining and learning is a key issue in the design of serious educational language learning games. However, designing a perfect game with the right combination of play and learning does not naturally guarantee its smooth implementation in educational contexts (Rice, 2007). The successful implementation of a serious language learning game relies heavily on the negotiation between the game and the particular instructional context. In this section, we will use the design and implementation of *Zon*, a MMORPG for Chinese language learning, as an example to illustrate these two issues in some depth.

Zon, a Chinese language learning MMORPG

Zon is a MMORPG specifically designed and developed for learning Chinese as a second language. It provides a game-based immersive Chinese learning environment in which the players engage in real-life quests to advance their identity in the gaming world (from tourist to resident, to citizen) and pick up language and cultural knowledge along the way. The overall goal of playing *Zon* is to advance socially and economically in this virtual world, just as people do in real life (see Zhao & Lai, 2009 for more information). The beta version of *Zon* was released to the public in April 2008 and an upgraded version of *Zon* 1.0 appeared in September 2009. In Spring 2010, *Zon* launched its K-12 school program that targeted students from upper elementary through lower high school level. As of Fall 2011, more than ten *Zon* servers have been set up in schools to support Chinese enrichment program and Chinese as foreign language courses for K-12 schools across the country.

Since its debut in K-12 Chinese classes, the *Zon* development team has been collecting feedback from students, teachers and *Zon* tutors.[1] Our discussion in this section is based on *Zon* tutors' feedback, discussions with school teachers, and interviews with students. Based on user feedback, *Zon* developers are making constant adjustments to the game design to create a better fit between the game and the K-12 instructional context. In the section below, we will discuss some of the lessons *Zon* development team learned about the design of serious language learning games to use in the K-12 context.

Fuse learning seamlessly with play

The primary challenge facing the design of serious language learning games is to strike the right balance between instruction and gameplay (Kiili, 2005; Neville et al., 2009). Some advocate keeping the instructional contents in gameplay to a minimum and leaving that to be dealt with outside the gaming environment, that is, on a game-related website or in the classroom (Neville et al., 2009). Others recommend seamlessly integrating learning into the gameplay by embedding the learning content as cognitive scaffolds for play (Johnson, 2007; Rankin et al., 2008; Sykes et al., 2010). Sykes, Reinhardt and Thorne (2010) recommend structuring learning content as skills and knowledge players must acquire for continued advancement in the game. This is the approach that *Zon* adopts to fuse learning and play. To play *Zon*, players need to solve various real-life quests to progress from 'tourists' to 'residents' and finally to 'citizens'. Communicative skills and cultural knowledge are resources that players need to pick up along the way to help them advance. For each quest, relevant learning content is placed right next to the quest at a click's distance so that students can access the learning content at any time. Rankin et al. (2008) further suggest providing the instructional content as game plug-ins to provide emergent language support to facilitate the gameplay. An example they give is to provide chat prompts with references on relevant expressions and explanations on conversation conventions to assist students' social interactions associated with game activities. *Zon* realizes this emergent support through using non-player characters (NPCs) and tutors to direct the players to the requested learning content when they get stuck in play. Furthermore, *Zon* seamlessly integrates learning into play by designing game failure states as genuine consequences of communication failures (Sykes et al., 2010). For instance, if the player fails the currency exchange communication at the bank, s/he will not get any money for use in the game.

Fit the game design to the K-12 instructional context

Digital games, even when they have been designed specifically for learning, do not fit naturally into the instructional context. Rice (2007) identified six barriers to classroom implementation of educational video games. Some barriers reside in the stakeholders' negative perceptions about digital games and learning. Some barriers come from constraints in the school context (e.g., the unsupportive information infrastructure at the school; limited instructional time in school periods). Other barriers originate in the game design itself (e.g., the affordances of the gaming environment do not fully support the desired learning objectives at school or the learning objectives in the game do not align well with the state and local standards the school observes). Thus, to ensure adoption of the game in the instructional context, various constraints in school context need to be taken considered.

Enhance the adaptability of the game to K-12 context

The adoption of a game in the classroom relies on the ease of its adaptability to the classroom instructional context. Deubel (2002) stressed that a game needs to possess the 'capabilities for dynamic teacher adjustments' in order to ensure its widespread adoption in the school context. To facilitate the dynamic teacher adjustments, a game may need to consist of a large amount of small episodes that target short learning objectives so that teachers could easily identify and integrate the episodes that align with a given instructional purpose for a certain day. *Zon* consists of a number of mini-tasks in each game scene, and, the mini-tasks are related but relatively independent. For instance, the airport scene consists of mini-tasks such as buying food or drinks at the snack store, exchanging currency at the bank, picking up luggage, making transportation arrangements, clearing customs and so on. Teachers can easily fit individual mini-tasks with specific instructional purposes. To further ease teachers' alignment of the mini-tasks with their classroom teaching objectives, a content map was introduced upon teachers' request, with all the mini-tasks labelled with targeted communicative functions and colour-coded according to difficulty levels. The communicative functions and the set-up of difficulty levels align with the state and local standards. Furthermore, the learning objectives are often kept small in scope so that they can be finished within a typical class period (Rice, 2007).

Restructure the game to meet K-12 institutional needs

Zon is designed to be a MMORPG that fosters transcultural and translingual interactions for language learning (Zhao & Lai, 2009). To realize this affordance, the game world needs to be open to the public to attract native speakers and learners of different cultures and linguistic backgrounds. However, when *Zon* was introduced to the K-12 context, concerns for students' privacy and safety led school administrators to request that the *Zon* school server be open only to the students within the school. Thus the envisioned open world had to be closed to meet K-12 institutional needs; this change greatly sacrificed a major contribution of MMORPG for language learning – transcultural and translingual interactions. To remedy the situation, the *Zon* development team had to recruit Chinese-speaking *Zon* tutors into the game to create the much-needed multicultural interaction opportunities.

Enhance the affordances of the game to support K-12 learner needs

Research studies show that the availability of sufficient scaffolding and guidance to prevent players from becoming overwhelmed is key to the success of a game, especially when adopted in the educational context (de Freitas, 2006; Frank, 2007; Kebritchi, 2010; Kenny & Gunter, 2011; Rice, 2007). In-game scaffolding mechanisms help players to play the game smoothly, take initiatives in creating language learning opportunities and tune in to the emergent language learning opportunities (Neville et al., 2009). To achieve in-game scaffolding, Neville et al. (2009) proposed incorporating embedded narrative as cognitive scaffolding for gameplay to supplement with the emergent narrative of the game. These embedded narratives could be in the form of 'prerendered or interactive' cut-scenes to direct players through the game environment or in the form of resources to help players get through a game quest.

The *Zon* development team's experience with *Zon* implementation in K-12 context supports the argument that balance must be achieved between emergent narrative and embedded narrative in game design (Dickey, 2007; Neville et al., 2009). When it was first piloted at a school to support the Chinese learning of about 40 5th–8th graders, *Zon* had an open-ended, overarching game narrative with only three major cut-scenes defined by players' game identities (tourist, resident and citizen). Players had unrestricted access to various game regions and scenes within each cut-scene and were immersed in a vast amount of quests and learning resources. Shortly after its school début, teachers and students complained about feeling overwhelmed by the freedom of exploration and felt at a loss about which quests to pick and enact. Students felt disoriented and expressed frustrations over too many quest choices.

Some of the most frequently asked questions from students in the computer lab were 'What's next?', 'What should I do now?'. Some students, frustrated at the complexity of the game environment, simply withdrew to repeat a limited number of quests with which they were already familiar to earn game rewards rather than continuing with the gameplay. These experiences showed that too wide an array of choices was overwhelming and to some extent demotivating to the K-12 students (Dickey, 2007). Students needed structure built into the game to scaffold them through the gameplay. To remedy the situation, an embedded narrative was built in: within each major cut-scene (e.g., the tourist world), sub-cut-scenes were added where players had to finish one sub-cut-scene (e.g., the airport) before moving on to another while preserving the emergent narrative within each sub-cut-scene. To provide further gameplay support, suggested lines of quests were built within each sub-cut-scene so that the storyline was unrolled gradually as players finished one quest after another. Optional quests were also available for players' free exploration to gain experience points. Furthermore, for each quest, a quest management tool bar was built to provide relevant background information and instructions on the locations of relevant language content for the quest, and to present visual displays so that the players would have a clear idea of the gaming objectives. Thus, instead of throwing the players directly into an intricate and strange world, an embedded narrative was built to scaffold their gameplay. This modification resulted in a drastic decline of complaints about disorientation and frustration. The enquiries to the *Zon* tutors were no longer on gameplay but rather requests for language support. One of the returning students, who had participated in the previous version of *Zon* told a tutor that: 'this is much better than what I had last year. Last year, I spent a lot of time to find the right task. There were too many of them . . . I had to ask tutors where is the next step. It took so much time to figure out by myself. But now I play at home too, because I know what to do'. Further, the gradual revelation of the gameplay served as a motivator to continue playing as students were eager to find out what challenge was waiting for them next.

In this section, we used *Zon* as an example to illustrate the two key issues around the design of serious language learning games: the seamless integration of learning and play and the accommodation of the affordances and constraints in the target educational context. Although we have identified the specific tension between ideal game design and the complexity of how to implement Zon in the K-12 educational context, we believe the lessons we learned actually apply more broadly to all educational contexts. Each context has its particular affordance and constraints that impact significantly on the game design.

Future development and research directions

The use of digital games in language learning, although developing quickly, is still a relatively young field. At this stage, the discipline's development is intertwined with research on the discipline itself. Current research has mainly focused on exploring the various affordances of digital games for language learning. To advance the field further, more systematic research on various issues related to the adaption of COTS and the design and the implementation of serious language learning games is needed.

Research on digital games and simulations has focused on understanding the cognitive and affective effects of digital games on language learners to establish their legitimacy in language learning. Evidence has been mounting on the positive effects of digital games on the affective domain, learning outcomes and social interaction. However, current evidence has relied heavily on retrospective self-report data from short-term studies, which is subject to a novelty effect (Hew & Cheung, 2010). Researchers are advocating broadening the scope of research to tap into the actual gaming process, such as the language learning strategies students employ when playing digital games (Lee & Key, 2008) and learner autonomy development in gameplay (Chik, 2011), and to understand how digital games foster and shape 'emerging social practices' for language learning through both in-gameplay and offline social activities around the gameplay (Sykes et al., 2010). Researchers also are calling for investigations into the effects of sociocultural factors on digital game-based language learning (Hew & Cheung, 2010; Thomas, 2011) and urging for longitudinal studies to examine the long-term effects of digital game-based learning (Hew & Cheung, 2010).

Research into game design is crucial but unfortunately still in its infancy. The design of digital game and simulation environments for language learning faces the challenge of several contentious relationships: the tension between scaffolding play and learning through imposing structures on gameplay and granting players personal agency and individual choice (i.e., embedded narrative vs emergent narrative in gameplay) (Neville et al., 2009); and the tension between fostering a flow experience through fun play and drawing learners' attention to instructional content (i.e., entertainment vs education) (Killi, 2005). Although various propositions have been put forth to balance the relationships (Neville et al., 2009; Sykes et al., 2010) systematic empirical studies are needed to examine and advance these propositions. Issues at the design of individual quest level also await evidence-based guidance. Such issues include the distribution of learning resources and instructional content within the questing structure, the feedback mechanisms and the reward systems (Sykes et al., 2010). Moreover, as facilitation and scaffolding strategies for language learning within a digital game are acknowledged as essential to its language learning potential, the kinds of facilitation and scaffolding strategies required need to be informed by research. Types of in-game learning supports might include on-demand cultural tips, pragmatic hints and language models, running collections of language and culture items acquired, and various focus-on-form techniques in learning resources and instructional contents. Future research studies are needed to investigate the effectiveness of various in-game facilitation and scaffolding strategies. When designing a game, we need guidance not only on maximizing the language learning potential of the game, but also on increasing its adoption in language classrooms. Deubel (2002) pointed out that to enhance the likelihood of a game being adopted as an instructional component in classrooms, a digital game needs to 'provide capabilities for dynamic teacher adjustments' (p. 257). An examination of various ways to provide such flexible adjustments in different instructional contexts is important to advance the adoption of serious language learning games in educational contexts.

Game implementation in language classrooms is another crucial area of research that awaits exploration. Although the general literature on educational games has provided some useful suggestions for effective implementation of digital games in classrooms (Rice, 2007), guidance at the pedagogical level is still lacking. The nature and levels of learner preparation and pedagogical scaffolding prior to, during and after gameplay and the approaches to learner training deserve a lot of attention (Chen, 2010; Lee & Key, 2008). Different instructional arrangements in aligning games with the language curriculum, such as the settings of game use and the strategies for implementing them (Johnson & Wu, 2008), and ways of connecting games and language curricula need to be subject to systematic investigation in order to inform classroom practice. Furthermore, the roles of facilitators and teachers in using games in language teaching at different stages of gameplay and for different types of language learners need to be empirically defined. Researchers should outline both the types of support game facilitators and teachers need to provide for scaffolded learning and define preparation strategies for teachers implementing COTS or serious educational games (Johnson & Wu, 2008).

Designing games requires significant investment, and it is not likely that one game or online simulation alone could satisfy all language learning needs. Thus, future research may need to focus on unravelling the affordances and pedagogical relevance of existing digital games and simulations (Sykes et al., 2010) and help teachers and learners make informed decisions about how to construct game-based experiences that serve their learning and teaching needs.

Note

1 *Zon* tutors, who are also learning content developers, are deployed in game space during class sessions to virtually support students and obtain feedback.

References

Balkun, M. M., Zedeck, M., & Trotta, H. (2009). Literary analysis as serious play in Second Life. In C. Wankel & J. Kingsley (Eds.), *Higher education in virtual worlds: Teaching and learning in Second Life* (pp. 141–57). Bingleym, UL: Emerald Group Publishing.

Bryant, T. (2007). Games as an ideal learning environment. Retrieved from http://dspace.nitle.org/handle/10090/6565

Bytheway, J. A. (2011). *Vocabulary learning strategies in massively multiplayer online role-playing games* (Unpublished Masters Thesis). Victoria University of Wellington, New Zealand.

Catel, M. (2008). Les Sims 2 – Langaming. [Web log comment]. Retrieved from www.freewebs.com/prcatel/
Chen, D. D. (2010). Enhancing the learning of Chinese with Second Life. *Journal of Technology and Chinese Language Teaching, 1*(1), 14–30.
Chen, H. H., & Huang, W. Y. (2010). Examining the potentials of computer games for English learning. *Proceedings of the 2010 third IEEE international conference on digital game and intelligent toy enhanced learning, DIGI'10* (pp. 134–8). Washington, DC, USA: IEEE Computer Society.
Chen, H. H., & Yang, C. (2011). Investigating the effects of an adventure video game on foreign language learning. *Proceedings of the 6th international conference on E-learning and games, edutainment technologies, edutainment'11* (pp. 168–75). Berlin, Heidelberg: Springer-Verlag.
Chen, H. J., & Su, C. C. (2011). Constructing a 3D virtual world for foreign language learning based on open source freeware. In M. Chang, W. Y. Hwang, M. P. Chen & W. Müller (Eds.), *Edutainment technologies: Educational games and virtual reality/augmented reality applications* (pp. 46–53). Berlin, Heidelberg: Springer Berlin Heidelberg.
Chik, A. (2011). Learner autonomy development through digital gameplay. *Digital Culture & Education, 3*(1), 30–45.
Clark, A. (2008). Genome island: A virtual science environment in Second Life, science, and recess. *Environment, 5*(1), 1–6.
Coleman, D. W. (1990). Computerized simulations and games for language learning: Part 1. *Simulation & Gaming, 21*(4), 443–4.
Connolly, T. M., Stansfield, M., & Hainey, T. (2011). An alternate reality game for language learning: ARGuing for multilingual motivation. *Computers & Education (57)*1, 1389–415.
Crookall, D. (2007). Editorial: Second language acquisition and simulation. *Simulation & Gaming, 38*(1), 6–8.
Dalgarno, B., & Lee, M. J. W. (2010). What are the learning affordances of 3D virtual environments? *British Journal of Educational Technology, 41*(1), 10–32.
de Freitas, S. (2006). Learning in immersive worlds: A review of game-based learning. Report prepared for the JISC eLearning programme. Retrieved from www.mendeley.com/research/learning-in-immersive-worlds-a-review-of-gamebased-learning/#
deHaan, J., Reed, W. M., & Kuwada, K. (2010). The effect of interactivity with a music video game on second language vocabulary recall. *Language Learning & Technology, 14*(2), 74–94.
Deubel, P. (2002). Selecting curriculum-based software: Valuable educational software can help students rise to the challenge of standardized testing and assessment. *Learning and Leading with Technology, 29*(5), 10–16.
Deutschmann, M., Panichi, L., & Molka-Danielsen, J. (2009). Designing oral participation in Second Life – a comparative study of two language proficiency courses. *ReCALL, 21*(02), 206–26.
Dickey, M. D. (2007). Game design and learning: A conjectural analysis of how massively multiple online role-playing games (MMORPGs) foster intrinsic motivation. *Educational Technology Research & Development, 55*(3), 253–73.
Frank, A. (2007). Balancing three different foci in the design of serious games: Engagement, training objective and context. *Situated play: Proceedings of the digital games research association conference* (pp. 567–74). Tokyo: The University of Tokyo.
Gee, J. P. (2008). Game-like learning: An example of situated learning and implications for opportunity to learn. In P. A. Moss, D. C. Pullin, J. P. Gee, E. H. Haertel & L. J. Young (Eds.), *Assessment, equity, and opportunity to learn* (pp. 200–21). Cambridge, UK: Cambridge University Press.

Hao, Y., Hong, J. C., Jong, J. T., Hwang, M. Y., Su, C. Y., & Yang, J. S. (2010). Non-native Chinese language learners' attitudes towards online vision-based motion games. *British Journal of Educational Technology, (41)*6, 1043–53.

Henderson, M., Huang, H., Grant, S., & Henderson, L. (2009). Language acquisition in Second Life: Improving self-efficacy beliefs. *Same places different spaces proceedings Ascilite Auckland 2009* (pp. 464–74). Retrieved from www.ascilite.org.au/conferences/auckland09/procs/henderson.pdf

Hew, K. F., & Cheung, W. S. (2010). Use of three-dimensional (3-D) immersive virtual worlds in K-12 and higher education settings: A review of the research. *British Journal of Educational Technology, 41*(1), 33–55.

Johnson, W. L. (2007). Serious use of a serious game for language learning. *Proceedings of the 2007 conference on artificial intelligence in education: Building technology rich learning contexts that work* (pp. 67–74). Amsterdam, The Netherlands: IOS Press.

Johnson, W. L., & Wu, S. (2008). Assessing aptitude for learning with a serious game for foreign language and culture. In B. P. Woolf, E. Aïmeur, R. Nkambou, & S. Lajoie (Eds.), *Intelligent tutoring systems* (pp. 520–9). Berlin, Heidelberg: Springer Berlin Heidelberg.

Kebritchi, M. (2010). Factors affecting teachers' adoption of educational computer games: A case study. *British Journal of Educational Technology, 41*(2), 256–70.

Kenny, R., & Gunter, G. (2011). Factors affecting adoption of video games in the classroom. *Journal of Interactive Learning Research, 22*(2), 259–76.

Kiili, K. (2005). Digital game-based learning: Towards an experiential gaming model. *The Internet and Higher Education, 8*(1), 13–24.

Kim, B., Park, H., & Baek, Y. (2009). Not just fun, but serious strategies: Using meta-cognitive strategies in game-based learning. *Computers & Education, 52*(4), 800–10.

Koenraad, A. L. M. (2008). How can 3D Virtual Worlds contribute to language education? Focus on the language village format. Unpublished manuscript. The Netherlands: Utrecht University of Applied Sciences.

Lee, J. J., & Hoadley, C. M. (2007). Leveraging identity to make learning fun: Possible selves and experiential learning in massively multiplayer online games (MMORPGs). *Innovate: Journal of Online Education, 3*(6).

Lee, Y. Y., & Key, S. (2008). Playing videogames: Do students choose specific foreign language learning strategies in playing these games? *TNTESOL Journal*, 30–7.

Lu, H. M., Lou, S. J., Papa, C., & Chung, C. C. (2011). Study on influence of adventure game on English reading confidence, motive and self-efficacy. *Proceedings of the 6th international conference on e-learning and games, edutainment technologies* (pp. 430–4). Heidelberg: Springer-Verlag Berlin.

Neville, D. O., Shelton, B. E., & McInnis, B. (2009). Cybertext redux: Using digital game-based learning to teach L2 vocabulary, reading, and culture. *Computer Assisted Language Learning, 22*(5), 409–24.

Oliver, M., & Carr, D. (2009). Learning in virtual worlds: Using communities of practice to explain how people learn from play. *British Journal of Educational Technology, 40*(3), 444–57.

Örngren Berglund, T. (2006). Att mötas online: Muntliga realtidsträffar i nätverket ITAS. In P. Svensson (Ed.), *Från vision till praktik: Språkutbildning och informationsteknik.* Stockholm: Nätuniversitetet.

Palmer, D. S. (2010). *Second language pragmatic socialization in World of Warcraft.* University of California, CA.

Peña, J., & Hancock, J. T. (2006). An analysis of socioemotional and task communication in online multiplayer video games. *Communication Research, 33*(1), 92–109.

Peterson, M. (2006). Learner interaction management in an avatar and chat-based virtual world. *Computer Assisted Language Learning, 19*(1), 79–103.

— (2010a). Computerized games and simulations in computer-assisted language learning: A meta-analysis of research. *Simulation & Gaming, 41*(1), 72–93.

— (2010b). Massively multiplayer online role-playing games as arenas for second language learning. *Computer Assisted Language Learning, 23*(5), 429–39.

Piirainen-Marsh, A., & Tainio, L. (2009). Collaborative game-play as a site for participation and situated learning of a second language. *Scandinavian Journal of Educational Research, 53*(2), 167–83.

Purushotma, R. (2005). Commentary: You're not studying, you're just . . . *Language Learning & Technology, 9*(1), 80–96.

Purushotma, R., Thorne, S. L., & Wheatley, J. (2009). *10 key principles for designing video games for foreign language learning.* Open Language & Learning Games Project, Massachusetts Institute of Technology Education Arcade. Retrieved from http://lingualgames.wordpress.com/article/10-key-principles-for-designin g-video-27mkxqba7b13d-2/

Ranalli, J. (2008). Learning English with 'The Sims': Exploiting authentic computer simulation games for L2 learning. *Computer Assisted Language Learning, 21*(5), 441–55.

Rankin, Y. A., Gold, R., & Gooch, B. (2006). 3D role-playing games as language learning tools. *Proceedings of the Eurographics Education Program 2006.*

Rankin, Y. A., McNeal, M. K., Shute, M. W., & Gooch, B. (2008). User centered game design: Evaluating massive multiplayer online role playing games for second language acquisition. *Proceedings of the 2008 ACM SIGGRAPH symposium on Video games* (pp. 43–9). New York, NY: ACM.

Rankin, Y. A., Morrison, D., McNeal, M. K., Gooch, B., & Shute, M. W. (2009). Time will tell: In-game social interactions that facilitate second language acquisition. *Proceedings of the 4th international conference on foundations of digital games* (pp. 161–8). New York, NY: ACM.

Rice, J. W. (2007). New media resistance: Barriers to implementation of computer video games in the classroom. *Journal of Educational Multimedia and Hypermedia, 16*(3), 249–61.

Roy, D. (2007). Warcraft teaches Spanish, part 1. Retrieved from www.educationarcade.org/node/239

Schaffer, D., Squire, K. D., Halverson, R., & Gee, J. P. (2005). Video games and the future of learning. *Phi Delta Kappan, 87*(2), 104–11.

Shih, Y. C. (2010). VEC 3D Home page. Retrieved from http://faculty.ndhu.edu.tw/~vec3d/

Shih, Y. C., & Yang, M. T. (2008). A collaborative virtual environment for situated language learning using VEC3D. *Journal of Educational Technology & Society, 11*(1), 56–68.

Sorensen, B. H., & Meyer, B. (2007). Serious games in language learning and teaching – A theoretical perspective. *Situated Play: Proceedings of the digital games research association conference* (pp. 559–66). Tokyo: The University of Tokyo.

Suh, S., Kim, S. W., & Kim, N. J. (2010). Effectiveness of MMORPG-based instruction in elementary English education in Korea. *Journal of Computer Assisted Learning 26*(5), 370–8.

Sykes, J. M. (2009). Learner requests in Spanish: Examining the potential of multiuser virtual environments for L2 pragmatics acquisition. In L. Lomicka & G. Lord (Eds.), *The next generation: Social networking and online collaboration in foreign language learning* (pp. 199–234). San Marcos, TX: CALICO.

Sykes, J. M., & Cohen, A. D. (2009). Learner perception and strategies for pragmatic acquisition: A glimpse into online learning materials. In C. Dreyer (Ed.), *Language and linguistics: Emerging trends* (pp. 99–135). Hauppauge, NY: Nova Science Publishers.

Sykes, J. M., Reinhardt, J., & Thorne, S. L. (2010). Multiuser digital games as sites for research and practice. In F. M. Hult (Ed.), *Directions and prospects for educational linguistics* (Vol. 11, pp. 117–35). Dordrecht: Springer Netherlands.

Taylor, M. (1990). Simulations and adventure games in CALL. *Simulation & Gaming, 21*(4), 461–6.

Thomas, M. (2011). Editorial: Digital games and second language acquisition in Asia. *Digital Culture & Education, 3*(1), 1–3.

Thorne, S. L. (2008). Transcultural communication in open internet environments and massively multiplayer online games. In S. S. Magnan (Ed.), *Mediating discourse online* (305–27). Philadelphia, PA: John Benjamins.

Thorne, S. L., & Reinhardt, J. (2008). 'Bridging activities', new media literacies, and advanced foreign language proficiency. *CALICO Journal, 25*(3), 558–72.

Thorne, S. L., Black, R. W., & Sykes, J. M. (2009). Second language use, socialization, and learning in internet interest communities and online gaming. *The Modern Language Journal, 93,* 802–21.

Tomlinson, B., & Masuhara, H. (2009). Playing to learn: A review of physical games in second language acquisition. *Simulation & Gaming, 40*(5), 645–68.

Waters, J. K. (2007). On a quest for English. *T.H.E. Journal, 34*(10), 27–8.

Wright, A., Betteridge, D., & Buckby, M. (2006). *Games for language learning.* Cambridge, UK: Cambridge University Press.

Yang, J. C., Chen, C. H., & Jeng, M. C. (2010). Integrating video-capture virtual reality technology into a physically interactive learning environment for English learning. *Computers & Education, 55*(3), 1346–56.

Yee, N., & Bailenson, J. (2007). The proteus effect: The effect of transformed self-representation on behavior. *Human Communication Research, 33*(3), 271–90.

Zhao, Y., & Lai, C. (2009). MMOPRG and foreign language education. In R. E. Ferdig (Ed.), *Handbook of research on effective electronic gaming in education* (pp. 402–21). Hershey, PA: Information Science Reference.

Zheng, D., Young, M. F., Wagner, M., & Brewer, R. A. (2009). Negotiation for action: English language learning in game-based virtual worlds. *The Modern Language Journal, 93*(4), 489–511.

11

Mobile-assisted language learning

Glenn Stockwell

Summary

As mobile technologies become more widely used in our everyday lives, it is perhaps not surprising that they have attracted the attention of language teachers as a means of providing learning opportunities that learners can take advantage of at a time and place that suits them. Mobile learning has the potential to not only increase the amount of time that individual learners spend engaged in language learning activities (Stockwell, 2010), but also to reduce the psychological distance that may be associated with more formal language learning situations (Bax, 2003). There are, however, a number of concerns that need to be taken into consideration when incorporating mobile learning. The smaller screen and limited input methods which are often associated with learning with mobile devices, for example, have an effect on the amount of information which can be provided to learners and the types of tasks and activities that learners can be expected to undertake. In addition to the physical characteristics, learners still exhibit some psychological barriers regarding learning which need to be overcome in order to make mobile learning come more into the mainstream, such as the distinction between private time and study time, and the difficulties associated with studying in public places, such as while commuting. This chapter will discuss the complexities of mobile learning, looking not only at the potential advantages of learning a language with mobile devices, but also outlining the factors which need to be kept in mind when learning through mobile devices. It also includes a discussion of the possibilities that current and emerging mobile technologies may have on the language learning process.

Introduction

In many ways, mobile learning has long been predicted as one of the next stages of education. Mobile technologies have become more and more a part of our everyday lives, and to this end, it seems natural to assume that they will take on a role in learning contexts as well. As in other areas of education (Ally, 2009), this change has been reflected in the steadily growing body of recent research that looks at language learning through various mobile devices, and research has appeared that capitalizes on the expanding functionalities of these devices, including short message system (SMS) (Kennedy & Levy, 2008), mobile-phone-based email (Kiernan & Aizawa, 2004), podcasting (Rosell-Aguilar, 2007), mobile phone Web browsers (Stockwell, 2007) and apps (Bateson & Daniels, 2012).

As the name suggests, mobile learning occurs predominantly out of class time, such as while commuting or waiting for friends (Stockwell, 2008), which entails a shift from the traditional concept of computer-assisted language learning (CALL) as a predominantly classroom activity. This redefinition of the learning context from more formal settings to something that occurs as an accessible – if not a natural – part of learning both in and out of the classroom is encompassed in Bax's description of what he terms *integrated CALL*, where technology is seen as being 'in every classroom, on every desk, in every bag' (2003, p. 21). Included in this idea is that learners carry devices around with them that they can access at a time that is convenient to them, and they can pick up the device to augment their learning in much the same way that one may pick up a pen or a book. This means, however, that learners must feel comfortable enough with the technology such that they do not have reservations about using it without supervision or assistance.

An underlying concept that may be considered as supporting the use of mobile devices in education is that of 'Digital Natives' as coined by Prensky (2001), who argues that this upcoming generation has been brought up in an environment where technologies around them are a natural part of life, and therefore using these technologies for studying may be seen as ordinary, if not expected. Prensky also suggests that these 'Digital Natives' are capable of carrying out multiple tasks at once, and therefore are able to utilize different channels of information simultaneously, such as engaging in text-chat at the same time as undertaking internet searches for an assignment. In mobile learning, this type of multitasking becomes essential, as learners need to negotiate with their surroundings at the same time as undertaking activities or tasks on their mobile devices, such as a student completing a vocabulary activity while riding on a train to commute to classes. While this might not seem like multitasking at first glance, when considering that the student needs to ensure that they listen or watch for information about which station they need to disembark the train while doing the activity, we can see that the learner needs to concentrate on two distinct sources of information – the mobile activity and the information about where they are – to be able to successfully complete both.

While Prensky's ideas have been subject to some degree of criticism, such as the fact that multitasking need not be a quality that is particular to so-called Digital Natives (Baron, 2008; Bennett, Maton & Kervin, 2008), the idea that technology will likely be less daunting to the majority of younger learners who have been brought up surrounded by – and, in the vast majority of cases, owning – mobile devices would seem to make sense. Mobile learning is, then, certainly something that is likely to be seen with increasing frequency in the language learning literature in the foreseeable future of CALL. Given this emerging trend, and the rather large number of books that have started to appear in the last few years regarding learning through mobile devices (Ally, 2009; Kidd & Chen, 2011; Kukulska-Hulme & Traxler, 2005), it is perhaps time to step back and take stock of the effects that mobile devices can have on learning a language, both positive and negative, give some thought to what we need to bear in mind when using mobile devices to learn a language and consider the possible future directions for mobile language learning.

Enabling aspects of mobile learning

One of the primary advantages that is given regarding mobile learning is that it allows learners to 'exploit small amounts of time and space for learning' (Traxler, 2007, p. 8). In order to do this, it means that these devices must become part of the everyday life of the user, so that it is at hand for when these often unanticipated 'small amounts of time and space' arise. To consider this further, it is helpful to think through the role that mobile devices now play in our lives. While there are of course new features and functions that did not exist before the development of many modern mobile devices, for the most part their functions replicate features of various tools that we carried with us before they appeared. To many, a single modern mobile device such as a mobile phone, a 3G MP3 player or a tablet computer now takes the place of the plethora of items that might be carried around – a camera, a watch, an alarm clock, a newspaper, a book, a diary, a CD player, a map, a train schedule and even a magnifying glass and a mirror – without needing to fill a backpack with all of the possible bits-and-pieces that were anticipated as necessary before leaving the house. In other ways, however, mobile devices allow for things that were not possible before the development of these technologies. While a camera previously needed images to be printed or transferred to a computer before distributing to family and friends, as Green and Haddon (2009) suggest, the mobile device itself acts like a photo album, in that photos can be viewed directly on the screen or they can be immediately emailed to others or posted on a social networking site such as *Facebook*. This broad range of functionalities makes mobile devices both a replacement and an extension of technologies which were in use beforehand.

Trivanova et al. (2004) suggest that a mobile device for learning can be 'any device that is small, autonomous and unobtrusive enough to accompany us in every moment and can be used for educational purposes' (p. 1). This carries with it the connotation that, given the fact that we generally have it with us at all times, the device is something that we can take out and use at any time or place. If we need to remind ourselves whether we are carrying a device that could be used for learning, in one sense, we already have a problem about using that device as a part of our learning. We should feel that we can reach into our bag or our pocket and take out the device when we want to engage in some form of learning in the same way that we might reach into our bag and pick up a textbook, pen or notepad on our way home from classes. The advantage that mobile devices that we continually carry around with us provide is that we do not necessarily have to prepare anything in advance of undertaking the learning. Rather than needing to carry our language textbook in our bags on the off-chance we have a spare few minutes and decide to use it constructively for learning purposes, if the mobile device that we are already carrying takes on this additional role, it makes learning something that can happen in a spontaneous way depending on circumstances, thus exploiting the gaps in time and place as described by Traxler (2007) above.

The device that is used will depend greatly on our own lifestyles. If we are used to carrying around a laptop or an MP3 player, then it makes sense that these devices are put towards educational uses. Even within the comparatively short history of mobile devices, it is becoming clear that, to a large extent, the modern mobile phone has already replaced the roles of many other mobile devices. While of course other devices may be used relatively widely in certain communities (such as palmtop computers for business people), mobile phones indisputably have the greatest penetration rate across the general population, reaching essentially 100% in recent studies where statistics are included, such as university-age students in Japan (Thornton & Houser, 2005), Korea (Nah, White & Sussex, 2008) and Austria (Ebner & Billicsich, 2011). Furthermore, mobile phones now contain relatively high-resolution cameras that not only enable quite clear photographs to be taken, but, as described above, these can be immediately distributed through email, *Facebook* or *Twitter*. Whereas many people – particularly the younger generation – have carried around MP3 players to listen to music while riding on trains, walking or even while sitting in libraries or cafes, recently we see that this functionality is also included in most mobile phones. Even many pre-smartphone era phones allowed users to listen to music, but this has become even easier with smartphones, most allowing learners to buy new songs or albums directly from their phone without needing to use a computer at all. Internet browsing, which was typically in the domain of laptop and tablet computers and personal digital assistants (PDAs), is possible from smartphones, although this was available on many earlier phones as well. Devices such as mobile phones (and PDAs) also have the advantage of no 'boot-up' time, making them even more appropriate for extremely short bursts of activity than devices such as laptop computers (see Stockwell, 2008; Trinder et al., 2005). Of course, the bigger screen of laptop and tablet computers makes scanning through large amounts of information easier, but as Weiss (2002) argues, 'wireless users may be using their leisure time to gather information, but they typically have immediate goals' (p. 66). What this suggests is that when people use a mobile device, in many cases, they wish to use to solve an immediate and comparatively simple problem, such as finding when the next train arrives, the weather for the day or what time a movie starts. If further information that involves more 'surfing' through multiple pages is needed, they are likely to do this in a more leisurely manner, using different technologies at a time and place more appropriate to the larger cognitive demands required of them.

Although the discussion above alludes to the fact that a mobile device should be something that we carry with us, how does this translate into enabling learning? Put simply, anything that makes opportunities for learning more accessible to learners must be considered as an enabling aspect. Because of the wide range of uses that are generally applied to mobile devices, it means that the device becomes a familiar part of the everyday routine of the user, and this in itself increases the chance for learning to take place. The main problem that arises, however, is how to alter the awareness of the device such that it is also applied to language learning purposes. As Healy (1999) so aptly points out, 'Technology alone does not create language learning any more than dropping a learner into the middle of a large library does' (p. 136). This is of course relevant also for learning through mobile devices, and it is important not only to provide the tools to learn, but also to provide the skills and the impetus for learners to do it.

Uses of mobile devices in language learning

As there has been a recent overview of different mobile technologies and how they have been used in language learning by Kukulska-Hulme and Shield (2008), the description here has been limited to the general trends that have started to emerge, and an overview of some recent examples from the literature. In short, research into mobile language learning has primarily focused on three main technologies: MP3 players, PDAs and mobile phones. Not surprisingly, the majority of research using MP3 players has been limited to listening through podcasts (e.g., Abdous, Camarena & Facer, 2009; Rosell-Aguilar, 2007), but there have also been studies that have explored their use for other language areas such as pronunciation (Ducate & Lomicka, 2009). While most of these studies have given positive results regarding the use of MP3 players (although this is mainly based on perceptions of usefulness rather than actual empirical data), it is a technology that has received perhaps less-than-expected attention in the literature, with the bulk of the research into mobile language learning looking at PDAs and mobile phones.

Until quite recently, the primary focus of mobile devices for language learning was the PDA, but over time there has been a shift more towards mobile phones. To illustrate this, we can look at two recent collections regarding technology use in learning: an edited volume from 2005 and a special journal issue in 2008. Although not all of the chapters were about language learning, in Kukulska-Hulme and Traxler's edited volume published in 2005, of 14 chapters where specific mobile devices were described or researched, 13 focused predominantly on the PDA (including 2 that also mentioned mobile phones or tablet computers) and only 1 focused on the use of a mobile phone. Three years later, in a special issue on mobile learning published in *ReCALL* in 2008, of the five research articles focusing on a particular technology, three described mobile phones and two described PDAs. This movement towards the mobile phone from PDAs is indicative of two factors. First, as described above, mobile phones have now developed to a point where they have caught up with the internet browsing and email capabilities that were previously more synonymous with PDAs. As stated earlier, the majority of university students these days seem to possess a mobile phone, and for the most part, mobile phones developed over the last decade or so have some kind of internet browsing capabilities, meaning that mobile phones are more than sufficient to complete the types of activities that were once only limited to PDAs. Second, as a PDA is generally not a device owned by most university students (who more frequently than not end up the focus of studies of mobile language learning), teachers and researchers are generally required to provide class sets for learners. This obviously entails the costs of putting together full sets of PDAs for learners to use, but at the same time, because the devices are generally on loan, learners are generally not able to use them in a completely unsupervised manner (i.e., take them home after class and use them in their own time as with privately owned mobile phones). As a result, studies into PDAs have the potential to be somewhat contrived, as they may not reflect the normal ways that learners would likely use mobile devices, unlike the use of mobile phones.

To provide an example of the nature of mobile language learning, the three main mobile devices used for language teaching, MP3 players, PDAs and mobile phones, are described below, including a brief overview of some recent studies using these devices.

MP3 players and podcasting

Although podcasting has not received an enormous amount of coverage in the second language learning literature, there have been a small number of studies. In most cases, the podcasts are created by the instructors, and learners are required to listen to these outside of class time, generally to support what has been covered in class. In one such example, O'Bryan and Hegelheimer (2007) used podcasts as a supplement to an ESL listening strategies course. The podcasts could be downloaded to MP3 players, but in keeping aware of the need to cater to those learners who did not possess an MP3 player, the podcasts could also be watched using a normal desktop computer. There were a total of 14 podcasts, 12 of which were audio only, and 2 which included video as well. These were intended as a supplement to the class material, and were typically intended to be completed as homework. Although the scale of the study was quite small with only six learners participating, the results of surveys and interviews with learners revealed that the podcasting was very well received. In another study, Weinberg, Knorr and Vandergrift (2011) examined perceptions of learners of French of the enjoyment and usefulness of podcasts through questionnaires and focus group discussions. There were a total of seven podcasts created by the instructors to give advice about how to listen to French lectures, but it was unclear whether the podcasts were listened to in class or for homework. Feedback regarding the podcasts was relatively neutral, but a criticism aimed at the podcasts was that they needed to be more professional in terms of the way in which they were recorded (i.e., use professional actors). In both of these examples, the focus of the podcasts is on how to learn rather than on providing actual language learning input itself, and learners were essentially required to listen to the podcast and to apply the content to their language learning situations. In addition, there was little or no information given about where the learners listened to the podcasts, and whether they used portable MP3 players to listen to them or not, or even how many of the learners owned them.

A study by Abdous, Camarena and Facer (2009), however, revealed some interesting statistics about learners' usage patterns with podcasts. They showed that while around two-thirds of learners had an iPod or other MP3 player, less than half this number used the device with any degree of consistency, with those who did opting to listen to them via a desktop computer in preference to a mobile device. The reason most commonly cited was that learners did not have time to download the podcasts, although others claimed that they either did not know how to download them or that they did not think that they would be useful. In this sense, while podcasting is often considered as being an activity that takes place on mobile devices, the research available suggested that it is more commonly carried out on desktop computers than on mobile devices such as MP3 players. The reasons behind this lack of use are discussed later in the section on limitations of mobile learning.

PDAs

Earlier research into PDAs (also known as handheld or palmtop computers) in second language learning contexts predominantly focused on the features of the technology itself, and as such a good deal was conducted within the language classroom. More recent research, however, has attempted to see PDAs used in more naturalistic settings, with some studies giving learners unlimited access to PDA devices for a set period of time, and others providing more closely supervised usage to complete a particular task or activity. One underlying commonality of most PDA studies, however, was that learners were provided with a PDA to use during the research rather than expected to use one that they themselves owned (although actual ownership was not mentioned). Given this point, quite understandably, studies in which learners were given unlimited access tended to be of a smaller scale, whereas larger scale studies tended to be more closely supervised, presumably to guarantee the safety of the devices. As an example of a small-scale study, C.-M. Chen and Chung (2008) developed a rather sophisticated system for learning vocabulary based on Item Response Theory (IRT) and learning memory cycles for 15 learners of English in Taiwan. Learners had completely free use of the system for a period of five weeks, and could access the PDA at any time or place that suited them. The system kept record of learner progress, and also tracked whether or not learners were regularly accessing the system. When learners failed to access the system for two days, they were sent an email reminder, and this resulted in learners accessing the system relatively consistently. The study yielded positive feedback from the learners, and learners who used the system showed an improvement in their vocabulary development compared with learners who did not.

A larger-scale study was carried out by I.-J. Chen and Chang (2011), where 162 Taiwanese learners of English carried PDA devices to Taipei City Zoo and engaged in animal observation while listening to an audio guide in English. This differed from a number of previous studies in that learners used the mobile device in such a way that it enabled them to interact directly with the environment around them, rather than being a tool to complete activities assigned to them by the teacher such as the C.-M. Chen and Chung (2008) example above, or to carry out internet searches (e.g., Song & Fox, 2008). Learners had the option of listening to the guide at the same time as reading it as they moved their way around the zoo. Of interest in the results was that a significant number of learners felt that the events at the zoo were distracting from the learning that they were undertaking, and that the text on the PDA was difficult to read, although the inclusion of the text did help in comprehending the audio guide. This has interesting implications for the use of mobile devices in public places, as it indicates that tasks and activities that require a degree of concentration can be difficult to complete unless the environment is appropriate.

Mobile phones

Recent studies into mobile phone use for language learning loosely fit into two categories: those that entail some kind of communication tool such as SMS or mobile email, and those that use applications either through an internet browser or a pre-installed application. Like many early studies into PDAs, research on mobile phones often took place in classroom situations (Thornton & Houser, 2005), although more recent research has also moved into more naturalistic settings. Despite the fact that the technologies themselves have started to resemble each other, one primary difference that defines them is the fact that PDAs were on loan whereas students used their own private mobile phones. There is an obvious psychological difference between using a device which is dedicated to language learning (as in the loaned PDA) and a device which is owned by the learner and has practical uses apart from learning. While this is discussed in more depth below, suffice to say that when the cost of using a technology is placed onto the learners, there is likely to be an adverse effect on how much they are willing to engage with it.

Regarding the content of research into using mobile phones, studies that have involved SMS usage generally involved sending information about vocabulary items much like a digital flashcard (N.-S. Chen, Hsieh & Kinshuk, 2008), but other uses have been more innovative. Kennedy and Levy (2008), for example, sent various text notifications related to their language learning, including information about what they had learned during class, details of upcoming television programmes and other interesting facts about the target language and culture. With the development of faster internet browsing and more user-friendly operating systems for mobile phones, application-based research has started to appear more frequently in recent years. Some of the online systems have been quite complex, including intelligent aspects that keep records of learner progress and match activities to suit individual learners (Stockwell, 2007). The system developed by Stockwell operated through the browser function on the phone and provided vocabulary activities for Japanese learners of English, adapting to the learner through detailed records of their progress. Learners in this study were given the option of using either their mobile phones or desktop computers, and while the mobile interface was simplified to make it easier to use given the smaller screen, the vast majority opted to use the desktop computer in preference to the mobile device to complete the activities. In a later study to investigate the possible causes for this, Stockwell (2008) found that cost factors, the small screen size and the study environment lead learners to feel that the desktop computer was sufficient for completing activities. Although learners generally gave a positive impression of the activities themselves, the fact that usage was very low was certainly a point for concern, as is discussed in the following section.

Issues of concern with mobile learning

Although mobile devices have the potential to give learners greater access to learning opportunities, there are also a number of issues which have the potential to shape the way in which they can be used. Obviously the portable nature of the technology means that it has certain physical characteristics which determine what it is and is not suited to, and this also affects how learners view it for learning purposes. There is also a psychological dimension to mobile learning, where the degree of acceptance by learners will depend very much on their skills, experiences, as well as their preferences for determining how these devices will be used. Finally, as mobile devices come to be used for educational purposes, there is also a need to consider their appropriateness for learning situations, particularly given their parallel non-learning uses. These points are described in more depth below.

Physical issues

The physical characteristics of mobile devices have been cited by many researchers, particularly with regard to the size of the screen and the inconvenient keypad (see Stockwell, 2008, for a discussion). While it is true that the screens of newer devices such as smartphones and PDAs are bigger and use different input methods from earlier ones, there are still obvious difficulties in reading from the screen, particularly when there are distractions (I.-J. Chen & Chung, 2011). Learners may be willing to read shorter texts on mobile devices, but when the text is longer there is definitely a clear preference for reading through desktop computers (Huang & Lin, 2011). In addition to these, as Koole (2009) points out, other issues that can have an effect on how mobile devices are used are the general size and weight, the file storage capacity, hardware and software malfunctions and processor speed. It is the total balance of all of these factors which will determine how a mobile device can be best used in language learning.

Psychological issues

As has been alluded to in the results of a number of the studies outlined above, there are also psychological considerations regarding the ways in which learners – and teachers – view mobile learning. A fundamental issue pertains to the assumption that learners are competent users of new technologies, and this is perhaps even more evident when learners themselves own these technologies. However, as Bennett, Maton and Kervin (2008, p. 779) point out, 'a significant proportion of young people do not have the levels of access or technology skills predicted by proponents of the digital natives idea', meaning that we cannot simply assume that learners will be able to use mobile devices just because they were brought up in an environment where they are surrounded by them. In the studies by Abdous, Camarena and Facer (2009) on podcasting and Stockwell (2008) on mobile phones, there was an unexpectedly low proportion of users who opted to use mobile devices. In both studies, there were learners who did not use the mobile tools available simply because they did not know how. In addition, as described in Stockwell (2008, 2010), many learners just did not feel that the mobile device (in this case a mobile phone) was an appropriate tool for language learning, and others preferred to engage in activities in a quieter environment where they could concentrate. When we think about this lack of use, we may conclude that the expectations that many teachers have of learners engaging in language learning tasks and activities using mobile devices may not match the skills, expectations and perceptions held by the learners, and at the same time, teachers may not have a clear idea of when and where learners will engage in them. If the discrepancy between teachers' and learners' views becomes too great, it is likely that it will result in learners forming negative images of mobile learning, and prevent them from undertaking it actively.

Pedagogical issues

The characteristics of the mobile device, the learners' skills and attitudes, and the way in which the device is used for non-educational purposes will all have an effect on the pedagogical value of language learning tasks and activities. A brief look through the literature reveals that there are very few studies that actually provide detailed training to learners in undertaking mobile learning outside of class time. With the exception of studies such as C.-M. Chen and Chung (2008), who provided their learners with 2 hours of detailed training with a PDA before asking them to study outside of class, the majority of studies provide little or no training, or at the very least, have no mention of this (see Hubbard, 2004, for a discussion of learner training). Knowledge of how to use a technology for personal purposes does not mean that they will know how to use it effectively for learning purposes, and this will obviously impact the pedagogical effectiveness of tasks and activities. Related to this is the supposition that because devices are used outside of class, then they will encourage learner autonomy. Learner autonomy is achieved only when a learner reaches a point where they are both willing and able to take responsibility for learning on their own, two points that do not necessarily coincide (see Stockwell, 2012, for a discussion). Finally, it is important to bear in mind the ways in which learners typically use mobile devices for personal purposes actually are, as this will likely affect how they are used for learning purposes. For example, Kemp (2010) found that around three-quarters of native-speaking users regularly used what is termed as *textisms* – abbreviations in spelling and spacing as a result of space limitations and typing difficulties – when writing SMS messages to one another. It is quite feasible, then, that learners may try to apply the same rules of textisms to messages that are written in a second language as well, sometimes with little idea of the appropriateness in the target culture.

In addition to these issues, the design of the tasks and activities themselves for mobile learning needs to consider the environment in which it is used. Given the potentially unstable environments in which mobile learning may take place, activities on mobile devices need to be short and succinct, with a very short start-up time as well as short-segmented sections that can be completed individually as a single unit (see Metcalf, 2006, for a discussion). In this way, learners can pick up mobile devices when they have a spare couple of minutes, without wasting time waiting for it to start up, and without worries about quitting a longer activity mid-way due to external interruptions. Issues regarding timing may be written into the software, such as the program that Cui and Bull (2005) designed for Chinese learners of English, *TenseITS*, which included a start-up screen which directly asked the learners where they were undertaking the activities (e.g., Restaurant/Hotel, etc.), the anticipated frequency of interruption and the expected amount of time to be spent on the activities, but more often than not, the onus is on the learner to make decisions about which activities to engage in.

Emerging directions

Making predictions about any developments in the future is difficult, and in essence can only be based on what we can see around us, and the developments that have already started to take place. With regard to mobile learning, as the field is still establishing itself in many ways, predictions become even more difficult. In saying this, however, it is possible to look back the short distance that we have already come and combine the knowledge we have accrued thus far with the developments in technology that are currently underway.

Capabilities of mobile devices have already developed dramatically since their introduction several decades ago, and of these, it is perhaps the mobile phone that carries the most promise. As Watson and Plymale (2011) argue, one of the major factors that is likely to contribute to expanding ubiquitous learning – that is, learning that is not constrained by time or place – is the development of new smartphones, which not only allow access to multiple wireless interfaces, but also are equipped 'with numerous hardware sensors capable of collecting contextual information about the user and their environment' (p. 11). One such example is a GPS (Global Positioning System), which can track where a person is, and can provide information such as maps and directions, or even trigger messages to be sent to the users' devices depending on their location. We might imagine a situation where a person is studying Japanese in Australia, for example. Their mobile phone has an application installed that accesses their location using the built-in GPS feature. As they walk down the street, the application senses that there is a Japanese restaurant nearby, and sends a message to the person along with a list of vocabulary that might be useful with regard to Japanese food, such as descriptions of menu items, or even terminology often used in ordering Japanese food. This type of feature would mean a change from the commonly used 'pull' style of learning, where learners need to seek information for themselves, to the 'push' style, where information is made available to learners without effort on their part. The use of mobile devices to act as a means of linking learning events and the real world has been termed 'augmented reality' (AR) (see Kukulska-Hulme, 2009), and one sense is considered as making the optimum use of the portability of mobile devices to learn.

A second factor that Watson and Plymale describe is the development of the 'Internet of Things', which is where people can interact with everyday objects (and in some cases objects can interact with other objects) through an infrastructure of 'networked sensors and actuators coupled with low-cost microcontrollers, wireless technologies, cloud services, and PMI [Physical Mobile Interaction] interfaces' (2011, p. 11). At the simplest end of the scale, a PMI may include a QR code, where users may bring up information about an object or even details of a task (see Rivers, 2009, for a discussion of QR codes in language learning). Other systems may be far more complex, where mobile devices can interact with one another using a LAN, WAN or even Bluetooth, which can send a signal that can be read by a mobile unit (Naismith & Smith, 2009). This type of interconnectedness means that learners can constantly be interacting with the things and people around them, and language learning tasks can be shaped so that they draw learners into interacting with their surroundings in new and innovative ways.

This type of environment makes it possible for mobile learning to take on a rather different nature from that which takes place through fixed technologies such as desktop computers, so that rather than simply replicating computer-based activities adapted for mobile technologies, learning can be interactive not only between the learner and the technology that they are holding, but also with their surroundings. In this way, the mobile phone goes beyond the current main uses of communication tools (such as email and chat) and internet tools, but can extend to uses which capitalize upon not only what the user consciously does for language learning, but at the same time also keep track of what the learner does for other purposes either through the phone itself, or simply by where they are when they carry it. Thus, learners are able to interact with their surroundings in a way that can facilitate language learning through relating it to potential opportunities that arise as a part of their daily lives rather than just what occurs in the classroom or in completing activities or tasks as a part of the class. These language learning opportunities have the potential to fit naturally into learners' everyday lives, thereby contributing to the lowering of barriers between what happens in the classroom and students' lives outside of class.

Conclusions

There is no doubt that research into mobile learning is both inevitable and necessary. As Hémard (2003) argues, the overall validity of CALL applications must be viewed as being acceptable by learners with regard to both usefulness and enjoyment in order to be accessed outside the classroom. This is of course relevant to mobile learning, and there is a need to ensure that the interface makes it comfortable to use, and at the same time capitalizes upon the mobile characteristics of the device. Simply adapting PC-based activities for mobile devices is unlikely to link to significant mobile usage due to their inherent psychological and physical limitations. This of course does not mean that mobile learning should not include some elements typically associated with more traditional forms of CALL, but these need to take into consideration not only what technologies are to be used, but also when, why and how. If the mobile device can act as a link between the learning world and the world that learners interact with in their daily lives, then there is a greater chance that the psychological link between mobile devices and learning can be broken down, and learners can capitalize more upon the opportunities for learning afforded them by the tools at their fingertips.

As Morris (2011) argues, one of the biggest pedagogical challenges then becomes finding ways to utilize available technologies to create a smooth combination of physical spaces and virtual environments, where knowledge can be imparted that is immediately relevant to the surrounding context. Finding the balance of how to do this successfully is likely to be an important issue in the future of mobile learning.

References

Abdous, M., Camarena, M. M., & Facer, B. R. (2009). MALL technology: Use of academic podcasting in the foreign language classroom. *ReCALL, 21*(1), 76–95.

Ally. M. (2009). *Mobile learning: Transforming the delivery of education & training.* Edmonton, AB: AU Press.

Baron, N. S. (2009). *Always on: Language in an online and mobile world.* New York: Oxford University Press.

Bateson, G., & Daniels, P. (2012). Diversity in technologies. In G. Stockwell (Ed.), *Computer-assisted language learning: Diversity in research and practice* (pp. 128–46). New York: Cambridge University Press.

Bax, S. (2003). CALL – past, present and future. *System, 31,* 13–28.

Bennett, S., Maton, K., & Kervin, L. (2008). The 'Digital Natives' debate: A critical review of the evidence. *British Journal of Educational Technology, 38*(5), 775–86.

Chen, C.-M., & Chung, C.-J. (2008). Personalized mobile English vocabulary learning system based on item response theory and learning memory cycle. *Computers & Education, 51,* 624–45.

Chen, I.-J., & Chang, C.-C. (2011). Content presentation modes in mobile language listening tasks: English proficiency as a moderator. *Computer Assisted Language Learning, 24*(5), 451–70.

Chen, N.-S., Hsieh, S.-W., & Kinshuk. (2008). Effects of short-term memory and content representation on mobile language learning. *Language Learning & Technology, 12*(3), 93–112.

Cui, Y., & Bull, S. (2005). Context and learner modeling for the mobile foreign language learner. *System, 33,* 353–67.

Ducate, L., & Lomicka, L. (2009). Podcasting: An effective tool for honing language students' pronunciation? *Language Learning & Technology, 13*(3), 66–86.

Ebner, M., & Billicsish, T. (2011). Is the iPhone a ubiquitous learning device?: First step towards digital lecture notes. In T. T. Kidd & I. Chen (Eds.), *Ubiquitous learning: Strategies for pedagogy, course design, and technology* (pp. 137–51). Charlotte, NC: Information Age Publishing, Inc.

Green, N., & Haddon, L. (2009). *Mobile communications: An introduction to new media.* Oxford: Berg.

Healey, D. (1999). Classroom practice: Communicative skill-building tasks in CALL environments. In J. Egbert & E. Hanson-Smith (Eds.), *CALL environments: Research, practice and critical issues* (pp. 116–36). Alexandria, VA: TESOL.

Hémard, D. (2003). Language learning online: Designing towards user acceptability. In U. Felix (Ed.), *Language learning online: Towards best practice* (pp. 21–42). Lisse: Swets & Zeitlinger.

Hembrooke, H., & Gay, G. (2003). The laptop and the lecture: The effects of multitasking in learning environments. *Journal of Computing in Higher Education, 15,* 46–64.

Huang, L.-L., & Lin, C.-C. (2011). EFL learners' reading on mobile phones. *The JALT CALL Journal, 7*(1), 61–78.

Hubbard, P. (2004). Learner training for effective use of CALL. In S. Fotos & C. Browne (Eds.), *New perspectives on CALL for second language classrooms* (pp. 45–68). Mahwah, NJ: Lawrence Erlbaum Associates.

Kemp, N. (2010). Texting versus txtng: Reading and writing text messages, and links with other linguistic skills. *Writing Systems Research, 2*(1), 53–71.

Kennedy, C., & Levy, M. (2008). L'italiano al telefonino: Using SMS to support beginners' language learning. *ReCALL, 20*(3), 315–50.

Kidd, T. T., & Chen, I. (2011). *Ubiquitous learning: Strategies for pedagogy, course design, and technology.* Charlotte, NC: Information Age Publishing, Inc.

Kiernan, P., & Aizawa, K. (2004). Cell phones in task based learning: are cell phones useful language learning tool? *ReCALL, 16*(1), 71–84.

Koole, M. (2009). A model for framing mobile learning. In M. Ally (Ed.), *Mobile learning: Transforming the delivery of education & training* (pp. 25–47). Athabasca: AU Press.

Kukulska-Hulme, A. (2009). Will mobile learning change language learning? *ReCALL, 21*(2), 157–65.
Kukulska-Hulme, A., & Shield, L. (2008). An overview of mobile assisted language learning: From content delivery to supported collaboration and interaction. *ReCALL, 20*(3), 271–89.
Kukulska-Hulme, A., & Traxler, J. (2005). *Mobile learning: A handbook for educators and trainers*. London: Routledge.
Levy, M., & Kennedy, C. (2005). Learning Italian via mobile SMS. In A. Kukulska-Hulme & J. Traxler (Eds.), *Mobile learning: A handbook for educators and trainers* (pp. 76–83). London: Routledge.
Metcalf, D. S. (2006). *mLearning: Mobile learning and performance in the palm of your hand*. Amherst, MA: HRD Press.
Morris, L.-D. (2011). Helping your lecturers to creatively introduce ubiquitous computing technologies into their teaching: What every lecturer should know. In T. T. Kidd & I. Chen (Eds.), *Ubiquitous learning: Strategies for pedagogy, course design, and technology* (pp. 209–28). Charlotte, NC: Information Age Publishing, Inc.
Naismith, L., & Smith, M. P. (2009). Using mobile technologies for multimedia tours in a traditional museum setting. In M. Ally (Ed.), *Mobile learning: Transforming the delivery of education & training* (pp. 247–64). Edmonton, AB: AU Press.
O'Bryan, A., & Hegelheimer, V. (2007). Integrating CALL into the classroom: The role of podcasting in an ESL listening strategies course. *ReCALL, 19*(2), 162–80.
Prensky, M. (2001). Digital natives, digital immigrants. *On the Horizon, 9*(5), 1–6.
Rivers, D. J. (2009). Utilizing the quick response (QR) code within a Japanese EFL environment. *The JALT CALL Journal, 5*(2), 15–28.
Rosell-Aguilar, F. (2007). Top of the pods: In search of a podcasting 'podagogy' for language learning. *Computer Assisted Language Learning, 20*(5), 471–92.
Song, Y., & Fox, R. (2008). Using PDA for undergraduate student incidental vocabulary testing. *ReCALL, 20*(3), 290–314.
Stockwell, G. (2007). Vocabulary on the move: Investigating an intelligent mobile phone-based vocabulary tutor. *Computer Assisted Language Learning, 20*(4), 365–83.
— (2008). Investigating learner preparedness for and usage patterns of mobile learning. *ReCALL, 20*(3), 253–70.
— (2010). Using mobile phones for vocabulary activities: Examining the effect of the platform. *Language Learning & Technology, 14*(2), 95–110.
— (2012). Introduction. In G. Stockwell (Ed.), *Computer-assisted language learning: Diversity in research and practice* (pp. 1–13). New York: Cambridge University Press.
Thornton, P., & Houser, C. (2005). Using mobile phones in English education in Japan. *Journal of Computer Assisted Learning, 21*(3), 217–28.
Traxler, J. (2007). Defining, discussing, and evaluating mobile learning: The moving finger writes and having writ. . . . *International Review of Research in Open and Distance Learning, 8*(2), 1–12.
Trifanova, A., Knapp, J., Ronchetti, M., & Gamper, J. (2004) Mobile ELDIT: Challenges in the transitions from an e-learning to an m-learning system. Trento, Italy: University of Trento.
Trinder, J., Magill, J., & Roy, S. (2005). Expect the unexpected: Practicalities and problems of a PDA project. In A. Kukulska-Hulme & J. Traxler (Eds.), *Mobile learning: A handbook for educators and trainers* (pp. 92–7). London: Routledge.
Watson, C. E., & Plymale, W. O. (2011). The pedagogy of things: Ubiquitous learning, student culture, and constructivist pedagogical practice. In T. T. Kidd & I. Chen (Eds.),

Ubiquitous learning: Strategies for pedagogy, course design, and technology (pp. 3–16). Charlotte, NC: Information Age Publishing, Inc.

Weinberg, A., Knorr, H., & Vandergrift, L. (2011). Creating podcasts for academic listening in French: Student perceptions of enjoyment and usefulness. *CALICO Journal, 28*(3), 588–605.

Weiss, S. (2002). *Handheld usability.* Chichester: John Wiley & Sons.

12

CALL in low-tech contexts

Dafne Gonzalez and Rubena St. Louis

Summary

Slow internet connections, the lack of limited finances or educational facilities with few resources have made it difficult, and in many cases impossible, for language learners to obtain the benefits of learning via computers. In foreign language learning where learners need to communicate with other speakers of the target language, it is essential that ways to promote authentic interaction be found. While the use of Web tools has made this interaction easier, an internet connection is, however, needed. Experience in distance education, carried out using snail mail with video cassettes and CD-ROMs has shown that learning in low-technology (low-tech) contexts is feasible and although poor internet access can be an obstacle, it is one that can be overcome. Radio, TV, telephones and more recently mobile phones are examples of mediums through which language can be accessed in low-technology contexts. The challenge facing teachers is to find a way in which these mediums can be used in conjunction with computers to facilitate learning.

Introduction

Language teaching has always made use of the technology available (Bates, 2005; Chapelle, 2001; Eyring, 2001; Hanson- Smith, 2001; Warschauer, 1996), and the emergence of digital technologies has not been an exception. As a result, computer-based learning can be found in most schools worldwide today; however, there are still vast numbers of students who have no, or limited access to technology and its benefits. The potential the internet has as a source and medium of learning is not being fully exploited. Furthermore, even if such technologies were available many teachers do not seem to have the 'know how' to integrate it into their educational praxis (Fawzi, 2010; Stevens, 2010; Yuildez & Tatar, 2010). This problem, faced by educators in low-tech contexts, also concerns those who would like to find ways of bridging this technological gap (Egbert & Yang, 2004; Venezky, 2000; Warschauer, 2003).

One of the main criticisms of e-learning has been the digital divide, which has been defined as 'Complex and dynamic factors that determine who has access to which computer-mediated technology' (Kaur Khalsa, Maloney-Krichmar & Kreeft Peyton, 2007, p. 24). It has been a source of concern since the implementation of information technology in the 1970s (Fong, 2009; Valdivia, 2008; Venezky, 2000; Warschauer, 2004). Access not only refers to the physical availability of hardware, networks and computer services, but also to conditional access to computer programs, applications and multimedia content which are often sold at a high cost or available as online resources for a fee. Computers and computer services may be more readily available to teachers and learners in developed countries through their schools, libraries, internet cafes or for personal use at home. Many educational facilities may be equipped with computer laboratories with broadband access and have budgets which cover the costs of educational software, either online or in DVD format.

Less-developed countries, on the other hand, may be plagued by a poor telecommunications infrastructure which may hinder internet access. Although an increase in the use of ICT is on the agenda of all developing countries (Parliamentary Office of Science and Technology, 2006) there are a few problems that these countries face. These include the implementation of government policy with regard to the role of technology in education, limited budgets for the purchase of educational software or computer hardware, a scarcity of human resources with the technological expertise to implement technology in the classroom, as well as a lack of technical skills on the part of the student at the receiving end (Dalha, 2010; Marandi, 2010; Yildiz & Tatar, 2010). As a result, it may be difficult, and in many cases impossible, for large numbers of foreign language learners worldwide to obtain the maximum benefits of learning via computers and other digital devices (Gulati, 1981; Hvorecky, 2004).

In the field of foreign language (FL) learning, where learners need to communicate with other speakers, both native and those competent in the target language, it is essential that ways to promote authentic interaction be found. The incorporation of Web 2.0 tools in education might help to achieve this by allowing language practitioners access to free software and educational resources available on the Web (Gonzalez & Almeida, 2006; Gonzalez & St. Louis, 2008; Motteram & Sharma, 2009; Peachey, 2009). While the use of Web-based resources has made this interaction easier, an internet connection is, however, needed. Problems of physical access to the internet may again be a major obstacle. Apart from these physical constraints, the digital divide can also be seen in situations in which teachers with all these technological resources lack the necessary skills to incorporate them into their pedagogical practice in such a way as to promote language learning (Egbert & Yang, 2004; Hanson-Smith, 2001; Motteram & Sharma, 2009).

Therefore, a digital divide may be said to exist, not only among teachers who work in environments in which there is insufficient access to ICT, but also in those environments where teachers are unable to use these resources adequately. Consequently, the digital divide can be said to refer to both physical and human constraints. It is important, therefore, to determine the characteristics of environments where these constraints are found in order to suggest possible ways in which they can be overcome.

This chapter examines the factors that describe low-tech contexts in computer-assisted language learning (CALL) today to determine if they are similar to those described in the literature. This will be done through the responses given by language practitioners from different countries worldwide to a survey entitled, 'Media and Language Teaching Context', which was created especially to obtain data for this chapter. The experience of some teachers who work in low-tech environments will also be described, since they can be used to help those who are facing similar challenges. Finally, some strategies that teachers in this type of setting can use to overcome the obstacles faced will be discussed.

Definition of low-technology contexts

Although language learning in low-technology contexts has been discussed (Dalha, 2010; Egbert & Yang, 2004; Kam, Ramachandran, Devanathan, Tewari & Canny, 2007; Tamela, Scolari & Bedient, 2000; Warschauer, 2004), the available literature does not provide a clear-cut definition for this term. According to *Webster's New World College Dictionary* low-tech means 'not involving specialized, complex technology in full'. This definition is not very enlightening as it does not explain what complex technology is. The *American Heritage Dictionary*, in turn, defines high technology as 'Technology that involves highly advanced or specialized systems or devices'. Therefore, what is advanced and specialized in one period, would be outdated in another, as in the case of the videocassette recorder (VCR), which was considered a 'high-tech' resource in the 1980s and is now 'low-tech' by twenty-first-century standards.

Rather than defining these terms, some authors (Egbert & Yang, 2004; Kelly, 2008) tend to describe the constraints that characterize the digital divide and which in turn, determine if the context is low-tech. Egbert and Yang (2004) mention several of these conditions which characterize 'limited' or 'low-tech' settings. They include the problem of access, which might range from no internet connection, to a general or limited access to the technology due to a slow connection, limited bandwidth, reduced contact hours as a result of computer lab availability and a low computer to student ratio. Censorship is also mentioned as a contributing factor as school administrators or government bodies might also prohibit access to certain sites (Marshall, 2009; Ngeow, 2010). Finally, software packages might also prove in time to be incompatible with newer operating systems or the activities might not provide students with sufficient and varied input for different learning styles. Egbert and Yang (2004) however, consider that it is precisely this type of environment that has 'unlimited potential to support learning opportunities in the language classroom' (p. 283). This is true if teachers possess the knowledge to use the limited resources at hand to promote learning. This connection seems to be reflected in the definition of technology offered by the United Nations Education,

Social and Cultural Organisation (UNESCO) (1985) in which the individual's 'know-how' and creative processes in the use of tools, resources and systems allows them to solve problems and improve their lives.

In the case of CALL, the know-how and creative processes could correspond to the approaches and techniques used by the teachers in the classroom, while the tools, resources and systems could be viewed as media through which learners come into contact and interact with the language.

Overview of how technology has been used in educational settings in the last few decades

The last 60 years has seen a revolution in the way the language learning field has evolved and it has gone hand in hand with the advances made in ICT. In this sense, Warschauer (1996) divides the history of CALL into three phases which correspond to movements in language learning acquisition theory: behaviourist, communicative and integrative.

The first stage, behaviourist CALL, was based on the movement of the same name and entailed the use of computers in language laboratories for the learning of language through repetitive drills. This was followed in the 1980s by the communicative CALL stage, and the use of computer programs which allowed students to be more actively involved with the language by stimulating creative thinking, discussion and the development of writing skills through simulations in games and the use of desk-top publishing (DTP).

Advances in technology and the public use of the internet, led to the third phase of Integrative CALL in the 1990s. Through multimedia, learners were exposed to a more authentic environment in which images and audio were incorporated into programs on CD-ROMs and hyperlinks within texts allowed students the freedom to explore varied content at their own speed.

The end of the twentieth century and the increased use of the internet saw the dawn of another phase of CALL, Intelligent CALL (ICALL) (Warschauer & Healey, 1998) in which it was hoped that the developments in software (speech-recognition, language corpus, concordances) and multimedia formats would create a rich language environment where learning would be more personal, catering to the individual styles and needs of students and which would allow them to hypothesize about, and use language, in more authentic ways.

Coming into the twenty-first century, rapid developments in technology have perhaps seen the arrival of this fourth phase in CALL in which high-speed internet connections, advances in digital technology and the reduction in size of computer hardware has made an impact on society. From laptop computers, MP3 players, multimedia mobile phones and tablets to the latest in software, the learning environment, as we know it, is changing. The development of Web 2.0 has increased communication by allowing users to connect with others through dynamic websites and networking communities like Facebook, My Space and Twitter (Borau, Ullrich & Shen, 2009; Harrison & Thomas, 2009). The use of Flash-based applications, open source programming and sites such as YouTube, Ustream and Flickr, along with text and video blogs and wikis have allowed users to express their creativity, search for and share information and learning resources, and more importantly, communicate with others around the world (Godwin-Jones, 2003; Martinez-Carillo & Pentikousis, 2008; Motteran & Sharma, 2009; Thorne & Payne, 2005). These online resources have also opened doors to an even more authentic environment for language learning through virtual worlds like Second Life (Gonzalez, Palomeque & Sweeney, 2011; Jauregi, Canto, de Graaff, Koenraad & Moonen, 2011; Motteran & Sharma, 2009; Sweeney, Palomeque & González, 2010), and online games (Peterson, 2010; Rankin, Gold & Gooch, 2006; Stanley & Mawer, 2008). The proliferation of blogs, wikis, chatrooms, social media networks and virtual environments reflect individuals' desire to interact with those around them and these are a rich source of language learning opportunities (Evans, 2009; McLoughlin & Lee, 2007; Sykes, Oskoz & Thorne, 2008; Thomas, 2009).

Although CALL has been present in language learning since the middle of the twentieth century, adapting to the changes in language learning theory, the digital divide has always existed between those who have the technology and use it adequately and those who do not.

CALL and low-tech environments

Although the literature refers to the characteristics of low-tech environments (Dalha, 2010; Egbert & Yang, 2004; Gulati, 1981; Kelly, 2008), and of the importance of the adequate use of technology in teaching in these contexts (Bonk, Ehman, Hixon & Yamagata-Lynch, 2002; Egbert & Yang, 2004; Hanson-Smith, 2001; Koehler & Mishra, 2009; Mishra & Koehler, 2006), we thought it necessary to learn from practitioners themselves, from around the world, whether they considered their context to be low-tech or not, the tools they used and how these were integrated into their praxis. Furthermore, individual teachers, who were chosen because of their different geographical locations and expertise in teaching language with technology, were asked to define low-technology and describe how CALL had been implemented in their classes.

A survey was sent out to teachers worldwide via the members' list of several international language learning groups. This survey required information on the country the participants were working in, student age group, language(s) taught and type of teaching and language context. Participants were also asked whether they considered their work environment to be low-tech and to describe the context. Finally, they were given a number of different resources ranging from blackboard and radio to videoconferencing and mobile phones, and were asked to choose the ones they worked with and describe the manner in which these resources were used in their classes. Participants were not asked to define a low-technology context but rather it was hoped that through an analysis of their work environment and the tools that they used, we could arrive at the factors which determine whether a teaching context was low-tech. As this survey was sent to distribution lists, it was a self-selecting process with regard to teacher participation over which there was no researcher control. The survey was open from the 29th of June to the 15th of October, 2011 and 100 replies were received.

Moreover, individual teachers from Sudan, Cyrus, Portugal, Tajikistan, Peru, Russia, Iran, Turkey, Venezuela and Colombia were asked to define low-technology and describe how CALL had been implemented in their praxis. These teachers were chosen because, apart from their experience in CALL, they were working in countries which could be considered to have technological constraints. Five of these teachers replied to this request.

It was hoped that the information obtained on country, level of education, type of educational institute, type of language taught (foreign or second language) and resources used by the teachers in the survey, would be factors in determining and helping to define a low-technology environment.

The results

Although this survey was sent to online CALL interest groups and teacher development communities, the data revealed that of the 100 respondents from 37 countries, 48% considered their language teaching environments to be low-tech (see Figure 12.1).

The data also showed (see Table 12.1) that in all educational levels represented in this survey there were low and non-low-technology contexts.

In Figure 12.2, we can see that this was also true for the type of language being taught, namely, Foreign Language (FL), (80%) or Second Language (SL), (20%).

What stands out in Figure 12.3 is that some teachers from within the same country believed their teaching environments to be low-tech while others did not. This was the

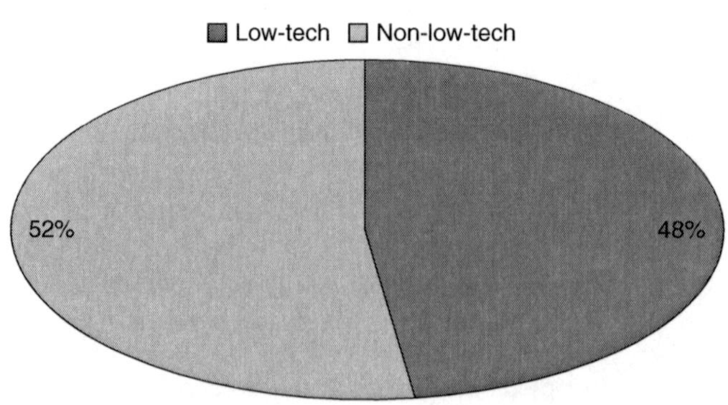

FIGURE 12.1 *Respondents in low-tech and non-low-tech contexts.*

TABLE 12.1 Low and non-low-tech respondents by levels taught

Level	Low-tech	Non-Low-tech
Adults	11	10
Academies	3	4
Primary	7	4
Secondary	9	9
Tertiary	15	20
Vocational	3	5
	48	52

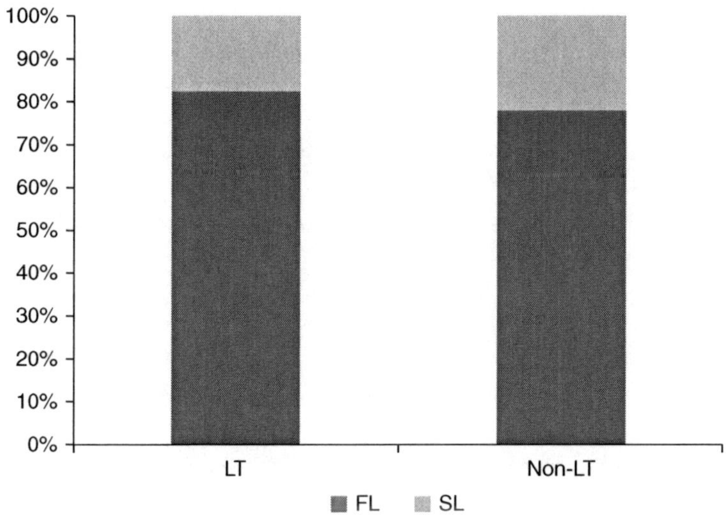

FIGURE 12.2 *Respondents teaching FL and SL in low-tech and non-low-tech contexts.*

case with Spain, Canada, France, the United States and Venezuela. This supports the argument that the perceived digital divide also exists *within* countries (Fong, 2009; Marandi, 2010; Venezky, 2000) regardless of the country's economic standing, as the United States is a developed country while Spain and Venezuela may be considered to be less developed.

Determining factors for a low-tech context

According to the data, neither the country, the level of education nor the foreign or second language context seem to be factors which indicate if the teaching context

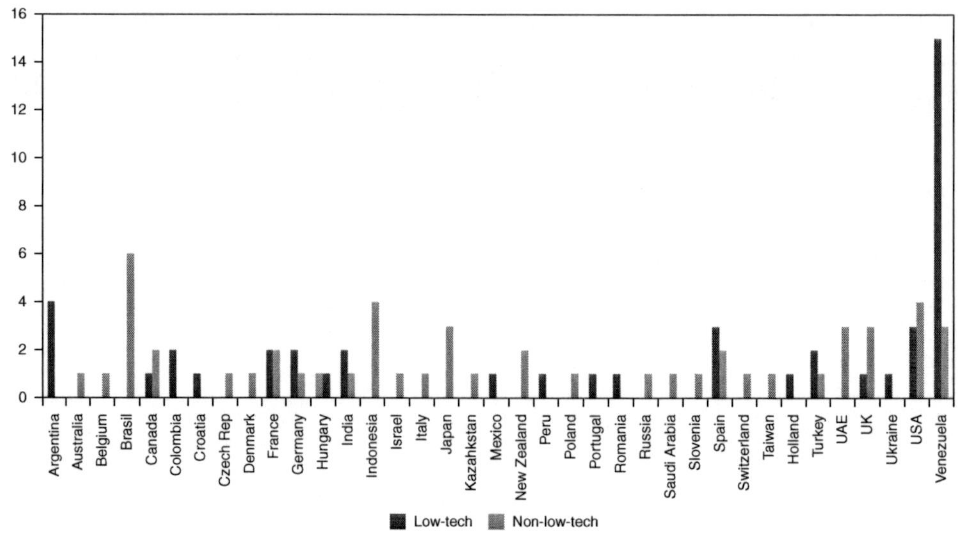

FIGURE 12.3 *Distribution of low-tech and non-low-tech contexts by countries.*

was low-tech or not. This is in contrast to what is found in the research literature on the digital divide in general, which mentions socio-demographic factors such as age (Bonfadelli, 2002; Cheng, 2007; Fox & Madden, 2005) and socio-economic status/ education (Hargittai & Walejko, 2008; Madden, 2003; Peter & Valkenburg, 2006; Van Dijk, 2005) as predictors of the digital divide.

Next, an analysis of the description of the teaching environment of the respondents, who considered that they worked in a low-technology context, was done. Human and institutional constraints were mentioned. It should be pointed out that the physical constraints mentioned in the literature (Kaur Khalsa, Maloney-Krichmar & Kreeft Peyton, 2007; Yildiz & Tatar, 2010) are found here under the category of institutional constraints, as we believe that it is the administration which controls the finances, and therefore the availability of those resources which permit the physical access to technology. The human and institutional constraints reported by the respondents are outlined below:

- Human constraints reported by 14.58% of the teachers
  - lack of teacher preparation for using technology in language teaching
  - teachers not interested in using technology
  - students associate technology with non-academic purposes

- Institutional constraints reported by 60.41% of the teachers
  - lack of institutional support
  - insufficient budget

- Physical constraints
  - only whiteboard, CD/DVD players
  - no computers for students
  - insufficient number of computers for students
  - outdated hardware
- High cost of internet access
  - limited or no internet access available

Most of these factors, which create a challenge when incorporating technology in the language classroom, correspond to those mentioned by Kaur Khalsa et al. (2007) when discussing the digital divide. Therefore, these teachers appear to be at a disadvantage with regard to their colleagues in other contexts who have an adequate infrastructure, that is, wireless internet access, internet access and computers for all the students or at least a connected PC in the classroom, as mentioned by respondents who rated their working environment as being non-low-tech. However, as Egbert and Yang (2004) point out, this scenario is not necessarily as negative as it may seem.

At this point, the first two factors which may incur in the description of a low-technology context, according to the replies given, are the human and institutional or physical constraints, which concur with the literature on the digital divide in the area of language learning.

Tools used in low and non-low-tech contexts

The survey also asked participants to select the tools that they used in their praxis. These ranged from the earliest audio and visual medium, the radio and blackboard, to the latest audio-visual gadgets, mobile phones and tablets. These tools were selected to reflect a cross-section of the different audio-visual medium used in language teaching in the last century (see Figure 12.4).

Specific Web 2.0 tools were not itemized in the survey but rather left for teachers to include in the category 'Other'. This was done to guarantee that these were included because the respondents knew and actually used them.

As Table 12.2 illustrates, teachers in both low-tech and non-low-tech groups used all of the tools listed in the survey to a greater or lesser extent.

However, the tools most used by those who considered their context to be low-tech were the stand-alone PC with overhead projector and CD-ROMs with 70.21% each, while the non-low-tech group used the whiteboard, email and DVD, all with 78.84%. The high number of respondents who reported using CD-ROMs may be due to first, their inclusion in materials bought from publishers and second, the fact that they can be used with a stand-alone PC without an internet connection. Most published materials come with a CD-ROM for use by the students while the DVD component

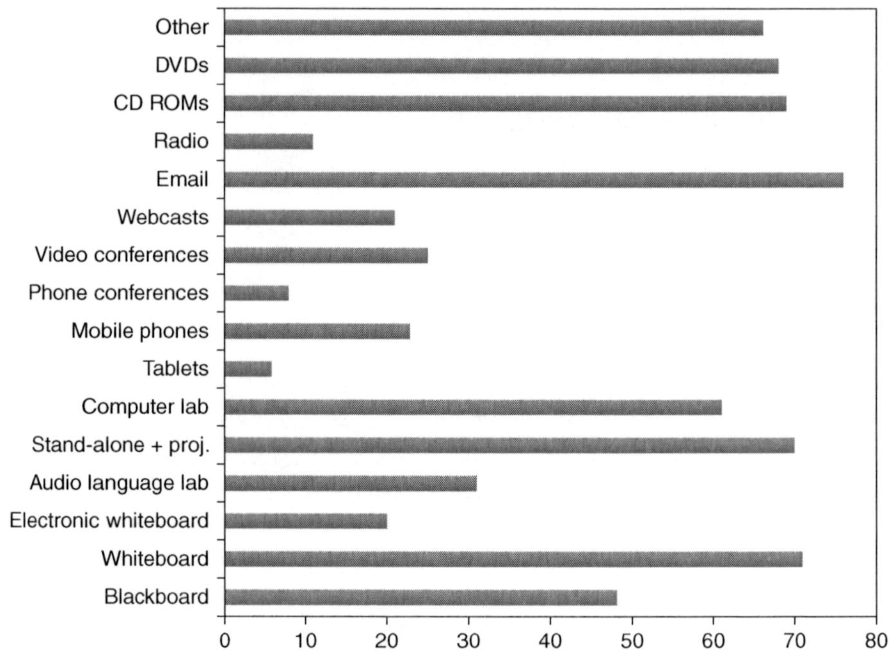

FIGURE 12.4 *Tools used by respondents in low and non-low-tech contexts.*

must be purchased additionally. This would incur an extra cost for the institution which may not be a problem for teachers working in a non-low-tech environment where the administration has invested in infrastructure, hardware and software. This may account for why 78.84% of the teachers in this group report the use of DVDs compared to 59.57% in the low-tech group.

Webcasts were used by 27% of the non-low-tech group compared to 15% in the low-tech group. This may be due to the difference in availability and quality of the internet connection for teachers in both groups.

It should be noted that mobile phones and phone conferences were used by 28% and 10.63% of teachers in the low-tech group. In the non-low-tech group, these resources were used by 11.52% and 3.84% respectively. This might be a result of the availability of telephone communication over internet access in their areas. This seems to support m-learning, the use of mobile phones for education, which is being explored and implemented in different locations around the world (MILLEE, 2004; Moura & Carvalho, 2009; Project ABC / IMAC, 2009; Yoza Project, 2009).

The data also revealed that there were a number of tools that were used by both groups. The blackboard is still a favourite with 51.06% of the respondents in the low-tech group and 48% in the non-low-tech. Tablets were also mentioned by 6.39% of teachers in the low-tech and 5.76% of those in the non-low-tech group. It is, however, the least used by both groups. 70.21% of the teachers in the low-tech group and 71.15% in the non-low-technology group reported the stand-alone PC as a medium for language teaching. Nevertheless, it should be noted that teachers in the first group

TABLE 12.2 Tools used in low and non-low-tech contexts

Tools	Low-tech	%	Non-Low-tech	%
Blackboard	24	51.06	25	48
Whiteboard	32	68.08	41	78.84
Electronic Whiteboard	7	15	10	19.23
Audio language lab	13	28	17	32.69
Stand-alone PC With OHP	33	70.21	37	71.15
Computer lab	25	53.19	33	63.46
Tablets	3	6.39	3	5.76
Mobile phones	13	28	6	11.52
Phone conferences	5	10.63	2	3.84
Video conferences	10	21.27	13	25
Webcasts	7	15	14	27
Email	32	68.08	41	78.84
Radio	5	10.63	6	11.53
CD-ROM	33	70.21	36	69.26
DVD	28	59.57	41	78.84

mentioned the stand-alone PC as the only computer resource in the classroom while teachers in the non-low-tech group remarked that they had classrooms with individual PCs for students.

The whiteboard, email and computer labs are widely used by both groups although there is a 10% difference in the figures for each tool when compared with the non-low-tech group. It should also be pointed out that the radio is still being used by teachers in both groups with 10.63% (low-tech) and 11.53% (non-low-tech) as it is a resource for authentic listening as reported in the survey.

An analysis of the tools found in the 'Other' category revealed that teachers in both groups incorporated Web 2.0 tools in their teaching. These included MP3 players, podcasting applications, blogs, wikis and Web-based video sites like YouTube. They also mentioned the use of LMSs (Learning Management Systems) mainly Moodle, for asynchronous communication, and as a gateway for course materials. 45.83% of the teachers in the low-tech group reported using these resources compared to 46.15%

of those in the non-low-tech group. A few teachers in the low-tech group also cited Twitter, Facebook and virtual worlds (Second Life) as a means of communicating with their students, practising language and for teacher development respectively. However, none of the teachers in the other group reported this use.

Only 46.15% of teachers in the non-low-tech group reported using Web 2.0 tools in their teaching. This may be considered low given the importance of these tools in promoting authentic interaction and communication among learners (Duffy, 2007; Peachey, 2009; Raith, 2009; Thomas, 2009). As one respondent stated 'they bring authenticity into the classroom'.

It could be inferred from the analysis of the data for this item that the teachers who considered their environment to be low-tech feel a more urgent need to overcome this obstacle, and so resort to finding other ways in which the missing or scarce resources could be incorporated into their teaching. This can be seen by the growth in the number of participants from South America, Eastern Europe and Asia who participate in online communities and online professional development sessions.

An example of this is 'Becoming a Webhead', a hands-on workshop on how to use Web communication tools for language teaching and learning (Gonzalez, 2004), which is offered for free as part of the yearly TESOL Electronic Village Online. Unlike second language teachers, those who teach foreign languages lack the language input that their SL counterparts have at their disposal for their students. As a result, they need to explore how a range of options could provide this target language exposure for their students and Web 2.0 has emerged as one of the best options available. Let us now take a closer look at how these practitioners are integrating ICT into their contexts.

Use of tools in low-tech contexts

The way technological tools are used in educational low-tech contexts is very important if we want to offer strategies to teachers working in this type of environment. To this end, based on the data received, the tools in Table 12.3 below (the stand-alone PC with overhead projector, CD-ROM, whiteboard, email, DVD, computer lab and blackboard) were selected. Although few teachers reported the use of Web 2.0 tools, it was considered important that they be included as these resources can be used by other teachers who are willing to incorporate them in their teaching. The same can be said for the inclusion of mobile phones, as this cutting-edge technology is quickly gaining ground in settings where other types of ICT might be difficult to access (MILLEE, 2004; Moura & Carvalho, 2009; Project ABC/IMAC, 2009; Yoza Project, 2009).

Table 12.2 shows that both teachers in low-tech and non-low-tech settings use the same tools, while Table 12.3 shows the way in which teachers in the low-tech group incorporate these resources in their teaching. On comparing this to the teachers in the non-low-tech group, it was found that both groups used them in the same way.

It should be noted that differences between the two groups have to do with physical constraints and not with the way in which the technological resources are implemented in the classroom. That it is to say, teachers who consider their environment to be

TABLE 12.3 How some tools are used in low-tech contexts

Resource	Ways in which it is used
Stand-alone PC with overhead projector	• To use with PPTs to introduce new topics and explain grammar and vocabulary • To show illustrations and images • To project quizzes
CD-ROM	• To develop listening comprehension skills in the language lab
Whiteboard	• To present and review vocabulary, grammar explanations • To brainstorm ideas
Email	• To communicate with students • To send reading materials • To send and receive student assignments
DVD	• To develop listening and speaking skills
Computer lab	• To play interactive games to develop grammar, vocabulary and reading • To write in wikis and blogs • To do various tasks using the internet • To use licensed audio-visual resources to develop language skills
Blackboard	• To teach vocabulary and syntax • To explain grammar
Mobile phones	• To make announcements • To keep in touch with students • To complete class activities (e.g., look up unknown vocabulary on android phones)
Web 2.0 tools (blogs, wikis, podcasts)	Wikis and blogs: • To post lessons and assignments • To do collaborative work Podcasts • To practise listening, speaking and pronunciation

non-low-tech, reported having more computers per student in the classroom as well as in the language lab, but there was no difference in the way the actual tools were used.

The information from the survey seems to indicate that institutional or physical constraints, and to a lesser extent human constraints, are important factors in determining the type of technological teaching context (Egbert & Yang, 2004; Kaur Khalsa, Maloney-Krichmar & Kreeft Peyton, 2007). Moreover, the fact that teachers in low-tech environments used the tools in the same way as their colleagues in non-low-tech settings may be due to the formers' involvement in online communities where knowledge sharing and scaffolding occur.

Let us now look at how five experienced teachers who work in low-tech environments describe their teaching situation in more detail to see what additional factors, if any, emerge.

Low-tech contexts according to practitioners

The individual teachers, who were asked to define what they considered to be a low-tech environment, described it in the following manner:

> A low-tech context for me includes schools with limited use of technology due to lack of appropriate equipment or even worse, due to lack of qualified trained staff. So, if there is no computer lab in a school, no laptops, no video projectors or maybe only one or two, or interactive whiteboards that would be a low-tech school. What is more, a school that is adequately equipped with all the aforementioned technology tools but has no trained teachers to use them is again defined as a low-tech school. There is no worse thing that teachers thinking that the use of PowerPoint presentations in the classroom is the ultimate way of implementing new technologies in their teaching. (Cyprus)

> Low-technology environment – is this an environment where technology is rarely used by people in their everyday life? If yes, then in such environment people value technology less because they do not know what it can do for them. The majority because of limited knowledge and conservative thinking do not see much value in technology; do not want changes in life which technology rich environment has. Such low-technology environments lag behind compared to rich technology environments. Those who are literate using technology may not be able to implement their ideas or face challenges working with the majority. (Tajikistan)

> Low-technology contexts are very difficult to describe as our context is very diverse. What I find as very strange is that our classes and working environment is full of technology. But no one uses the technology. Sudan is an example of a country where telecommunication services are the best in Africa. But the 'low know how' and the use of technology in services other than education makes our contexts very low-tech. (Sudan)

> I considered my one computer classroom a low-tech context, basically because there was only my laptop for 28 students. Is it correct to define this context as low-tech considering we had access to other technology, namely, a video projector? I think so in terms of the very limited student/computer ratio. (Portugal)

> I consider I work in a low-tech environment. Although the university has a certain number of rooms equipped with computers and access to the internet, the number of rooms is limited considering the number of students. Therefore, professors need to compete for the availability of those rooms. Besides that,

> there are certain restrictions in campus regarding the kind of websites and services that can be accessed. For example, Second Life cannot be used inside campus. 'Aula virtual', our LMS, has many restrictions and does not offer full functionality. Many professors need to resort to free-access platforms (Yahoo, Google, Wikispaces etc.) and often have to deal with advertising and other problems. A final aspect is the availability of wireless internet. The university has just two or three wireless networks and they don't work all the time and are available in specific parts of the campus. Some are blocked even for professors. To sum up, there is technology access in my context but this comes with serious limitations if compared with other contexts. Most professors have to put their creativity and virtuosity to [work to] provide effective ICT tools and support for their students. (Venezuela)

As can be seen from these comments, there are three aspects which standout: the lack of adequate physical resources, trained staff and those who resist the incorporation of technology in their teaching. These comments confirm the constraints (human and institutional) found when analysing the working environment of teachers in the low-tech group. In this case, institutional constraints correspond to the hardware, available software and internet connection (physical resources) as it is the administration that provides them. It is interesting to note, that in both the survey and the replies to the question posed to specific teachers, mention was made of this human factor, relating to practitioners and students. The lack of teacher training and/or the lack of motivation to incorporate technology into their teaching seems to be an important element for some of the respondents when describing a low-tech setting. Teacher resistance to integrating technology, even when having both technological skills and resources, seems to be another relevant issue (Fawzi, 2010; Yildez & Tatar, 2010). These problems could be the result of psychological barriers such as personality, attitude, motivation, self-efficacy, anxiety, stress and locus of control (Correa, 2008), as teachers are required to move outside of their comfort zone when confronting technology. Students also appear reluctant to use technology for language learning and seem to consider it only as a source of entertainment (Yildez & Tatar, 2010). Therefore, it would sound reasonable to include both the physical and the human factors when attempting to describe a technological environment in education, and in language teaching in particular. This seems relevant given that some practitioners seem to link the use of computers with a certain type of technological environment. That is to say, if computers are used in a classroom, then it is a no low-tech context. However, they do not seem to consider the pedagogical use that should be given to these tools.

Low-tech or non-low-tech?

On analysing the responses of those practitioners who consider their work environment to be non-low-tech, the following examples came to our attention:

> Most of my work nowadays involves classes in which the computer attached to a data projector is the main technology; many of them use PowerPoint as the basic tool to introduce the points of the class, supported by sound (MP3, CD or occasionally, cassettes). (Czech Republic)
>
> Book, blackboard, whiteboard, CD-ROM, DVD, Webcast, Stand-alone PC (mostly teacher centric activities and transmission mode-explanation/illustration/reinforcement. Recalling data, making students react, understanding meaning – written and oral. (Brazil)
>
> New vocabulary written on whiteboard; use of DVDs and YouTube to introduce new structures/vocabulary and to practise listening comprehension; OHP and PowerPoint for introduction/repetition of new material and exercises/answers. (New Zealand)
>
> The students access the materials via Moodle either in the PC lab or in their own computer. I usually communicate with them via email for anything related to class-work. The whiteboard is only used when I can't explain a concept using MS PowerPoint. (Indonesia)
>
> I use PPT, email, videos, blogs and DVDs for the adults. I have used blogs and DVDs for the pupils but to a much lesser degree, mainly because of the limited possibilities (room, three computers at my disposal, large classes). (Switzerland)
>
> I take my office laptop to class and use it for many purposes. I use it for listening activities, for showing resources from the net and for modeling some activities. (Turkey)
>
> Data show: To display images, photos for clarifications or for presentations
>
> Email: to exchange info and circulars + to communicate with parents and admin. (UAE)

Considering the factors found in the survey, these descriptions would best suit a low-tech environment given that they appear to have similar physical constraints. However, this is because we have placed them in this category due to the types of devices they use and not by how they are used. This raises the question of the characteristics that define a low-tech environment in CALL. Considering the two major factors of physical and human constraints, we can now list the basic features needed in a low-tech setting in a language classroom.

The results of the analysis to the two sources of information point to low-tech environments as those in which there are:

- physical constraints with regard to:
  - the number of computers per student;
  - insufficient and inadequate internet access which would allow for the productive use of language learning resources on the Web;

 - lack of interest on the part of the administration for the use of technology in learning.

- human constraints in the form of:

 - untrained teachers and those unwilling to incorporate ICT in their praxis;
 - students who are reluctant to use technology in their language learning.

In this way, for example, a classroom in which students have computers and adequate access to internet, but where the teachers do not maximize the use of the online resources available and stick to their comfort zone, would be considered a low-tech environment. This brings us back to the definition of technology given by UNESCO (1985) in which the 'know-how' and 'creative process' play very important roles. So, how the resources are used is as important, if not more important than the tool, system or resource itself.

How to use CALL in low-tech contexts

Egbert and Yang (2004) point out the advantages of studying and teaching in a low-tech environment. They include the fact that students can learn a few technologies well and use these to support the development of their metacognitive skills and can concentrate on their tasks and interaction with other learners without the distraction of the 'bells and whistles' (p. 283). Teachers can also benefit from this environment because 'more emphasis can be placed on the use of the technology than on its functions' (p. 283). These authors propose a framework based on the eight conditions needed for language learning (Egbert & Hanson-Smith, 1999) which include opportunities for social interaction and negotiation of meaning, varied input and involvement with authentic tasks and with authentic audiences. These conditions, necessary for language learning, should be incorporated into CALL and do not depend on the level of technology available in the classroom. Teachers should devise a class plan based on clear learning objectives, the needs and strengths of their students, both linguistically and cognitively, and develop activities that would promote authentic interaction through the discovery and use of the language. Once this has been done, the appropriate technological tools from those available can be used to facilitate the learning process.

Strategies to use in low-tech contexts with physical restraints

With this in mind, let us now look at the way in which teachers in low-technology settings can use the resources available on the internet to maximize learning in classrooms with physical and human restraints. Table 12.3 shows the resources used by teachers for introducing new topics or vocabulary, explaining or reviewing grammar, for presentations and testing. However, below are more comprehensive examples, some taken from teachers who have used them successfully in their classrooms, where students play a more active role. Teachers can:

- Use downloadable interactive exercise generators (e.g., Hot potatoes) which can be used to create a number of different exercises offline. Other free software providers allow activities to be created on external memory (CDs, DVDs or memory stick).
    - These exercises can then be shown to the students and different group games can be played. These games will encourage student co-operation and collaboration.
- Send and reply to videos using email (e.g., Eyejot)
    - Invite students to practise and then use the language by sending audio and video emails to other students.
    - Show students how to use free downloadable audio-editing programs (e.g., Audacity) and encourage them to be used for recording activities such as interviews, radio programmes, and storytelling or advertising slots. These recordings can then be collected and burnt to a CD or DVD for students.
    - Encourage students to make videos with their mobile phones or cameras and show these on the PC. These can be individual or project based.
- Create a blog and send entries via email (e.g., Posterous).
    - Have students work in small groups, discuss the information and write what they would like to post to the blog. Have them take turns at posting, during the term.
    - Have students work in small groups or pairs creating a text which they will later record using the available tools (MP3 player, mobile phone or computer microphone) and then post to a blog.
    - Invite other students and teachers to visit the class blog and post their comments.
    - Encourage students to work on blogs at home through the creation of interesting extra-curricular activities based on students' age and interests.

- Download videos and podcasts with topics of interest and authentic language use and then create activities for students. These videos and podcasts can be obtained from a number of online sites, either dedicated to foreign language learning or authentic sources of the language (news, museums, specific professional areas, like nursing, architecture or engineering or social sites like YouTube).
    - The information from these videos and audios can be used as input for discussion, or writing (using downloadable dictionaries like Wordweb), and a number of activities for listening comprehension, vocabulary building, dictations and cultural awareness among others.
- Create after school programmes, for example language clubs, where students can use the computers to do research and project-based activities and communicate with other language learners and teachers both locally and internationally.

These activities involve students' active involvement with the language through interaction with text, audio, video and their peers. In this way, they are using the language communicatively, for personal use which increases motivation and helps foster learning. These activities can be done offline thereby giving students multiple exposure to both input and output.

Strategies to use in low-tech contexts with human restraints

Although the majority of the respondents to the survey reported physical constraints as the main obstacle to the implementation of CALL in low-technology environments, several teachers stressed the human constraints as well. Lack of teacher training and/or peer scaffolding, insufficient practice in the use of online resources and fear of using new tools and finding a new methodology to fit with the changes in language learning are some of the factors which might inhibit teachers and prevent them from using, or making the most of these resources.

Researchers such as Harris, Mishra and Koehler (2009), Guerrero (2005), Kelly (2008), Mishra and Koehler (2006) and Koehler and Mishra (2009), propose a framework for teacher development in technology in which knowledge of content, technology and pedagogy are integrated to optimize learning and argue that teachers should master each of these areas. In the case of language learning, this would mean that teachers should know about the theories of second language acquisition and language learning to know how to teach the content and then use their knowledge of the technology to design activities to mediate between the two.

The following are some suggestions that might help teachers to overcome these obstacles and become better practitioners in the use of ICT in language learning and teaching:

- More experienced teachers can volunteer to help those with less experience in the use of ICT in education. Teachers can hold informal meetings with colleagues, who have more expertise in the implementation of CALL in their context to express their doubts, ask for advice and receive scaffolding.
- Teachers can join free existing online communities or even begin their own local or national group with other interested teachers. In this way they can share experiences, describe challenges and ask for suggestions for overcoming them.
- Special Interest Groups of worldwide English teachers associations are another source of professional development that can enrich teachers new to teaching with technology.
- Self-access professional development sites (blogs, wikis, webcasts) are other sources of contact and knowledge sharing.
- Online communities, Special Interest Groups and professional development sites are sources which can enrich teachers by providing them with support and keeping them abreast of new developments with regard to both tools and teaching techniques. It is essential for teachers who work in low-tech environments to share their knowledge and expertise with those who might need it.

Another point raised by the respondents to the survey dealt with students' response to the use of CALL in their language classes. Students appeared to be either unmotivated or to consider technology as only for entertainment or for personal use. Here are some suggestions which might encourage students to take an interest in the use of ICT resources in language learning:

- Propose activities to be done at home. This is recommended when there are limited or no ITC resources in the classroom. It is important that the topics for these activities be based on learner needs and interests and not on the official curriculum.
- Create wikis and blogs for learners to post their work.
- Design authentic tasks which will require students to be creative with their use of both the language and the technological resources.
- Encourage healthy competition between and among students through meaningful projects that reflect the culture of the country and the students' interests.

- Encourage peers and other target language speakers to visit the students' blogs and wikis and leave comments or to act as judges.

These types of activities will motivate students as they will help them to see the need to use the technological resource as a medium for authentic communication in the target language.

Learners of English as a second language (ESL) are exposed to more target language input when they interact with the society in which they live. This, however, is not possible for learners of English as a foreign language (EFL) who must find and exploit all the opportunities available for exposure to, and interaction with, the language. To this end, the role of CALL and ICT in EFL is essential and Web 2.0 resources can be used in an attempt to bridge this gap. For those who work and live in environments in which physical and human constraints might pose a challenge, it is important that viable solutions be found. These include downloading resources from the Web which can be used in computers without the need for an internet connection or using software programs which can be downloaded to a computer's hard drive to generate activities which also do not need an internet connection.

Conclusions

Today's 'high-tech' devices are continually being replaced by newer and more innovative ones. From the printing press, to radio and TV, to electronic devices, new developments in science have taken us from print, to audio, to moving images and finally to interconnectivity. All of these have been used, and will continue to be used, in language teaching. But, these are just tools, media to connect with others. What is important is the 'know-how', the way in which these tools are used. In this way, it is perhaps the human constraints that are more important than the physical obstacles when we look at the implications of the digital divide in language learning. In this sense, many teachers in low-tech settings understand the importance of the integration of ICT, which is the hardware and online resources, in language learning. Nevertheless, most still do not know how to achieve this, especially when it comes to promoting interaction and communication for meaningful purposes.

There is, however, a widespread interest in professional development right now as can be seen in the growing number of participants who view presentations on the use of technology in language learning, webinars from international professional teaching associations and commercial publication houses, as well as interest in online Special Interest Groups (SIGs) (e.g., TESOL and IATEFL). To sum up, while teaching languages with the use of technology in a low-tech environment can sometimes be discouraging for practitioners, as the respondents to the survey used for this chapter, as well as the wider literature have shown (Fawzi, 2010; Marandi, 2010; Yildez & Tatar, 2010), there are many ways in which these obstacles can be overcome.

References

Bates, A. W. (2005). *Technology, e-learning and distance education.* London: Routledge.

Bonfadelli, H. (2002). The internet and knowledge gaps: A theoretical and empirical investigation. *European Journal of Communication, 17*(1), 65–84.

Bonk, C. J., Ehman, L., Hixon, E., & Yamagata-Lynch, L. (2002). The pedagogical TICKIT: Teacher institute for curriculum knowledge about the integration of technology. *Journal of Technology and Teacher Education, 10*(2), 205–33.

Borau, K., Ullrich, C., Feng, J., & Shen, R. (2009). Microblogging for language learning: Using Twitter to train communicative and cultural competence. *Advances in Web Based Learning, Lecture Notes in Computer Science, 5686*, 78–87.

Chapelle, C. (2001). *Computer applications in second language acquisition: Foundations for teaching, testing and research.* Cambridge: Cambridge University Press.

Chen, H. T. (2007). *Sharing, connection, and creation in the Web 2.0 era: Profiling the adopters of video-sharing and social-networking sites.* Paper presented at the Association for Education in Journalism and Mass Communication, Washington DC.

Correa, T. (2008). *Literature review: Understanding the 'second-level digital divide'.* Unpublished manuscript prepared for the class Mass Communication Theory I. School of Journalism. UT-Austin.

Dalha, L. (2010). Unmet promises, outmoded models and inadequate support in Nigeria. In J. Egbert (Ed.), *CALL in limited technology contexts* (pp. 167–77). Texas: CALICO.

Duffy, P. (2007). *Engaging the YouTube Google-eyed generation: Strategies for using Web 2.0 in teaching and learning.* In D. Remenyi (Ed.), *Proceedings of the 6th European Conference on E-Learning.* Academic Conferences Limited, Reading, UK.

Egbert, J., & Brander, B. (2010). A framework for situated online language teacher education: Learning to engage diverse students through culturally responsive CALL. In J. Egbert (Ed.), *CALL in limited technology contexts* (pp. 135–44). Texas: CALICO.

Egbert, J., & Yang, Y. F. (2004). Mediating the digital divide in CALL classrooms: Promoting effective language tasks in limited technology contexts. *ReCALL, 16*, 280–91.

Evans, M. (Ed.) (2009). *Foreign language learning with digital technology.* London: Continuum.

Eyring, J. (2001). Technology with a human touch: Reaching ESL students in their own communities through interactive television. In L. Henrichsen (Ed.), *Distance-learning programs* (pp. 13–25). Alexandria, VA: TESOL, Inc.

Fawzi, Hala. (2010). Bleeding edge challenges in Sudan: Limits on using CALL in EFL classrooms at the tertiary level. In J. Egbert (Ed.), *CALL in limited technology contexts* (pp. 189–200). Texas: CALICO.

Fong, M. (2009). *Digital divide: The case of developing countries. Issues in informing science and information technologies* (Vol. 6). Retrieved from http://iisit.org/Vol6/IISITv6p471-478Fong597.pdf

Fox. S., & Madden, S. (2005). *Generations online. Washington*, DC: Pew Internet and American Life Project.

Godwin-Jones, R. (2003). Emerging technologies: Blogs and wikis environments for online collaboration. *Language, Learning and Technology, 7*(2), 12–16.

González, D. (2004). Bringing colleagues into Web-based learning and teaching. *TESOL Essential Teacher, 1*(4), 24–8.

González, D., & Almeida d'Eca, T. (2006). Becoming a Webhead: Bridging the gap from classroom to blended or online teaching. *CALICO Journal, 2*(3), 569–80.

González, D., & St. Louis, R. (2008). *The use of Web 2.0 tools to promote learner autonomy. Independence, 43*, 28–32.

González, D., Palomeque, C., & Sweeney, P. (2011). Teaching Spanish in Second Life. In M. Thomas (Ed.), *Digital education: Opportunities for social collaboration* (pp. 143–66). London & New York: Palgrave Macmillan.

Guerrero, S. (2005). Teacher knowledge and a new domain of expertise: Pedagogical technology knowledge. *Journal of Educational Computing Research*, *33*(3), 249–67.

Gulati, D. V. (1981). Computer education and the needs for developing countries. In R. Lewis & D. Tagg (Eds.), *Computer in education* (pp. 551–5). Amsterdam, North Holland Publishing Company.

Hanson-Smith, E. (2001). The role of technological environments in language education. In E. Hanson-Smith (Ed.), *Technology-enhanced learning environments* (pp. 1–6). Alexandria, VA: TESOL Inc.

Hargittai, E., & Walejko, G. (2008). The participation divide: Content creation and sharing in the digital divide age. *Information, Communication & Society*, *11*(2), 239–56.

Harris, J., Mishra, P., & Koehler, M. J. (2009). Teachers' technological pedagogical content knowledge and learning activity types: Curriculum-based technology integration reframed. *Journal of Research on Technology in Education*, *41*(4), 393–416.

Harrison, R., & Thomas, M. (2009). Identity in online communities: Social networking sites and language learning. *International Journal of Emerging Technologies & Society*, *7*(2), 109–24.

Hvorecky, J., (2004). 'Can e-learning break the digital divide?' *European Journal of Open, Distance and E-learning*, *2*. Retrieved from www.eurodl.org/materials/contrib/2004/Hvorecky.htm

Jauregi, K., Canto, S. de Graaff, R., Koenraad, T., & Moonen, M. (2011). Verbal interaction in Second Life: Towards a pedagogic framework for task design. *Computer Assisted Language Learning*, *24*(1), 77–101.

Kam, M., Ramachandran, D., Devanathan, V., Tewari, A., & Canny, J. (2007). *Localized iterative design for language learning in underdeveloped regions: The PACE framework*. Proceedings. Designing for Specific Cultures. 28 April 28–3 May. San Jose, CA, USA.

Kaur Khalsa, D., Maloney-Krichmar, D., & Kreeft Peyton, J. (2007). Theory and research: Interaction via computers issue. In J. Egbert & E. Hanson-Smith (Eds.), *Call environments research practice and critical issues* (pp. 19–31). Alexandria, VA: Teachers of English to Speakers of Other Languages (TESOL) Inc.

Kelly, M. A. (2008). Bridging digital and cultural divides. In American Association of Colleges for Teachers (Ed.), *Handbook of technological pedagogical content knowledge (TPCK) for educators* (pp. 31–9). New York, NY: Routledge.

Koehler, M. J., & Mishra, P. (2009). What is technological pedagogical content knowledge? *Contemporary Issues in Technology and Teacher Education*, *9*(1). Retrieved from www.citejournal.org/vol9/iss1/general/article1.cfm

Madden, M. (2003). *America's online pursuits*. Washington, DC: Pew Internet & American Life Project.

Marandi, S. (2010). Bravely stepping forward: Creating CALL communities to support teachers and learners in Iran. In J. Egbert (Ed.), *CALL in limited technology contexts* (pp. 179–88). Texas: CALICO.

Marshall, G. (2009). *From China to the UK: Net censorship worldwide*. Retrieved from www.techradar.com/news/internet/from-china-to-the-uk-net-censorship-worldwide-622428

Martinez-Carrillo, C., & Pentikousis, K. (2008). An application of wikis for mediated collaborative learning to Spanish L2. In *Proceedings of the international conference on internet and multimedia systems and applications* (EuroIMSA) (pp. 39–44). Innsbruck, Austria.

McLoughlin, C., & Lee, M. J. W. (2007). Listen and learn: A systematic review of the evidence that podcasting supports learning in higher education. In C. Montgomerie & J. Seale (Eds.), *Proceedings of world conference on educational multimedia, hypermedia and telecommunications* (pp. 1669–77). Chesapeake, VA: AACE.

Mishra, P., & Koehler, M. J. (2006). Technological pedagogical content knowledge: A new framework for teacher knowledge. *Teachers College Record, 108*(6), 1017–54.

Motteran, G., & Sharma, P. (2009). Blending learning in a Web 2.0 world. *International Journal of Emerging Technologies & Society,* 7(2), 83–96.

Moura, A., & Carvalho, A. (2009). Mobile learning: Two experiments on teaching and learning with mobile phones. In R. Hijón-Neira (Ed.), *Advanced learning* (pp. 89–103). Vukovar, Croatia: In-Tah. *Mobile and immersive learning for literacy in emerging economies* (MILLEE) (2004–11). Retrieved from www.cs.cmu.edu/~mattkam/lab/millee.html

Ngeow, K (2010). Restricted internet access and censorship: CALL alternatives and initiatives. In J. Egbert (Ed.), *CALL in limited technology contexts* (pp. 93–105). Texas: CALICO.

O'Reilly, T. (2005). *Design patterns and business models for the next generation software.* Retrieved from http://oreilly.com/web2/archive/what-is-web-20.html

Parliamentary Office of Science and Technology Post note (2006). *ICT in developing countries, 261*, March. Retrieved from www.parliament.uk/documents/post/postpn261.pdf

Peachey, N. (2009). *Web 2.0 tools for teachers.* Retrieved from www.scribd.com/doc/19576895/Web-20-Tools-for-Teachers

Pentikousis, K., & Martinez-Carrillo, C. (2008). Mediated collaborative learning. In *ERCIM News, 75*, 60–1.

Peter, J., & Valkenburg, P. M. (2006). Adolescents internet use: Testing the 'Disappearing digital divide' versus the 'Emerging digital differentiation' approach. *Poetics, 34*(4–5), 293–305.

Peterson, M. (2010). Massively multiplayer online role-playing games (MMORPGs) as arenas for second language learning. *Computer Assisted Language Learning, 23*(5), 429–39.

Projet ABC / IMAC. (2009). Retrieved from http://mobileactive.org/using-mobiles-rural-literacy-and-market-information-niger-projet-abc-imac

Raith, T. (2009). The use of Weblogs in language education. In M. Thomas (Ed.), *Handbook of research on Web 2.0 and second language learning.* Hershey, PA: Information Science Reference.

Rankin, Y., Gold, R., & Gooch, B. (2006). *3D role playing games as language learning tools.* Retrieved from http://webhome.cs.uvic.ca/~bgooch/Publications/PDFs/Rankin_Gold_Gooch.pdf

Reske, S. (2005). Using radio scripts in English language learning. *Proceedings of the CATESOL State Conference, 2005.* Rocklin, CA: Sierra College.

Stanley, G., & Mawer, K. (2008). Language learners and computer games: From Space Invaders to Second Life. *TESL-EJ, 11*(4), 1–12.

Stevens, V. (2010). Shifting sands, shifting paradigms: Challenges to developing 21st century learning skills in the United Arab Emirates. In J. Egbert (Ed.), *CALL in limited technology contexts* (pp. 227–39), Texas: CALICO.

Sweeney, P., Palomeque, C., & González, D. (2010). Task design for language learning in an embodied environment. In V. Giovanni & B. James (Eds.), *Teaching through multiuser virtual environments: Applying dynamic elements to the modern classroom* (pp. 259–82). Hershey, PA: Information Science Reference.

Sykes, J. M., Oskoz, A., & Thorne, S. L. (2008). Web 2.0, synthetic immersive environments and mobile resources for language education, *CALICO Journal, 25*(3), 528–56.

Tamela, R., Scolari, J., & Bedient, D. (2000). Too few computers and too many kids. *Learning and Leading with Technology, 27*(7), 50–3.

Thomas, M. (Ed.) (2009). *Handbook of research on Web 2.0 and second language learning.* Hershey, PA: Information Science Reference.

Thorne, S. L., & Payne, S. (2005). Evolutionary trajectories, internet-mediated expression and language education. *CALICO Journal, 22*(3), 171–97.

UNESCO (1985). *Definition of technology.* Retrieved from www.pa.ash.org.au/tefa/wite.html

Valdivia, I. J. (2008). *Las políticas de tecnología para escuelas en América Latina y el mundo: visiones y lecciones.* Economic Commission for Latin America and the Caribbean. Retrieved from www.eclac.org/ddpe/publicaciones/xml/8/34938/W214.pdf

Van Dijk, J. (2005). *The deepening divide inequality in the information society.* Thousand Oaks: Sage.

Venezky, R. (2000). *The digital divide within formal school education: Causes and consequences in learning to bridge the Digital Divide.* OECD Publishing.

Warschauer, M. (1996). Computer-assisted language learning: An introduction. In S. Fotos (Ed.), *Multimedia language teaching* (pp. 3–20). Tokyo: Logos International.

— (2001). On-line learning in second language classrooms. An ethnography study. In M. Warschauer & R. Kern (Eds.), *Network-based language teaching: Conceps and practice* (pp. 41–58). Cambridge: Cambridge University Press.

— (2003). *Technology and social inclusion: Rethinking the digital divide.* Cambridge: MIT Press.

— (2004). *Of digital divides and social multipliers: Combining language and technology for human development. Information and communication technologies in the teaching and learning of foreign languages: State of the art, needs and perspectives* (pp. 46–52). Moscow: UNESCO Institute for Information Technologies in Education.

Warschauer, M., & Healey, D. (1998). Computers and language learning: An overview. *Language Teaching, 31*, 57–71.

Yildiz, S., & Tatar, S. (2010). Overcoming limited planning and vision in Turkish schools. In J. Egbert (Ed.), *CALL in limited technology contexts* (pp. 201–13). Texas: CALICO.

Yoza Project (2009–10). Retrieved from http://yozaproject.com/about-the-project/

PART THREE

CALL in language education

Section introduction

Michael Thomas, Hayo Reinders and Mark Warschauer

The diversity of CALL has led to a growing number of specialized areas of teaching and research. These areas include intelligent computer-assisted language learning (ICALL) (Heift & Schulze, 2007); technology-enhanced reading and writing environments (Abraham, 2008; Chen & Cheng, 2008; Kol & Schcolnik, 2008); less commonly taught languages (LTCTs) (Davidson, 2010); the use of technology to enhance learner feedback (Ware & Warschauer, 2006); task-based language teaching (TBLT) (Thomas & Reinders, 2010); and self-directed learning and learner autonomy (Reinders & White, 2011). While many of these areas were only partially in evidence 20 to 30 years ago, the intervening period has seen a significant growth in their research and application. In the final section, we provide a discussion of these areas of research and note how they have each developed sophisticated approaches to the study of foreign language learning and a significant body of empirical research and scholarship.

In Chapter 13, Schulze and Heift discuss developments in intelligent computer-assisted language learning, providing a historically informed analysis of the last decade in particular, highlighting the importance of ICALL resources for both the language learning classroom and language researcher. Throughout their discussion of the former connections between second language acquisition theory are made with ICALL especially in relation to noticing and interaction in second language learning. Examples of ICALL are provided which incorporate a range of activities from vocabulary acquistion to grammar development, as well as comphrension skills in relation to reading and writing in the second language classroom. Moreover, the use of ICALL applications in relation to corpora for learners and reference purposes are identified and the future of ICALL research is considered based on recent developments in new intelligent and interactive technologies.

Developing from ICALL, the subject of Park, Zheng, Lawrence and Warschauer's chapter is the use of new technologies to enhance and support reading environments for learners of English. Carefully identifying the factors necessary to understand and read in English, the chapter discusses the significance of skills related to word decoding, reading comprehension, as well as interpretation and summarizing skills and the way technology can be used to augment learners' engagement with each of these components. Having established this context, the chapter pursues two concrete examples utilizing digital media to aid visual-syntactic text formatting (VSTF). VSTF is concerned with the presentation of reading text which attempts to overcome barriers learners have in relation to syntactic knowledge. In the second example, strategies for using blogs (or Weblogs) to support a collaborative and supportive approach to learning are discussed. A study utilizing mixed methods is explored in which blogs are advanced as tools to aid communication, interpretation and cognitive reading skills. The chapter makes a significant contribution to current research on the topic and discusses a future agenda for research on reading and technology-enhanced environments as we move forward with developments in tablet and mobile devices.

Having addressed technology-enhanced reading, Chapter 15 turns to consider the role of technology in teaching and researching writing with language learners. Hegelheimer and Lee describe the transition from approaches based on grammatical accuracy and form to process-oriented strategies in which students develop skill sets related to 'organization, development and expression'. The process approach uses technology to develop writing strategies for language learners in which they engage in multiple drafts or iterations in the development of their work, and receive formative feedback from instructors and/or peers. The chapter draws on recent research studies to provide a map of scholarship in the field of technology-assisted writing instruction, engaging with automated essay evaluation technologies as well as the potential of collaborative writing applications such as Google Docs.

While most discussions in the volume have focused on the dominance of research on the use of CALL with English language learning, Chapter 16 incorporates important research on CALL in less commonly taught languages (LCTLs) from both the learner and instructor perspective. The main focus is the use of Web-based resources and technologies and those languages such as Russian, Chinese and Japanese which while marginal are still taught in college curricula particularly in the United States. A number of issues in the context of Web 2.0 are highlighted, including copyright and debates surrounding the use of non-Roman scripts in computer applications for these languages.

Running throughout the chapters in this section is the underlining importance of new technologies to aid and enhance learner feedback. Chapter 17 confronts this important subfield by offering an extended discussion and overview of CALL and digital feedback. Ware and Kessler discuss the different ways that digital feedback has been defined, covering a number of areas including individual tutorial approaches focused on discrete language skills or pronunciation, to the use of computers as a medium for feedback utilizing synchronous and asynchronous forms of communication. The chapter discusses these developments and offers a comphrehensive overview of the field encompassing the ways that digital feedback has been used in particular to enhance learner-instructor communication in the productive language skills of writing and speaking.

At the same time as CALL has developed over the last three decades, task-based approaches which emphasize the importance of authentic learning environments in which meaning rather than form-based instruction is the primary purpose of instruction have become one of the most important developments in foreign language education. Chapter 18 examines the relationship between task-based approaches and CALL, noting that while they have often been separated, they each have a good deal in common. This chapter provides a historical overview of this relationship, discussing the main research areas that have been evident during this period. A case study of a task-based language learning approach utilizing CALL in Asia is introduced to illustrate developments in the field and to outline a future research agenda.

In the final chapter a number of the themes developed in the previous chapters are brought together in the discussion of technologies that have been used to develop and support learner autonomy. Reinders and Hubbard discuss how the role and responsibilities given to learners has developed and how research on learner autonomy has been engaged in attempting to understand learners' active contributions to the learning process (Breen, 2001). Autonomous, self-directed and informal language learning as the name implies largely occurs in environments removed from traditional educational spaces. While autonomous learning like technology often has significant potential to aid the language learning process, it needs to be targeted via precise strategies and often overcome any technical barriers that learners may have. The final chapter in the volume outlines a detailed overview of research in the field, the role of technology within it and identifies ways in which the 'potentially symbiotic relationship' of learner autonomy and CALL can produce mutually beneficial relationships.

References

Abraham, L. B. (2008). Computer-mediated glosses in second language reading comprehension and vocabulary learning: A meta-analysis. *Computer Assisted Language Learning, 21*(3), 199–226.

Breen, M. (2001). *Learner contributions to language learning. New directions in research.* Harlow: Longman.

Chen, C. E., & Cheng, W. E. (2008). Beyond the design of automated writing evaluation: Pedagogical practices and perceived learning effectiveness in EFL writing classes. *Language Learning & Technology, 12*(2), 94–112.

Davidson, D. (2010). Study abroad: When, how long, and with what results? New data from the Russian front. *Foreign Language Annals, 43*(1), 6–26.

Heift, T., & Schulze, M. (2007). *Errors and intelligence in CALL: Parsers and pedagogues.* New York: Routledge.

Kol, S., & Schcolnik, M. (2008). Asynchronous forums in EAP: Assessment issues. *Language Learning & Technology, 12*(2), 49–70.

Reinders, H., & White, C. (2011). Learner autonomy and new learning environments. *Language Learning & Technology, 15*(3), 1–3.

Thomas, M., & Reinders, M. (2010). *Task-based language learning and teaching with technology.* London & New York: Continuum.

Ware, P., & Warschauer, M. (2006). Electronic feedback and second language writing. In K. Hyland & F. Hyland (Eds.), *Feedback on ESL writing: Context and issues* (pp. 105–22). Cambridge: Cambridge University Press.

13

Intelligent CALL

Mathias Schulze and Trude Heift

Summary

This chapter provides a historical overview of ICALL over the last decade by focusing on two key areas: resources for the language learning classroom and resources for the researcher. With respect to resources for the language learning classroom, we discuss and link ICALL developments to contemporary theories in Second Language Acquisition (SLA) by focusing on the importance of interaction and noticing (Gass, 1997; Long, 1996; Schmidt 1990, 1994). The ICALL projects described support a wide range of language learning activities in vocabulary and grammar acquisition, writing and reading comprehension. With regards to resources for researchers, we focus on learner and reference corpora. The chapter concludes with a discussion of new directions in ICALL research.

What is ICALL?

Intelligent Computer Assisted Language Learning (ICALL) is a field within CALL that applies concepts, techniques, algorithms and technologies from artificial intelligence to CALL (Gamper & Knapp, 2002; Heift & Schulze, 2007; Nerbonne, 2003; Schulze, 2008a). Artificial intelligence (AI) describes the science and engineering of making intelligent machines (McCarthy, 2007). This includes work in robotics, intelligent agents and computer vision. Most relevant to CALL is research in four branches of artificial intelligence: (1) natural language processing, (2) user modelling, (3) expert systems and (4) intelligent tutoring systems.

Natural language processing deals with both natural language understanding and natural language generation. In natural language understanding, written or spoken language input is turned into a formal representation that captures phonological/graphological, grammatical, semantic and pragmatic features of the input. For example, when a written sentence is submitted to a natural language understanding system, frequently to a parser, then the output likely consists of a syntactic tree that describes the grammatical structure of this sentence including specifications of immediate dominance (phrase structure) and linear precedence (word order). In contrast, in natural language generation, a formal representation of an information structure, commonly stored in a database, is turned into natural written and/or spoken language output. For instance, given the relevant syntactic, semantic and pragmatic rules of certain utterance types and a lexicon, the information from a database on a city's geography can then be provided in adequate prose (e.g., 'Berlin is located in eastern Germany). Within natural language processing, software that turns spoken utterances into written text is subsumed under *speech recognition* or speech-to-text systems; the reverse process is called *speech synthesis* or text-to-speech (Jurafsky & Martin, 2000).

Another branch of AI relevant to CALL is user modelling. It can also be described as a sub-area of human-computer interaction (HCI) research because it strives to adapt computational systems to their users. Of the different research domains in user modelling, student modelling is, of course, of particular relevance to CALL. A student model observes the student's actions, maintains a data structure with this information and infers beliefs about the student's knowledge and abilities based on these data (Self, 1994).

Expert systems capture relevant knowledge about a particular (learning) domain. Most ICALL applications therefore contain information about the grammatical system of the target language (a parser grammar). The expert's system is the module that enables the program to process the student input and turn it into a formal representation that contains detailed information about its form (phonological/graphological, morphological, syntactic features) and meaning (semantic, discoursal, pragmatic features). This representation can then be used to maintain a more detailed record of the learner's grammatical knowledge including both correct forms as well as misconceptions. Other ICALL applications use the expert system to communicate knowledge about linguistic structures to the student upon request (Zock, 1988, 1992; Zock, Sabah & Alviset, 1986).

Both the student model and the expert model are essential modules of intelligent tutoring systems (ITSs), another branch of AI. These systems are tutors in the context of Levy's (2009) tutor-tool distinction in CALL. ITSs are used in the teaching of various subject matters, domains and instructional settings. Intelligent Language Tutoring Systems (ILTSs) have been developed for the past 30 years for a wide range of first, second and additional languages as well as different proficiency levels (Heift & Schulze, 2007). For instance, *Robo-Sensei* is a commercial ILTS for Japanese for all proficiency levels (Nagata, 2009); *Tagarela* teaches beginner learners of Portuguese (Amaral, 2007; Amaral & Meurers, 2007) and *The E-Tutor* is a comprehensive language learning environment for all proficiency levels of German (Heift, 2010b).

In the following, we focus on the main contributions and progress that ICALL has made over the past decade. First, we discuss resources for the language classroom by linking them to some of the contemporary theories of second language acquisition (SLA), more specifically, to the importance of interaction and noticing. Second, we discuss resources for researchers by focusing on learner and reference corpora. Our conclusion provides a discussion of new directions in ICALL research.

ICALL resources for the language learning classroom

ICALL is a young, but highly interdisciplinary field of research that draws on a number of disciplines in applied linguistics and computing (see Levy, 1997, p. 49). The article by Weischedel, Voge and James (1978) is commonly cited as the first publication that reports on an ICALL system the authors developed for L2 German. Since then, two printed ICALL bibliographies (Bailin, 1995; Matthews, 1992b) in addition to a more up-to-date set of bibliographies which can be found at the *Integrated Digital Language Learning* website (www.noe-kaleidoscope.org/group/idill/) have been published. More recently, the monograph by Heift and Schulze (2007) provides a comprehensive overview of the main concepts and research questions in the field. For instance, the authors surveyed the ICALL literature and identified 119 ICALL projects that were documented in English and German publications between 1978 and 2004/5. Shorter overviews of ICALL can be found in Nerbonne (2003), Matthews (1992a, 1993) and Gamper and Knapp (2002). A number of edited volumes contain collections of articles on different projects in ICALL. Of particular importance in this respect are two books (Holland, Kaplan & Sams, 1995; Swartz & Yazdani, 1992) because they provide a useful snapshot of important research and development at the time. Other collections of articles appeared in special issues of journals on CALL (Bailin, 1991; Bailin & Levin, 1989; Chanier, 1994; Heift & Schulze, 2003; Meurers, 2009; Schulze, 2008c; Schulze, Hamel & Thompson, 1999; Tokuda, Heift & Chen, 2002). Beginning in 2000, both EuroCALL (2000, 2001, 2002, 2004) and CALICO (2006, 2007, 2008, 2009, 2010) provided one-day pre-conference workshops with a series of paper presentations on various aspects of ICALL which were organized on behalf of the special interest groups of Natural Language Processing and ICALL, respectively. As is common in Computer Science and in Computational Linguistics, collections of refereed papers appeared in proceedings volumes (e.g., Maritxalar, Ezeiza & Schulze, 2007; Thompson & Zähner, 1992). More recently, the annual conferences of the Association for Computational Linguistics included workshops on the building of educational applications whose refereed papers are available through the ACL Anthology (ACL, 2011). The contributions of ICALL research to Applied Linguistics were discussed at a symposium during the world congress AILA 2008 (Schulze, 2008b) and at an invited panel at the American Applied Linguistics Conference in 2009 (Heift, 2010a). However, it is not only at such conferences that the link between SLA and ICALL is apparent.

ICALL and the importance of interaction

Warschauer and Healey (1998) argued that two issues would become important for the future of CALL: electronic literacies and intelligent CALL. They discuss the latter almost exclusively in the context of online writing and tutorial CALL, that is, CALL in a more structured, operationalized instructional environment. Nevertheless, more than ten years ago their outlook was rather sceptical: 'we've still got a very long way to go before CALL can be accurately called "intelligent" ' (p. 67). A few years later, however, Nerbonne (2003), in his chapter on NLP in CALL in the *Oxford Handbook of Computational Linguistics*, argues that advances in NLP have much to contribute to CALL. Especially in tutorial CALL (Hubbard & Bradin-Siskin, 2004), in which students interact directly with the computer during language learning activities, ICALL has been a major impetus (Schulze, 2008a).

Even in one of the early ICALL studies, Nagata (1996, 1998a) concludes from one of her learner studies that only CALL programs that make use of the full potential of the computer, mainly by providing immediate and informative feedback, will produce higher learning results. Over many years, error detection and diagnosis resulting in corrective feedback have been the main focus of research and development in ICALL (Heift & Schulze, 2007). The main advantage of ILTSs over more traditional CALL environments lies in the error-specific feedback that an ILTS can provide in response to learner output. Traditional CALL programs are generally based on string matching algorithms, that is, the student response is compared letter by letter against an answer key. In contrast, and based on sophisticated NLP technologies, an ILTS identifies and interprets errors as well as correct constructions in learner input and then generates appropriate, informative learner feedback. Over the past decades, research has sought evidence that feedback in CALL makes a difference in language development, and more specifically what kind of feedback makes a difference. Following Nagata's (1996) study, a number of publications on the value of informative feedback followed (e.g., Bowles, 2005; Heift, 2001, 2004, 2010c; Pujola, 2002; Rosa & Leow, 2004) and the results generally support the claim that students benefit from the more explicit feedback because they subsequently perform better on particular target-language structures and/or because students' grammatical awareness is subsequently raised.

But language awareness not only results from ICALL applications that provide feedback in the more traditional sense. Lewis (1997), for instance, claimed that some familiarity with machine translation software would be beneficial for modern language students because it increases language awareness and their knowledge about the language system. Moreover, and on a very practical level, 'for a student graduating with a culture-based modern language degree, familiarity with MT has proved to be a point of interest for prospective employers' (p. 271). Niño (2008) provides a comprehensive overview of projects that investigated the use of machine translation in second language learning. She concludes from her quasi-experimental study with learners of Spanish that her 'results advocate that for advanced students . . . the target language MT post-editing was especially good for creating opportunities for producing comprehensible and acceptable output and for raising language awareness through error detection and correction' (p. 44). Machine translation plays a role when it comes to task designs that involve translation, text critiquing and commenting, language awareness, error analysis and correction. It can facilitate language learning and increase students' awareness of and familiarity with modern language technologies such as online translation engines, which many of them use anyway, but might not always do so in the most appropriate way (Williams, 2006).

After more than 30 years of development and research (for a chronology of ICALL systems, see Heift and Schulze, 2007), ILTSs nowadays are rarely limited to form-focused instruction but instead allow for more diverse learning environments. For instance, Dickinson, Eom, Kang, Lee and Sachs (2008) designed an ILTS that is embedded in a synchronous computer-mediated communication environment. The system provides feedback on particle usage for first-year L2 Korean learners during online chat. Harbusch, Itsova, Koch and Kuhner (2008) designed a virtual writing environment for German for elementary-school children, *The Sentence Fairy*, which deploys natural language generation technology to evaluate and improve the grammatical well-formedness of student output. Most other ICALL systems provide a combination of form-focused and meaning-focused instruction. For instance, the activity types in the *E-Tutor* (Heift, 2010b) allow for grammar practice as well as reading comprehension and/or cultural knowledge and also supports discovery learning in the form of exploration of learner language. For this, user submissions over five years were compiled and from those a common learner corpus was constructed that allows students to explore learner language according to various parameters. Thus, learners can examine interlanguage or task-specific phenomena and the benefits in this respect have been well documented (Granger, 2003a). Moreover, these large data sets also allow language instructors and/or researchers to examine the design of language learning material in addition to a wide range of additional research topics (e.g., use of help options, interlanguage studies).

Similarly, *Robo-Sensei* developed by Nagata (2009) for L2 learners of Japanese analyses student input for selected exercises, performs an itemization (separating tokens for later linguistic analysis) and a morphological analysis, and parses the sentential input syntactically using a context-free grammar. Finally, *Tagarela* (Amaral & Meurers, 2011) an ICALL system for Portuguese is similar to the *E-Tutor* and *Robo-Sensei*, in that it uses the metaphor of an electronic textbook. The system provides practice with grammar and listening comprehension and students receive feedback on spelling, morphological, syntactic and semantic errors. These three systems are used in the regular L2 language classroom.

The ICALL examples mentioned above have already illustrated the fact that ICALL systems offer a wide variety of interactions both tutorial, commonly associated with ILTSs, and non-tutorial. The non-tutorial interactions fall into two broad categories: dialogue systems and language tools.

In dialogue systems, the computer generally takes on the role of a conversation partner. ICALL has always seen some interest in dialogue systems that engage language learners in short linguistic interactions (Hamburger, 1994; Hamburger & Hashim, 1992; Hamburger, Schoelles & Reeder, 1999; Hamburger, Tufis & Hashim, 1993; Jehle, 1987; Underwood, 1982; Walker, Trofimovich, Cedergren & Gatbonton, 2011). Many systems make use of relatively limited NLP capabilities such as keyword searches and shallow parsing. However, if the dialogue has a grammar focus, such as the grammatically well-formed and pragmatically appropriate use of personal pronouns in Māori, then deep syntactic processing might be necessary. The *Te Kaitito* dialogue system (Vlugter, Knott, McDonald & Hall, 2009), for instance, uses an HPSG-based grammar of Māori and the Linguistic Knowledge Building system as its parser. It engages students in short dialogues that require them to include personal pronouns. If the student uses a pronoun incorrectly, the system provides feedback in the form of a metalinguistic dialogue sequence. The system was tested in the classroom and the researchers suggest that the *Te Kaitito* system helps students achieve the same results as human tutoring.

The dialog system *FLUENT I* (Hamburger & Hashim, 1992) asks students to move objects in a bathroom per request. Hamburger and his team also developed an interface for teachers to create exercises that utilize the natural language processing tools of *FLUENT-2*, both written and spoken. The teacher can use the tutorial schema tool to design interactive exercises, the language tool to influence the language generated by *FLUENT-2* and the drawing tool to manipulate the graphical microworlds (Schoelles & Hamburger, 1996).

With respect to language tools, we find grammar and spell checkers (Gamon et al., 2009; L'Haire, 2007; L'Haire & Vandeventer Faltin, 2003; Rimrott & Heift, 2008) morphological analysers (ten Hacken & Tschichold, 2001) as well as corpus look-up tools that can be employed in many different interactional settings. In a number of systems, students have contingent access to online dictionaries (Hamel, 2010; Nerbonne & Dokter, 1999; Roosmaa & Prószéky, 1998), they can retrieve inflectional paradigms of words that are generated on the fly and displayed to the student (Dokter & Nerbonne, 1998; Heift, 2006, 2010b; Wood, 2011), and/or can gain access to contextualized examples in large text corpora and other online resources such as target language versions of Wikipedia (Wood, 2011). In addition to using language technology to augment language learning materials with additional lexical and morpho-syntactic information the student can access, similar techniques from artificial intelligence can be used to make linguistic features of a text more salient and to help students develop their language awareness (e.g., Amaral, Metcalf & Meurers, 2006). For instance, *ELDIT* (Knapp, 2004) is an electronic learner dictionary for German and Italian intended for reading activities and vocabulary acquisition. The system supports a number of reading tasks that aim to prepare students for bilingual proficiency examinations. More recently, Wood (2011) developed *QuickAssist* that supports reading and vocabulary acquisition for L2 learners of German through the automatic annotation and lemmatization of texts selected by the students or their instructor. Students have one-click access to an online dictionary in which the lemma of the word in context will be looked up. Learners can also retrieve collocations of the word from a German corpus including a morphological deconstruction of the word and the paradigm of relevant word forms. In addition, students have direct access to the German version of Wikipedia to look up proper nouns and related concepts. Thus the system reuses proven, reliable and robust human language resources that are freely available (see Wood, 2008).

However, in addition to the development of language tools in isolation, we meanwhile also see applications that provide a combination of a number of tools. For instance, Knutsson, Cerrato Pargman and Severinson Eklundh (2003) adapted and tested *Granska*, a grammar checker for learners of Swedish as a foreign language, which originally had been developed for Swedish native speakers. They reported that *Granska* 'detected about 35% of all errors' (n.p.). Students noted that they had difficulties using the program because of a lack of advanced computer training and due to the high number of false alarms the program generated. Later *Granska* became the main language technology component of *Grim* (Karlström, Cerratto-Pargman, Lindström & Knutsson, 2007), a tool for learners of Swedish. *Grim* combines the grammar checker Granska with a surface syntactic parser, a concordance interface to the Swedish version part of the Parole corpus, a dictionary and an interface to a tool for automatic word inflection (Knutsson, Cerratto Pargman, Severinson Eklundh & Westlund, 2007).

Another area in ICALL, which has received increased interest more recently, is that of automated essay scoring (Coniam, 2009; Cotos, 2011; Ware & Warschauer, 2006; Warschauer & Grimes, 2008; Warschauer & Ware, 2006). For instance, Lonsdale and Strong-Krause (2003) present a parser-based essay rater for beginning learners of English as a Foreign or Second Language, which achieved an inter-annotator agreement with human raters of 62.1% to 69.5%. The authors conclude that a 'purely syntactic parse does not always assure appropriate ratings' (n.p.). They identified possible improvements of the linguistic processing and argue that 'the output from a non-traditional syntactic parser can be used to grade ESL essays. With a robust enough parser, reasonable results can be achieved, even for highly ungrammatical text' (n.p.).

Coniam (2009) evaluates BETSY with ESL examination essays from Hong Kong students. BETSY's scores correlated highly with those given by human raters and thus Coniam concludes that essay scoring software is an efficient tool for the evaluation of word-processed essays. His focus on automated essay scoring for assessment purposes is complemented by the studies by Warschauer and colleagues (Ware & Warschauer, 2006; Warschauer & Grimes, 2008; Warschauer & Ware, 2006) who focus on the feedback capabilities of such systems and their use in the language classroom. Warschauer and Grimes (2008) investigated the in-class use of two systems, *Criterion* and *My Access*, in secondary schools. In their study, the teachers' highly positive perception of the benefits of AES in the classroom was contradicted by their limited and infrequent use of the systems in class. Although students clearly benefited in a number of ways from their work with the two systems, 'almost all of the revisions that students made were narrow in scope' (p. 29). Warschauer and Ware (2006) summarize their findings as follows:

> We believe that both of the above-described potentials – technology that empowers by providing instant evaluation and feedback, and technology that dehumanizes by eliminating the human element – exist in automated writing evaluation software. Where on the continuum between these two outcomes AWE might fall depends on how such software is used in specific teaching and learning contexts, a matter subject to empirical investigation. (p. 20)

Cotos (2011) situates her study of IADE, a system that provides feedback on discourse moves in academic texts (Pendar & Cotos, 2009), in the interactional framework of

SLA. She states that IADE has 'the potential to trigger noticing and focus on discourse form [and will thus] enhance learning' (p. 444). Like IADE, TechWriter (Napolitano & Stent, 2009) provides assistance for specialized text genres, in this case, technical writing. It relies on the public part of the American National Corpus and is tagged for parts of speech. Learner texts are then checked against n-gram sequences of stemmed words and part-of-speech tags. Their relative and absolute frequencies in the corpus are then compared to the respective frequencies in the student text. Differences signal the probable occurrence of an error. Feedback is provided through offering alternative n-gram sequences from the corpus data. Although the system has not yet been evaluated formally, it is used by students at Stony Brook University.

These applications described above are excellent examples of theory-based ICALL. Their functionalities, such as the highlighting not only of errors but also of important morpho-syntactic features of the text, are all grounded in relevant SLA theories. The researchers/developers are well cognizant of the importance of focus on form (Long, 1991), interaction (Gass, 1997; Long, 1996) and the noticing of linguistic features (Schmidt, 1990). They conceptualize the mediating role of technology by relying on an understanding of Activity Theory (Lantolf & Thorne, 2006) that can depict both language learning processes as well as human computer interaction. Moreover, in interpreting 'interaction' not only in the context of SLA but also in terms of human computer interaction, it becomes apparent that ICALL systems provide many different types of student input from fill-in-the-blank (cloze exercises) through sentential input to the handling of large texts. Computer reactions to this input also vary from system to system. Error detection and feedback are very common. Language generation systems (Bailin & Thomson, 1988; Harbusch et al., 2008; Zock, 1992; Zock et al., 1986) provide students with well-formed examples of the L2. Systems that augment texts with linguistic information, for example, by displaying a paradigm of a verb in the text, react with contextualized help and additional information to a student's request. Grammar, style and spelling checkers provide guidance during form-focused learning activities and phases. Thus ICALL systems have engaged or at least have the potential to engage language learners in a wide selection of interactions. For a number of ICALL systems such interactions happen in the well-defined context of a communicative, language learning task. This aspect of ICALL as a venue for language learning interaction is complemented by the role of ICALL connecting learners, instructors and researchers with electronic language resources. One of the most important sets of such resources are corpora, principled, electronic collections of texts.

Reference and learner corpora

Reference and learner corpora are at the nexus of Applied Linguistics and ICALL. Electronic corpora have become a widely used research tool not just in Corpus Linguistics but also in many other linguistic disciplines. For example, researchers in descriptive and formal linguistics (e.g., Biber, Conrad & Reppen, 1998), lexicography (e.g., Baker,

Francis, Sinclair & Tognini-Bonelli, 1993) and translation studies (e.g., Olohan, 2003) use large corpora to study examples of language use. Such large electronic corpora for a variety of different languages and with texts of a wide range of genres have become more widely available in recent years. Consequently, we have seen more frequent corpus use both in NLP research and development and in language learning.

Generally, there are three different ways of employing corpora in NLP and CALL.

First, the use of corpora to *evaluate* NLP tools in CALL is relatively common. However, the limited amount of linguistic data used does commonly not approximate the size of modern electronic corpora. Usually, the data consist of small collections of sentences or samples of student essays. Examples of parser-based projects that have utilized electronic collections of sentences or texts produced by learners will be given.

Second, corpora are employed in the *design* of NLP tools. Here both types – learner corpora (collections of L2 texts produced by a population of language learners) and reference corpora (representative and relatively clean samples of L1 texts) – can be utilized. The work by Granger and her team who examined errors in second language texts is an example of using a learner corpus in an ICALL project. Their *FRIDA* (French Interlanguage Database) corpus was analysed to extract detailed error statistics and to perform concordance-based analyses of specific error types (Granger, 2003b). The results were then used to improve the error diagnosis system integrated in the *FreeText* ICALL program (Hamel, 1996; L'Haire & Vandeventer Faltin, 2003; Schulze & Hamel, 2000; Vandeventer, 2001; Vandeventer Faltin, 2003). In a different project, Dagneaux, Denness and Granger (1998) also performed an analysis of learner errors to advance research in computer-aided error analysis. The authors hope that this approach will give a new impetus to Error Analysis research and re-establish it as an important area of study. The data employed to demonstrate the technique consist of a 150,000-word corpus of English written by French-speaking learners at the intermediate and advanced levels. After the initial native speaker correction, the corpus is annotated for errors using a comprehensive error classification. This stage is a computer-aided process supported by an 'error editor'. The error-tagged corpus can then be analysed by using standard text retrieval software tools and to obtain lists of the different types of errors and error counts in a matter of seconds (p. 163). While other projects have used similar information on learner errors, they are usually extracted from significantly smaller samples of learner text.

In recent years, the ICALL research community recognized that a robust and standardized annotation of errors in learner corpora becomes increasingly important. The two pre-conference workshops of the CALICO special interest group in ICALL in 2008 and 2009 focused on the theme 'Automatic Analysis of Learner Language' and selected papers were published in a special issue of the *CALICO Journal* (Meurers, 2009). Interesting approaches emerged but the 'gold standard' of learner corpus annotation and/or automatic analysis learner texts is still elusive.

In the design of the NLP components of ICALL systems, the exploitation of learner corpora of different sizes has played a role. The use of reference corpora, however, has had much less influence. Statistical NLP (Manning & Schütze, 1999) and statistical machine translation (Dale, Moisl & Somers, 2000) have relied on large text corpora including parallel corpora that display the same texts in more than one language. These approaches have also played an important role in automated essay scoring (Attali & Burstein, 2006; Shermis & Burstein, 2003; Warschauer & Grimes, 2008) and have been employed especially to determine the lexical and morpho-syntactic accuracy level of student essays (Kaplan et al., 1998). It is rare, however, that the usefulness of statistical approaches in ICALL has been explored. Comparing chunks of learner texts (n-grams of various sizes) to large, clean reference corpora is a fruitful avenue of current and future research. This has already been exemplified for the detection of lexical errors (Tsao & Wible, 2009), sentence analysis (Sun et al., 2007), error correction of selected linguistic phenomena (De Felice & Pulman, 2008; Gammon, 2010; Gamon et al., 2009), error detection in essays (Chodorow & Leacock, 2000) and the application of statistical machine translation methods to error correction (Brockett, Dolan, & Gamon, 2006).

The third and last approach to using corpora in ICALL is probably the most straightforward. A number of projects have successfully combined NLP tools and corpora and applied them to CALL environments. The *Glosser* project (Dokter & Nerbonne, 1998; Nerbonne, Dokter & Smit, 1998; Roosmaa & Prószéky, 1998), the Irakazi project (Aldabe & Maritxalar, 2005) and *OuickAssist* (Wood, 2011), for instance, combine tools for morphological analysis (lemmatizer, morphological analyser) with the opportunity for the language learner and/or teacher to consult a relevant corpus. This combination enables the user to select a word and then look up instances of different inflected forms as well as potentially related words of the same word family as they appear in the corpus.

Future research

ICALL has undoubtedly added a new dimension to more traditional CALL environments due to its sophisticated underlying technologies. NLP and AI modelling techniques provide the analytical complexity underpinning an ILTS thereby resulting in a more learner-centred, individualized language learning environment. Unlike earlier applications that primarily focused on grammar taught in more traditional learning environments, more recent applications reflect a wide range of teaching and learning approaches by also addressing a variety of language skills.

During the 30 years of its existence, ICALL has become a major impetus for tutorial CALL (Hubbard & Bradin-Siskin, 2004). A turn towards more applied research questions in computational linguistics (ten Hacken, 2003), and a sustained interest in CALL in both modern language technology and tutorial CALL coupled with the improved availability of robust linguistic and computational resources for natural language processing should imply that this positive trend will continue.

As evident from the examples provided in this chapter, progress in terms of widespread and sustained use of ICALL applications in real language learning situations (Amaral & Meurers, 2011) has been slow and sketchy. This is mainly due to the immense complexities of the computational processing of human language and the nature of language itself coupled with the complexity of foreign language learning processes. However, ICALL has added and will continue to add innovative and interesting facets to (tutorial) CALL in particular, and to Applied Linguistics in general through its capability to analyse student input and observe and support students' language learning behaviour. Continued progress in developing robust, effective and widely used ICALL systems can only be made if the 'communication problem and a mutual lack of interest' (Zock, 1996) between researchers in CALL and SLA on one side and Computational Linguistics on the other are superseded by joint discussions and projects.

Nerbonne (2003) expressed some surprise that available NLP-based language resources which are very robust such as parallel corpora, part-of-speech taggers, lemmatizers and morphological analysers are not more widely used and integrated in CALL software. This has, however, changed since the ICALL community has moved away from its almost exclusive focus on the diagnosis and correction of lexical and syntactic errors and, as we saw with the examples in this chapter, has applied NLP to the support of reading activities, increasing language awareness, supporting writing processes, and providing rich, contextualized examples of current language use. This focus on scaffolding and the provision of learning resources makes good use of established and often widely available NLP tools and thus stimulates further progress in ICALL research and development by, at the same time, providing innovative language learning artefacts for students and instructors.

Finally, the different aspects of quality of ICALL systems need to be measured against emerging standards and by widely accepted and established methods. More empirical studies such as the ones by Heift (2001, 2002, 2003, 2004, 2005, 2010c) and Nagata (1992, 1996, 1998a, 1998b) are required to evaluate the effectiveness of ICALL systems, provide insight into SLA processes and outcomes, measure learning outcomes and inform software design decisions. These need to take into consideration the entire bandwidth of language learning activities supported by ICALL systems. Moreover, aspects such as the grammatical and lexical coverage and error detection rate of ICALL systems need to be well documented to establish gold standards.

References

Aldabe, I., & Maritxalar, M. (2005). IRAKAZI: A Web-based system to assess the learning process of Basque language learners. Paper presented at the Eurocall 2005 conference. *EUROCALL 2005*, Krakow, Poland.

Amaral, L. (2007). *Designing intelligent language tutoring systems for integration into foreign language instruction.* PhD Thesis, The Ohio State University, United States.

Amaral, L., & Meurers, D. (2011). On using intelligent computer-assisted language learning in real-life foreign language teaching and learning. *ReCALL, 23*(1), 4–24.

Amaral, L., & Meurers, W. D. (2007). Conceptualizing student models for ICALL. In C. Conati, K. McCoy & G. Paliouras (Eds.), *User Modeling 2007. 11th International Conference, UM 2007, 25–29 June 2007, Corfu, Greece* (pp. 340–4). Berlin; Germany: Springer-Verlag.

Amaral, L., Metcalf, V., & Meurers, W. D. (2006). Language awareness through re-use of NLP technology. Paper presented at the Pre-conference Workshop on NLP in CALL – Computational and Linguistic Challenges. *CALICO 2006,* Honolulu, Hawaii.

Attali, Y., & Burstein, J. (2006). Automated essay scoring with e-rater® V.2. *Journal of Technology, Learning, and Assessment, 4*(3). Retrieved from http://escholarship.bc.edu/jtla/vol4/3/

Bailin, A. (Ed.) (1991). Special Issue of the CALICO Journal on ICALL. *CALICO, 9 (1).*

Bailin, A. (1995). Intelligent computer-assisted language learning: A bibliography. *Computers and the Humanities, 29*(5), 375–87.

Bailin, A., & Levin, L. S. (Eds.) (1989). Intelligent computer-assisted language instruction. *Computers and the Humanities, 23.*

Bailin, A., & Thomson, P. (1988). The use of natural language processing in computer-assisted language instruction. *Computers and the Humanities, 22,* 99–110.

Baker, M., Francis, G., Sinclair, J. M., & Tognini-Bonelli, E. (1993). *Text and technology: In honour of John Sinclair.* Amsterdam/Philadelphia: John Benjamins.

Biber, D., Conrad, S., & Reppen, R. (1998). *Corpus Linguistics: Investigating language structure and use.* Cambridge: Cambridge University Press.

Bowles, M. (2005). *Effects of verbalization condition and type of feedback on L2 development in a CALL task.* PhD dissertation, Georgetown University, Washington, DC.

Brockett, C., Dolan, W. B., & Gamon, M. (2006). Correcting ESL errors using phrasal SMT techniques. *Proceedings of the 21st International Conference on Computational Linguistics and 44th Annual Meeting of the ACL,* (pp. 249–56), Sydney.

Chanier, T. (1994). Special issue on language learning. *Journal of Artificial Intelligence in Education, 5.*

Chodorow, M., & Leacock, C. (2000). An unsupervised method for detecting grammatical errors. *Proceedings of the 1st North American Chapter of the Association for Computational Linguistics conference* (pp. 140–7). Seattle.

Coniam, D. (2009). Experimenting with a computer essay-scoring program based on ESL student writing scripts. *ReCALL, 21*(2), 259–79.

Cotos, E. (2011). Potential of automated writing evaluation feedback. *CALICO Journal, 28*(2), 420–59.

Dagneaux, E., Denness, S., & Granger, S. (1998). Computer-aided error analysis. *System, 26*(2), 163–74.

Dale, R., Moisl, H., & Somers, H. (Eds.) (2000). *Handbook of natural language processing.* New York: Marcel Dekker.

De Felice, R., & Pulman, S. G. (2008). A classifier-based approach to preposition and determiner error correction in L2 English. *Proceedings of the 22nd International Conference on Computational Linguistics (Coling 2008)* (pp. 160–76). Manchester, UK.

Dickinson, M., Eom, S., Kang, Y., Lee, C., & Sachs, R. (2008). A balancing act: How can intelligent computer-generated feedback be provided in learner-to-learner interactions? *Computer Assisted Language Learning, 21*(4), 369–82.

Dokter, D., & Nerbonne, J. A. (1998). A session with Glosser-RuG. In S. Jager, J. A. Nerbonne & A. van Essen (Eds.), *Language teaching and language technology* (pp. 89–95). Lisse: Swets & Zeitlinger.

Gammon, M. (2010). Using mostly native data to correct errors in learners' writing: A meta-classifier approach. *Human Language Technologies: The 2010 Annual Conference of the North American Chapter of the ACL,* (pp. 163–71). Los Angeles.
Gamon, M., Leacock, C., Brockett, C., Dolan, W. B., Gao, J., Belenko, D., & Klementiev, A. (2009). Using statistical techniques and Web search to correct ESL errors. *CALICO JOURNAL, 26*(3), 491–511.
Gamper, J., & Knapp, J. (2002). A review of intelligent CALL systems. *Computer Assisted Language Learning, 15*(4), 329–42.
Gass, S. M. (1997). *Input, interaction, and the second language learner.* Mahwah, NJ: Lawrence Erlbaum Associates.
Granger, S. (2003a). The international corpus of learner English: A new resource for foreign language learning and teaching and second language acquisition research. *TESOL Quarterly, 37*(3), 538–46.
— (2003b, 10–11 October). *Learner corpora for SLA.* Paper presented at the Conference on Technology for SLL, Memorial Union, Iowa State University.
Hamburger, H. (1994). Foreign language immersion: Science, practice, and a system. *Journal of Artificial Intelligence in Education, 5*(4), 429–53.
Hamburger, H., & Hashim, R. (1992). Foreign language tutoring and learning environment. In M. L. Swartz & M. Yazdani (Eds.), *Intelligent tutoring systems for foreign language learning: The bridge to international communication* (pp. 201–18). Berlin: Springer Verlag.
Hamburger, H., Schoelles, M., & Reeder, F. (1999). More intelligent CALL. In K. Cameron (Ed.), *Computer-Assisted Language Learning* (pp. 183–202). Lisse: Swets & Zeitlinger.
Hamburger, H., Tufis, D., & Hashim, R. (1993). Structuring two – medium dialog for learning language and other things. In O. Rambow (Ed.), *Intentionality and structure in discourse relations. Proceedings of a workshop sponsored by the Special Interest Group on generation of the Association of Computational Linguistics* (pp. 27–30). Columbus, Ohio.
Hamel, M.-J. (1996). NLP tools for NLP in CALL for error diagnosis. *Canadian Journal of Applied Linguistics, 18*(2), 125–41.
— (2010). Prototype d'un dictionnaire électronique de reformulation pour apprenants avancés de français langue seconde. *Cahiers de l'APLIUT, XXIX*(1), 73–82.
Harbusch, K., Itsova, G., Koch, U., & Kuhner, C. (2008). The sentence fairy: A natural-language generation system to support children. *Computer Assisted Language Learning, 21*(4), 339–52.
Heift, T. (2001). Error-specific and individualized feedback in a Web-based language tutoring system: Do they read it? *ReCALL, 13*(2), 129–42.
— (2002). Learner control and error correction in ICALL: Browsers, peelers and adamants. *CALICO Journal, 19*(3), 295–313.
— (2003). Multiple learner errors and feedback: A challenge for ICALL systems. *CALICO Journal, 20*(3), 549–60.
— (2004). Corrective feedback and learner uptake in CALL. *ReCALL, 16*(2), 416–31.
— (2005). Inspectable learner reports for Web-based language learning. *ReCALL, 17*(1), 32–46.
— (2006). Context-sensitive help in CALL. *Computer Assisted Language Learning, 21*(4), 243–59.
— (2010a). Bridging computational and applied linguistics: Implementation challenges and benefits. *Language Teaching, 43*(1), 102–5.
— (2010b). Developing an intelligent tutor. *CALICO Journal, 27*(3), 443–59.

— (2010c). Prompting in CALL: A longitudinal study of learner uptake. *Modern Language Journal, 94*(2), 198–216.

Heift, T., & Schulze, M. (Eds.) (2003). *Error Analysis and Error Correction. Special Issue of the CALICO Journal, 20 (3).*

Heift, T., & Schulze, M. (2007). *Errors and intelligence in CALL. Parsers and pedagogues.* New York: Routledge.

Holland, V. M., Kaplan, J. D., & Sams, M. R. (Eds.) (1995). *Intelligent language tutors: Theory shaping technology.* Mahwah, NJ: Lawrence Erlbaum Associates.

Hubbard, P., & Bradin-Siskin, C. (2004). Another look at tutorial CALL. *ReCALL, 16*(2), 448–61.

Jehle, F. (1987). A free-form dialog program in Spanish. *CALICO Journal, 5*(2), 11–22.

Jurafsky, D., & Martin, J. H. (2000). *Speech and language processing: An introduction to natural language processing, computational linguistics, and speech recognition.* Upper Saddle River, NJ: Prentice Hall.

Kaplan, R., Wolff, S., Burstein, J., Lu, C., Rock, D. A., & Kaplan, B. A. (1998). Scoring Essays Automatically Using Surface Features (GRE Board Professional Rep. No 94–21P; ETS RR-98–39). Princeton, NJ: ETS.

Karlström, P., Cerratto-Pargman, T., Lindström, H., & Knutsson, O. (2007). Tool mediation in focus on form activities: Case studies in a grammar-exploring environment. *ReCALL, 19*(1), 39–56.

Knapp, J. (2004). *A new approach to CALL content authoring.* Doctoral Dissertation, Universität Hannover, Hannover.

Knutsson, O., Cerrato Pargman, T., & Severinson Eklundh, K. (2003). Transforming grammar checking technology into a learning environment for second language writing *Proceedings of the Workshop on Innovative Use of NLP for Building Educational Applications*: Association for Computational Linguistics.

Knutsson, O., Cerratto Pargman, T., Severinson Eklundh, K., & Westlund, S. (2007). Designing and developing a language environment for second language writers. *Computers & Education, 49*(4), 1122–46.

L'Haire, S. (2007). FipsOrtho: A spell checker for learners of French. *ReCALL, 19*(2), 137–61.

L'Haire, S., & Vandeventer Faltin, A. (2003). Error diagnosis in the FreeText project. *CALICO Journal, 20*(3), 481–96.

Lantolf, J. P., & Thorne, S. L. (2006). *Sociocultural theory and the genesis of second language development.* Oxford & New York: Oxford University Press.

Levy, M. (1997). *Computer-assisted language learning. Context and conceptualisation.* Oxford: Clarendon.

— (2009). A tutor-tool framework. In P. Hubbard (Ed.), *Computer assisted language learning: Critical concepts in linguistics* (45–78). New York: Routledge.

Lewis, D. (1997). Machine translation in a modern languages curriculum. *Computer Assisted Language Learning, 10*(3), 255–71.

Long, M. H. (1991). Focus on form: A design feature in language teaching methodology. In K. de Bot, D. Coste, R. Ginsberg & C. Kramsch (Eds.), *Foreign language research in cross-cultural perspectives.* Amsterdam: John Benjamins.

— (1996). The role of the linguistic environment in second language acquisition. In W. C. Ritchie & T. K. Bhatia (Eds.), *Handbook of second language acquisition* (pp. 413–68). San Diego: Academic Press.

Lonsdale, D., & Strong-Krause, D. (2003). Automated rating of ESL scores *proceedings of the workshop on innovative use of NLP for building educational applications*: Association for computational linguistics.

Manning, C. D., & Schütze, H. (1999). *Foundations of statistical natural language processing*. Cambridge, MA: MIT Press.
Maritxalar, M., Ezeiza, N., & Schulze, M. (Eds.) (2007). *Proceedings of the workshop NLP for educational resources at the international conference recent advances in natural language programming 2007*. Borovets, Bulgaria: Bulgarian Academy of Sciences.
Matthews, C. (1992a). Going AI. Foundations of ICALL. *CALL, 5*(1–2), 13–31.
— (1992b). *Intelligent CALL (ICALL) bibliography*. Hull: CTI Centre for Modern Languages.
— (1993). Grammar frameworks in intelligent CALL. *CALICO Journal, 11*(1), 5–27.
McCarthy, J. (2007). What is Artificial Intelligence? Retrieved 17 November 2009, from www-formal.stanford.edu/jmc/whatisai/whatisai.html
Meurers, W. D. (Ed.) (2009). *Automatic analysis of learner language. Special issue of the Calico* Journal, *26*(3). San Marcos, TX: Calico.
Nagata, N. (1992). *A study of the effectiveness of Intelligent CALI as an application of natural language processing*. PhD Thesis, University of Pittsburgh, Pittsburgh.
— (1996). Computer vs. workbook instruction in second language acquisition. *CALICO Journal, 14*(1), 53–75.
— (1998a). Input vs. output practice in educational software for second language acquisition. *Language Learning & Technology, 1*(2), 23–40.
— (1998b). The relative effectiveness of production comprehension practice in second language acquisition. *Computer Assisted Language Learning, 11*(2), 153–77.
— (2009). Robo-Sensei's NLP-based error detection and feedback generation. *CALICO JOURNAL, 26*(3), 562–79.
Napolitano, D. M., & Stent, A. (2009). TechWriter: An evolving system for writing assistance for advanced learners of English. *CALICO Journal, 26*(3), 611–25.
Nerbonne, J. A. (2003). Natural language processing in computer-assisted language learning. In R. Mitkov (Ed.), *The Oxford handbook of computational linguistics* (pp. 670–98). Oxford: Oxford University Press.
Nerbonne, J. A., & Dokter, D. (1999). An intelligent word-based language learning assistant. *Traitement Automatique des Languages, 40*(1), 125–42.
Nerbonne, J. A., Dokter, D., & Smit, P. (1998). Morphological processing and computer-assisted language learning. *Computer Assisted Language Learning, 11*(5), 543–59.
Niño, A. (2008). Evaluating the use of machine translation post-editing in the foreign language class. *Computer Assisted Language Learning, 21*(1), 29–49.
Olohan, M. (2003). *Introducing corpora in translation studies*. London: Routledge.
Pendar, N., & Cotos, E. (2009). Automatic identification of discourse moves in scientific article introductions. *Proceedings of the third ACL workshop on innovative use of NLP for building educational applications*. Columbus, OH: Association for Computational Linguistics.
Pujola, J.-T. (2002). CALLing for help: Researching language learning strategies using help facilities in a Web-based multimedia program. *ReCALL, 14*(2), 235–62.
Rimrott, A., & Heift, T. (2008). Evaluating automatic detection of misspellings in German. *Language Learning & Technology, 12*(3), 73–92.
Roosmaa, T., & Prószéky, G. (1998). GLOSSER – Using language technology tools for reading texts in a foreign language. In S. Jager, J. A. Nerbonne & A. van Essen (Eds.), *Language teaching and language technology* (pp. 101–7). Lisse: Swets & Zeitlinger.
Rosa, E., & Leow, R. (2004). Computerized task-based exposure, explicitness and type of feedback on Spanish L2 development. *Modern Language Journal, 88*, 192–217.
Schmidt, R. W. (1990). The role of consciousness in second language learning. *Applied Linguistics, 11*(2), 129–58.

Schoelles, M., & Hamburger, H. (1996). Teacher-usable exercise design tools. In C. Frasson, G. Gauthier & A. Lesgold (Eds.), *Intelligent tutoring systems. Second international conference, ITS'96, Montréal, Canada, June 1996, proceedings* (pp. 102–10). Berlin: Springer Verlag.

Schulze, M. (2008a). AI in CALL – Artificially inflated or almost imminent? *CALICO JOURNAL, 25*(3), 510–27.

— (2008b). Instruction and modeling in ICALL. Retrieved 7 October 2011, from www.aila2008.org/public/pdf-dokumente-aila/tagungsband-abstract/abstracts(2)symposia.pdf

— (Ed.) (2008c). *Interfaces in intelligent CALL. Special issue of computer assisted language* Learning, *21*(4). London: Routledge.

Schulze, M., & Hamel, M.-J. (2000). Towards authentic tasks and experiences. The example of parser-based CALL. *Canadian Journal of Applied Linguistics, 3*(1–2), 79–90.

Schulze, M., Hamel, M.-J., & Thompson, J. (Eds.) (1999). *Language processing in CALL. ReCALL special publication (Proceedings of a one-day conference 'natural language processing in computer-assisted language learning' Held at UMIST, 9 May 1998, Organised by the Centre of Computational Linguistics, UMIST, in Association with Eurocall).* Hull: CTICML.

Self, J. A. (1994). The role of student models in learning environments. *IEICE Transactions on Information and Systems, 77*(1), 8.

Shermis, M. D., & Burstein, J. (2003). *Automated essay scoring: A cross-disciplinary perspective.* Mahwah, NJ; London: Lawrence Erlbaum Associates.

Sun, G., Liu, X., Cong, G., Zhou, M., Xiong, Z., Lee, J., & Lin, C.-Y. (2007). Detecting erroneous sentences using automatically mined sequential patterns. *Proceedings of the 45th Annual Meeting of the Association of Computational Linguistics* (pp. 81–8). Prague.

Swartz, M., & Yazdani, M. (Eds.) (1992). *Intelligent tutoring systems for foreign language learning.* New York: Springer Verlag.

ten Hacken, P. (2003). Computer-assisted language learning and the revolution in computational linguistics. *Linguistik online, 17*(5), 23–39.

ten Hacken, P., & Tschichold, C. (2001). Word Manager and CALL: Structured access to the lexicon as a tool for enriching learners' vocabulary. *ReCALL, 13*(1), 121–31.

Thompson, J., & Zähner, C. (Eds.) (1992). *Proceedings of the ICALL Workshop, UMIST, September 1991.* Hull: University of Hull, CTI Centre for Modern Languages.

Tokuda, N., & Chen, L. (2002). *Special issue on ICALL. Computer-assisted language learning, 15*(4). Lisse: Swets & Zeitlinger.

Tsao, N.-L., & Wible, D. (2009). A method for unsupervised broad-coverage lexical error detection and correction. *Proceedings of the NAACL HLT workshop on innovative use of NLP for building educational applications* (pp. 51–4). Boulder, Colorado.

Underwood, J. H. (1982). Simulated conversation as CAI strategy. *Foreign Language Annals, 15*, 209–12.

Vandeventer, A. (2001). Creating a grammar checker for CALL by constraint relaxation: A feasibility study. *ReCALL, 13*(1), 110–20.

Vandeventer Faltin, A. (2003). Natural language processing tools for computer assisted language learning. *Linguistik online, 17*(5), 137–53.

Vlugter, P., Knott, A., McDonald, J., & Hall, C. (2009). Dialogue-based CALL: A case study on teaching pronouns. *Computer Assisted Language Learning, 22*(2), 115–31.

Walker, N. R., Trofimovich, P., Cedergren, H., & Gatbonton, E. (2011). Using ASR technology in language training for specific purposes: A perspective from Quebec, Canada. *CALICO Journal, 28*(3), 721–43.

Ware, P., & Warschauer, M. (2006). Electronic feedback and second language writing. In K. Hyland & F. Hyland (Eds.), *Feedback and second language writing*. Cambridge: Cambridge University Press.

Warschauer, M., & Grimes, D. (2008). Automated writing assessment in the classroom. *Pedagogies: An International Journal, 3*, 22–36.

Warschauer, M., & Healey, D. (1998). Computers and language learning: An overview. *Language Teaching, 31*, 57–71.

Warschauer, M., & Ware, P. (2006). Automated writing evaluation: Defining the classroom research agenda. *Language Teaching Research, 10*(2), 157–80.

Weischedel, R. M., Voge, W. M., & James, M. (1978). An artificial intelligence approach to language instruction. *Artificial Intelligence, 10*, 225–40.

Williams, L. (2006). Web-based machine translation as a tool for promoting electronic literacy and language awareness. *Foreign Language Annals, 39*(4), 565–78.

Wood, P. (2008). Developing ICALL tools using GATE. *Computer Assisted Language Learning, 21*(4), 383–92.

— (2011). Computer assisted reading in German as a foreign language. Developing and testing an NLP-based application. *CALICO Journal 28*(3), 662–76.

Zock, M. (1988). Language learning as problem solving. Modeling logical aspects of inductive learning to generate sentences in French by man and machine. *Proceedings of the Twelfth International Conference on Computational Linguistics* (Vol. 2, pp. 806–11). Budapest: John von Neumann Society for Computing Sciences.

— (1992). SWIM or Sink: The problem of communicating thought. In M. L. Swartz & M. Yazdani (Eds.), *Intelligent tutoring systems for foreign language learning. The Bridge to International Communication* (pp. 235–47). Berlin: Springer Verlag.

— (1996). Computational linguistics and its use in real world: The case of computer assisted language learning. *Proceedings of Coling'96: The Sixteenth International Conference on Computational Linguistics* (pp. 1002–4). Copenhagen: Center for Sprogteknologi.

Zock, M., Sabah, G., & Alviset, C. (1986). From structure to process. Computer-assisted teaching of various strategies for generating pronoun constructions in French. *Proceedings of COLING* (pp. 566–9). Bonn.

14

Technology-enhanced reading environments

Youngmin Park, Binbin Zheng, Joshua Lawrence and Mark Warschauer

Summary

Although we live in a globalized information society where the ability to read in English is more important than ever before, many learners of English as a second or foreign language still struggle with this important skill. This chapter presents an overview of research on computer-supported reading. We first present the major components of reading, including word decoding, language comprehension and text interpretation, and summarize research on computer-assisted reading in each of these areas. We then hone in on two examples of recent approaches to the use of digital media to support second language reading. In the first example, we introduce visual-syntactic text formatting (VSTF), which presents texts in a cascaded version that helps compensate for limitations in explicit or implicit syntactic knowledge among second language learners. Empirical studies in classroom settings demonstrate the effectiveness of this syntactically cued text formatting on reading comprehension, retention and proficiency. The second example, capitalizing on the interactive and collaborative nature of blogs, demonstrates the benefits of sociocultural learning in support of reading. Both quantitative and qualitative analysis of fifth-grade students' blog posts reveals that online communication not only engages English learners, but also helps them develop text interpretation abilities by enriching cognitive skills and students' sense of audience and authorship. We conclude by discussing directions for future research, drawing on a typology that identifies eleven types of digital resources that can be used to enhance reading comprehension.

Introduction

In a global economy and information-based society, the ability to read well in English is more important than ever before, and one that has significant consequences for non-native speakers of the language. In English as a foreign language (EFL) contexts English language reading is an increasing necessity for global interaction, especially with an estimated 80 to 90% of the world's scientific research printed in English (Montgomery, 2004). Yet achievement of high standards of English reading is beyond the reach of most EFL learners, especially those whose native language is not Indo-European and does not use the Latin script. Countries such as China, Korea and Japan continually find that even ten years of English instruction is not sufficient to enable people to read needed English-language material in their field of study (see, for example, Kim, Chin & Goodman, 2004; Sheu, 2003; Tanaka & Stapleton, 2007).

In ESL settings, the ability to read English is even more critical, shaping young people's likelihood of graduating from high school and being able to pursue further studies or a career. Yet, in the United States, for example, only 25% of English language learners achieve even a basic level of English reading proficiency by eighth grade; the remaining 75% hardly make basic sense of reading materials, make obvious connections between texts and their previous experiences or make simple inferences when reading grade-appropriate texts (National Center for Educational Statistics, 2011).

To help address these challenges, applied linguists and educators have introduced diverse approaches to improve second language reading, including extensive reading (Day & Bamford, 1998; Iwahori, 2008; Sheu, 2003), strategy-based instruction (Anderson, 1999; Souvignier & Mokhlesgerami, 2006; Sung, Chang & Huang, 2008), motivational approaches (Carreira, 2006; Kim, 2010; Warden & Lin, 2000), and text modification (Oh, 2001; Rahimi, 2011; Wang, 2011). In the last 20 years with the growing diffusion of multimedia computing and the internet, computer-based approaches to the teaching and learning of second language reading have also gained in popularity.

In this chapter, we examine research on the use of computers and digital media in second language reading instruction. First, we elaborate on the components of second language reading and briefly review computer-assisted reading research consistent with these components. Then discuss at more length two particular examples – syntactic text formatting and blogging – that represent recent approaches to promoting reading with technology. We then introduce a typology that presents a broad array of resources for digitally scaffolded reading.

Components of second language reading

Learning to read is a complex, multifaceted process, and even more so in a second language. Theoretical frameworks analysing the process of learning to read (e.g.,

Cummins, 2008; Luke & Freebody, 1999; Scarborough, 2001) suggest three critical components of this process: word recognition, language comprehension and text interpretation.

Word recognition

Word recognition – either through phonological decoding or sight-reading – is widely recognized as a vital skill for early reading development (Hoover & Gough, 1990; Joshi & Aaron, 2000; McBride-Chang & Kail, 2002; Ziegler & Goswami, 2005). Paradoxically, though, this skill is comparatively less important for L2 learners than for English native speakers (L1). Most adolescent or adult L2 learners already have sufficient word recognition skills, and even very young L2 learners sometimes outperform their L1 peers in word decoding (see Lesaux & Siegel, 2003). Software to promote word recognition thus may not be particularly important for all L2 learners. So while a number of studies suggest that technology-supported automaticity training can facilitate faster lexical access during reading among L2 learners (see, for example, Fukkink, Hulstijn & Simis, 2005; Li, 2010; Tozcu & Coady, 2004), it is far from clear that improvements in automatic word recognition can facilitate improved textual comprehension without concomitant improvement in language comprehension skills (Hulstijn, 2000; Fukkink, Hulstijn & Simis, 2005). We interpret these findings as suggesting that the biggest challenge facing L2 readers is not the area of word decoding, but in that of language comprehension, an area we turn to next.

Language comprehension

There has been extensive research on how technology can be used to support language comprehension, using tools such as electronic dictionaries, computer software, Web-based activities and materials, and Web 2.0 tools. Given Hu and Nation's (2000) finding that readers need to know 98% of vocabulary in a text to comprehend it and infer unknown words from the context, it is not surprising that this has been an important area of computer-assisted language learning (CALL) research.

Types of multimedia used in vocabulary learning studies vary from electronic dictionaries, to multimedia glossing, to online word lists and corpus analyses, to video trailers and short readings. A wide range of CALL-supported conditions have been explored: the effect of access to internal glossary vs. external dictionary (Chun, 2011); the effect of sentence-level translation vs. word-level basic translation on vocabulary retention (Gettys, Imhof & Kautz, 2001; Grace, 1998); the effect of multimedia glosses (e.g., graphics, videos or audio) vs. textual translations (Abraham, 2008; Al Seghayer, 2001; Yoshii & Flaitz, 2002); and learners' multimedia preferences (Chun & Plass, 1996; Yanguas, 2009). Although the use of multimedia glosses is positively related to proximal outcomes, such as better vocabulary acquisition (Gettys et al., 2001;

Proctor et al., 2011), relationships with more global outcomes like enhanced reading comprehension have been harder to establish (Abraham, 2008; Proctor et al., 2011).

Text interpretation

Understanding of text genres, text structures, formality, metaphor, register and culturally related aspects of language interact with word and sentence awareness in intricate ways; it is especially difficult for L2 learners to acquire these competencies. How then do we help them in recognizing topics, making inferences and understanding text structures and discourse organization? Kitajima (2002) proposed that computer-assisted reading materials could help learners improve their higher-order interpretation skills for constructing coherent text representation. It may be possible to use strategy prompts embedded in digital texts to lead students to more effectively apply reading strategies (e.g., those of predicting, questioning, clarifying, summarizing, visualizing and empathizing) and to acknowledge text organizational patterns, but little research has been conducted in these areas to date.

Cultural and textual background knowledge can also be built through classroom discussion and interaction. Interventions, such as reciprocal teaching have been used to help facilitate structured discussion about texts, leading to robust learning outcomes (Palincsar & Brown, 1984; see Lawrence & Snow, 2010 for a review of similar studies). It may be that similar results can be obtained through conversational writing (e.g., of 'Experience Stories', as Allen and Allen, suggested as long ago as 1976). Literacy is a transaction between readers and writers who have mutual awareness and shared expectations (Nystrand, 1986). Studies have shown that writing during reading potentially leads to more critical thinking (Tierney & Shannahan, 1991), helps readers to be more active, reflective and evaluative (Salvatori, 1985), and encourages students to be more engaged in thinking more deeply about what they read (Colvin-Murphy, 1986).

Requiring some form of digital written interaction, textual feedback or annotation can potentially offer such language learning opportunities (see discussion in Chun, 2011). For example, a blogging environment that encourages participants to negotiate their understanding of the meaning of a text may encourage better understanding of sociocultural aspects of meaning. Online interaction can also provide students with opportunities to explore comprehensible language while building reading fluency, which can also help to keep L2 learners more motivated and focused on authentic texts and tasks (Brandl, 2005; Chun, 2011; Lyman-Hager, 2000). For example, Carico and Logan's study (2004) on online discussion among university students and eighth graders suggested that these students helped each other clarify confusing texts, figure out together both plot elements and relationships and make connections among readings. Another study by Grisham and Wolsey (2006) also suggested that online threaded book discussions assisted eighth-grade students to engage in and think deeply about the reading materials. In addition, the synchronous nature of online threaded discussion enabled students to rapidly give and receive feedback, a process that can lead to greater reflection, metacognition and more thoughtful construction of ideas (Downes, 2004; Jacobs, 2003).

New approaches to computer-supported reading

In the last decade, new approaches to computer-supported reading have emerged which appear to hold great promise. We present and discuss two approaches that our research team has investigated: VSTF and blogging to learn.

Visual-syntactic text formatting

In contrast to the considerable amount of research on vocabulary learning with multimedia scaffolding (Abraham, 2008; Chun, 2011; Chun & Payne, 2004; Yanguas, 2009), much less work has been done to support reading development through digital scaffolding of syntax. Digital technology has enabled a text to be presented in various ways by changing font size and style, text and background colour, line and page length, and page layout (Anderson-Inman & Horney, 2007). For the past several decades, researchers and educators have sought to see if such easily customizable texts could be a more effective way to help improve reading comprehension. Such alterations of text format have varied from simple changes in letters, line space or capitalization (Marks & Taylor, 1966), to insertion of additional spaces between phrases (Bever, Jandreau, Burwell, Kaplan & Zaenen, 1990; Jandreau & Bever, 1992; Jandreau, Muncer & Bever, 1986; O'Shea & Sindelar, 1983), to linguistically informed text reformatting using computer software (Straub, 2009). Another alternative, VSTF, uses several of these approaches simultaneously to present text in a cascading pattern formed into visual clusters as seen in Figure 14.1.

What specific information do readers gain through this unusual format? Using natural language processing techniques, VSTF automatically breaks sentences up at salient clause and phrase boundaries, and presents visual clusters across multiple rows to denote syntactic hierarchies (Walker et al., 2005). This text formatting is believed to help readers retain and integrate multi-phrase images in their mind, as it seems to facilitate more efficient eye movement and syntactic processing (Warschauer, Park & Walker, 2011).

In contrast to conventional text formatting that does not correspond to the limits of human eye spans, VSTF specifically fits each row of text into one or two fixation eye spans. Due to limitations of the human eye span, readers can typically only take in nine to fifteen characters at a time before moving to the next fixation (Demb, Boynton & Heeger, 1997). Everything else outside this limited space competes for visual attention, leading readers – and especially struggling or L2 readers – to get lost in a sea of words. Reading thus consists of a series of saccades or rapid eye movements as meaning

Four score
and seven years ago
our fathers
brought forth
upon this continent
a new nation,
conceived in liberty
and **dedicated**
to the proposition
that all men
are created equal.

FIGURE 14.1. *Visual-syntactic text formatting (VSTF).*

shifts in a reader's glance to the next textual fixation. Because of skipped words at the edge of fixations (Rayner & Sereno, 1994), combined with limitations of working memory (Garrod, 1992), readers often have to re-examine previously viewed words as they make these saccade shifts while encountering new blocks of reading text. These repeated regressions not only slow down reading, but also impede reading comprehension, especially for L2 learners and others with reading challenges.

One way to overcome this problem is by grasping words in clausal or phrasal units, a process that helps skilled readers anticipate what comes next, and thus avoid confusion at fixation boundaries (Warschauer & Park, 2012). In contrast, poor readers read one word at a time (Cromer, 1970) and rarely parse words into phrases or clauses (Fuchs, Fuchs, Hosp & Jenkins, 2001). This need to comprehend text first at a clausal or phrasal level helps explain why learners' syntactic knowledge is significantly related to both reading fluency and reading comprehension (Mokhtari & Thompson, 2006; Ravid & Mashraki, 2007). In other words, possessing the phonetic ability to decode individual phonemes and words is a *necessary* skill for effective reading, but not a *sufficient* skill (Cain, Oakhill, Barnes & Bryant, 2001; Catts, Fey, Zhang & Tomblin, 1999; Nation & Snowling, 2000). Syntactic awareness remains important, not only at a beginning level, but also at more advanced levels, as readers encounter texts of greater variety and complexity (Bowey, 1986; Gaux & Gombert, 1999). At all levels, more efficient syntactic parsing frees up working memory for semantic processing (Larkin & Simon,

1987; Webb, Thornton, Hancock & McCarthy, 1992). For all these reasons, formatting changes that provide syntactic clues have consistently been shown to improve reading fluency and speed (Bever et al., 1990; Jandreau & Bever, 1992; Jandreau, Muncer & Bever, 1986; LeVasseur, Macaruso & Shankweiler, 2007).

The value of syntactic awareness in reading is closely related to that of prosodic awareness, which interacts with syntax at the phrase level and with semantics at the passage level (Esser, 1988). A number of studies have found that knowledge of prosody – knowing about a language's rhythm, stress and intonation patterns – is highly correlated with a learner's reading rate, accuracy and comprehension (Dowhower, 1987; Miller & Schwanenflugel, 2006). Prosody in oral communication is indicated in a variety of ways, including through pauses, word stress, and changes in pitch, pacing and flow. Unfortunately, in written communication, most of these clues are either absent or substituted for by much more limited orthographic conventions, such as punctuation and typographic emphasis (e.g., via italics, underlining or bold typeface).

Just as L1 speakers carry out syntactic parsing while reading, aided by their knowledge of prosody and rhetorical patterns, so do L2 learners. However, this process is much more challenging for L2 learners, who either lack explicit knowledge of the target language syntax or, in more cases, may know the rules but cannot automatically use those rules to mentally process language. Due to this lack of syntactic knowledge or skill, as well as interference from their first language, learners make significantly more parsing errors when reading in a foreign language (Mack, 1986; White, 1989). Thus, not surprisingly, knowledge of syntax has been proven to be a salient factor in determining second language reading ability (Shiotsu, 2010), and the more dissimilar the syntactic rules of a target language are from one's native language, the more difficult reading in the target language becomes (Frenck-Mestre & Pynte, 1997). All these reasons explain why the use of visual syntactic cues embedded in texts can potentially be of greater benefit to second language learners than more typical approaches to text modification, such as the simplification or elaboration of content (Oh, 2001).

Empirical research on VSTF

Studies among college students have found that reading text in VSTF improves reading comprehension, with readers using that format scoring 40% higher than block format readers (Walker et al., 2005). Other studies suggest that VSTF is effective in improving students' reading speed. The participants wearing eye-tracking equipment showed a 20% increase in their average reading speeds when using VSTF as opposed to reading in block format (Warschauer, Park & Walker, 2011). Not only did their reading rates and comprehension improve, but better academic content retention was also reported in VSTF studies with high school students in World History classes (Walker & Vogel, 2005; Walker et al., 2007). Most interestingly, a number of studies have found that students who read regularly with VSTF can also transfer such skills they have learned, and thereby tend to become more proficient readers of material in traditional block format, presumably due to gaining increased confidence in their reading, or perhaps also due to how such explicit training helps to raise their awareness of the importance of implicit language structural patterns (Vogel, 2002; Walker & Vogel, 2005; Walker et al., 2005; Walker et al., 2007).

Though VSTF has been used with both L1 and L2 speakers of English, evidence suggests it is particularly effective with the latter. In a study with high school students, greater gains were seen with lower proficient students than among those who were already good readers (Walker et al., 2005). Many of these were L2 learners who were able to achieve the same reading proficiency level at the end of the year as the control group of L1 readers. Walker and Vogel (2005) also reported that the use of VSTF had a positive effect on L2 learners' reading development across all secondary grades, allowing these L2 learners' reading with VSTF to close between one-half to the entire gap between themselves and L1 speakers who did not use VSTF.

In summary, though there has been broader attention to the value of multimedia scaffolding to assist reading comprehension, there are also very promising signs of the value of syntactic scaffolding.

Blogging to learn

Blogging first emerged as a social phenomenon in about 1999 and was introduced in classrooms soon thereafter (for review and discussion, see Warschauer & Grimes, 2007). A number of studies have shown the benefits of using blogs to support second language writing (Arslan & Şahin-Kızıl, 2010; Bloch, 2007). In one of our recent studies, we examined the use of blogging to support the reading process. The study analysed 37 fifth-grade students' literacy development in a classroom blogging environment over the course of a school year. Twenty-five of the thirty-seven students were designated as English language learners. Students were engaged in reading and writing connection activities in real-time blogging during twice-a-week 20-minute sessions. A Web-based live blogging tool, *CoverItLive*, was embedded into blog entries to support synchronous online discussions (as shown in Figure 14.2). During these sessions, students were encouraged to write simultaneously, while one of their teachers read a chapter aloud or while the whole class watched a video together. Students' posts on their blogs in the first two months and the last two months of the school year were selected and analysed to examine students' literacy development as reflected in their cognitive skills development, degree of interaction, as well as their sense of audience and authorship.

Cognitive skills development

Using a cognitive analysis model adapted from Henri (1992) and Hara, Bonk and Angeli (2000), we analysed students' cognitive skills in five categories: elementary

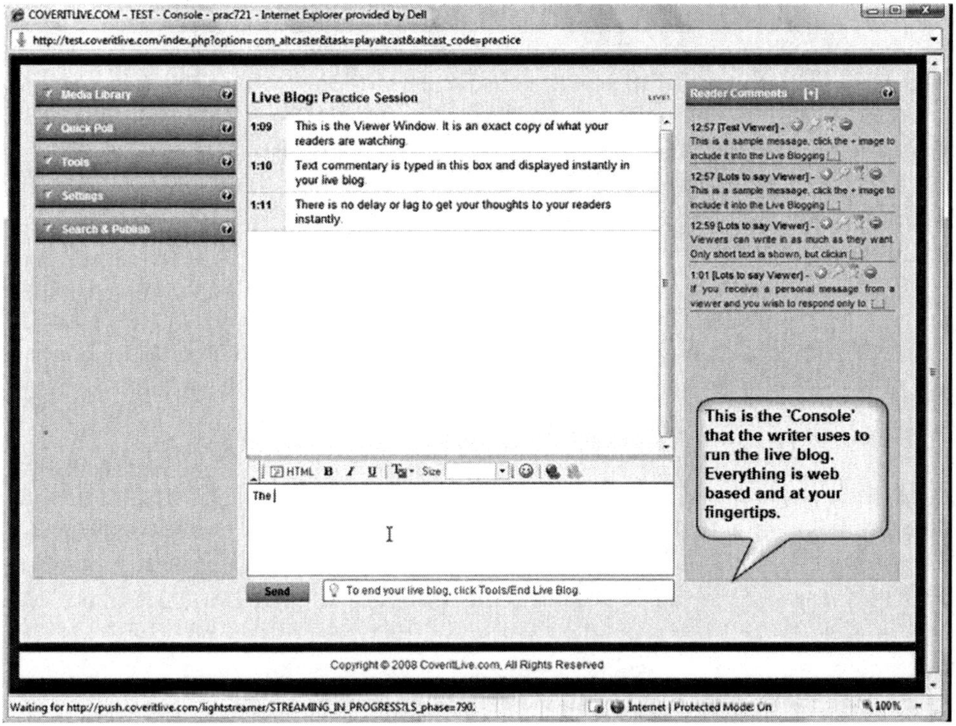

FIGURE 14.2. *Interface of 'CoveritLive' discussion board. (Used with permission of The CoverItLive™ live-event publishing platform).*

clarification, in-depth clarification, inferencing, judgement and application of strategies. All of the students' posts from the first and last two months of the year were coded into the most appropriate of the five above categories.

The results suggested that students used higher-level cognitive skills at the end of the year as compared to the beginning of the year. Students applied skills of *elementary clarification* (e.g., raising simple questions or describing basic facts) much more in the first two months than in the last two months. Posts involving *in-depth clarification* (e.g., interpreting information, offering explanations, expressing opinions or brainstorming ideas) remained at the same level from beginning to end and overall were the most frequents types of posts at both the beginning and the end of the blogging activity. The largest growth in types of cognitive skills applied in student posts occurred in *inferencing* (e.g, summarizing, making connections, making predictions and reflecting) and in *judgement* (e.g., indicating substantial agreement or disagreement, evaluating arguments, offering criticism); the percentage of posts involving these two sets of skills tripled in the last two months as compared to in the first two months. This increased amount of inferencing and judgement reflected a shift from stating simple questions and basic ideas to making connections, reflecting upon reading materials and making comparisons and evaluations. These results align well with previous studies indicating that deeper cognitive processing occurs among students as their communication skills grow through participation in online discussions (Hara et al., 2000). Application of strategies rarely occurred in student posts in our study, which is consistent with previous research by Garrison et al. (2001). Garrison's study showed that application of strategies did not occur among college students, and it is thus not surprising that this particularly high level of cognitive processing did not occur among fifth-grade students either.

Teacher–student and student–student interactions

This study's findings also suggested that both teacher–student interaction and student–student interactions facilitated students' deeper engagement and higher-order thinking. Analysis of discourse indicated that the teachers constantly encouraged students to 'push their thinking', and use their writing to dig deeper into the motivations of authors, the meanings of texts and the relationships among texts and contexts. Over time, a decrease in teacher participation revealed a transformation from teacher mentoring to peer scaffolding, as students gradually learned, not only how to write better, but also how to support their peers' thinking processes. The following conversation between two students illustrates how students encouraged each other and how students took the stance of facilitator during their reading and writing activities:

> A: I like the book so far. I think that writing about a little boy who was invisible was a good topic for the author to pick.
>
> B @ A: Why do you think it is a good topic? Also, what else do you like about the book because I know there are more than one reason.
>
> A @ B: I think it is a good topic because some people might want to know what happens and being invisible is cool. I also like the book because I want to know how well of friends Alisha and Bobby will become. I also like Alisha.

At the beginning, student A only wrote one sentence about why she liked their reading on that day. Several minutes later, student B replied and pushed her to think more about why she liked this topic. As a consequence, student A thought more deeply and wrote another three sentences about the reasons. Student B here took the stance of facilitator and scaffolded student A's writing development. This example strengthens Tierney and Shannahan's (1991) claim that writing during reading leads to more critical thinking.

Another example shows how students encouraged each other and how students took on the role of facilitator. After one student, Tyler, posted a paragraph of more than 200 words about a topic, many students expressed their compliments to him and some also encouraged him to keep it up, as the exchange below indicates:

> Student C@Tyler: Way to go! Just keep putting things like that up!
>
> Student D@Tyler: Great Job!!! You are a great writer!
>
> Student E@Tyler: I think you did a good job. I wish I would write like you Tyler. Nice job and keep up the good work.

The next day when student Tyler did not participate too much, student C responded:

> Student C@Tyler: You are on fire with comments the past couple of days and I am really impressed! But what is your opinion on this book? How do you like it?

In this example, student C took on the stance of a mentor and encouraged peers to actively participate in the discussion. The teachers did not directly teach students how to scaffold each other. Rather, students spontaneously learned about scaffolding and facilitating through apprenticeship and modelling from the teachers. During the process of interacting with peers and facilitating each other's thinking, students became more motivated and engaged, developed more critical thinking skills and gained confidence in their reading and writing.

Sense of audience and authorship

Furthermore, during the process of blogging about readings, students built a better sense of how to communicate with an audience through collective examination of the authoring process. They discussed the strategies of authors that they read, and actively connected their personal experience with characters in the readings. For example, when reading a story about how the boy was ignored by his parents when he was trying to participate in an adult conversation, one student wrote, 'I have connection trying to get in a adult conversation. One day this ADT security guy came over and said about the security and i tryed to go in the conversation but I got ignored [sic].' Students discussed the characters in books, related the stories in books with their own stories, learned from how the authors told stories and strategized about how this learning would change their own writing. As one student wrote, 'I really like how the author use description words. Maybe I can use lots more description words in my writing [sic].' Another student added, 'the author is using actions to tell the readers that they like each other. Maybe I'll use that technique in my writing next time.' Through these interactive conversations, students appeared to develop a more critical understanding of what they read, as well as a sense of audience and authorship in their own writing. This latter point was reflected in our study as well; L2 learners who blogged the most improved their writing the most over the course of a year.

This study is of course not definitive, but it does offer empirical evidence that the benefits that seem to be afforded by computer-mediated interaction for scaffolding reading development (Carico & Logan, 2004; Grisham & Wolsey, 2006) also apply to L2 learners. Indeed in our study, whether measured by growth in participation throughout the year, or by impact on test score outcomes, L2 learners in the classrooms received the greatest benefits and achieved greater average gains.

Broader approaches

The above examples indicate the great promise of digital media for supporting L2 reading. At the same time, the examples discussed in this chapter represent only a fraction of the potential ways that new technologies can support the reading process. To consider this broader range of possibilities, a useful starting point is the typology developed by the *National Center for Supported eText* (Anderson-Inman & Horney, 2007; see Table 14.1). Though this typology was developed for general purposes rather than particularly for L2 learning, the digital resources it discusses are certainly applicable for an L2 setting. These include presentational resources that enable text and graphics to be presented in varying and customizable ways; navigational resources that facilitate movement within documents (e.g., to glossaries); translational resources that make available alternative versions of texts such as through VSTF or text-to-speech; explanatory resources that provide supplemental clarifications or descriptions; illustrative resources that provide visual support; summarizing resources, such as through presentation of key ideas or timelines; instructional resources such as tutorial or prompts; notional resources that enable electronic highlighting or drawing; collaborative resources, such as blogs or threaded discussions; evaluational resources that provide formative assessments of student progress.

As Anderson-Inman and Horney (2007) point out, a good deal of research is necessary to determine which of these types of resources and in what combinations, are most valuable with particular types of learners. This will be especially important in new digital reading environments that potentially combine several of these types of resources. For example, new types of e-textbooks might include multimedia glossaries, tools for highlighting, social tools for sharing notes and highlights, use of visual animations and formative assessments. There is a huge potential for embedding data capturing tools within these electronic texts so that researchers can better understand which of these resources students use and how that correlates with reading comprehension, retention and proficiency outcomes.

TABLE 14.1. Typology of resources for supported eText

Resource	Description	Examples
Presentational	Enables the text and accompanying graphics to be presented in varying ways, hence customizable to meet the needs of individual readers.	Font size and style, text and background colour, line and page length, page layout and juxtaposition with other pages, graphics in relationship to text.
Navigational	Provides tools that allow the reader to move within a document or between documents.	Within-document links, across-document links, embedded menus, links from other resources such as Table of Contents, Glossary, Bibliography.
Translational	Provides a one-to-one equivalent or simplified version that is more accessible or familiar to the reader. May focus on a word, phrase, paragraph, picture or whole document. May be of same or different modality or media.	Synonyms, definitions, digitized or synthesized text-to-speech, alternate language equivalents (Spanish), video of American Sign Language translation, simplified version at lower reading level, text descriptions for images, captions for video.
Explanatory	Provides information that seeks to clarify the what, where, how, or why of some concept, object, process or event.	Clarifications, interpretations, or descriptions that point to causes, operations, components, mechanisms, parts, methods, procedures, context or consequences; list of influencing factors.
Illustrative	Provides a visual representation or example of something in the text. Designed to support, supplement or extend comprehension of the text through illustrations or examples.	Drawings, photos, simulations, video, photos, re-enactments, sounds, music, information that something is representative of its type ('. . . is a typical example of . . .').
Summarizing	Provides a summarized or condensed way of viewing some feature of the document.	Table of contents, concept map, list of key ideas, chronology, timeline, cast of characters, abstract.
Enrichment	Provides supplementary information that is not strictly needed to comprehend the text, but adds to the readers' appreciation or understanding of its importance or historical context.	Background information, publication history, biography of the author, footnotes, bibliography, influence on other writers.

Continued

TABLE 14.1. Cont'd

Resource	Description	Examples
Instructional	Provides prompts, questions, strategies or instruction designed to teach some aspect of the text or how to read and interpret the text.	Tutorials, self-monitoring comprehension questions, annotations, instructional prompts, study guides, embedded study strategies, online mentoring, tips for effective reading.
Notational	Provides tools for marking or taking notes on the text to enable later retrieval for purposes of studying or completing assignments.	Electronic highlighting, bookmarking, margin notes, outlining, drawing. Ways to gather and group these notes for post-reading review.
Collaborative	Provides tools for working or sharing with other readers, the author or some other audience.	Threaded discussion, online chat, email links, podcasts, blogs.
Evaluational	Provides materials, prompts and assignments designed to assess student learning from the text.	Questions, quizzes, tests, surveys, online interviews, assignments leading to products.

Note: Adapted from: Supported eText: Assistive technology through text transformations. In L. Anderson-Inman & M. A. Horney (2007). *Reading Research Quarterly*, *42*(1), 154. Copyright 2007 by National Center for Supported eText, University of Oregon.

Conclusion

Previously, efforts to improve reading through use of new technologies have been hampered by a lack of broad access to digital tools and content. Today, however, with desktop and laptop computers widely available at affordable prices, low-cost e-readers and tablets expanding into new markets, broadband internet access ubiquitous in much of the world and a vast array of mass-market and educational reading material available in digital format, the age of e-reading is fully upon us. Furthermore, new tools for presenting and scaffolding texts, as well as for facilitating social interaction around texts, are also available. As this review suggests, the use of such tools to promote second language reading holds great promise. Given the need to improve second language reading, as well as the vast array of new CALL tools available, this will be an important area of further research for many years to come.

References

Abraham, L. B. (2008). Computer-mediated glosses in second language reading comprehension and vocabulary learning: A meta-analysis. *Computer Assisted Language Learning, 21*(3), 199–226.

Allen, R. V., & Allen, C. (1976). *Language experiences activities.* Boston: Houghton Mifflin.

Al Seghayer, K. (2001). The effect of multimedia annotation modes on L2 vocabulary acquisition: A comparative study. *Language Learning & Technology, 5*(1), 202–32.

Anderson, N. J. (1999). *Exploring second language reading.* Boston, MA: Newbury House.

Anderson-Inman, L., & Horney, M. A. (2007). Supported eText: Assistive technology through text transformations. *Reading Research Quarterly, 42*(1), 153–60.

Arslan, R. Ş., & Şahin-Kızıl, A. (2010). How can the use of blog software facilitate the writing process of English language learners? *Computer Assisted Language Learning, 23*(3), 183–97.

Bever, T. G., Jandreau, S., Burwell, R., Kaplan, R., & Zaenen, A. (1990). Spacing printed text to isolate major phrases improves readability. *Visible Language, 25*, 74–87.

Bloch, J. (2007). Abdullah's blogging: A generation 1.5 student enters the blogosphere. *Language Learning & Technology, 11*(2), 128–41.

Bowey, J. A. (1986). Syntactic awareness in relation to reading skill and ongoing reading comprehension monitoring. *Journal of Experimental Child Psychology, 41*(2), 282–99.

Brandl, K. (2005). Are you ready to 'MOODLE'? *Language Learning & Technology, 9*(2), 16–23.

Cain, K., Oakhill, J. V., Barnes, M. A., & Bryant, P. E. (2001). Comprehension skill, inference making ability and their relation to knowledge. *Memory and Cognition, 29*, 850–9.

Carico, K. M., & Logan, D. (2004). A generation in cyberspace: Engaging readers through online discussions. *Language Arts, 81*(4), 293–302.

Carreira, J. M. (2006). Motivation for learning English as a foreign language in Japanese elementary schools. *JALT Journal, 28*(2), 135–58.

Catts, H. W., Fey, M. E., Zhang, X., & Tomblin, J. B. (1999). Language basis of reading and reading disabilities: Evidence from a longitudinal investigation. *Scientific Studies of Reading, 3*, 331–61.

Chun, D. M. (2011). CALL technologies for L2 reading post Web 2.0. In N. Arnold & L. Ducate. (Eds.), *Present and future promises of CALL: From theory and research to new directions in language teaching* (pp. 131–70). San Marcos, TX: CALICO.

Chun, D. M., & Payne, J. S. (2004). What makes students click: Working memory and look-up behavior. *System, 32*(4), 481–503.

Chun, D. M., & Plass, J. L. (1996). Effects of multimedia annotations on vocabulary acquisition. *Modern Language Journal, 80*, 183–98.

Colvin-Murphy, C. (1986, December). *Enhancing critical comprehension of literacy texts through writing.* Paper presented at the National Reading Conference, Austin, TX.

Cromer, W. (1970). The difference model: A new explanation for some reading difficulties. *Journal of Educational Psychology, 61*, 671–83.

Cummins, J. (2008). Technology, literacy, and young second language learners: Designing educational futures. In L. L. Parker (Ed.), *Technology-mediated learning environments for young English learners: Connections in and out of school* (pp. 61–98). New York, NY: Lawrence Erlbaum Associates.

Day, R., & Bamford, J. (1998). *Extensive reading in the second language classroom.* Cambridge: Cambridge University Press.

Demb, J. B., Boynton, G. B., & Heeger, D. J. (1997). Brain activity in the visual cortex predicts individual differences in reading performance. *Proceedings of The National Academy of Science, 94*, 13363–6.

Dowhower, S. L. (1987). Effects of repeated reading on second-grade transitional readers' fluency and comprehension. *Reading Research Quarterly, 22*(4), 389–406.

Downes, S. (2004). Educational blogging. *EDUCAUSE Review, 39*(5), 14–26.

Esser, J. (with Polomski, A.) (1988). *Comparing reading and speaking intonation.* Amsterdam: Rodopi.

Frenck-Mestre, C., & Pynte, J. (1997). Syntactic ambiguity resolution while reading in second and native languages. *Quarterly Journal of Experimental Psychology, 50A*(1), 119–48.

Fuchs, L. S., Fuchs, D., Hosp, M. K., & Jenkins, J. R. (2001). Oral reading fluency as an indicator of reading competence: A theoretical, empirical, and historical analysis. *Scientific Studies of Reading, 5*(3), 239–56.

Fukkink, R. G., Hulstijn, J., & Simis, A. (2005). Does training of second-language word recognition skills affect reading comprehension? An experimental study. *Modern Language Journal, 89*(1), 54–75.

Garrison, D. R., Anderson, T., & Archer, W. (2001). Critical thinking, cognitive presence, and computer conferencing in distance education. *American Journal of Distance Education, 15*(1), 7–23.

Garrod, S. (1992, April). *Reconciling the psychological with the linguistic in accounts of text comprehension.* Paper presented at the NORDTEXT symposium, Espoo, Finland.

Gaux, C., & Gombert, J. E. (1999). Implicit and explicit syntactic knowledge and reading in preadolescents. *British Journal of Developmental Psychology, 17*(2), 169–88.

Gettys, S., Imhof, L. A., & Kautz, J. O. (2001). Computer-assisted reading: The effect of glossing format on comprehension and vocabulary retention. *Foreign Language Annals, 34*(2), 91–106.

Grace, C. A. (1998). Retention of word meaning inferred from context and sentence-level translations: Implications for the design of beginning-level CALL software. *Modern Language Journal, 82*(4), 533–44.

Grisham, D. L., & Wolsey, T. D. (2006). Recentering the middle school classroom as a vibrant learning community: Students, literacy, and technology intersect. *Journal of Adolescent & Adult Literacy, 49*, 648–60.

Hara, N., Bonk, C. J., & Angeli, C. (2000). Content analysis of online discussion in an applied educational psychology course. *Instructional Science, 28*(2), 115–52.

Henri, F. (1992). Computer conferencing and content analysis. In A. R. Kaye (Ed.), *Collaborative learning through computer conferencing: The Najaden papers* (pp. 117–36). New York, NY: Springer.

Hoover, W. A., & Gough, P. B. (1990). The simple view of reading. *Reading and Writing, 2*(2), 127–60.

Hu, M., & Nation, I. (2000). Unknown vocabulary density and reading comprehension. *Reading in a Foreign Language, 13*(1), 403–30.

Hulstijn, J. H. (2000). The use of computer technology in experimental studies of second language acquisition: A survey of some techniques and some ongoing studies. *Language Learning & Technology, 3*(2), 32–43.

Iwahori, Y. (2008). Developing reading fluency: A study of extensive reading in EFL. *Reading in a Foreign Language, 20*(1), 70–91.

Jacobs, J. (2003, July). *Communication over exposure: The rise of blogs as a product of cybervoyeurism.* Paper presented at the ANZCA 03, Brisbane, Australia.

Jandreau, S. M., & Bever, T. G. (1992). Phrase-spaced formats improve comprehension in average readers. *Journal of Applied Psychology, 77*, 143–6.

Jandreau, S. M., Muncer, S. J., & Bever, T. G. (1986). Phrase-sensitive formatting. *British Journal of Educational Technology, 17*(2), 128–33.
Joshi, R. M., & Aaron, P. G. (2000). The component model of reading: Simple view of reading made a little more complex. *Reading Psychology, 21*(2), 85–97.
Kim, K., Chin, C., & Goodman, Y. (2004). Revaluing the reading process of adult ESL/EFL learners through critical dialogues. *Colombian Applied Linguistics Journal*, (6), 42–57.
Kim, K. J. (2010). Reading motivation in two languages: An examination of EFL college students in Korea. *Reading and Writing. 24*(8), 861–81.
Kitajima, R. (2002). Enhancing higher order interpretation skills for Japanese reading. *CALICO Journal, 19*(3), 571–81.
Larkin, J. H., & Simon, H. (1987). Why a diagram is (sometimes) worth ten thousand words. *Cognitive Science, 11*, 65–99.
Lawrence, J., & Snow, C. (2010). Oral discourse and reading comprehension. In M. Kamil, D. Pearson, E. Moje, P. Aflerback & P. Mosenthal (Eds.), *Handbook of reading research.* (Vol. 4, pp. 320–37). London: Routledge.
Lesaux, N., & Siegel, L. (2003). The development of reading in children who speak English as a second language. *Developmental Psychology, 39*(6), 1005–19.
LeVasseur V. M., Macaruso, P., & Shankweiler, D. (2007). Promoting gains in reading fluency: A comparison of three approaches. *Reading and Writing, 21*, 205–30.
Li, J. (2010). Learning vocabulary via computer-assisted scaffolding for text processing. *Computer Assisted Language Learning, 23*(3), 253–75.
Luke, A., & Freebody, P. (1999). A map of possible practices: Further notes on the four resources model. *Practically Primary, 4*(2), 5–8.
Lyman-Hager, M. A. (2000). Bridging the language-literature gap: Introducing literature electronically to the undergraduate language student. *CALICO Journal, 17*(3), 431–52.
Mack, M. (1986). A study of semantic and syntactic processing in monolinguals and fluent bilinguals. *Journal of Psycholinguistic Research, 15*, 463–89.
Marks, M. B., & Taylor, P. (1966). Reading through better format. *The Journal of Educational Research, 60*(4), 147–51.
McBride-Chang, C., & Kail, R. V. (2002). Cross-cultural similarities in the predictors of reading acquisition. *Child development, 73*(5), 1392–407.
Miller, J., & Schwanenflugel, P. J. (2006). Prosody of syntactically complex sentences in the oral reading of young children. *Journal of Educational Psychology, 98*(4), 839–53.
Mokhtari, K., & Thompson, H. B. (2006). How problems of reading fluency and comprehension are related to difficulties in syntactic awareness skills among fifth graders. *Reading Research and Instruction, 46*(1), 73–94.
Montgomery, S. (2004). Of towers, walls, and fields: Perspectives on language in science. *Science, 303*(5662), 1333–15.
Nation, K., & Snowling, M. J. (2000). Factors influencing syntactic awareness skills in normal readers and poor comprehenders. *Applied Psycholinguistics, 21*, 229–41.
National Center for Educational Statistics (2011). *The Nation's Report Card: NAEP 2009 Year in Review* (NCES Number 2011471).
Nystrand, M. (1986). *The structure of written communication: Studies in reciprocity between writers and readers.* Orlando, FL: Academic Press.
Oh, S. (2001). Two types of input modification and EFL reading comprehension: Simplification versus elaboration. *TESOL Quarterly, 35*(1), 69–96.
O'Shea, L. J., & Sindelar, P. T. (1983). The effects of segmenting written discourse on the reading comprehension of low- and high-performance readers. *Reading Research Quarterly, 18*, 458–65.

Palincsar, A. S., & Brown, A. L. (1984). Reciprocal teaching of comprehension-fostering and comprehension-monitoring strategies. *Cognition & Instruction, 1*(2), 117–75.

Proctor, C., Dalton, B., Uccelli, P., Biancarosa, G., Mo, E., Snow, C., & Neugebauer, S. (2011). Improving comprehension online: Effects of deep vocabulary instruction with bilingual and monolingual fifth graders. *Reading and Writing, 24*(5), 517–44.

Rahimi, M. A. (2011). Use of syntactic elaboration techniques to enhance comprehensibility of EST texts. *English Language Teaching, 4*(1), 11–17.

Ravid, D., & Mashraki, Y. E. (2007). Prosodic reading, reading comprehension and morphological skills in Hebrew-speaking fourth graders. *Journal of Research in Reading, 30*(2), 140–56.

Rayner, K., & Sereno, S. (1994). Eye movements in reading: Psycholinguistic studies. In M. A. Gersbacker (Ed.), *Handbook of psycholinguistics* (pp. 57–81). San Diego, CA: Academic Press.

Salvatori, M. (1985). The dialogical nature of basic reading and writing. In D. Bartholomae & A. Petrosky (Eds.), *Facts, artifacts and counterfacts: Theory and method for a reading and writing course* (pp. 137–66). Upper Montclair, NJ: Boynton.

Scarborough, H. (2001). Connecting early language and literacy to later reading (dis) abilities. In S. B. Neuman & D. K. Dickinson (Eds.), *Handbook of early literacy research* (pp. 97–110). New York, NY: Guilford.

Sheu, S. P-H. (2003). Extensive reading with EFL learners at beginning level. *TESL Reporter, 36*(2), 8–26.

Shiotsu, T. (2010). *Components of L2 reading: Linguistic and processing factors in the reading test performances of Japanese EFL learners.* Cambridge: Cambridge University Press.

Souvignier, E., & Mokhlesgerami, J. (2006). Using self-regulation as a framework for implementing strategy instruction to foster reading comprehension. *Learning and Instruction, 16*, 57–71.

Straub, K. (2009). *Kindle2: Crack for readers . . . until you start reading: How text formatting can ruin (or enhance) the readability and persuasiveness of text.* Fairfield, IA: Human Factors International.

Sung, Y. T., Chang, K. E., & Huang, J. S. (2008). Improving children's reading comprehension and use of strategies through computer-based strategy training. *Computers in Human Behavior, 24*, 1552–71.

Tanaka, H., & Stapleton, P. (2007). Increasing reading input in Japanese high school EFL classrooms: An empirical study exploring the efficacy of extensive reading. *The Reading Matrix, 7*(1), 115–31.

Tierney, R., & Shannahan, T. (1991). Research on the reading/writing relationship: Interactions, transactions, and outcomes. In P. E. Pearson, M. Barr, & P. B. Mosenthal (Eds.), *Handbook of reading research* (pp. 246–80). New York, NY: Longman.

Tozcu, A., & Coady, J. (2004). Successful learning of frequent vocabulary through CALL also benefits reading comprehension and speed. *Computer Assisted Language Learning, 17*(5), 473–96.

Vogel, C. A. (2002). *A program evaluation of the Live Ink format.* (Unpublished doctoral dissertation). Denver, CO: University of Denver.

Walker, R., & Vogel, C. (2005, June). *Live Ink: Brain-based text formatting raises standardized test scores.* Paper presented at the National Educational Computing Conference, Philadelphia, PA.

Walker, R., Gordon, A. S., Schloss, P., Fletcher, C. R., Vogel, C., & Walker, S. (2007, October). *Visual-syntactic text formatting: Theoretical basis and empirical evidence for impact on human reading.* Paper presented at the IEEE Professional Communication Conference, Seattle, WA.

Walker, S., Schloss, P., Fletcher, C. R., Vogel, C. A., & Walker, R. (2005). Visual-syntactic text formatting: A new method to enhance online reading. *Reading Online, 8*(6).

Wang, Y. (2011). The effect of text length on students' reading comprehension. *Theory and Practice in Language Studies, 1*(9), 1160–6.

Warden, C. A., & Lin, H. J. (2000). Existence of integrative motivation in an Asian EFL setting. *Foreign Language Annals, 33*(5), 535–45. Retrieved from http://doi.wiley.com/10.1111/j.1944–9720.2000.tb01997.x

Warschauer, M., & Grimes, D. (2007). Audience, authorship, and artifact: The emergent semiotics of Web 2.0. *Annual Review of Applied Linguistics, 27*(2007), 1–23.

Warschauer, M., & Park, Y. (2012). Re-envisioning reading in English as a foreign language. *JACET-CANTO Journal.*

Warschauer, M., Park, Y., & Walker, R. (2011). Transforming digital reading with visual-syntactic text formatting. *The JALT CALL Journal, 7*(3), 255–70.

Webb, J. M., Thornton, N. E., Hancock, T. E., & McCarthy, M. T. (1992). Drawing maps from text: A test of conjoint retention. *Journal of General Psychology, 119*, 303–13.

White, L. (1989). The adjacency condition on case assignment: Do L2 learners observe the subset principle? In S. M. Gass & J. Schachter (Eds.), *Linguistic perspectives on second language acquisition* (pp. 134–58). Cambridge: Cambridge University Press.

Yanguas, I. (2009). Multimedia glosses and their effect on L2 text comprehension and vocabulary learning. *Language Learning & Technology, 13*(2), 48–67.

Yoshii, M., & Flaitz, J. (2002). Second language incidental vocabulary retention: The effect of picture and annotation types. *CALICO Journal, 20*(1), 33–58.

Ziegler, J. C., & Goswami, U. (2005). Reading acquisition, developmental dyslexia, and skilled reading across languages: A psycholinguistic grain size theory. *Psychological Bulletin, 131*(1), 3–29.

15

The role of technology in teaching and researching writing

Volker Hegelheimer and Jooyoung Lee

Summary

Writing is arguably an essential skill for language learners to be successful, especially in the context of university studies in the United States. Since the widespread introduction of the process approach to writing, the emphasis has shifted from a focus on grammatical accuracy to a focus on organization, development and expression. Additionally, the process approach to writing prescribes multiple iterations that include peer and instructor feedback on several drafts. In this chapter, we will summarize how various technology developments have been used in teaching writing and discuss the advantages and caveats of such approaches. In particular, we will outline how technology-assisted writing tools such as automated essay evaluation and collaborative writing environments have been used in the classroom and highlight the key findings from recent research studies.

Introduction

'Despite the inability to give a definitive, universal answer to the question "How does technology affect student writing?" we still pursue an answer' (Bloch, 2008, p. 2). Many agree with Bloch (2008) that there is no conclusive evidence that technology has produced better writers. Just as many, perhaps, would argue that this is not a question that should be pursued. Rather, the more important question is how technology can (and should – or should not) effect change in writing practices and in the teaching of writing. In a special issue of the journal *Language Learning & Technology* (LLT) published in 2008, various researchers contributed articles dealing with the effect of technology on writing. They explored issues related to corpus technology (Yoon, 2008), using blogging to help generate ideas for writing (Kol & Schcolnik, 2008), and automated writing evaluation (AWE) programs (Chen & Cheng, 2008). In particular, Chen and Cheng's

(2008) results as to whether additional feedback iterations provided by AWE programs can help relieve teachers of some of their tasks and provide enough substance to help revise essays remain inconclusive. In fact, the results are not unexpected since many studies on the effectiveness of technology on (improved) writing performance have equally yielded uncertain results.

Yet, technology continues to be used in daily interactions as well as in teaching writing. Indeed, in many parts of the world, the use of technology is now integral to every day living and no longer restricted to privileged countries. Bloch (2008), in introducing the special issue of LLT, supports this observation by noting that there was a surprisingly large number of abstracts from EFL contexts, which may be part of a continuing trend whereby technology gets adopted more rapidly in many different countries, and that adoption leads to technology use in teaching in general – including teaching writing. Interestingly, though, Bloch also pointed out that there was minimal interest in Web 2.0 technologies reflected in the abstracts submitted for the special issue. Keeping in mind that the special issues was published in 2008, research for these papers was conducted at a time when Web 2.0 technologies were perhaps (a) not as common as they are in 2012 and (b) many users employed these technologies for personal (i.e., social networking) purposes and not necessarily for writing (or writing instruction).

Another aspect is the prevalence of dissimilarities with regard to the teaching of writing to native speakers versus language learners. We see a much higher proficiency level and a focus on obtaining writing skills to succeed in their jobs for the former and lower proficiency levels with a focus on either getting into a university or obtaining skills to make it through the university classes without receiving a penalty for 'non-native' essays and lab reports for the latter group. Consequently, there is more of a debate on whether grammar and word level errors should receive attention within the ESL/EFL community than within the group of L1 composition researchers.

Yet, CALL and writing have arguably come a long way in the last decade. In the early days, learners were able to type a word on a computer and the notion of copying, pasting and editing changed writing pedagogy. Now, the range of ever expanding possibilities is staggering. In addition, being able to receive various types of feedback on a word or a sentence (e.g., synonyms/antonyms, translation, definition, pronunciation, usage, pictorial depiction, etc.), writers can also rely on constant lexical and grammatical 'supervision' in all major word-processing applications.

As with all technologies – be it CALL for writing, listening or reading – teachers play a crucial role in introducing the technology and helping students use it appropriately. Writing, however, is a skill most language learners, particularly those in an ESL context wanting to secure employment, work on even after completing their language courses as it is an essential skill in the job market. To help teachers identify and interpret aspects suggested by research findings, Chapelle and Jamieson (2008, p. 95) outline six tips for teaching writing with CALL:

1. Select appropriate writing texts as models;
2. Choose CALL programs that teach genre as well as linguistic knowledge and strategies;
3. Teach learners how to benefit in terms of interactive help and feedback when using computers;
4. Create learners' opportunities to expand knowledge of English through writing and to write for a real audience;
5. Include explicit evaluation;
6. Help learners develop their writing strategies.

First, it is important to select appropriate writing texts as models. Asking students to read and write texts they will never encounter in their life outside of the language course they are taking is not recommended. This applies to the writing genre and to the level of writing. CALL can help by providing appropriate and relevant texts that can serve as models for language learners.

Second, Chapelle and Jamieson recommend choosing CALL activities that teach genre as well as linguistic knowledge and strategies. Following Swales' (1991) discovery of specific 'moves' within research articles, they argue that it is important to explicitly teach these conventions 'through examination of the language used to accomplish specific purposes' (p. 101). Teachers can use CALL programs that highlight specific forms as required by the genre of writing. For example, Chapelle and Jamieson highlight the CALL program 'Click into English', which is meant to help learners write postcards using only essential words and forms.

A third aspect revolves around learner training. More specifically, learners need to be taught how to benefit from interactive help and feedback from the computer. Learners often get inundated with automated help and feedback and teachers must be able to discern feedback that is helpful at a particular time from feedback that is not. Therefore, Chapelle and Jamieson argue, 'teacher guidance is essential' (p. 106), especially when using more advanced writing tools such as AWE tools such as *MY Access!* (by Vantage Learning) or *Criterion* (by ETS). However, guidance is needed even for more common word processing applications like MS Word.

The fourth tip is to create opportunities to expand knowledge of English through writing and to write for a real audience. A key aspect needed for the development of language ability is the opportunity to use the language for a meaningful task. In the case of writing, this means being able to write for a real and expanded audience beyond the classroom teacher. CALL tools that support this include wikis (Raith, 2009) and other shareable documents (via technologies such as GoogleDocs). This, however, also leads to a change in the role the teacher plays as a facilitator, which at times can be an issue as students are not used to teachers occupying that role and often want them to be more directing and instructing.

Explicit evaluation, tip number five, and feedback has been identified as a factor that positively influences student learning (Skehan, 1998). Furthermore, knowing that their writing will be evaluated leads to other aspects that enhance learning, that is, planning and self-correction, which Crookes (1989) has pointed out as being beneficial. CALL programs do provide feedback ranging from MS Word-type feedback to specific feedback from automated writing evaluation tools (e.g., *Criterion*). The key is to help learners understand how to make use of the feedback they receive. However, much more research is needed as we see a growing use of AWE tools in writing instruction. How to best use such tools needs to be investigated.

Sixth, teachers are charged with helping learners develop their writing strategies. It is important for writers to be able to evaluate the purpose and the audience and to evaluate if the goals have been achieved. Without this, the ultimate goal of self-sufficiency as a writer cannot be met. Writing strategies fall into three categories (psychological, sociological and linguistic) and CALL programs are able to provide teachers with assistance with the development of all three strategies. Further evaluation of CALL writing tools and approaches should involve looking at whether these tips are integrated.

In the remainder of this chapter, we examine two prevalent technologies that have taken a (at times controversial) foothold in writing instruction, automated writing evaluation tools and collaborative writing environments, and discuss them in terms of current practice, merits and additional research requirements.

Automated writing evaluation

Automated scoring systems evaluate essays and provide feedback by identifying relevant linguistic evidence in essays and then analyse and combine it in a way that approximates human scoring based on language recognition technologies and statistical procedures (Chapelle & Chung, 2010). Such systems have drawn the attention of English teachers and researchers due to a combination of increased affordability (i.e., relatively low per student cost) and the promise of reduced amounts of time spent correcting errors in student writing. At the same time, however, some researchers are decidedly pessimistic about such approaches, arguing that machines cannot perform as well as human raters. CCCC (2006), for instance, rejected machine scoring for any assessment purpose and launched harsh criticisms, mainly arguing that 'while AWEs may promise consistency, they distort the very nature of writing as a complex and context-rich interaction between people' (Guiding Principles of Assessment, para. 2). However, given that the use of technology in the field of language education is an irreversible trend and that AWE not only has gone through significant refinements since its first appearance about 50 years ago but also was found to help students revise and improve their writing (e.g., Chodorow, Gamon & Tetreault, 2010; Cotos, 2011; Grimes & Warschauer, 2006), it is worth examining its current use in the language classroom as well as the relevant research findings and considering the way such applications may best benefit ESL/EFL students.

Current practice

Although automated scoring engines remain under constant revision, some standardized exams already use them as a second rater to complement human scoring. For instance, the Analytic Writing Section of both Graduate Management Admissions Test (GMAT) and Graduate Record Examination (GRE) as well as the independent writing task of the Test of English as a Foreign Language (TOEFL) has been using *e-rater* as one of the two raters. E-rater, developed by the Educational Testing Service (ETS), evaluates grammar, style, organization and lexical complexity of the essay and then produces a holistic score based on regression analysis. The Analytical Writing portion of the GMAT has also employed *IntelliMetric* to evaluate cohesiveness, content and logic of discourse as well as syntactic variety and accuracy. Besides *e-rater* and *IntelliMetric*, there are other scoring engines such as *PEG, IEA* and *BETSY*, and different systems focus on and assess different aspects of writing based on different statistical approaches (Chapelle & Chung, 2010; see Warschauer & Ware, 2006, for an overview of various AWE tools).

The use of AWE systems in such high-stakes exams has been justified and supported by psychometric studies, which show that machines can rate as well as human raters do. The majority of these studies endorse the validity of AWE programs by demonstrating high correlations between the scores given by machines and human raters. Although different systems show different correspondence rates, they generally range from 0.80 to 0.85 (Cohen, Ben-Simon & Hovav, 2003), which is similar to those between two expert human raters. Another line of psychometric research also demonstrates, by examining criterion-related validity, that the scores given by the machine and those by other measures of the same writing construct are strongly correlated (Dikli, 2006; Keith, 2003; Phillips, 2007). Finally, some studies investigated the reliability of the scoring engines by examining the scores assigned to multiple essays of the same examinee and found, for instance, that the reliability of *e-rater* is higher than that of a single human rater and fairly equivalent to the average of two human raters (Attali & Burstein, 2006).

Based on such encouraging findings in psychometric research, the use of AWE programs in the language classroom has received some attention (Dikli, 2006; Phillips, 2007; Valenti, Nitko & Cucchiarelli, 2003). In addition, given that programs such as *Criterion*, *My Access* and *WriteToLearn* (see Warschauer & Grimes, 2008) can provide not only final numerical scores but also evaluative feedback for various aspects of writing, thus helping learners revise initial drafts, their incorporation into classroom instruction seems promising. As Warschauer and Ware (2006) pointed out, however, positive findings based on statistical estimates are necessary conditions for adopting software in the classroom, but they are not sufficient ones. Instead, we need to evaluate the validity and usefulness of AWE programs in the context of classroom dynamics including students and teachers' learning/teaching styles and their willingness to use them. We also need to judge the appropriateness of the feedback given by such programs in light of pedagogical contexts such as the lesson goals and specificity and explicitness of the feedback.

Fortunately, an increasing number of pedagogically oriented AWE studies have recently been conducted (Grimes & Warschauer, 2010). The first strand of research shows whether and how much AWE programs contribute to improving student writing. Elliot and Mikulas (2004), for example, had one group of students use *My Access* 4–5 times a week, a second group use it 2–3 times a week and a third group not use it. The results indicate that those who took advantage of *My Access* passed a district writing test more often than those who did not. Interestingly, however, the medium-use group exhibited better results than the high-use one. On the other hand, some researchers compared the first and last draft of student writing and found that feedback given by *Criterion* and *ESL Assistant* helped students reduce article and preposition errors to a significant extent (Chodorow, Gamon & Tetreault, 2010). In addition to grammatical and mechanical aspects, AWE feedback was also found to encourage students to make corrective modifications in terms of rhetorical development in academic writing (Cotos, 2011) as well as write a more insightful and creative essay (Grimes & Warschauer, 2006).

A second strand of pedagogical research shows how such AWE programs are actually employed by students and teachers in the classroom. For instance, Attali (2004) observed that nearly seven out of ten students submitted their essay only once without further modification although AWE software was available and it was originally meant to motivate and guide subsequent revisions. On the other hand, some teachers use AWE software not for encouraging multiple revisions as a part of process writing, but for practising timed essay writing to get students prepared for high-stakes exams.

A third line of studies explores the relationship between the (perceived) effectiveness of AWE and diverse instructional contexts. The implementation of AWE was not perceived positively when the program was used in the later stages of writing process or when it was not complemented by teacher feedback (Chen & Cheng, 2008). Also, teachers' basic attitude towards AWE and their familiarity with using technology as well as students' learning styles and goals determine its effectiveness to a great extent (Chen & Cheng, 2008). In addition, students' prior experience of and familiarity with technologies also showed a close relationship with the frequency of using AWE and its perceived helpfulness (Grimes & Warschauer, 2006).

Merits and caveats

As software developers claim, AWE programs indeed help students revise their writing and contribute to improved quality by providing individualized corrective feedback about diverse aspects of writing (e.g., Chodorow, Gamon & Tetreault, 2010; Cotos, 2011; Grimes & Warschauer, 2006). In addition, the mere presence of such programs as well as the availability of instant feedback increases students' motivation to write a good paper, making them view their work more critically and seriously revise it before final submission (Grimes & Warschauer, 2006). On the part of teachers, the programs constitute a teaching assistant helping an extraordinarily time-consuming job of providing individual feedback on multiple drafts for many students (Warschauer & Ware, 2006).

At the same time, however, it is not without problems. AWE programs currently available were found to be good at providing feedback with respect to grammatical and mechanical elements, but were not promising as far as content and organization are concerned. *Criterion*, for instance, provides accurate and specific feedback about grammar problems such as article errors, subject-verb agreement problems, run-on sentences and spelling but only offers very generic comments about organization and development; for example,

> Is this part of the essay your thesis? The purpose of a thesis is to organize, predict, control, and define your essay. Look in the *Writer's Handbook* for ways to improve your thesis. (*Criterion* feedback)

This is probably why few previous studies discuss the improvement of student writing at the content or discourse level. Another caveat that teachers should keep in mind is that students using AWE software may write for the 'machine', which is against the very social and interactive nature of writing. Unless learners do not have additional readers such as teachers, friends or readers outside the classroom, they may lose a sense of audience and end up writing a formulaic essay.

Important considerations and future research

In addition to the advantages and caveats of using AWE programs suggested above, teachers need to carefully consider course objectives when deciding whether to incorporate them into writing instruction or which AWE software to use. As different programs evaluate different aspects of writing as well as provide different types of feedback, teachers need to judge if what is evaluated by algorithms aligns with what is covered in the lesson as well as if the types of feedback given by a particular AWE program are appropriate for the level of target students.

In order to help teachers make an informed decision about the use of AWE, more research is needed. Considering that the validity should be discussed based on the uses of and inferences made from the test scores and that no test is valid for all purposes or in all situations (Kane, 2006; Messick, 1989), the validity of AWE also needs to be discussed in the context of particular classrooms. Therefore, future studies are expected to investigate and evaluate the use of diverse AWE programs with students, teachers and classes from various linguistic, social and cultural backgrounds. In doing so, research methods also need to be diversified to obtain more comprehensive findings so that they include detailed and qualitative analysis of student drafts, classroom observations, think-aloud protocols, video documentation and ethnographic studies in addition to surveys, interviews and quantitative comparison of multiple drafts in terms of holistic score and error correction rate. A series of such studies is underway at several research universities (e.g., Iowa State University). Last but not least, longitudinal research is also required to see if the evaluative feedback offered by AWE software has a lasting effect to subsequent writing and ultimately, second/ foreign language learning. A second area of interests to teachers, learners and CALL researchers dealing with writing is the rapidly growing realm of collaborative writing environments.

Collaborative writing environments

Since around 2005 the emergence of Web 2.0 and social media have added a participatory and collaborative dimension to the internet, turning it into a social Web (Brown & Adler, 2008; Richardson, 2006; Tan, 2011). These technologies not only transform how we interact with others in everyday life but also provide second/ foreign language learners with new ways to engage in collaborative practices (Thomas, 2009), particularly in relation to writing. Since content on Web 2.0 is created by users/consumers, learners can take advantage of that space to practise and post their writings. In addition, this newly added dimension enables learners to practise writing in collaboration with other students. Furthermore, as Warschauer (1997) predicted 15 years ago, computer-mediated communication (CMC) has the potential to shift our focus from form to the meaning of language. As all of these changes are pertinent to the process writing approach, the predominant approach to writing instruction, CMC tools deserve further attention. In this subsection, therefore, we will first examine the use of these technologies in current classrooms and the advantages and caveats of such approaches, as well as provide suggestions for teachers and future research.

Current practice

The new technologies include both synchronous and asynchronous tools such as blogs, wikis, chat, MSN, Blackboard and whiteboard, among which wikis and blogs are more extensively used in the classroom and have received considerable attention (Elola & Oskoz, 2010; Kessler, 2009; Kost, 2011; Murray & Hourigan, 2008; Raith, 2009; Ward, 2004). Although the discussion on collaboration often focuses on the revision process, more recent studies have begun to investigate how these tools aid the brainstorming and planning stages of writing as well. According to Kost (2011), for instance, some students used MSN for content brainstorming while others used a separate wiki page for the same purpose. According to Kost (2011), students took advantage of MSN and wikis to brainstorm ideas and create an outline with their group members. In this process, some groups collaboratively made an outline for the entire paper whereas other groups discussed only the main points together and then worked individually on the supporting details. It was also observed that some students inserted links to useful resources such as online dictionaries and grammar references. Without any specific guidelines or regulations, students demonstrated various ways of engaging in the initial stages of process writing.

With regard to actually composing a draft, students were required to either write an essay individually or submit one essay as a group. Even in the former case, however, collaboration among peers was required in the process of revision. Without detailed guidelines prescribed by teachers, different groups demonstrated different collaboration patterns. Sometimes, students did not collaborate at all. In fact, Bradley, Lindstrom and Rystedt (2010) reported that other classmates never visited several essays posted on the class wiki. On other occasions, students mechanically took turns to complete a draft (Bradley et al., 2010), or they divided up their roles at the beginning according to each person's strength (Bradley et al., 2010; Forsyth, 1999; Kost, 2011). That is, students with better grammar tended to assume the role of editor while the others focused on content for the initial draft. Findings indicated that only a few groups worked in a truly collaborative manner.

When it comes to revision, students provided peer feedback in the blog by leaving a meta-comment next to the relevant part of the essay, adding or deleting a text, or giving a general final comment regarding whether the arguments were feasible and well communicated, the last of which was found to the most common strategy as it provides an easy exit from the task (Bradley et al., 2010). However, making clarifications of already posted ideas was not a frequent type of feedback because direct editing is impossible in the blog, and therefore, even teachers had to give detailed language feedback on a separate piece of paper (Bradley et al., 2010). On the other hand, Elola and Oskoz's (2010) compared individual and collaborative writing via wiki and chat in terms of students' revision process. Interestingly, while writing individually, students focused on grammar in the revision and they tended to add extra information to improve their essay. Moreover, they also fleshed out the paragraph around the established thematic sentence defined in the first draft rather than changing the topic sentence. In terms of the thesis statement and supporting evidence of the entire essay and conclusion, learners constantly modified their essay. In contrast, while working collaboratively, students tended to reduce the amount of content and searched for ways to express existing ideas more precisely. In addition, they decided on a macro structure of the essay including a thesis and conclusion of the entire essay at the beginning of their joint work and followed through, but made major and minor modifications at the paragraph level in the course of elaborating the content. Moreover, those who worked collaboratively paid attention to grammar and vocabulary throughout the whole writing process, whereas those who worked individually did the editing job predominantly in the final draft.

As far as students' focus in the revision process is concerned, some researchers found that learners still pay more attention to grammar or linguistic form on Web 2.0 technologies (Arnold, Ducate & Kost, 2009; Bradley et al., 2010; Kost, 2011; Lee, 2010), and word choice and spelling received the most attention according to Lee (2010). Also, form-related errors are usually identified by peers rather than the original writer, and it appears to be easier to discuss and reflect on form-related errors in asynchronous online spaces than in synchronous ones as they allow greater time for learner reflection (Kessler, 2009). However, other researchers argue that learners tend to focus more on global concerns such as content and organization than on grammar in Web 2.0-based writing (Elola & Oskoz, 2010; Hewett, 2006; Kessler, 2009; Murray & Hourigan, 2008), and that unless a grammatical error hinders communication, it is normally ignored (Elola & Oskoz, 2010; Kessler, 2009). Some of them further point out that even if teachers required students to focus on form rather than meaning while providing peer feedback, they paid more attention to content (Kessler, 2009; Storch, 2005). Although students exchange comments on content and organization not only in asynchronous tools but also in synchronous ones such as chat, MSN and whiteboard, they preferred the latter (chat) to the former (wiki) when they were given both tools at the same time (Elola & Oskoz, 2010).

Advantages and disadvantages

Many researchers generally report that such collaborative effort resulted in higher quality papers, especially in terms of content development (Arnold et al., 2009; Kessler, 2009; Lee, 2010) and organization (Elola & Oskoz, 2010). As Wells (2000) and Swain (2000) note, learners can jointly construct a performance that surpasses their individual competence. With respect to linguistic form, however, prior studies report uncompromising findings. For instance, Storch (2005) argued that collaborative texts were better in terms of grammatical accuracy and complexity compared with individual writing, whereas Kessler (2009) found that 48% of word choice revisions resulted in an erroneous correction.

Perhaps most importantly, it is students who report several advantages of collaborative writing. With respect to the effect of collaborative writing on learner anxiety, some students reported that they felt less pressure when completing a writing assignment in pairs or groups because it enabled them to share the workload, thus reducing their burden (Mulligan & Garofalo, 2011). Also, peer feedback was viewed to be less intimidating than teacher feedback (Lee, 2010). This is not the case for all learners, however. Some students felt very nervous about their classmates looking at their writing although they did not feel embarrassed about their work being examined and evaluated by teachers who are assumed to have superior knowledge (Storch, 2005). In addition, some students were not comfortable with criticizing their peers' work and pointing out their mistake as they viewed it as a face-threatening activity (Dippold, 2009; Hyland & Hyland, 2006). Interestingly, however, the account of embarrassment and discomfort was normally reported from the learners of particular cultures (Japanese and Chinese in particular) (Nelson & Carson, 1998; Storch, 2005). A collaborative writing approach also influences learners' identity. As learners were able to reach a real and wider audience beyond the teacher, they began to see writing not merely as an assignment but as a purposeful communicative activity, and accordingly they viewed themselves as multilingual/multicultural speakers as well as language learners (Blake, 2008). Furthermore, with traditional assignments that require each student to write on a piece of paper, students have always been an individual writer, but with the new type of assignments that encourages several students to complete one paper collaboratively, they began to develop a sense of co-authorship (Elola & Oskoz, 2010).

Such an awareness of the audience may influence learners' sense of responsibility, which encourages them to start writing earlier and faster as well as to generate more content (Kost, 2011). Sharing their own drafts with peers raises a sense of audience, which motivates learners to write a high-quality paper (Lee, 2010; Ward, 2004) and examine their essay from a critical point of view, anticipating readers' response (Dippold, 2009; Nicol & Macfarlane-Dick, 2006; Rolliston, 2005). Moreover, collaboration among peers not only helps students learn from each other by noticing the gap (Kost, 2011; Lee, 2010) but also develop learner autonomy as the process is more student-centred. That is, each group can decide when and how to write and they can decide on the format of the final draft (Dippold, 2009; Lee, 2010). Finally, the experience of jointly writing an essay helps students learn what co-ownership means and how to incorporate plural voices into one single essay (Mishan, 2004; Murray & Hourigan, 2008).

This type of collaborative writing, however, is not without complaints from the students. Most of them preferred individual work due to the difficulties inherent in collaboration, that is, the rather cumbersome procedure of reaching agreement and resolving disagreement (Elola & Oskoz, 2010; Lee, 2010). In addition, learners do not feel comfortable with providing peer feedback not only because they lack confidence in detecting lexical and grammatical errors (Dippold, 2009; Hyland & Hyland, 2006; Lee, 2009), but also because they are reluctant to threaten others' face by correcting errors or deleting sentences in their essays (Dippold, 2009; Liu & Carless, 2006). Furthermore, they value teacher feedback more than peer feedback because the latter neither pinpoints what types of errors are involved nor provides specific suggestions.

Important considerations and future research

Writing in Web 2.0 environments was generally reported to produce positive results, not only promoting process writing and collaboration with peers, but also in terms of students' focus on content and organization as well as grammar. Differences were observed across different studies, however, in terms of collaboration patterns while brainstorming and writing an initial draft, specific methods of delivering comments, aspects of writing receiving students' attention in revision and success rate of revision effort. That is, in most research contexts, teachers did not provide detailed enough guidelines about how to use wikis or blogs. As a result, different groups used the tools differently, which led to varying success rates. These anomalies may be attributed to different instructional contexts in various classes, a point which deserves further attention in order for teachers to make informed decisions rather than indiscriminately implementing collaborative writing based on new tools merely to follow recent trends.

To begin with, teachers should consider the goal of their writing lessons, especially the genre of essay. Since the online environment is often perceived as an informal context and exhibits low-impact in terms of errors (Kessler, 2009), it might not be the best environment for learning formal and academic writing. In addition, collaborative writing is not ideal for practising particular types of writing such as book reviews, which highly value individual judgement over collective thoughts (Tan, 2011).

Second, writing tasks should be carefully selected and designed because it is not the technology itself, but the nature of the tasks that eventually promotes a high level of interaction (Lund, 2008). In line with this, Lee (2007) suggests that open-ended and problem-oriented tasks give students more opportunities to collaborate with peers.

Third, teachers should be able to choose the most appropriate tools for their purpose. For instance, a blog is good for providing general comments but not for detailed linguistic feedback. In contrast, wikis provide a suitable environment for fine-tuning comments or revision as anyone can directly edit content. On the other hand, synchronous environments including chat, MSN and Whiteboard are ideal for macro-level discussion such as brainstorming, topic development and the overall structure of the essay rather than micro-level issues such as grammar, vocabulary and minor editing.

Fourth, teachers should take into account students' learning style and personality. Even though an online space provides a perfect environment for collaboration, the collaboration may not occur in a pedagogical setting. That is to say, as Kessler (2009) notes, such a system can only work with learners who are serious about collaborating and willing to follow agreed group conventions and practices.

Fifth, teachers need to reconsider their roles when implementing this new approach of teaching writing. Given that there is very little follow-up interaction when teachers take a back seat (Prins, Sluijsmans, Kirschner & Strijbos, 2005), they need to offer explicit guidelines regarding how to give, use and react to the feedback (Dippold, 2009). In addition, considering that feedback from peers is unevenly distributed, which can affect learners' motivation to further revise and collaborate (Catera & Emigh, 2005), it is also the teacher's job to teach learners how to direct peers to issues where feedback is needed (Baggentun & Wasson, 2006). Furthermore, if the teacher is also to intervene and provide feedback, when to do so should constitute another important consideration given Dippold's (2009) study in which the teacher's earlier feedback dramatically reduced peer involvement.

Last but not least, assessing students' writing becomes more complicated under the collaborative approach especially when they are asked to submit one final product as a group. Since everyone depends on another person for their grade (Elola & Oskoz, 2010), assessment may be a sensitive issue among students. In addition, on the part of teachers, it is not always easy to determine how much each group member contributed to the writing process. Furthermore, it is up to teachers whether to grade only the final product or to evaluate the whole process.

Despite a very close relationship between these instructional contexts and the success of collaborative writing via Web 2.0, many questions remain unanswered. This relationship deserves further attention in future research so that teachers can make an informed decision regarding how to incorporate available technologies in the teaching of writing.

Conclusions

In this chapter, we have highlighted research in the areas of automated writing evaluation and collaborative writing and outlined more generally construed tips for teaching writing with technology. Technology has played and will continue to play a role in writing instruction. What that role is depends on various factors, including access to technology, administrative mandates and teacher and student goals. It remains important to integrate technology prudently and cautiously and to train teachers and students to recognize what various CALL applications can do and how they may be of assistance in students' writing development and, more importantly, what these applications cannot do or where flaws may exist and thus not enhance writing. Even then, language learning potential lies in students being able to recognize that automatically generated feedback on their writing cannot always be trusted. The bigger question, however, is to see if the feedback can lead to increased writing proficiency and learner autonomy. The potential of automated writing evaluation systems and collaborative writing tools remains significant. Longitudinal studies following students and teachers of actual writing classrooms will be able to shed light on the effects of the approaches to writing outlined in this chapter. We especially encourage case studies researching on-going (post-instruction) development of ESL writers and learner use of various technology tools to help identify useful technology-integration-in-writing-instruction models.

References

Arnold, N., Ducate, L., & Kost, C. (2009). Collaborative writing in wikis. In L. Lomicka, & G. Lord (Eds.), *The next generation: Social networking and online collaboration in foreign language learning. CALICO Monograph Series, 8,* 115–44.

Attali, Y. (2004). *Exploring the feedback and revision features of* Criterion. Paper presented at the National Council on Measurement in Education Annual Meeting, San Diego, CA.
Attali, Y., & Burnstein, J. (2006). Automated essay scoring with e-rater® V.2.0. *Journal of Technology, Learning, and Assessment, 4*(3). Retrieved from www.jtla.org
Baggetun, R., & Wasson, B. (2006). Self-regulated learning and open writing. *European Journal of Education, 41*(3–4), 453–72.
Blake, R. J. (2008). *Brave new digital classroom: Technology and foreign language learning.* Washington, DC: Georgetown University Press.
Bloch, J. (2008). *Technologies in the second language composition classroom.* Ann Arbor: University of Michigan Press.
Bradley, L., Lindstrom, B., & Rystedt, H. (2010). Rationalities of collaboration for language learning in a wiki. *ReCALL, 22*(2), 247–65.
Brown, S., & Adler, R. P. (2008). Minds on fire: Open education, the long trail, and learning 2.0. *Educause Review, 43*(1), 16–32.
Catera, E., & Emigh, R. (2005). Blogs, the virtual soapbox. *Essential Teacher, 2*(3), 46–9.
CCCC (2006). Position statement on writing assessment. Retrieved from www.ncte.org/cccc/resources/positions/writingassessment
Chapelle, C. A., & Chung, Y. R. (2010). The promise of NLP and speech processing technologies in language assessment. *Language Testing, 27*(3), 301–15.
Chapelle, C. A., & Jamieson, J. (2008). *Tips for teaching with CALL: Practical approaches to computer-assisted language learning.* New York: Pearson-Longman.
Chen, C. E., & Cheng, W. E. (2008). Beyond the design of automated writing evaluation: Pedagogical practices and perceived learning effectiveness in EFL writing classes. *Language Learning & Technology, 12*(2), 94–112.
Chodorow, M., Gamon, M., & Tetreault, J. (2010). The utility of article and preposition error correction systems for English language learners: Feedback and assessment. *Language Testing, 27*(3), 419–36.
Cohen, Y., Ben-Simon, A., & Hovav, M. (2003, October). *The effect of specific language features on the complexity of systems for automated essay scoring.* Paper presented at the International Association of Educational Assessment Annual Conference, Manchester.
Cotos, E. (2011). Potential of automated writing evaluation feedback. *CALICO Journal, 28*(2), 420–59.
Crookes, G. (1989). Planning and interlanguage variation. *Studies in Second Language Acquisition, 11*, 367–83.
Dikli, S. (2006). An overview of automated scoring of essays. *The Journal of Technology, Learning, and Assessment, 5*(1), 3–35.
Dippold, D. (2009). Peer feedback through blogs: Student and teacher perceptions in an advanced German class. *ReCALL, 21*(1), 18–36.
Elliot, S., & Mikulas, C. (2004, April). *The impact of MY Access! use on student writing performance: A technology overview and four studies.* Paper presented at the annual meeting of the American Educational Research Association, San Diego, CA.
Elola, I., & Oskoz, A. (2010). Collaborative writing: Fostering foreign language and writing conventions development. *Language Learning & Technology, 14*(3), 51–71.
Forsyth, D. R. (1999). *Group dynamics.* Belmont, CA: Wadsworth Publishing.
Grimes, D., & Warschauer, M. (2006, April). *Automated essay scoring in the classroom.* Paper presented at the American Educational Research Association, San Francisco, California.
— (2010). Utility in a Fallible Tool: A Multi-Site Case Study of Automated Writing Evaluation. *Journal of Technology, Learning, and Assessment, 8*(6). Retrieved (2012, July 12) from www.jtla.org

Hewett, B. (2006). Synchronous online conference-based instruction: A study of whiteboard interactions and student writing. *Computers and Composition, 23,* 4–31.
Hyland, F., & Hyland, K. (2006). State of the art article: Feedback on second language students' writing. *Language Teaching, 39,* 83–101.
Kane, M. (2006). Validation. In R. Brennan (Ed.), *Educational measurement* (4th ed., pp. 17–64). Washington, DC: American Council on Education and National Council on Measurement in Education.
Keith, T. Z. (2003). Validity of automated essay scoring systems. In M. D. Shermis & J. C. Burstein (Eds.), *Automated essay scoring: A cross-disciplinary perspective* (pp. 147–207). Mahwah, NJ: Lawrence Erlbaum.
Kessler, G. (2009). Student-initiated attention to form in wiki-based collaborative writing. *Language learning & Technology, 13*(1), 79–95.
Kol, S., & Schcolnik, M. (2008). Asynchronous forums in EAP: Assessment issues. *Language Learning & Technology, 12*(2), 49–70.
Kost, C. (2011). Investigating writing strategies and revision behavior in collaborative wiki projects. *CALICO Journal, 28*(3), 606–20.
Lee, L. (2007). Fostering L2 oral communication through constructivist interaction in desktop videoconferencing. *Foreign Language Annals, 40,* 635–49.
— (2009). Promoting intercultural exchanges with blogs and podcastings: A study of Spanish-American telecollaboration. *Computer Assisted Language Learning, 22*(5), 425–43.
— (2010). Exploring wiki-mediated collaborative writing: A case study in an elementary Spanish course. *CALICO Journal, 27*(2), 260–76.
Liu, N., & Carless, D. (2006). Peer feedback: The learning element of peer assessment. *Teaching in Higher Education, 11*(3), 279–90.
Lund, A. (2008). Wikis: A collective approach to language production. *ReCALL, 20*(1), 35–54.
Messick, S. (1989). Validity. In R. L. Linn (Ed.), *Educational measurement* (3rd ed., pp. 13–103). New York: Macmillan.
Mishan, F. (2004). A task-based approach to Web authoring for learning languages. In A. Chambers, J. E. Conacher & J. Littlemore (Eds.), *ICT and language learning: Integrating pedagogy and practice* (pp. 121–44). Birmingham: University of Birmingham Press.
Mulligan, C., & Garofalo, R. (2011). A collaborative writing approach: Methodology and student assessment. *The Language Teacher, 35*(3), 5–10.
Murray, L., & Hourigan, T. (2008). Blogs for specific purposes: Expressivist or socio-cognitivist approach? *ReCALL, 20*(1), 82–97.
Nelson, G., & Carson, J. G. (1998). ESL students' perceptions of effectiveness in peer response groups. *Journal of Second Language Writing, 7(2),* 113–31.
Nicol, D., & Macfarlane-Dick, D. (2006). Formative assessment and self-regulated learning: A model and seven principles of good feedback practice. *Studies in Higher Education, 31*(2), 199–218.
Phillips, S. M. (2007). Automated essay scoring: A literature review. Retrieved from www.saee.ca
Prins, F., Sluijsmans, D., Kirschner, P., & Strijbos, J. W. (2005). Formative peer assessment in a CSCL environment: A case study. *Assessment & Evaluation in Higher Education, 30*(4), 417–44.
Raith, T. (2009). The use of Weblogs in language education. In M. Thomas (Ed.), *Handbook of research on Web 2.0 and second language learning* (pp. 274–91). Hershey, PA: Information Science Reference.
Richardson, W. (2006). Blogs, wikis, podcasts, and other powerful Web tools for classrooms. Thousand Oaks, CA: Corwin Press.

Rolliston, P. (2005). Using peer feedback in the ESL writing class. *ELT Journal, 59*(1), 23–30.

Skehan, P. (1998). *A cognitive approach to language learning*. Oxford: Oxford University Press.

Storch, N. (2005). Collaborative writing: Product, process and student's reflections. *Journal of Second Language Writing, 14*, 153–73.

Swain, M. (2000). The output hypothesis and beyond. In J. Lantolf (Ed.), *Sociocultural theory and second language acquisition* (pp. 97–114). Oxford, UK: Oxford University Press.

Swales, J. (1991). *Genre analysis: English in academic and research settings*. Cambridge, UK: Cambridge University Press.

Tan, A. (2011). Why write with wikis? In C. M. L. Ho, K. T. Anderson & A. P. Leong (Eds.), *Transforming literacies and language: Multimodality and literacy in the new media age* (pp. 207–22). London: Continuum.

Thomas, M. (Ed.) (2009). *Handbook of research on Web 2.0 and second language learning*. Hershey, PA: Information Science Reference.

Valenti, S., Nitko, A., & Cucchiarelli, A. (2003). An overview of current research on automated essay grading. *Journal of Information Technology Education, 2*, 319–29.

Ward, J. (2004). Blog assisted language learning (BALL): Push button publishing for the pupils. *TEFL Web Journal, 3*(1), 1–16.

Warschauer, M. (1997). Computer-mediated collaborative learning: Theory and practice. *Modern Language Journal, 81*(4), 470–81.

Warschauer, M., & Grimes, D. (2008). Automated writing assessment in the classroom. *Pedagogies: An International Journal, 3*(22), 22–36.

Warschauer, M., & Ware, P. (2006). Automated writing evaluation: Defining the classroom research agenda. *Language Teaching Research, 10*(2), 1–24.

Wells, G. (2000). Dialogic inquiry in education. Building on the legacy of Vygotsky. In C. Lee & P. Smagorinsky (Eds.), *Vygotskian perspectives on literacy research: Constructing meaning through collaborative inquiry* (pp. 51–85). Cambridge, UK: Cambridge University Press.

Yoon, H. (2008). More than a linguistic reference: The influence of corpus technology on L2 academic writing. *Language Learning & Technology, 12*(2), 31–48.

16

CALL and less commonly taught languages

Richard M. Robin

Summary

This chapter discuss the technological issues facing both learners and instructors of the less commonly taught languages with an emphasis on the impact of the latest Web-based technology on less commonly taught languages (LCTLs) that are a traditional part of college curricula (e.g., Russian, Chinese, Japanese) as opposed to those that are taught much more rarely. Technological measures applicable to those who must resort to self-instruction are also considered. Finally, issues specific to LCTLs in the current Web 2.0 environment are discussed, such as the representation of non-Roman scripts and copyright clearance for materials coming from sources in countries where intellectual property law is less clearly defined.

Introduction

The maturation of digital technology and the internet has changed the nature of foreign language instruction, but few areas have reaped greater cumulative benefits than those involved in the teaching and learning of LCTLs in nearly all facets. These include (1) the availability of materials for specifically pedagogical input, (2) the creation of modular learning materials and (3) the ability to use raw Web materials for self-instruction. Of course, such benefits flow not only to LCTLs, but to all other languages. Nevertheless, the significance of the technological changes for LCTLs is greater. Instructors in the commonly taught languages (CTLs) have an embarrassment of riches that can address all modalities and appeal to a number of learning styles. The materials available for LCTLs, especially those not taught traditionally, are sparser, and require greater forbearance and search strategies.

In this chapter we will examine the specific technological issues facing teachers and learners of LCTLs with emphasis on the materials currently available, barriers to use of intelligent CALL (ICALL), the need for independent learning strategies, the technical and pedagogical demands posed by non-Roman script and possible directions where technology might lead LCTL learners.

What are less commonly taught languages?

In North America, the acronym LCTLs commonly applies to all languages other than English, Spanish, French and German. However, that definition is a bit too encompassing for the purposes of this chapter for it fails to capture features subject to the offerings and challenges posed by the current technology. A clearer picture emerges when we consider additional characteristics.

Language level difficulty

The commonly taught languages, 'cognate' languages as defined by Jorden and Walton (1987), are acquired by English speakers relatively quickly. Most LCTLs, as per Jackson and Kaplan (2007)[1] are not. The most notable exceptions are Italian and Portuguese, which rank fifth and ninth respectively on the MLA college enrolment list (Furman et al., 2010). Both are ILR Category I languages for which general proficiency is deemed achievable in less than 600 hours of small-group instruction. Additionally both these languages have a significant instructional tradition in the United States and large internet footprints as described below.

Proficiency expectations

Most LCTLs are harder than French, Spanish and German, for speakers of English, but the proficiency expectations of LCTL learners can be assumed to be higher. It is reasonable to posit that most students of CTLs will not use the languages they are learning in more than a perfunctory way. If, as Swender's (2003) data suggests, a minority of college CTL *majors* break through the ACTFL Advanced threshold by graduation, the proficiency attained by CTL students with less exposure than that of a college major – and consequently lower levels of oral proficiency – prepares them for competent tourism. On the other hand, high-level proficiency in LCTLs (especially in 'critical' languages) represents a largely unmet demand (Brecht, 2002; Malone et al., 2005). That presents a paradox. LCTL learners are more likely than CTL students to need their language for specific purposes – those which require minimal working proficiency (ACTFL Advanced). And yet as many have pointed out (e.g., Blake et al., 2008; Leaver et al., 2004; Rifkin, 2005, 2006) higher-level proficiency in most LCTLs, is often beyond the learning capability, given the resources at hand, of most learners without additional intensive residential courses, often in the form of in-country practice. In addition, data from longitudinal studies such as Davidson (2010) shows that in-country training for difficult languages bears fruit only when extended – at least a semester and significantly more productive if for a year – and after basic proficiency (Intermediate Mid or High) has been attained. Similar results for Russian are reported by Golonka (2001). (We should note that some studies on in-country experience with CTLs provide evidence of greater gains, see for example: Allen (2002) and Yager (1998); see also DeKeyser (2007) for a summary of study abroad results in a number of languages.) Moreover, the modalities that provide the fundamental infrastructure for content-rich learning, reading and writing, especially where non-Roman script is involved, make these competencies particularly difficult to achieve (Larson, 2006).

Traditional treatment

Less commonly taught does not mean *not widely* taught. Materials development for a number of LCTLs has a long academically based tradition that extends back to before the appearance of the World Wide Web in the early 1990s or Web 2.0, which is more gated and populated with user-produced content. This includes languages such as Russian, Chinese and Japanese, which have had or still have enrolments high enough to spur the production of materials, dedicated teacher-training workshops, assessment workshops, such as ACTFL tester certification programs and so on. In short, instructors and materials developers need not start from scratch. Further down in this branch of the hierarchy is Arabic, whose scarcity in college language programs before the post-2001 boom in enrolments (637% in the decade leading up to 2009 – Furman et al., 2010) had not provided the demand required for a variety of finely crafted materials. Moreover, until quite recently, Arabic suffered from a relatively small internet footprint, as discussed next. Nevertheless, with adjustments for individual areas of difficulty (see, for example, the discussion of writing systems below), the electronic mediation of instructional materials for *traditionally if less commonly* taught LCTLs bears greater similarity to that of CTLs than to those of those languages which are taught more rarely, as taxonomized by Brecht and Walton (1993): much more rarely taught (39 languages including Armenian, Turkish, Hindi), least commonly taught (80 languages, for example, Malay and Aymara – Carreira, 2011) and those that are never or almost never taught (Galician, Asturiano – Carreira, 2011).

Internet footprint

A language's internet footprint is an amalgam of internet infrastructure and number of users as a percentage of the population. A rough measure of internet footprint is the number of Wikipedia articles available in the target language (valid except for simplified Chinese – as Wikipedia is blocked in the People's Republic of China). A language's internet footprint is important both for materials developers and independent learners alike. A small footprint limits pedagogical choice.

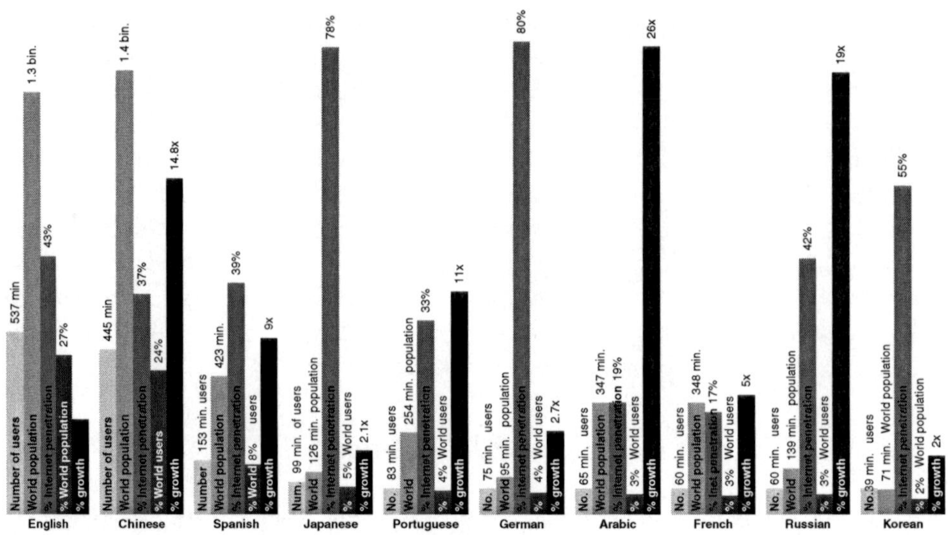

TABLE 16.1. *Internet footprint of major languages*

(Based on statistics from World Internet Stats, 2011)

As Table 16.1 makes clear, after English, Chinese and Spanish, the difference in footprint is not great, neither in terms of percentage of the target language population using the internet nor in the raw number of users. It is notable only that current penetration of internet use is significantly smaller than for the other major LCTLs. But this is offset by a high internet expansion rate – by a factor of 26, the highest of the languages surveyed. However, a wholly different picture emerges when we look at non-traditional LCTLs. The availability of language-specific internet radio is indicative. TuneIn.com lists 95 internet accessible radio stations for Russian, a traditional LCTL with 144 million native speakers (NSs), according to Ethnologue, but only 6 for Bengali with 181 million NSs (Lewis, 2009).[2]

A large internet footprint is important because it affords materials developers and independent learners a wide choice of input. But it also suggests a wide variety of ready-made pedagogical materials, whether in gated textbook ancillaries or in openly available add-ons. In this regard, little difference exists between traditional LCTLs like Russian and Chinese on the one hand, and Spanish, French and German on the other. Non-traditional LCTLs, however, lack an abundance of such materials, many of which must be put together ad hoc.

Available resources

The internet provides a wealth of material for many LCTLs, but the issues of finding and developing material for use vary depending on the language. Bartoshesky (2004) found that in terms of integration of Web-based materials, a positive correlation was found between LCTL teachers' Web surfing time and the ease of locating materials, both as raw source material and ready-made modules. For the more common LCTLs, ready-made material abounds and includes much for special purposes.

Pedagogical packages

Coordinators, instructors and students can seek out material through a number of LCTL clearinghouses, such as the University of Minnesota's Centre for Advanced Research on Language Acquisition (CARLA), LangMedia, National Association of Self-Instructional Language Programs (NASILP), Speech and Language Technology for Minority Languages (SALTMIL) and similar sites. See Appendix A – Pedagogical Site Thumbnail Descriptions.

One area of languages for specific purposes in the traditional LCTLs that has received lavish attention and considerable funding is business language. A number of Centres for International Business Education and Research (CIBERs) have developed business-oriented materials in several LCTLs, including internet sourcebooks for business topics in strategic languages such as Korean and Japanese, online interviews with business figures in Chinese (Kelm, 2008), Japanese (Kelm & Tanaka, 2007) and Turkish (Kelm, Wang & Chen, 2007). Full-scale business-language projects for complete courses to be used with students who have reached ACTFL Intermediate are underway for Arabic, Chinese, Korean, Japanese and Russian at the George Washington University CIBER. Within the CIBER community, Gonglewski and Helm (2010) have introduced business case templates for use in the strategic languages.

Pedagogical packages for listening comprehension (presentational mode) in the form of podcasts aimed at ACTFL Intermediate listeners are available for Russian, Chinese and Arabic from the National Capital Language Resource Centre (2012).[3]

Intelligent CALL (ICALL)

Despite the vast array of pedagogical material available for a wide range of languages, LCTL learners are hard-pressed to find appropriate materials (Lim et al., 2011); even rarer are ICALL materials that are capable of natural language processing (NLP). To begin with, NLP, especially that capable of handling learner errors, is still largely an unfinished work, whose commercial application for dedicated language learning projects has been limited. Unlike processing based on *string matches* in which student responses are compared to the expected response character by character, NLP requires extraordinary effort in advance. String-match exercises are easy to create, but their processing power is narrow.[4] They require that the exercise writer produce all possible variants for an answer – often an impossible task, especially in languages with free word order. The *statistical approach to NLP*, used in Web-based sites such as the Google translator, requires enormous efforts in collecting and manually tagging large translated corpora for each language or set of languages involved. Statistically based natural language processors improve as more tagged data is entered. This allows a wide range of user input (in this case L2 from the learner), although false positives occur. For most LCTLs statistics-based NLP is far too costly an endeavour without initial groundwork from well-financed commercial software producers. *Rule-based NLP* dates back to the era of mainframe computing. It requires programmers to supply the language processor with the vocabulary, rules and major exceptions. However, such an approach cannot cover every aspect of the language, and learner input must be limited to that subset of language that falls within the NLP's rule base. Despite that drawback, rule-based NLP has been predominant in CALL-based applications because of its relative economy. But as Shalaan (2005, pp. 87–8) points out, rule-based NLP comes with a sense of grammaticality, based on hand-constructed rules. That avoids the pitfalls of non-grammatical language from being included into the language processor's repertoire of permitted language, a problem that plagues statistics-based NLP.

While rule-based NLP has advantages over other methods, it nevertheless requires a significant investment in advance. Therefore it is no surprise that true ICALL projects for LCTLs are scarce. They include *Robo-Sensei* for Japanese (Nagata, 2002; Ushida, 2007), Arabic ICALL (Shalaan, 2005), an intelligent CMC and the Portuguese Tagarela (Amaral Meurers, 2009). Vlugter et al. (2009) describe a more specialized Māori CMC project for New Zealand English speakers. The program is similar to a chatbot, which is capable of playing several chat partners in one Instant Messenger (IM) conversation and which can parse student errors and suggest corrections, targeting Māori pronouns.[5]

If NLP has begun to make its way into reliable educational and commercial products only since the dawn of the twenty-first century, work on corpora, which lay the basis for statistic-based NLP, is underway thus providing the framework for the production of pedagogical materials for LCTLs. For example, the MILE project is a small, structured English corpus designed for translation into LCTLs, and a set of re-usable tools for the creation of similar corpora (Alvarez et al., 2006). Simpson et al. (2009) describe the creation of language packs for eight diverse Asian LCTLs (from Indo-European Punjabi to Austronesian Tagalog) that include basic data processing and conversion tools, such as tokenizers, sentence segmenters, character encoding converters and name transliterators, as well as more advanced tools, such as part of speech taggers (POS), named entity taggers and morphological analysers.

Web-based ICALL resources aside, even the most pedestrian of Web-based material with wrap-around pedagogical activities may be hard to come by in the non-traditional LCTLs. Armitage and Bowerman (2005) investigated the possibility of creating learning object modules (LOMs) – reusable pieces that can be applied as needed. The LOM approach rests on three principles: (1) standardization of metadata files so that search agents can assemble potential learning objects (such as Flash animations) into a suitable course; (2) the development of adaptive systems to match the data profiles of learners and institutions to provide highly targeted materials; (3) the consequent assembly of the content of the adaptive courses created on the basis of the metadata files. Such a library would be malleable with courses assembled ad hoc, based on automated decisions. However, the authors note the shortcomings of current NLP and bemoan the loss of instructor input.

No discussion of instruction in LCTLs would be complete without addressing commercial packages such as Rosetta Stone, if for no other reason because the company has published so many courses for LCTLs – nearly 30. Unfortunately, the profession has chosen largely to ignore the product. Reviews from the field are few and only Nielson (2011) has investigated whether the product works. Her main finding was severe attrition among adult learners and 'Despite beginning with large n-sizes, a wide range of enthusiastic participants from different positions within the [US Government], and researcher encouragement and support, this method of language training yielded very limited proficiency gains in only a handful of learners' (p. 125). Reviewers (all teachers of CTLs) have been critical. Erickson (2004, p. 1027) sees the program as worthy enhancement for *classroom* teaching but along with Bidlake (2009) bemoans the mechanical nature of the exercises. In Bidlake's words, 'Rosetta Stone has replaced "boring memorization" . . . and "the endless tedium of . . . grammar drills" with boring multiple choice questions and the endless tedium of mouse-clicking' (p. 163). Only VanBuren (2008) is less critical but nevertheless assigns Rosetta Stone a preliminary or supplementary role, one which prepares learners for initial interaction with native speakers.

The raw Web

The paucity of ready-made pedagogical materials for the more rarely taught LCTLs means that '[l]earners of LCTLs will necessarily manage significant portions of their own study' (Walker & McGuiness, 1995, p. 2). That requires learners to master raw, unfiltered materials available on the Web. For digital natives (Prensky, 2001) honing skills for such learning enhancement is not difficult, although learners might need some initial direction. While digital natives might find and use material with greater initial ease, facility with digital technology does not guarantee the concerted long-term effort required for real proficiency gains.

Writing and lexicon: Google as a corpus and concordancer

Students can use the Google search engine as an immense corpus tool and concordancer (Guo & Zhang, 2007; Robb, 2003; Shei, 2008; Wu, 2009; Wu et al., 2012; Zengin, 2009). Sha (2010) outlines the differences between traditional static annotated corpora, such as the British National Corpus, and the unannotated, statistics-based Google search engine. He presents recommendations on Google use for English, which can be adapted to other LCTLs: be guided by the number of hits returned for a phraseological unit (e.g., discard phrases of four words that return fewer than 30 hits); (2) compare phraseological preference when in doubt (e.g., *quit* *smoking* vs **quit from smoking*); (3) use the search engine to check the original context.

Reading: The Google translator

Machine translation based on statistical NLP is rapidly coming of age. While machine translators produce clunky text, they are now sophisticated enough to prompt Pym's (2011, p. 4) remark that a 'true translation' becomes one that is 'revised by a professional translator'. But, he adds, the technology is here to stay. If the Google translator betrays a lazy student's written production in L2 fairly quickly right now, that will not always be the case. Even more importantly, with some language pairings, the Google translator allows non-L2 readers to understand simple text at the paragraph level without much difficulty. That probably should be seen as an advantage to diligent students learning a LCTL where resources are limited. (How an eventually improved Google translator will develop in both CTL and LCTL learning situations remains to be studied.) It should be noted because statistics-based translators require so much training based on extant texts, the more widespread the language, the better they work. This has obvious consequences for the rarer LCTLs.

Writing: The Google translator

We discussed search engines such as Google's as tools for writing immediately above. The translator itself can act as a writing check when used in reverse. Remember that L2 writers, especially those without ready access to native readers, are shooting at a target almost entirely blind. They cannot determine when they have hit the mark. A statistically based translator can remove the blindfold, at least partly. L2 writers can have Google translate their attempts back into L1. When they see idiomatic English as translations for their L2, they can be assured that they got it right. Awkward or nonsense English prose is no guarantee that the L2 attempt was inaccurate, but it serves as a warning sign that something might be wrong.

Authentic listening

The availability of authentic audio is probably the greatest technological boon to language learning, especially around the intermediate level. For LCTLs with a large internet footprint, the menu of choices is for all intents and purposes equal to that of the CTLs. Listeners can find speech on a variety of topics, often with side-by-side audio transcripts from major news and public affairs outlets, whether from within the target-speaking area or outside (e.g., the BBC's language services). Of course, the selection of material in non-traditional LCTLs is sparser, as alluded to in the discussion

TABLE 16.2 Percentage of participants that use Web-based materials to teach language areas (as per Bartoshesky, 2004, p. 78)

Language area	ESL	CTL	LCTL
Culture	64	93	85
Grammar	77	62	24
Reading	70	71	74
Writing	35	70	43
Speaking	41	23	17
Listening	53	31	40
Vocabulary	77	60	43
Literature	24	37	37
Pronunciation	30	15	15
Language functions	20	28	20

of internet footprint at the beginning of this chapter. The relative paucity of authentic audio in the rarer LCTLs means that the appropriate audience – those who have reached the ACTFL Intermediate Mid-High borderline might have to resort to extraordinary measures to manipulate audio material that exceeds i+1 difficulty. Such measures include using an audio player (or editor) to repeat or slow down or select the audio text in question and finding additional written background material, both in L1 and L2 to fill gaps in the information. Background material might include both original scripts and literary works that serve as the basis for the material. See Robin (2007) for a complete description of such ameliorating devices.

The availability of material is only one side of the coin however. Instructors' decisions about what to use is the other. Bartoshesky (2004), for example, compared LCTL teacher use to that of CTL and ESL teachers (see Table 16.2). She found that overwhelmingly, LCTL teachers – 85% – turned to the Web for culturally authentic materials, reading, and, to a lesser extent, listening materials. This closely mirrored the patterns reported by CTL teachers. But CTL teachers were more likely to turn to the Web to enhance other facets of instruction as well.

Non-Roman writing systems

Many LCTLs, both traditional and non-traditional, employ non-Roman script. In CALL, the main issue over the last two decades, even before pedagogical questions, has been the reliable cross-platform representation of non-Roman script. The introduction of Unicode in the 1990s was meant to alleviate incompatibilities among computing platforms due to language code pages (in use from the early 1980s to the early 2000s). Each code page covered one alphabet with space for 127 alphanumeric symbols in addition to standard Roman. Two or more code pages could not be combined in a single document. Thus a document containing three separate alphabets required extraordinary measures. Moreover, a lack of standardization often led to code page 'wars': several competing code pages, one for each computer platform. That prevented free exchanges in non-Roman LCTLs between Macintosh and Windows users. Unicode, based on 16-bit computing provided for over 65,000 glyphs, enough to cover every character ever used in all writing systems with room to spare for new glyphs. However, Unicode has made its way into computing slowly. It requires explicit support for all parts of a computing system. For example, while http-based mail systems (e.g., Gmail, Yahoo mail, MSN-mail) are fully Unicode compliant, some proprietary email systems, such as those set up by individual universities, are still code page-dependent, resulting in gibberish in email exchanges.[6] As recently as the early and mid-2000s, Arabic writers had to resort to transliteration in email and instant messaging (Alosh, 2001; Palfreyman & Khalil, 2003; Warschauer, El Said & Zohry, 2002).

Even full Unicode compliance is no shield against problems relating to glyph variations not covered by agreed-to Unicode conventions. Consider, for example, the issue of stress notation in East Slavic languages (Russian, Belorussian and Ukrainian). East Slavic languages have unpredictable dynamic stress, which must be marked for beginning students. But Unicode provides no error-free standard cross-platform convention for this.[7]

Finally, students attempting to access non-Roman scripts on computers that they themselves do not own face locked-down systems on which they cannot add foreign-language input. In such cases, they have no alternative but to turn to tools such as Google Transliteration.

Once the technical problems are solved, students must master keyboard input. For alphabetic languages, users must decide between a target-language native keyboard and a 'student' or 'phonetic' keyboard. While keyboards in which L2 letters are mapped to their closest Roman equivalents are easy to master, users may want to consider whether they will need to eventually enter text on devices where a pre-installed keyboard cannot be modified. Even with phonetic layouts, keyboard-induced mistakes will pose further challenges. For example, Hopp and Hopp's (2004) NewSlate program, which can be adapted to non-Roman alphabets, targets keyboard practice in Hebrew.

For logographic writing systems, such as Chinese and Japanese, native-like keyboard entry eases character-creation because entry starts as Roman transliteration. For each character, users then select from a menu of computer-generated choices. In the early 2000s, Hourser et al. (2002) introduced a version of keyboard entry for Japanese and Chinese which added English glosses to the menu of possible characters generated by each word entered in Romanization, while Okuyama (2007) investigated the usefulness of allowing students of Japanese to put off learning both kana syllabaries and Kanji. Chikamatsu (2003), on the other hand, found that American students of Japanese were more accurate in their production of Kanji on screen than in handwriting, especially if they had a higher language skill set. But greater concentration on keyboard input may mean less attention to handwriting skills. This affects LCTLs such as Russian, where handwriting is graphically similar to print but nevertheless requires additional instruction and practice, or Arabic, Pashto, Dari, Persian and Hebrew, all of which have difficult-to-produce cursive forms. Hindi, too, causes problems. While not cursive, the script is complicated by the use of conjuncts, which makes the beginnings and ends of letters somewhat opaque for first-time learners (Tozcu, 2008).

The level of difficulty of the writing system is germane to other activities involving on-screen text and listening comprehension. It is true that some, such as Vandergrift (2007, p. 7) find that on-screen captions can turn into a crutch that might inhibit the development of compensatory skills. But other studies suggest that on-screen captioning, whether in the form of original on-screen text or as a pedagogical device, has salutary effects on immediate comprehension (Borrás & Lafayette, 1994; Danan, 1992, 2004; Garza, 1991; Markham, 1993, 1999; Neuman & Koskinen, 1992; Price, 1983; Shen, 1991; Vanderplank, 1992) and serves as a strong motivator for learners (Chai & Erlam, 2008; Chung, 1999; Taylor, 2005; Vandergrift, 2008; Winke et al., 2010).

But unfamiliar writing systems can lead to cognitive overload in multimedia activities. Gruba (2004, pp. 76–7) investigated the use by Australian learners of on-screen visual elements in Japanese newscasts. He noted difficulties in the rapid decoding of graphic information in Kanji. Similarly, Winke et al. (2010) investigated the effectiveness of captions on comprehension for students of four languages: Spanish, Russian, Arabic and Chinese. In all cases captioned clips were more comprehensible than uncaptioned clips. For Spanish and for Russian (whose alphabet is Roman-like, morphophonemically based and easily mastered), captioning in a first viewing was generally more effective than when captioning was withheld until the second viewing. In Arabic and Chinese, where the writing systems are more problematic, captioning for the second viewing was more effective. Lee and Kalyuga (2011) successfully reduced cognitive overload brought on by the simultaneous on-screen presentation of pinyin Romanization and Chinese characters by reducing the amount of pinyin on screen. For the more experienced learners partial pinyin transcription facilitated more effective comprehension than full pinyin or no-pinyin conditions.

Distance learning and hybrid courses

Distance learning (DL) could be the engine that helps to save and even expand the teaching of LCTLs. Distance learning activities and assessment take place in one of two modes: synchronous (real time, direct, for example through audio-video conferencing, live whiteboarding and so on) or asynchronous (external internet sources for input material and assignments and email and dropboxes for the delivery of assignments). Hybrid courses usually involve some face-to-face instruction with many of the less interactive parts of the course – reading, listening to presentational texts (flow-of-speech, non-interactive listening), homework, especially mechanical, machine gradable exercises – farmed out to remote DL activities. But specialized LCTL courses with a large DL component often face two main difficulties:

1 **Technical support.** Synchronous activities require reliable high-speed connections. While free or low-cost products such as Skype work for individual tutoring sessions, classroom conferencing software capable of creating a virtual classroom with dozens of participants, such as Wimba or Ellimunate, require institutional support. Therefore it comes as no surprise that many DL conference efforts focus on pair-work or small groups (Fu Zhilai, 2010). The internet connection itself becomes an issue when remote locations include sites with slower speeds.

2 **Tuition issues.** The cost of electronic DL continues to fall. Reliable conferencing software and the required subscriptions are not cheap, but they are cost-efficient. And one-on-one video chat is essentially free. Individual tuition costs, however, are another matter. Fleming et al. (2002) took note of the problems caused by the uneven tuition rates for member campuses of the University of Hawai'i ITV courses. (ITV, or interactive television, was a 1990s precursor to academic videoconferencing.) The issue was through a United States National Security Education Program (NSEP) grant, but without such funding or without tuition relief for DL on the part institutions with higher tuition rates, materials developers at expensive schools have less incentive to develop DL for use by those outside the college.

Copyright issues

The birth of the digital age in the 1980s and 1990s brought with it a host of copyright issues. For CTLs, many of these issues have now been solved. Garrett (2009, p. 721) notes: 'In 1991 copyright concerns focused chiefly on the copying, or pirating, of software, but that is less of an issue now; publishers have well-established licensing procedures and password protection is more sophisticated.' The main issue these days, Garrett continues, is teachers' concerns about violating copyright. That concern is echoed by Hefferman and Wang (2008) in relation to CALL materials from Japan, where the culture of intellectual property rights is quite strict. However, many LCTL instructors will have to face copyright issues similar to those faced by CTL instructors 20 years ago because in many LCTL target countries intellectual property law is not well established, and few market channels for intellectual property exist. This especially applies to countries where piracy is rampant and widely tolerated. In such societies, copyright holders may be hard to identify. When identified, they may be hard to contact or, given their inexperience in the commercial copyright market, may be unrealistic in their negotiations for copyright release. Such issues do not plague the everyday classroom teacher. Here the provisions of Fair Use[8] and the TEACH Act of 2002 (American Library Association, 2012) allow the use of almost any material in a classroom setting, even if DL-based. Even asynchronous activities requiring storage of protected material might be permissible depending on the nature and length of the material used and how widely it is distributed. For example, the use of a recent downloaded copyrighted newscast in a copy-protected environment in which only the students in the course have access and cannot retain the material once the assignment is completed is likely to be permissible. On the other hand, issues of copyright regularly trouble materials developers who wish to publish pedagogical scaffolding materials for already existing Web-based material. The more daring of authors might embed an existing YouTube video clip into a webpage. More cautious authors might create a separate page with separate links to the material cited in the exercises. In either case, materials writers always run the risk that previously existing input material on the Web (audio, video, text, games) will disappear tomorrow – unless the authors have secured the rights and reuploaded the material on their own sites. But that is often an impossible task.

Conclusions

The current technology has gone a long way in levelling the playing field for learners of CTLs, traditionally taught LCTLs, and the rarer LCTLs from the standpoint of the availability of authentic input. While materials are still sparser for the rare LCTLs, the expansion of the Web, both in the number of sites and users and the variety of supported platforms, has brought a wealth of source material, much of it free of charge, to anyone with a good internet connection. The technological component of pedagogical materials has graduated from platform-specific specialized software, often on CD and DVD, to Web-based applications. But complete sets of pedagogical materials for the rarer LCTLs are not plentiful. The potential of the technology in such cases requires that independently minded users hone their strategies, technological and pedagogical, for setting their own language learning agenda. Learners cannot take full advantage of what is available unless they can construct a cogent learning package out of the disparate materials they find. Whether the acquisition of independent learning techniques based on available material in the Cloud is realistic is a matter for future observation. If success in such endeavours is rare, then would-be independent learners will require much more in the way of supplemental instruction, whether from a live instructor at a remote location or from carefully crafted pedagogical materials. And while the dissemination of rare LCTL packets is greatly eased by the technological revolution, their creation still requires time and financing.

Predicting the further development of technology in second language acquisition is dangerous. The literature from the late 1990s and early 2000s is filled with descriptions of pedagogical projects that did not anticipate the all-pervasive presence of YouTube (launched 2005), the Google translator (from 2006), social websites (Facebook went live 2005) or the growing penetration of mobile computing.

It would appear, however, that much of the future will centre on statistically based natural language processing (NLP), specifically the processing of human speech with the earliest availability to the most widespread LCTLs from language areas with the largest internet footprints. If that technology trickles down to the rarer LCTLs, the possibilities for more effective self-instruction or machine-based supplemental instruction widens.

But for the immediate future the challenge facing teachers and learners is no longer a matter of who can author the most targeted pedagogical software, but rather who can intertwine the newest mainstream technologies into strands that best serve LCTL learners.

Appendix A: Pedagogical Site Thumbnail Descriptions

CARLA (Centre for Advanced Research on Language Acquisition) Less Commonly Taught Languages, www.carla.umn.edu/lctl): Sharable resources in 25 languages, lists of university courses. Multimedia activities in Chinese, Japanese, Korean and Persian. North American Course Listings for Less Commonly Taught Languages, searchable database of course offerings at colleges and universities, K-12 programs, distance education courses, study abroad programs and summer language courses; LCTL classroom materials development; instructional materials; CARLA Summer Institute information.

CIBERweb (Language, http://ciberweb.msu.edu/events/language): Pedagogical LCTL initiatives for business language.

LangMedia (http://langmedia.fivecolleges.edu): Various multimedia pedagogical resources in 41 languages; mentored courses in eight LCTLs (available to Five College students only); independent study courses in twenty languages through the Five College Supervised Independent Language Program (Amherst, Hampshire, Mt. Holyoke, Smith, University of Massachusetts).

NASILP (National Association of Self-Instructional Language Programs, www.nasilp.net): Fosters the study of less commonly taught languages through self-instructional principles utilizing a 'prochievement' modality developed for an academic setting for 82 languages. See Dunkel (2002).

SALTMIL (Speech and Language Technology for Minority Languages, http://ixa2.si.ehu.es/saltmil/): Emphasis on corpora and linguistic analysis of data from SCOLA (www.scola.org) which provides rebroadcasts of the news from across the world. Some material is accompanied by transcripts and exercises. SCOLA requires an institutional subscription.

UCLA Language Materials Project (http://lmp.ucla.edu/): Provides pedagogical materials and teaching hints for over 100 LCTLs.

Michigan State University Foreign Language Resource Centre (nflrc.msu.edu): Materials, many online, for dozens of LCTLs.

WebCorps Live (www.webcorp.org.uk/live): Serves as a concordance front-end for Bing or Google search sites by reorganizing the information in hits so that users can see all the contexts at a glance.

Notes

1 Originally the US State Department, along with most government entities making up the Interagency Language Roundtable (ILR) classified languages by difficulty for American English speakers into four categories, based on the number of hours of small-group instruction required to reach ILR 3 (roughly equivalent to ACTFL Superior) across all skills: Category 1, for example, Romance languages – 575–600 hours, Category 2, for example, German and Malay – 750–900 hours, Category 3, for example, most Slavic languages – 11 hours and Category 4, for example, Chinese, Japanese, Arabic – 220 hours with a year in country. In the mid-2000s, the State Department reduced the number of categories to three, folding Category 2 into Category 1. But the four-tier taxonomy, for all intents and purposes, remains in effect, because the number of instructional hours allotted for former Category 2 languages is significantly higher than for other Category 1 languages: 750–900 class hours.

2 Total population figures vary from those cited for Table 16.1 because the figures come from 2011 estimates and are rounded off.

3 The NCRLC webcasts, The Simplified News, address the changes in media stylistics that has made newscasting in these languages more difficult over the last 20 years. Before globalization, much of the news delivery for the target audiences was slow, deliberate and predictable in terms of content. With the importation of Western media conventions, delivery has become faster, while redundancy and predictability have fallen. The Simplified News restores the previous delivery to the news in bimonthly news summaries accompanied by pedagogical wrap-arounds.

4 Unlike the NLP-based CALL projects discussed here, string-matching exercises can be put together from scratch by computer novices through such exercise creation sites as Quia, Hot Potatoes or on the test and assessment portions of course management software, such as Blackboard.

5 Common chatboxes are not showcases for NLP. Most recombine user input in an attempt at conversation and can be made to fail the artificial intelligence Turing test (they cannot fool a human interlocutor) without difficulty.

6 Problems with non-Roman email confound some users (usually outside the target countries) even today, despite the existence of Unicode.

7 The Unicode non-spacing characters confound spell-checkers and often fail to reproduce properly in print or on screen.

8 For a full and accessible discussion of the issue of copyright in pedagogy, see Harper (2007).

References

Allen, H. (2002). *Does study abroad make a difference? An investigation of linguistic and motivational outcomes.* Unpublished dissertation, Emory University.

Alosh, M. (2001). Learning language at a distance: An Arabic initiative. *Foreign Language Annals, 34*(4), 347–54.

Alvarez, A., Levin, L., Frederking, R., Fung, S., Gates, D., & Good, J. (2006). The MILE Corpus for less commonly taught languages. In *Proceedings of the Human Language Technology Conference of the North American Chapter of the ACL* (pp. 5–8). New York: Association for Computational Linguistics.

Amaral L., & Meurers, W. D. (2009). Little things with big effects: On the identification and interpretation of tokens for error diagnosis in ICALL. *CALICO Journal 26*(3), 580–91.

American Council for the Teaching of Foreign Languages (ACTFL) (2012). ACTFL Proficiency Guidelines.

American Library Association (2012). Distance education and the TEACH Act. Retrieved from www.ala.org/Template.cfm?Section = Distance_ Education_ and_the_TEACH _Act&Template= /ContentManagement/ ContentDisplay.cfm &ContentID=25939

Armitage, N., & Bowerman, C. (2005). The LOM approach: A call for concern? *Computer Assisted Language Learning, 18*(1/2), 109–18.

Bartoshesky, A. (2004). Cyber resources for language education: Accessing and using Web-based target language materials. Unpublished dissertation. ProQuest Dissertations & Theses (PQDT).

Bidlake, E. (2009). 'This is the biggest blue cake': A technology review of Rosetta Stone® Version 3. *ARECLS, 6*, 156–64.

Blake, R., Wilson, N., Cetto, M., & Pardo-Ballester, C. (2008). Measuring oral proficiency in distance, face-to-face, and blended classrooms. *Language Learning & Technology, 12*(3), 114–27.

Borrás, I., & Lafayette, R. C. (1994). Effects of multimedia courseware subtitling on the speaking performance of college students of French. *The Modern Language Journal, 78*(1), 61–75.

Brecht, R. (2002). Foreword to B. L. Leaver & B. Shekhtman (Eds.), *Developing professional-level language proficiency.* Cambridge: Cambridge University Press.

Brecht, R., & Walton, A. R. (1993). National strategic planning in the less commonly taught languages. Washington, D C: National Foreign Language Centre and University of Maryland.

CARLA (Centre for Advanced Research on Language Acquisition) (2009). 'Less Commonly Taught Languages are . . .'. Retrieved from www.carla.umn.edu/lctl/definition.html

Carreira, M. (2011). Preserving the less commonly taught languages: One size does not fit all. Presentation at *What Future for the Less Commonly Taught Languages?* New York: Columbia University 30 April.

Chai, J., & Erlam, R. (2008). The effect and the influence of the use of video and captions on second language learning. *New Zealand Studies in Applied Linguistics, 14*(2), 25–44.

Chi-Chiang, S. (2008). Discovering the hidden treasure on the internet: Using Google to uncover the veil of phraseology. *Computer Assisted Language Learning, 21*(1), 67–85.

Chikamatsu, N. (2003). The effects of computer use on L2 Japanese writing. *Foreign Language Annals, 36*(1), 114–27.

Chung, J. (1999). The effects of using video texts supported with advance organizers and captions on Chinese college students' listening comprehension: An empirical study. *Foreign Language Annals, 32*(3), 295–308.

Danan, M. (1992). Reversed subtitling and dual coding theory: New directions for foreign language instruction. *Language Learning, 42*(4), 497–527.

— (2004). Captioning and subtitling: Undervalued language learning strategies. *Meta, 49*(1), 67–77.
Davidson, D. (2010). Study abroad: When, how long, and with what results? New data from the Russian front. *Foreign Language Annals, 43*(1), 6–26.
DeKeyser, R. (2007). Study abroad as foreign language practice. In R. DeKeyser (Ed.), *Practice in a Second Language: Perspectives from applied linguistics and cognitive psychology* (pp. 208–26). Cambridge: Cambridge University Press.
Dunkel, A., Brill, S., & Kohl, B. (2002) The impact of self-instructional technology on language learning: A view of NASILP. In C. A. Spreen (Ed.), *New technologies in language learning: Cases in the less commonly taught languages* (pp. 97–120). Honolulu: University of Hawai'i, Second language teaching & Curriculum Centre.
Erickson, L. O. (2004). Review of Rosetta Stone, Personal Edition: Level I and II. *The French Review, 77*(5), 1027–8.
Fleming, S., Hiple, D., & Du, Y. (2002). Foreign language distance learning education: The University of Hawai'i experience. In C. A. Spreen (Ed.), *New technologies in language learning: Cases in the less commonly taught languages* (pp. 13–54). Honolulu: University of Hawai'i, Second language teaching & Curriculum Centre.
Fu, Z. (2010). Distance learning for foreign language teaching. 2010 Second International Conference on Multimedia and Information Technology. *IEEE Computer Society* (pp. 259–61).
Furman, N., Goldberg, D., & Lusin, Natalia. (2010). Enrollments in languages other than English in United States institutions of higher education, Fall 2009. New York: Modern Language Association.
Garrett, N. (2009). Computer-assisted language learning trends and issues revisited: Integrating innovation. *The Modern Language Journal, 93*, 719–40.
Garza, T. (1991). Evaluating the use of captioned video materials in advanced foreign language learning. *Foreign Language Annals, 24*, 239–58.
Golonka, E. (2001). Identification of salient linguistic and metalinguistic in the prediction of oral proficiency gain at the advanced-level threshold among adult learners of Russian. Unpublished dissertation, Bryn Mawr College.
Gonglewski, M., & Helm, A. (2010). An examination of business case methodology: Pedagogical synergies from two disciplines. *Global Business Languages, 15*(3).
Google Transliteration. Retrieved from www.google.com/transliterate
Gruba, P. (2004). Understanding digitized second language videotext. *Computer Assisted Language Learning, 17*(1), 51–82.
Guo, S., & Zhang, G. (2007). Building a customised Google-based collocation collector to enhance language learning. *British Journal of Educational Technology, 38*(4), 747–50.
Harper, G. K. (2007). The copyright crash course. Austin: University of Texas Libraries. Retrieved from http://copyright.lib.utexas.edu/index.html
Heffernan, N., & Wang, S. (2008). Copyright and multimedia classroom material: A study from Japan. *Computer Assisted Language Learning, 21*(2), 167–80.
Hopp, M., & Hopp, T. (2004). newSLATE: Building a Web-based infrastructure for learning non-Roman script languages. *CALICO Journal, 21*(3), 541–55.
Jackson F. H., & Kaplan, M. A. (2007). Theory and practice in government language teaching. Retrieved from www.govtilr.org/Publications/TESOL03ReadingFull.htm#_ftn1
Jorden, E. H., & Walton, A. R. (1987). Truly foreign languages: Instructional challenges. *The Annals of the American Academy of Political and Social Science, 490*, 110–24.
Kelm, O. (2008). *Cultural interviews with Turkish-speaking executives.* Austin: University of Texas CIBER.
Kelm, O., & Tanaka, M. (2007). *Cultural interviews with Japanese-speaking executives.* Austin: University of Texas CIBER.

Kelm, O., Wang, H., & Chen, J. (2007). *Cultural interviews with Chinese-speaking executives*. Austin: University of Texas CIBER.

Internet World Stats (2011). Internet world users by language. Retrieved from www.internetworldstats.com/stats7.htm

Larson, P. (2006). The return of the text: A welcome challenge for less commonly taught languages. *The Modern Language Journal, 90*(2), 255–8.

Leaver, B. L., Ehrman, M., & Lekic, M. (2004). Distinguished-level learning online: Support materials from LangNet and RussNet. *Foreign Language Annals, 37*(4), 556–66.

Lee, C. H., & Kalyuga, S. (2011). Effectiveness of on-screen pinyin in learning Chinese: An expertise reversal for multimedia redundancy effect. *Computers in Human Behavior, 27*(1), 11–15.

Lewis, P. M. (Ed.) (2009). *Ethnologue: Languages of the World* (16th ed.). Dallas: SIL International. Retrieved from www.ethnologue.com

Lim, J., Campbell, C., & Smala, S. (2011). Technology enhanced scaffolding in language teaching: Using LessonLAMS for Korean as a foreign language. In L. Cameron & J. Dalziel (Eds.), Proceedings of the 6th international LAMS & learning design conference 2011: Learning design for a changing world (pp. 128–34). Sydney: LAMS Foundation.

Malone, M., Rifkin, B., Christian, D., & Johnson, D. (2005). Attaining high levels of proficiency: Challenges for foreign language education in the United States. Washington, DC: Center for Applied Linguistics.

Markham, P. (1993). Captioned television videotapes: Effects of visual support on second language comprehension. *Journal of Educational Technology Systems, 21*(3), 183–91.

— (1999). Captioned videotapes and second-language listening word recognition. *Foreign Language Annals, 32*(3), 321–8.

Nagata, N. (2009). Robo-Sensei's NLP-based error detection and feedback generation. *CALICO Journal, 26* (3), 562–79.

NASILP (National Association of Self-Instructional Language Programs). Retrieved from www.nasilp.net

National Capital Language Resource Centre (2012). The Simplified News. Retrieved from http://nclrc.org/webcasts/

Neuman, S. B., & Koskinen, P. (1992). Captioned television as comprehensible input: Effects of incidental word learning from context for language minority students. *Reading Research Quarterly, 27*, 94–106.

Nielson, K. (2011). Self-study with language learning software in the workplace: What happens? *Language Learning & Technology, 15*(3), 110–29.

Okuyama, Y. (2007). CALL vocabulary learning in Japanese: Does Romaji help beginners learn more words? *CALICO Journal, 24*(2), 355–79.

Palfreyman, D., & Khalil, M. A. (2003). 'A funky language for teenzz to use': Representing Gulf Arabic in instant messaging. *Journal of Computer-Mediated Communication, 9*(1).

Prensky, M. (2001). Digital natives, digital immigrants. In *On the Horizon, 9*(5), 1–6.

Price, K. (1983). Closed-captioned TV: An untapped resource. *MATSOL Newsletter, 12*, 7–8.

Pym, A. (2011). What technology does to translation. *Translation & Interpreting, 3*(1), 1–9. Retrieved from www.trans-int.org/index.php/transint/article/view/121/81

Renouf, A. (2009). Corpus linguistics beyond Google: The WebCorp linguist's search engine. *Digital Studies/Le champ numérique, 1*(1).

Rifkin, B. (2005). A ceiling effect in traditional classroom foreign language instruction: Data from Russian. *The Modern Language Journal, 89*(1), 3–18.

— (2006). A ceiling effect for communicative language teaching? *The Modern Language Journal, 90*(2), 262–4.

Robb, T. (2003). Google as a quick'n dirty corpus tool. TESL-EJ. *Teaching English as a Second or Foreign Language, 7*(2).

Robin, R. (2007). Learner-based listening and technological authenticity. *Language Learning & Technology 11*(1), 109–15.
Rosetta Stone, Ltd. (2012). *Rosetta Stone* (language learning software editions for each of thirty languages). Retrieved from www.rosettastone.com
Sha, G. (2010). Using Google as a super corpus to drive written language learning: A comparison with the British National Corpus. *Computer Assisted Language Learning, 23*(5), 377–93.
Shalaan, K. (2005). An intelligent computer assisted language learning system for Arabic learners. *Computer Assisted Language Learning, 18*(1/2), pp. 81–108.
Shen, C. D. (1991). The effects of captioning on listening comprehension of English as a Second Language in a computer-based interactive videodisc system.
Simpson, H., Maeda, K., & Cieri, C. (2009). Basic language resources for diverse Asian languages: A streamlined approach for resource creation. In *Proceedings of the 7th Workshop on Asian Language Resources*, ACL-IJCNLP (pp. 55–62). Suntec, Singapore: ACL and AFNLP.
Swender, E. (2003). Oral proficiency testing in the real world: Answers to frequently asked questions. *Foreign Language Annals, 36*(4), 520–26.
Tagarela. Retrieved from http://sifnos.sfs.uni-tuebingen.de/tagarela
Taylor, G. (2005). Perceived processing strategies of students watching captioned video. *Foreign Language Annals, 38*(3), 422–7.
Tozcu, A. (2008). The use of interactive whiteboards in teaching non-Roman scripts. *Computer Assisted Language Learning, 21*(2), 143–66.
Ushida, E. (2007). Robo-Sensei personal Japanese tutor, version 1.0. *CALICO Journal, 24*(2), 408–20.
Van Buren, P. (2008). Review of Rosetta Stone: Español (Latinoamérica). *Hispania, 91*(3), 633–5.
Vandergrift, L. (2007). Recent developments in second and foreign language listening comprehension research. *Language Teaching, 40*, 191–210.
Vandergrift, L. (2008). Learning strategies for listening comprehension. In S. Hurd & T. Lewis (Eds.), *Language Learning Strategies in Independent Settings* (pp. 84–102). Bristol, England: Multilingual Matters.
Vanderplank, R. (1992). Non-native speaker viewers' use of teletext subtitles in English: Some exploratory studies. In G. Davies & M. Husey (Eds.), *New technology in language learning* (pp. 89–102). Frankfurt: Peter Lang.
Vlugter, P., Knotta, A., McDonald, J., & Hall, C. (2009). Dialogue-based CALL: A case study on teaching pronouns. *Computer Assisted Language Learning, 22*(2), 115–31.
Walker, G., & McGuiness, S. (1995). *Learning less commonly taught languages: An agreement on the basis of training for teachers.* Columbus, OH: Ohio State University. Pathway Series.
Warschauer, M., El Said, G. R., & Zohry, A. (2002). Language choice online: Globalization and identity in Egypt. *Journal of Computer-Mediated Communication, 7*(4).
Wikipedia (opening page). Retrieved from www.wikipedia.org/
Winke, P., Gass, S., & Sydorenko, T. (2010). The effects of captioning videos used for foreign language listening activities. *Language Learning & Technology, 14*(1), 65–86.
Wu, S., Franken, M., & Witten, I. (2009). Refining the use of the Web (and Web search) as a language teaching and learning resource. *Computer Assisted Language Learning, 22*(3), 249–68.
Yager, K. (1998). Learning Spanish in Mexico: The effect of informal contact and student attitudes on language gain. *Hispania, 81*(4), 898–913.
Zengin, B. (2009). Benefit of Google search engine in learning and teaching collocations. *Eurasian Journal of Educational Research, 34,* 151–67.

17

CALL and digital feedback

Paige Ware and Greg Kessler

Summary

In the field of CALL research, the term digital feedback has been used in a variety of ways. In some cases, feedback refers to individualized computer-based tutorials programmed to offer information about a targeted set of discrete language skills such as grammar or pronunciation. Other research has viewed technology not as a tutor, but as the mode by which human feedback is delivered (Kern, Ware & Warschauer, 2004; Ware & Warschauer, 2006). Such research focuses on the various ways that synchronous and asynchronous forms of interaction provide language users with information on their language and content. This chapter examines recent research across these various definitions of digital feedback with a specific focus on the promotion of the skills of writing and speaking.

Introduction

The term *digital feedback* is not easily defined. Scholars examining face-to-face feedback on student writing and speaking have developed various definitions of feedback according to particular pedagogical and theoretical orientations (see discussion in Ferris, 2004; Hyland & Hyland, 2006). This chapter therefore begins by situating digital feedback within an overview of three main dimensions of feedback: mode of feedback delivery, focus of feedback provided and strategies for delivering feedback (see Table 17.1). The subsequent review of current studies on digital feedback reflects various combinations of these three dimensions as they pertain to feedback on writing and on speaking.

The first dimension pertains to mode of delivery. Early research on modes often examined teacher and peer feedback provided through face-to-face discussions as compared with delivery through various forms of technology-mediated delivery (Kern & Warschauer, 2000). A range of technology modes were examined, such as word-processing software, real-time chatting sessions and delayed-time interaction in course management systems. Later research on mode of delivery introduced a new

TABLE 17.1 Three dimensions of feedback

Dimension 1: Modes of feedback delivery	
Face-to-face feedback	Writing or speaking workshop Teacher response (one-on-one conferencing) Classmate response (peer review)
Human feedback delivered electronically	Teacher response Within-class peer response Distally located peer response
Computer-generated feedback	Automated evaluation software Automated scoring engines Automated speech recognition Automated speech transcription
Dimension 2: Focus of feedback provided	
Error correction	Focus on morphological forms *(verb forms, noun endings, subject-verb agreement, etc.)* Focus on syntactic forms (*fragments, punctuation, missing words, redundancy, etc.*) Focus on lexical forms (*spelling, pronouns, word choice, informal register, idioms, etc.*)
Idea development	Focus on generating meaning by engaging in discussions Focus on global organization through phases of drafting, responding and revising
Genre awareness	Focus on awareness of register, rhetoric and audience Focus on understanding variety of language and literacy practices specific to particular contexts of use
Dimension 3: Strategies for delivering feedback	
Instructor-directed strategies	Use of transcripts of student production or other examples to draw attention to particular linguistic, organizational and rhetorical features Choice among feedback types: direct (changing the error) or indirect (highlighting errors without immediate correction) Modelling of effective feedback strategies
Peer-interaction strategies	Allowing peer comments to draw attention to particular linguistic, communicative or interactional features Developing collaborative projects and apprenticeships Focusing on form primarily as it impedes meaning Producing multiple types of purposeful writing
Autonomous strategies	Providing rubrics and evaluation guides Providing sample essays Encouraging autonomous editing

element, as the provider of feedback no longer needed to be the teacher or immediate peers. Rather, the efficiency and affordability of network-based technologies allowed for distally located peers to provide feedback, while the development of automated software programs provided the option of computer-generated feedback (Ware & Warschauer, 2006).

The second dimension examines the focus of feedback. First, error correction research locates the focus of feedback as students' control of specific morphological, syntactic and lexical forms. Error correction studies are typical in second language acquisition (SLA) and second language (L2) writing research (Ferris, 2004, 2006) and examine key questions on the provider of feedback (teachers, peers, computer or combination), the feedback cycle (whether revisions are required or not), the explicitness of feedback (direct correction of error or indirect awareness-raising of error), the frequency of feedback and the type of error (Ferris, 2004). Two other major foci of feedback in writing are on idea development and on genre awareness (Hyland & Hyland, 2006). A focus on idea development, for example, was born out of composition theory and suggests that feedback occurs as a discussion that helps writers generate meaning and organize their ideas as they move through a process approach to writing: drafting, receiving feedback, revising, receiving additional, feedback, editing and publishing. Finally, situating genre as the focus of feedback seeks to foster greater audience and register awareness by having students critically analyse the rhetorical strategies used across genres within specific contexts of use (Gebhard & Harman, 2011). Research that directly examines digital feedback on idea development and genre awareness for essay writing is not frequent, yet two critical features of this dimension of feedback include (1) the shift away from primary concerns with mechanical accuracy, and (2) the movement towards a critical exploration of new genres beyond an emphasis on the academic essay.

The third and final dimension lays out three overarching instructional strategies: instructor-directed, peer-interactional and autonomous. In face-to-face classes, language instructors likely employ these strategies in combination. Where the strategies primarily differ is a key issue in digital feedback, because the degree to which the instructor is involved shifts, typically towards more peer-interactional and autonomous strategies. In traditional instructor-directed strategies, for example, an instructor can promote metacognitive awareness of linguistic, organizational or rhetorical features by using transcripts of student discourse-generated online (Sengupta, 2001). However, with the shift towards more peer interaction through chat rooms and asynchronous discourse, peer-interactional strategies tend to dominate the feedback cycle (Ware & Warschauer, 2006). Finally, autonomous strategies are the hallmark of computer-generated feedback, as most automated evaluation programs rely on students to interpret and act upon feedback with limited support from the teacher (Chen & Cheng, 2008; Dikli, 2006).

Across these three dimensions of feedback, what constitutes quality is still largely undetermined, though a few patterns have emerged as promising (Ferris, 2004; Hyland & Hyland, 2006). In L2 writing, for example, research on whether and how error correction in L2 writing best takes place has been described as 'incomplete and inconsistent' (Ferris, 2004, p. 49), yet Ferris offers several 'predictions' (ibid.) about what might later prove important through empirical work: the need for the systematic presence of feedback, an emphasis on providing indirect over direct feedback, differentiation of feedback according to error types and the augmentation of metacognitive and metalinguistic awareness among learners. Characteristics of feedback on speaking that are viewed as influencing quality include the frequency of feedback (Engwall & Bålter, 2007), the frequency of interruptions (McCrickard & Chewar, 2003), the pace of correction (Eskenazi, 1999; Farmer, 2005), the timing of feedback as occurring during or after speech (Engwall & Bålter, 2007) and the potential for uptake and transfer (Eskenazi, 1999). Such considerations are unique to individual learners and instructors, and cultural appropriateness is also likely to be a factor.

Digital feedback in CALL on writing

This section examines digital feedback on writing in the three areas in which much of the research has taken place: computer-generated feedback through automated software, electronically delivered peer feedback with a focus on form and electronically delivered peer feedback with a focus on idea development.

Automated evaluation software: From assessment to assistance

Computer-generated assessment is commonly referred to as automated machine scoring or automated essay scoring. In terms of the dimensions laid out earlier, the mode of feedback delivery is almost entirely computer-generated, and the focus of feedback provided is primarily that of error correction, although pre-writing tools also make available a focus on idea development. Finally, the strategies for providing feedback rely almost entirely on student autonomy.

Computer-generated feedback allows for the provision of holistic and analytic scores on student writing that are derived from mathematical models based on any combination of organizational, stylistic and mechanical aspects of writing (for details see Brock, 1990, 1993; Burston, 2001; Chung & Baker, 2003; Leacock, 2004). Early models relied on word counts, word anomalies, spelling aberrations and sentence length to calculate a score (for an extended history, see Page, 2003; Warschauer & Ware, 2006), whereas current approaches can detect lexical-grammatical errors (Chodorow & Leacock, 2000) and awkward shifts between phrases (Miltsakaki & Kukich, 2000).

The tools offered include summative scoring as well as a range of formative assessment features. Pre-writing tools include graphic organizers and sample essays linked to scoring rubrics. During writing, students can access translation tools, writing checklists, spell checkers, writing manuals, dictionaries and word banks. After essay submission, students receive a combination of holistic and analytic trait scores, as well as graphic bar chart displays and text-based pop-up boxes that provide explanations for how to improve problematic areas. Newer versions of the programs allow for students to interact asynchronously with their instructor by sending private messages that show up as question flags for the instructor's feedback.

Instructors have flexibility in managing the settings. They can choose between importing their own prompts or selecting from a large number of prepared prompts classified by grade level and by genre and can disable the automated summative scoring feature. Computer-generated feedback can be enhanced or overridden by instructor feedback using delivery mechanisms similar to those found in most word-processing software programs such as *track changes* and *insert comments*. Time limits and limits on the number of revisions possible can also be set. In short, automated feedback programs bundle together many of the features that instructors might use when providing feedback electronically to students through word-processing software or email. A caveat in how the programs differ from these modes of electronic feedback, however, is the software's data storing capability, which allows for ease in longitudinal tracking of student writing.

The research base on the impact of automated feedback programs on improving student writing is limited but growing. Studies conducted by the developers suggest that intensive use of the programs might impact writing scores on formal essay features (Attali & Burstein, 2006; Elliot, Darlington & Mikulas, 2004; Lee, Gentile & Kantor, 2010; Shermis & Burstein, 2003). A few recent classroom-based studies (Chen & Cheng, 2008; Fang, 2010; Warschauer & Grimes, 2008), all using *MYAccess!* software, have described the instructor's role in implementation and in the perceptions held by students. Chen and Cheng (2008) documented the differences in how three post-secondary EFL teachers integrated the software and found that students who held positive perceptions of the feedback were in a class in which the program was used on a regular basis as a pre-writing and drafting tool, but not as an assessment mechanism. Warschauer and Grimes's (2008) study of secondary teachers showed that teachers generally endorsed the programs, but nonetheless did not use them on a regular basis, as pressure was high to prepare students for other state exams. Finally, Fang (2010) found that post-secondary EFL students in Taiwan appreciated the program feedback on form-related issues, though they felt it lacked as much assistance on organization and content and were also sceptical about its usefulness as a grading tool.

Automated feedback programs provide a form of digital feedback that might complement a larger, comprehensive instructional approach. Much is still to be learned, however, about the contexts in which the programs are best used (Chen & Cheng, 2008), the learners for whom the feedback is optimal (Dikli, 2006), the possibility of misuses of scoring systems to track students (Herrington & Moran, 2001) and the potential of a washback effect on instruction (Cheville, 2004).

Error correction by peers: Focus on form studies

A subset of the large research base on focus-on-form feedback is comprised of studies that embed a focus on form as learners interact through computers. The mode of delivery in these studies is primarily human feedback delivered electronically through peer response provided either by peers in the same class or by peers who are distally located partners. The focus of feedback is on morphological, lexical and syntactic error correction. The strategies are primarily peer interactional in which peers draw attention to linguistic, communicative or interactional features as they occur in real-time or delayed-time discussion.

Studies of corrective feedback between distally located peers are called a type of telecollaborative partnerships that take place using synchronous interaction in chat rooms or in asynchronous interaction through course management systems such as Moodle or Blackboard. While the main focus of such telecollaborative projects has typically been on developing intercultural competence (Belz, 2002; O'Dowd, 2003; Ware, 2005), a few researchers have launched an inquiry into the potential for such exchanges to provide a forum for peers to provide corrective feedback, either incidentally through ongoing written dialogue, or explicitly because of the instructor's course requirements.

Research on real-time interaction indicates that, although the medium provides opportunities for peer feedback on form, learners tend to focus on meaning over form. In his early study on chat-based corrective feedback, O'Rourke (2005) contends that a weekly, semester-long synchronous exchange between students in Ireland and Germany promoted opportunities for learners to develop metalinguistic awareness of grammatical forms. However, in their study of a bilingual 'e-Tandem' project that linked students in Japan and Australia for three chat sessions, Bower and Kawaguchi (2011) analysed chat logs and found that learners focused mostly on communication, not on the implicit provision of corrective feedback, except when given the task of providing explicit corrective feedback on transcripts of their chat interactions. Similarly, Sotillo (2005) found that learners using Yahoo! Messenger did indeed make feedback available and did, at least in part, utilize the feedback within the context of the chat. Finally, Darhower (2008) examined the linguistic affordances of a bilingual chat project between students in North Carolina and Puerto Rico and concluded that, although students reported satisfaction and engaged in some feedback, their typical interactions were characterized by a focus on communication rather than a focus on form.

In examinations of delayed time, or asynchronous, interactions in telecollaborative projects, researchers have also found that students typically focus on meaning, not on the provision of feedback on forms. For example, Ware and O'Dowd (2008) analysed transcripts of the asynchronous communication of students in Spain, Chile and the United States by comparing two types of telecollaboration: one approach that required students to provide a focus on form, and another approach that merely suggested a focus on form without an instructional mandate. They found that only the group which was given the explicit instructions to provide corrective feedback actually did so, and even then only provided feedback on form sparingly. Paradoxically, despite the limited attention students gave to one another's language form, the majority of participants in the project indicated in their surveys that they would have liked to receive feedback on form from their partner.

While the above studies rely on transcripts of interaction, surveys and interview data, a handful of researchers have used formal assessment to examine how such online interactions might foster the possibility of learner uptake of particular forms. In one of the first of such studies, Smith (2005) found that task-based chatting did not seem to lead to learner uptake of particular vocabulary, and he therefore cautioned instructors to look for 'nuances' (p. 33) of successful uptake rather than to expect specific lexical acquisition. Sauro (2009) investigated two types of corrective feedback, recasts and metalinguistic information, on a group of 23 high intermediate and advanced learners of English who engaged in online chatting with native English speakers. Using a pre-, post- and delayed-post design that measured the omission of the zero article with abstract non-count nouns, she found no statistically significant advantage for either type of feedback on immediate or sustained gains; however, the metalinguistic corrective feedback group did show immediate significant gains relative to the control group. Sauro and Smith (2010) investigated whether and how learners use the added time for planning during online chatting with their peers as an opportunity for self-correction. They examined 23 post-secondary students learning German in dyadic task-based chat and found that learners who self-corrected their own output after writing a message showed significantly greater lexical variety and linguistic complexity.

To summarize, research on error correction from peers in online chatting and in asynchronous writing is still at an early stage. Studies have begun the process of documenting the type of feedback and uptake in telecollaborative projects and in within-class contexts and have come to the general conclusion that corrective feedback does take place, but it occurs less frequently when not explicitly encouraged or mandated by the teacher. In the cases in which it does occur, findings are inconclusive as to the short- and long-term impact on learner uptake and retention of particular forms. Follow-up research is needed to examine which types of peer feedback designs promote most feedback, and whether and how such peer feedback opportunities might result in gains on learners' control of the targeted forms.

Idea development with peers: Academic essays, blogs and wikis

Research reviewed in this section shares with the peer feedback studies above a mode of delivery that is primarily peer-to-peer. However, the focus of feedback is mainly on idea generation, rather than on error correction. Studies of feedback on academic essays have focused on peer review online and on the instructor's changing role in that process. The next, more recent wave of studies examines newer technologies of blogs and wikis in an expanded repertoire of writing genres.

Peer review through online chatting and asynchronous writing has become a staple of many writing classes. In a recent summary of research conducted on the potential for asynchronous and synchronous electronic feedback to improve formal academic writing, Ware and Warschauer (2006) concluded that studies showed that peer review online is associated with a greater quantity of student writing, higher student motivation, a less threatening environment and more instructor control over peer response (DiGiovanni & Nagaswami, 2001; Kamhi-Stein, 2000; Tuzi, 2004). They document the convergence of study findings that peers tend to provide stronger written feedback on local issues at the mechanical or paragraph level, but that oral feedback tends to be the preferred mode for advice on more global changes (Ho & Savignon, 2007; Schultz, 2000). They describe teachers who have creatively used the transcripts of technology-mediated peer review to accomplish a wider set of goals, including promoting student autonomy (Lamy & Goodfellow, 1999), encouraging metalinguistic awareness (Yuan, 2003) and raising student attention to audience and communicative purpose (Sengupta, 2001).

The instructor's role in this shift towards human feedback delivered electronically by peers has been an important area of study. In their study of a 22 post-secondary ESL students in a writing class, for example, Guardado and Shi (2007) argue that instructors likely need to play a stronger role during face-to-face instruction in order to help maximize the benefits of peer review sessions online. Even though student comments on one another's essays were balanced, students' scepticism about peer review in general and their avoidance of requests to clarify their peer review comments manifested in what the researchers termed a 'one-way communication process' (p. 443). Also, Matsumura and Hann (2004) examined how computer anxiety might impact the quality of EFL student writing. In study in which students were given the choice between face-to-face teacher feedback and online peer and teacher feedback, students who were anxious about online feedback did better when they were provided with a choice over the preferred mode of feedback. Both of these studies underscore the importance of the instructors' role in making behind-the-scene pedagogical choices about individual differences and about maximizing in-class time.

A few years ago, Ware and Warschauer (2006) noted that research in the area of more interactive forums such as blogs and wikis had 'just begun' (p. 115), and indeed, since then a number of studies has explored the potential of these newer technologies to promote peer feedback. Research has focused on the choice of technology forum for promoting formal academic writing (Kessler, 2009; Oladi, 2005; Woo, Chu, Ho & Li, 2011), and other work has emphasized writers' perceptions of these modes rather than their skill development per se (Bloch, 2007; Ducate & Lomicka 2008; Lowe & Williams, 2004; Mak & Coniam, 2008; Parks, Huot, Hamers & Lemonnier, 2003).

Research that addresses feedback on writing in blogs tends to focus either on positive case-study experiences of individual students and classes or on descriptions of how the literacy practices and types of feedback differ from more conventional writing. Oladi (2005), for example, studied how students in Tehran interacted through blogging and found that it tended to coincide with their confidence in writing. Ducate and Lomicka (2008) analysed data from a year-long project in which students wrote and read blogs on a regular basis. They found that students explored different types of self-expression and creativity, and the German and French participants obtained a unique perspective on their partners' culture. In his case study of a Somali immigrant who used blogging in his writing class, Bloch (2007) argues that blogging may help students become active producers of writing on the internet, in addition to serving as a bridge into more academic writing. Lee (2006) documented two learners of Korean who self-reported an increase in their proficiency and in their comfort level in receiving feedback. For the most part, these studies document positive perceptions of participants and high student enthusiasm for blogging.

Research on wikis is of particular interest to instructors interested in peer feedback on formal writing, as wikis have been described as promoting 'more formal, topic-centric, depersonalized interaction' (Warschauer & Grimes, 2007, p. 12). The structure of wikis creates a writing environment that is distinct from either asynchronous or synchronous modes, which rely on some form of turn-taking. Rather, wikis allow for students to collaboratively create and edit a document, and instructors can track each individual's contribution.

The medium itself, then, seems to shift students away from conventional norms of authorship and towards more autonomy in their writing. Kessler (2009) examined students' attention to form in collaborative wiki writing among in-service EFL teachers in Mexico who were encouraged, but not required, to make use of a course wiki as they developed their English writing proficiency on a variety of topics across a 16-week period. He found that students did, in fact, attend to one another's grammatical forms, but almost exclusively when such attention to form impeded meaning. In follow-up interviews, he asked if participants knew the correct form of particular errors in the wiki; they did, in fact, but indicated that unless meaning was impeded, such errors were better left unaddressed, leading Kessler to conclude that there may be an 'acceptable level of tolerance for errors' (p. 91) as students focus the bulk of their attention to meaning and to design.

In a similar use of the wiki as an autonomous learner space, Mak and Coniam (2008) emphasize the potential for wikis to promote creative, authentic, collaborative writing. They describe the phases of writing, editing and publishing that grade 7 ESL learners in Hong Kong moved through, 'with minimal input and support from their teachers' (p. 437) as they collaboratively created a brochure of their school. In a case study of a class of fifth-grade EFL students in Hong Kong, Woo, Chu, Ho and Li (2011) examined participants' perceptions of writing and found it useful for fostering teamwork, enjoyment and scaffolding. The teacher also used the tracking features as a formative feedback opportunity to better determine the areas of writing in which students needed support and editing feedback.

In sum, interactive writing technologies may well be opening up different notions of what constitutes writing instruction, feedback on writing and the nature of writing itself (Godwin-Jones, 2003; Richardson, 2006; Warschauer & Grimes, 2007). Warschauer and Grimes make a strong case that these newer technologies are shifting three main areas of writing: audience, authorship and artefact. They argue that blogs, for example, reach a much wider audience than ever before and promote a view of the text as 'dialogic interaction' (p. 16). The new environments of blogs are viewed as potential sites for peer feedback, particularly to encourage peer interaction strategies such as drawing attention to linguistic, communicative and interactional features and to develop collaborative projects and writing apprenticeships. Wikis are seen as collaborative spaces that might foster learner autonomy as well as opportunities for joint authorship in the social construction of texts and of norms for interpreting and valuing those texts (Kessler, 2009; Mak & Coniam, 2008; Warschauer & Grimes, 2007).

Digital feedback in CALL on speaking

The second section explores digital feedback in tasks focused upon speaking and pronunciation. Although this research base is less extensive than that of digital feedback on writing, over the past decade there has been a noticeable increase in Web-based oral skills development. With the introduction of technologies such as Flash and Java that support the exchange of video and audio, there has been a rise in the use of new tools to support oral skills and a consequent increase in research that examines both automated as well as human-delivered modes of feedback.

Automated feedback on speaking

Many projects have incorporated automated speech recognition (ASR) to produce automated feedback for language learners. Notable among these are the automated system for accent reduction (AZAR), TELL ME MORE®, My English Teacher (MyET) and the Carnegie Mellon FLUENCY project. While other systems have been developed, there has been little evidence of research into their use or effectiveness. Therefore, these will serve as samples for the purpose of this discussion.

Recent systems developed through the lineage of the FLUENCY project include NativeAccent®, SpeakIraqi™, SpeakFarsi™ and SpeakRussian™, which all share the same interface and functionality. According to the company that created these products, Carnegie Speech (2011), they offer, 'pinpointed speech analysis [that] provides users with immediate, understandable and actionable feedback, and the Intelligent Tutor personalizes NativeAccent® speech training' (n.p.). Figure 17.1 is a screenshot from Native Accent that illustrates feedback following a student's incorrect production of a word-initial /m/ sound.

As Figure 17.1 illustrates, while the intelligent tutor within the Native Accent system does an assessment to determine which segmental and suprasegmental characteristics an individual student needs to work on, this feedback is the same for all users with an error regarding word-initial /m/. This lack of individualized situation-specific detail in automated feedback is common. In fact, Chen (2011) revisited the FLUENCY project and found that teachers requested significant

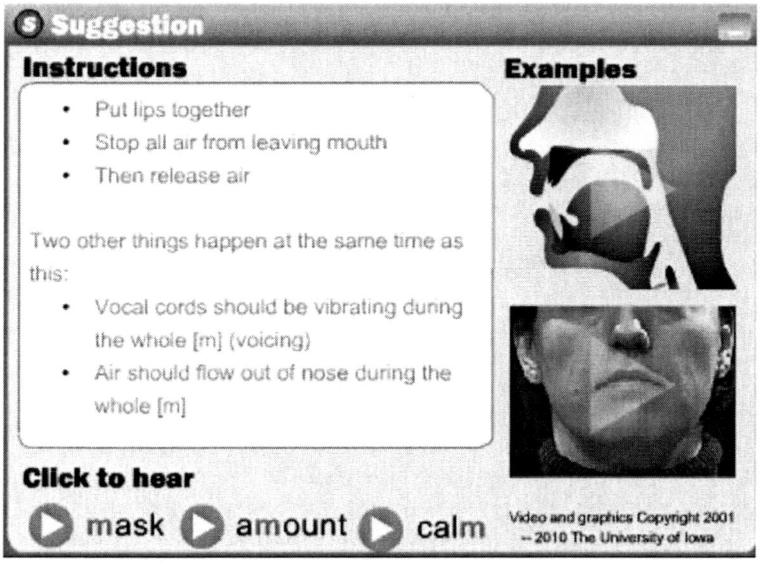

FIGURE 17.1 *NativeAccent® Feedback for Word Initial /m/.*

improvements to the feedback system, particularly regarding specific details about segmentals and suprasegmentals. While there has been a generally positive response from students using these systems for extensive pronunciation practice, the one consistent complaint has related to the limited nature of feedback (Chen, 2006; Chiu, Liou & Yeh, 2007; Liao, 2009). Some previous researchers have discussed the implications of a student's ability to adjust the acceptability threshold within these systems. While this may result in more accurate recognition, the feedback is largely unaffected. Further, students may be likely to adjust this as either too accepting or too demanding based on their emotional choices rather than on their language needs (Chen, 2001, 2011; O'Brien, 2006).

Another sample project is the AZAR Project for teaching German, which utilizes a lip recognition process that provides distinct user feedback, including lip width and height. This system provides students with visual feedback related to these phenomena. One study into the use of this system examined native Russian speakers who were learning German (Jokisch, Koloska, Hirschfeld & Hoffman, 2005). Their article highlights the unique nature of the AZAR system, which is based upon lip recognition. Investigation into its use concluded that varied means of feedback provides additional beneficial information to students.

Recent developments in ASR have found their way into various mainstream products, including those used for dictation and automated phone systems. Google® Voice offers a free voicemail transcription service that can be integrated with an existing or virtual phone number. Using English, the system automatically identifies clearly understood speech with dark black text while speech that is not understood is grayed.

This means of automated feedback may be most beneficial when integrated within a classroom context, as research has concluded that even when students are satisfied with automated feedback, they may still be concerned about the ability to be understood by native speakers (Hirata, 2004). Further, Chen (2011) identified that the rigidity of exercises using automated feedback did not allow for individual learner's interlanguage production, a concern that can be addressed by classroom teachers.

Human-generated feedback on speaking

In recent years we have witnessed the development of numerous opportunities for human-generated digital speech interaction. Many of the same principles that apply to feedback in automated systems should be considered in a mode of delivery that is delivered by people. In fact, it may be more difficult to predict, manage and track the feedback provided by teachers and student peers, since they are likely to respond on occasion in ways that are potentially distracting, demanding, emotional, personal or confusing. Further, due to the limited nature of feedback provided by automated systems, it may be most important that instructors are able to intervene when necessary and elaborate upon feedback.

Some recent technologies that have expanded the potential for human-generated oral production feedback include both free and commercial products as well as standalone Web-based tools, subscription services and tools embedded within learning management systems (LMS) such as Moodle and Blackboard. Figure 17.2 provides an example of feedback in an Indonesian language class within the Moodle Module Nanogong.

The Moodle/Nanogong combination allows students to record their speech, and the teacher clicks on the speaker icon to listen. Students can leave messages for the teacher as well. The teacher can leave comments, a grade and their own response message. The interaction is organized in tabular format for each assignment in a course. Another example within an LMS context is the Portable (PoodLL). While the Moodle/Nanogong and Moodle/PoodLL combination was designed for instructional use, it was not intended specifically for language learning, but CALL has often benefited from adopting such technology tools intended for varied purposes and audiences to fit the

Student Name 1

Submit Date		Message	Comments	Score
Friday, 19 November 2010, 11:09 AM		Pemdapat saya dari presentasi oleh Katie	Memperlambat	95

Student Name 2

Submit Date		Message	Comments	Score
Friday, 19 November 2010, 01:31 PM			Sangat baik	100

FIGURE 17.2 *Moodle/Nangong audio recording and teacher feedback.*

field's needs. Other examples of similar voice boards include Wimba (www.wimba.com/assets/videos/VoiceBoard/ VoiceBoard.html) and Voxopop (www.voxopop.com).

Engwall and Bålter (2007) compared pronunciation feedback between real and virtual language teachers. They noted that some successful strategies used by automated systems would not succeed when used by teachers (and vice versa). They noted that the lack of corrective feedback within class might necessitate the integration of automated feedback. Consequently, automated feedback may best be used out of class. They suggest that students may benefit most when they are allowed to define the amount of feedback they receive from an automated system. Allowing students to make decisions about their feedback interaction is likely to enhance their overall experience.

Challenges and future expectations of feedback on speaking

One limitation that has been recognized across a range of automated feedback systems is the lack of distinct individualized feedback (Engwall & Bålter, 2007; Mitra, Inamdar & Dixond, 2003). While a wide variety of automated responses may be available within a system, there is often a gap between the specific feedback needs of a learner and the information offered by the system. It is quite possible that language teachers without extensive phonological knowledge and experience working with feedback may also lack the ability to provide the optimal information in any given situation. This is particularly likely given that numerous researchers have concluded that language teachers are often inadequately prepared to teach pronunciation (Derwing & Munro, 2005). It is also important that teachers recognize the benefits of ASR systems and make attempts to incorporate them into instruction as is appropriate. Due to the limited nature of feedback offered by these systems, they are most likely to be useful when used in the context of a language class. Technologies will continue to be developed that support teachers in providing quality feedback that is accessible and appropriate for individual learners.

Conclusions

This chapter has presented an overview of the scholarship that has examined the role of feedback in the language classroom in both writing and speaking contexts. Different perspectives, purposes and implementation practices in using digital feedback inform this wide range of research. The research and practice presented here offer a starting point for understanding the role of feedback in the teaching of writing and speaking. As research, pedagogy and automated technologies continue to receive scholarly attention, convergence on some of the dimensions explored here is likely to take place and offer a better understanding of optimal feedback conditions across language learning contexts, learners and modes of delivery. There is still much to be learned about what constitutes quality and effective feedback across the three dimensions of mode of delivery, focus of feedback provided and strategies for feedback delivery. However, the growth in technological tools that provide new modes for delivery and expanded strategies for providing feedback make this area of research an intriguing field of inquiry for CALL researchers.

References

Attali, Y., & Burstein, J. (2006). Automated essay scoring with e-rater v.2. *Journal of Technology, Learning and Assessment, 4*(3), 1–30.

Belz, J. A. (2002). Social dimensions of telecollaborative foreign language study. *Language Learning & Technology, 6*(1), p. 60–81.

Bloch, J. (2007). Abdullah's blogging: A generation 1.5 student enters the blogosphere. *Language Learning & Technology, 11*(2), 128–41.

Bower, J., & Kawaguchi, S. (2011). Negotiation of meaning and corrective feedback in Japanese/English eTandem. *Language Learning & Technology, 15*(1), 41–71.

Brock, M. (1990). Customizing a computerized text analyzer for ESL writers: Cost versus gain. *CALICO Journal, 8*(2), 51–60.

— (1993). Three disk-based text analyzers and the ESL writer. *Journal of Second Language Writing, 2*(1), 19–40.

Burston, J. (2001). Computer-mediated feedback in composition correction. *CALICO Journal, 19*(1), 37–50.

Carnegie Speech (2011). Native Accent. Retrieved from www.carnegiespeech.com/products/nativeaccent.php

Chen, H-J. (2001). Evaluating five speech recognition programs for ESL learners. Paper presented at the ITMELT 2001 Conference, Hong Kong. Retrieved from http://elc.polyu.edu.hk/ conference/papers2001/chen.htm

— (2011). Developing and evaluating an oral skills training website supported by automatic speech recognition technology. *ReCALL, 23*(1), 59–78.

Chen, M-W. (2006). The impact of automatic speech technology on contrastive stress among adult EFL learners. Unpublished Masters thesis, Da-Yeh University.

Chen, C-F., & Cheng, W-Y. (2008). Beyond the design of automated writing evaluation: Pedagogical practices and perceived learning effectiveness in EFL writing classes. *Language Learning & Technology, 12*(2), 94–112.

Cheville, J. (2004). Automated scoring technologies and the rising influence of error. *English Journal, 93*(4), 47–52.

Chiu, T., Liou, H., & Yeh, Y. (2007) A study of Web-based oral activities enhanced by automatic speech recognition for EFL college learning. *Computer Assisted Language Learning, 20*(3), 209–33.

Chodorow, M., & Leacock, C. (2000). An unsupervised method for detecting grammatical errors. In *Proceedings of the 1st Annual Meeting of the North American Chapter of the Association for Computational Linguistics* (pp. 140–7).

Chung, K. W. K., & Baker, E. L. (2003). Issues in the reliability and validity of automated scoring of constructed responses. In M. D. Shermis & J. C. Burstein (Eds.), *Automated essay scoring: A cross-disciplinary perspective* (pp. 23–39). Hillsdale, NJ: Lawrence Erlbaum Associates.

Darhower, M. (2008). The role of linguistic affordances in telecollaborative chat. *CALICO Journal, 26*, 48–69.
Derwing, T. M., & Munro, M. J. (2005). Second language accent and pronunciation teaching: A research-based approach. *TESOL Quarterly, 39*(3), 379–97.
DiGiovanni, E., & Nagaswami, G. (2001). Online peer review: An alternative to face-to-face? *ELT Journal, 55*(3), 263–72.
Dikli, S. (2006). An overview of automated scoring of essays. *Journal of Technology, Learning, and Assessment, 5*(1), 1–35.
Ducate, L., & Lomicka, L. (2008). Adventures in the blogosphere: From blog readers to blog writers. *Computer Assisted Language Learning, 21*(1), 9–28.
Elliot, S., Darlington, K., & Mikulas, C. (2004). *But does it really work? A national study of MYAccess! Effectiveness.* Paper presented at the National Council on Measurement in Education in San Diego, CA. April, 2004.
Engwall, O., & Bålter, O. (2007). Pronunciation feedback from real and virtual language teachers. *Computer Assisted Language Learning, 20*(3), 235–62.
Eskenazi, M. (1999). Using automatic speech processing for foreign language pronunciation tutoring: Some issues and a prototype. *Language Learning & Technology, 2*(2), 62–76.
Fang, Y. (2010). Perceptions of the computer-assisted writing program among EFL college learners. *Educational Technology & Society, 13*(3), 246–56.
Farmer, R. A. (2005). Multimodal speech recognition errors and second language acquisition: An activity theoretic account. *Sixieme colloque des Usages des Nouvelles Technologies dans l'Enseignement des Langues Etrangeres* (UNTELE).
Ferris, D. (2004). The grammar correction debate in L2 writing: Where are we, and where do we go from here? (and what do we do in the meantime . . . ?). *Journal of Second Language Writing, 13*, 49–62.
— (2006). Does error feedback help student writers? New evidence on the short-and long-term effects of written error correction. In K. Hyland & F. Hyland (Eds.), *Feedback on ESL writing: Context and issues* (pp. 81–104). Cambridge: Cambridge University Press.
Gebhard, M., & Harman, R. (2011). Reconsidering genre theory in K-12 schools: A response to school reform in the United States. Special Edition of *Journal of Second Language Writing, 20*(1), 45–55.
Godwin-Jones, R. (2003). Blogs and wikis: Environments for online collaboration. *Language Learning & Technology, 7*(2), 12–16.
Guardado, M., & Shi, L. (2007). ESL students' experiences of online peer feedback. *Computers and Composition, 24*, 443–61.
Herrington, A., & Moran, C. (2001). What happens when machines read our students' writing? *College English, 63*(4), 480–99.
Hirata Y. (2004). Computer assisted pronunciation training for native English speakers learning Japanese pitch and duration contrasts. *Computer Assisted Language Learning, 17*(3), 357–76.
Ho, M-C., & Savignon, S. J. (2007). Face-to-face and computer-mediated peer review in EFL writing. *CALICO Journal, 24*(2), 269–90.
Hyland, K., & Hyland, F. (2006). *Feedback in second language writing: Contexts and issues.* New York, NY: Cambridge University Press.
Kamhi-Stein, L. D. (2000). Looking to the future of TESOL teacher education: Web-based bulletin board discussions in a methods course. *TESOL Quarterly, 34*, 423–55.
Kern, R., & Warschauer, M. (2000). Theory and practice of network-based language teaching. In M. Warschauer & R. Kern (Eds.), *Network-based language teaching: Concepts and practice* (pp. 1–19). New York: Cambridge University Press.

Kern, R., Ware, P., & Warschauer, M. (2004). Crossing frontiers: New directions in online pedagogy and research. *Annual Review of Applied Linguistics, 24*, 243–60.

Kessler, G. (2009). Student-initiated attention to form in wiki-based collaborative writing. *Language Learning & Technology, 13*(1), 79–95.

Jokisch, O., Koloska, U., Hirschfeld, D., & Hoffmann, R. (2005). Pronunciation learning and foreign accent reduction by an audiovisual feedback system. *Proceedings of 1st Intern. Conference on Affective Computing and Intelligent Interaction (ACII)*, Beijing (pp. 419–25).

Lamy, M.-N., & Goodfellow, R. (1999). 'Reflective conversation' in the virtual language classroom. *Language Learning & Technology, 2*(2), 43–61.

Leacock, C. (2004). Scoring free-responses automatically: A case study of a large-scale assessment. *Examens, 1*(3).

Lee, L. (2006). A study of native and nonnative speakers' feedback and responses in Spanish-American networked collaborative interaction. In J. Belz & S. Thorne (Eds.), *Internet-mediated intercultural foreign language education* (pp. 147–76). Boston, MA: Thomson & Heinle.

Lee, Y-W., Gentile, C., & Kantor, R. (2010). Toward automated multi-trait scoring of essays: Investigating links among holistic, analytic, and text feature scores. *Applied Linguistics, 31*(3), 391–417.

Liao, C. F. (2009). EFL Learners' use of contrastive stress supported with automatic speech analysis system. Unpublished Masters Thesis, Da-Yeh University.

Mak, B., & Coniam, D. (2008). Using wikis to enhance and develop writing skills among secondary school students in Hong Kong. *System, 36*, 437–55.

Matsumura, S., & Hann, G. (2004). Computer anxiety and students' preferred feedback methods in EFL writing. *The Modern Language Journal, 88*, 403–15.

McCrickard, D. S., & Chewar, C. M. (2003). Attuning notification design to user goals and attention costs. *Communication of the ACM, 46*(3), 67–72.

Miltsakaki, E., & Kukich, K. (2000). Automated evaluation of coherence in student essays. Paper presented at LREC-2000, Linguistic Resources in Education Conference. Athens, Greece.

Mitra, S., Tooley, J., Inamdar, P., & Dixond, P. (2003). Improving English pronunciation: An automated instructional approach. *Information Technologies & International Development, 1*(1), 75–84.

O'Brien, M. (2006). Teaching pronunciation and intonation with computer technology. In L. Ducate & N. Arnold (Eds.), *Calling on CALL: From theory and research to new directions in foreign language teaching* (pp. 1–20). San Marcos, TX: Computer Assisted Language Instruction Consortium.

O'Dowd, R. (2003). Understanding the 'other side': Intercultural learning in a Spanish-English email exchange. *Language Learning & Technology, 7*(2), 118–44.

O'Rourke, B. (2005). Form-focused interaction in online tandem learning. *CALICO Journal, 22*, 433–66.

Oladi, S. (2005). *Study of Tehran medical students' social interaction in cyber blogging environment and its effect on IELTS writing proficiency.* Unpublished Masters thesis. Tehran University, Tehran.

Page, E. (2003). Project essay grade: PEG. In M. D. Shermis & J. Burstein (Eds.), *Automated essay scoring: A cross-disciplinary perspective* (pp. 43–54). Hillsdale, NJ: Lawrence Erlbaum Associates.

Parks, S., Huot, D., Hamers, J., & Lemmonier, F. (2003). Crossing boundaries: Multimedia technology and pedagogical innovation in a high school class. *Language Learning & Technology, 7*(1), 28–45.

Richardson, W. (2006). *Blogs, wikis, podcasts, and other powerful Web tools for classrooms*. Newbury Park, CA: Corwin Press.
Sauro, S. (2009). Computer-mediated corrective feedback and the development of L2 grammar. *Language Learning & Technology, 13*(1), 96–120.
Sauro, S., & Smith, B. (2010). Investigating L2 performance in text chat. *Applied Linguistics, 31*(4), 554–77.
Schultz, J. M. (2000). Computers and collaborative writing in the foreign language curriculum. In M. Warschauer & R. Kern (Eds.), *Network-based language learning: Concepts and practice* (pp. 121–50). Cambridge, UK: Cambridge University Press.
Sengupta, S. (2001). Exchanging ideas with peers in network-based classrooms: An aid or a pain? *Language Learning & Technology, 5*(1), 103–34.
Shermis, M. D., & Burstein, J. (2003). Introduction. *Automated essay scoring: A cross-disciplinary perspective* (pp. xiii–xvi). Hillsdale, NJ: Lawrence Erlbaum Associates, Inc.
Smith, B. (2005). The relationship between negotiated interaction, learner uptake, and lexical acquisition in task-based computer-mediated communication. *TESOL Quarterly, 39*(1), 33–58.
Sotillo, M. S. (2005). Corrective feedback via instant messenger learning activities in NS-NNS and NNS-NNS dyads. *CALICO Journal, 22*(3), 467–96.
Tuzi, F. (2004). The impact of e-feedback on the revisions of L2 writers in an academic writing course. *Computers and Composition, 21*, 217–35.
Ware, P. (2005). 'Missed' communication in online communication: Tensions in a German-American telecollaboration. *Language Learning & Technology, 9*(2), 64–89.
Ware, P., & O'Dowd, R. (2008). Peer feedback on language form in telecollaboration. *Language Learning & Technology, 12*(1), 43–63.
Ware, P., & Warschauer, M. (2006). Electronic feedback and second language writing. In K. Hyland & F. Hyland (Eds.), *Feedback on ESL writing: Context and issues* (pp. 105–22). Cambridge: Cambridge University Press.
Warschauer, M., & Grimes, D. (2007). Audience, authorship, and artifact: The emergent semiotics of Web 2.0. *Annual Review of Applied Linguistics, 27*(1), 1–23.
— (2008). Automated writing assessment in the classroom. *Pedagogies, 3*(1), 52–67.
Warschauer, M., & Ware, P. (2006). Automated writing evaluation: Defining the classroom research agenda. *Language Teaching Research, 10*(2), 1–24.
Woo, M., Chu, S., Ho, A., & Li, X. (2011). Using a wiki to scaffold primary school students' collaborative writing. *Journal of Educational Technology & Society, 14*(1), 43–54.
Yuan, Y. (2003). The use of chat rooms in an ESL setting. *Computers and Composition, 20*, 194–206.

18

Task-based language teaching and CALL

Michael Thomas

Summary

At the same time as computer-assisted language learning (CALL) has developed over the last three decades, task-based language teaching (TBLT) has emerged as one of the most important methodologies in second and foreign language learning. The chapter provides a brief overview of the relationship between CALL and TBLT focusing on the extant and potential pedagogical implications. The review suggests that both have a great deal to learn from each other, particularly in relation to the design, sequence and understanding of tasks, as well as the behaviour of learners in a task cycle. In the second half of the chapter, the potential relationship between CALL and TBLT is analysed via a case study of a group of Japanese learners of English and their use of Web 2.0 digital media applications. Two of the aims of the study were to examine L2 learner identity and the challenges faced by learners within a task-based environment utilizing technology. The research found that (1) contrary to essentialist accounts of Asian English language learners as resistant to interactive learning environments, learners were highly engaged by the collaborative task-based approach and were successful at producing completed tasks in English, but (2) they remained over-reliant on their L1 (Japanese) during the planning and processing phases of the technology-enhanced tasks. The latter finding calls into question the ability of the learners to benefit from a task-based approach if their existing language skills are insufficiently developed.

Introduction

Often seen as a natural evolution of the communicative language teaching approach (CLT), TBLT has been growing in influence since the early 1980s (Van den Branden, Bygate & Norris, 2009). TBLT is concerned with a process-based language learning pedagogy that emphasizes the importance of learner communication in the target language and attempts to embody these principles by designing highly structured syllabi and curricula with clear objectives for instructors and learners. While understanding linguistic forms remains important, meaning is considered primary and real-world tasks are used to establish the importance of authentic learning environments (Ellis, 2003).

TBLT is an experiential approach to language learning, as exemplified by the Digital Kitchen project at the University of Newcastle-upon-Tyne, United Kingdom, where researchers have developed a fully functioning kitchen with sophisticated sensor technology to teach learners French while also engaged in their weekly catering course (Price, 2011; Seedhouse, Ali, Jackson, Ploetz & Olivier, 2011). By following the steps in the recipe and interacting with real cooking equipment, learners' actions activate audio recordings of the instructions in French. As the Digital Kitchen suggests, TBLT is based on the principle that by engaging the learners in real processes they will be able to interact, enhance their motivation for language learning and engage in negotiation of meaning in the target language. As Seedhouse argues, the Digital Kitchen 'tackles the fundamental problems you have when learning a language. In a classroom you're only rehearsing it; the kitchen means that people can learn language while they're performing a real-world task' (Price, 2011, n.p.). It is typical therefore to see TBLT described as a combination of communicative tasks, non-linguistic goals and engagement in real-world activities, as Seedhouse continues

> If you take the approach that we're using – which is task-based learning and teaching. . . . The basic idea is that you learn a language best while you're engaged in a physical task, performing something tangible rather than the way we traditionally think of foreign languages being taught in a classroom, where the teacher tells you how to put a sentence together. It's not terribly motivating for most people. It's not something physically real. Whereas the kitchen, in effect, is taking task-based learning out of the classroom and into the kitchen. (Price, 2011, n.p.)

The Digital Kitchen project would appear to be one way of developing a relationship between technology and TBLT, though one that is dependent on highly sophisticated and expensive technology at the current time. Such an innovative project is clearly not an option in many language teaching contexts, particularly outside the developed world or in low-tech contexts (see Gonzales & St. Louis, this volume). While the Digital Kitchen project demonstrates the instructional goals of the process-oriented approach, the project also foregrounds a number of significant challenges for TBLT. These include the fact that learners are typically asked to engage with TBLT in their normal classrooms, an assumption that requires them to suspend knowledge of their actual context and to imagine they are somewhere else (Ellis, 2003). This attempt to replicate real-work environments though admirable can be difficult to realize in traditional teaching contexts, where learners are more fully conscious of their location and its parameters and thus find it challenging to be immersed in their environment, particularly if it is an EFL one (e.g., a Chinese person studying English in China). Other challenges relate to the characteristics required of learners in TBLT, such as more independence and confidence in the target language, as well as simple classroom management issues facing teachers if they are required to control large classes of foreign language learners who may all be talking at the same time.

Historically the emergence of TBLT coincided with that of personal computers in educational institutions. Strikingly, however, research over the last three decades often reveals that CALL and TBLT have been running in parallel lines that rarely crossed until the mid-1990s. From that point onwards, more research started to be undertaken and it has sought to uncover ways in which TBLT can provide a pedagogical framework or rationale for work in CALL, as well as how CALL can help to overcome a number of the challenges and critiques aimed at TBLT (Chapelle, 2001; Ellis, 2003; Lai & Li, 2011; Ortega, 2009). In this more recent research it is clear that five areas of interest can be identified, including learner motivation, opportunities to develop authentic environments, the use of digital feedback, opportunities to afford learners' greater choices and the potential to participate in enriched learner communities (Ortega, 2009).

The role of computer-mediated communication (CMC) has played a central role in these five areas and offers learners opportunities to engage in real-time communication (via synchronous text and instant messaging) as well as reflective engagement via asynchronous applications (such as discussion forums and email). While research has discussed a number of points at the intersection of SLA and TBLT, including noticing, negotiation of meaning, and strategies for focusing on form (Skeehan, 2003), the approaches have often developed pedagogical practices that would be more appropriate for presence-based learning contexts than for those required by technology-mediated environments (Hampel, 2005). A second gap in existing research relates to the lack of studies on TBLT and CALL in non-Western contexts such as Asia. Typically essentialist arguments suggest that Asian learners demonstrate greater passivity in instructional contexts such that they would not fit well with task-based approaches (Vallance, 2009). Consequently, TBLT may be more challenging with Asian learners who are considered to be more reliant on teacher direction. Third, more research is required on lower-level learners, who simply do not possess the language skills to interact in sophisticated ways regardless of whether the environment is authentic or not.

In her keynote address at the TBLT 2009 conference, Ortega argued that future research on TBLT and technology needs to consider more 'real-world' spaces such as online 'open social spaces, gaming, [and] immersive environments' if the potential encounter is to be realized. This chapter is divided into three sections, the first two of which focus on providing a brief overview of research on TBLT and CALL and the pedagogical implications of TBLT for CALL. In the final part, and by way of a response to Ortega (2009), case-study research utilizing Web 2.0 collaborative technologies with lower-intermediate-level Asian learners of English in an EFL setting in Japan is discussed, focusing in particular on how TBLT with technology can influence L2 learner identity.

Task-based language teaching (TBLT)

The provenance of task-based approaches lies outside language learning and in more general theories of education which underline the importance of experiential or 'hands-on' learning. The American philosopher of education, John Dewey, is typically identified as an influential early advocate of TBL and there are strong interrelationships between his notion of problem-based learning, the value of experience, enhancing learner motivation and task-based approaches. Dewey's (1938) philosophy of education was collaborative in outlook, emphasizing that meaning emerges from collective experience and the willingness of people to work together. It also attempted to deconstruct prevailing binary thinking that marginalized the value of experience or practical knowledge in relation to theoretical knowledge. Engaging learners rather than wasting their time on impractical tasks that are likely to have no bearing on their lives or work was a central organizing principle for Dewey, such that TBL is expected to draw on the rich experience learners already have. Task-based approaches are therefore not new and there is thus a strong line of influence running from Dewey to Bruner (1960) through to constructivist thought (Vygotsky, 1978) and contemporary TBL.

In language learning, TBL owes a great deal to early research by Prabhu (1987) who posited the importance of problem-solving activities and the task as a structuring principle of syllabus design in opposition to the then prevalent form of linguistic syllabus, which was organized according to the linear mastery of linguistic forms. Prabhu's early work in India has clear lines of influence from interactionist theories in SLA theory to sociocultural and ecological approaches which also place an emphasis on learner interaction, the importance of the learning environment for supporting and scaffolding learner development and the real-world implications of the process.

TBLT, then, evolved by placing an emphasis on interaction, cognitive processing and authentic language use through negotiation of meaning (Bygate, Skehan & Swain, 2001; Nunan, 2004). Long (1990) focused on meaning negotiation in relation to problem-solving tasks. Pica, Kanagy and Falodun (1993) similarly indicated that negotiation of meaning is related to increased levels of interactive tasks. Research on interactive tasks emphasized how they produced greater complexity and accuracy in terms of output than non-interactive tasks, which tended to focus more on fluency (Skehan & Foster, 1997). Moreover, research on task planning indicates that it improves performance in accuracy and fluency (Ortega, 1999). Other important areas of research include the use of task repetition to enhance syntactic quality and use of the target language. Research on task-based approaches, as Willis (1996) argued, emphasizes the importance of exposure to authentic input, and sustained meaningful use of the target language for aiding output and learner motivation. In this respect Klapper's (2003) definition of task has become influential and representative of this approach:

> Tasks . . . are meaning-based activities closely related to learners' actual communicative needs and with some real-world relationship, in which learners have to achieve a genuine outcome (solve a problem, reach a consensus, complete a

puzzle, play a game etc.) and in which effective completion of the tasks is accorded priority. (p. 35)

To this definition we must also add the dimension of learner–learner collaboration and what Meskill (1999) calls sociocollaborative learning tasks. Based on this wider definition it is also worthwhile to highlight Lamy's (2007) definition, one which strikes a cord with Ortega's (2009) interest in the collective problem-solving aspects associated with Web-based gaming and immersive environments. According to this broader working definition, which is highly cognizant of the potential of technology to produce sociocollaborative interaction, Lai and Li (2011) suggest that tasks should be seen as 'holistic activities in which learners make use of their language and (cross-) cultural and communicative resources to achieve some nonlinguistic outcome through stretching their linguistic, (cross-) cultural, internet-based communication, and digital literacy skills' (p. 502).

TBLT and CALL: Reality and potential

As the Digital Kitchen project reminds us, technology can provide opportunities to transcend the limitations of the traditional classroom context. Online materials and applications can significantly enhance the types, authenticity and range of tasks that learners engage in. Moreover, through Web 2.0 technologies likes blogs and wikis and other collaborative tools, learners can emphasize their creative skills, author and produce outputs for an external audience and engage in activities which underline their active rather than passive participation (Lankshear & Knobel, 2011). Technology can promote learner agency in language learning contexts, corroborating constructivist goals and marginalizing the notion that learners are merely empty vessels to be filled with knowledge poured into them by more knowledgeable instructors.

Earlier research by Chun (1994) and Kern (1995) suggests that learners in CMC environments found them to be more motivating and resulted in lower levels of learner anxiety than interacting in presence-based environments. Abrams' (2003) findings indicate that synchronous CMC could enhance the amount of output produced by learners. In terms of the quality of output, there is also research which argues that text-based chatting can result in enhanced accuracy and complexity of target language use (Salaberry, 2000). One of the main foci of research on CMC in language learning contexts has been on the differences between synchronous and asynchronous performance. Studies indicate an opportunity for real-time spoken CMC to produce creative dialogues and conversation (Hwang, 2008), whereas written asynchronous studies have found that learners benefit from greater opportunities to reflect on their outputs and grammatical errors (Yamada, 2009). Key studies from Doughty and Long (2003), González-Lloret (2007) and Skehan (2003) elaborate on this potential for closer connections between CALL and TBLT.

While Chapelle (2003) called for greater consideration of research on CALL in second language acquisition, more studies on TBLT need to be aware of this potential in relation to the critiques often levelled at it. Van den Branden, Bygate and Norris' (2009) otherwise milestone reader on key TBLT research over the last three decades, significantly does not include a chapter on research utilizing technology. This is a striking omission given that leading CALL scholars such as Levy and Stockwell (2006) argue that research on language learning tasks has been a 'pivotal component in [CALL] design' (p. 14) since the mid-1980s.

Developments over the last five years in Web 2.0 applications suggest a renewed interest in a task-based approach utilizing technology (Mak & Coniam, 2008; Thomas & Reinders, 2010). According to O'Reilly (2005), Web 2.0 is related to a new attitude towards the use of internet technology, emphasizing the development of a truly networked environment in which new applications are automatically updated online and users actively contribute to content in what he calls an 'architecture of participation'. Whereas the first generation of the Web was popularly conceived of as a one-dimensional 'read only' experience, the applications associated with Web 2.0 enable users to interact with the 'read-write' Web in which they can actively contribute and interact (Warschauer & Grimes, 2007). Web 2.0 consists of a series of new technologies with a powerful social outlook with one of the aims being to promote community building in authentic online environments (Mak & Coniam, 2008).

Virtual worlds and language learning

Among these emerging Web 2.0 technologies are three-dimensional (3D) virtual worlds (VWs). Whereas early versions of virtual worlds such as Multiple User Domains Object Oriented (MOOs) were dependent on interaction via text chat, the latest generation uses a 3D landscape complete with buildings and land for new development. A number of virtual worlds such as Active Worlds and World of Warcraft have become popular, while Second Life has been used most often by presence based and distance learning educators, particularly in language education (Wankel & Kingsley, 2009; see also Sadler & Dooly, this volume).

For researchers who examine language learning in virtual worlds, a number of areas of interest emerge. These include research on improvements in learner attentiveness to pedagogical activities as well as general classroom behaviour and participation (Molka-Danielsen & Deutschmann, 2009). Learners engage in text and audio-based interaction, design and personalize 3D representations of themselves in the form of avatars and engage in the construction of objects. Research by Jarmon (2010) confirms that students' satisfaction with learning in VWs like Second Life was high when using authentic tasks, and that learners reported on significant opportunities for enhanced levels of engagement in online environments. Typically VWs have been identified as learning environments which promote opportunities for constructivist-led pedagogies in which learners can engage in text and voice chat activities connected with problem-solving, collaborative learning, knowledge-building and role-playing activities. Building on MOOs and their emphasis on encouraging a first person level of engagement, VWs continue this by developing a richer experience for participants. Typically constructivist approaches which underline the importance of collaborative or social engagement as the basis for learning, have been closely identified with the use of Web 2.0 applications in education. Svensson (2003), for example, found that learners in a virtual world were more focused on their learning and were less likely to be distracted by interaction unrelated to the main tasks.

Building on research into the use of text-based MOOs, research on VWs has indicated their positive potential in relation to reducing resistance to learning from students and aiding a less inhibited space where role-playing activities can be encouraged (Jarmon, 2010). Other features which are conducive to research on CMC include the ability to track learner input via chat logs and video screen recording. These can also provide useful documents for learners to reflect on their language use. Typically researchers have employed ethnographic approaches utilizing video recording and chat logs in order to understand learners' in-world behaviour and perception of virtual worlds and a range of disciplines, age-ranges and types of virtual world have thus far been examined (Molka-Danielsen & Deutschmann, 2009).

Case study on Web 2.0 digital media and TBL

The context for this research was an intensive English language communication course spread over one calendar week with 25 third- and fourth-year undergraduates at a university in Japan. From this group of lower intermediate learners, one pair of students aged 21, 1 male (henceforth *Yoshiaki*) and 1 female (henceforth *Eri*), were selected at random for the case-study research. In this case I had previously taught and observed the pair working both individually and with other partners in a non-technology-mediated context during a year-long English language module. Yoshiaki had significantly less oral fluency in English than Eri, who had studied abroad for one semester on a language exchange programme in the United Kingdom. Yoshiaki also scored over 150 points lower on the TOEIC proficiency test. A survey at the beginning of the class identified that none of the students from the cohort had previously used Second Life, were familiar with the Web 2.0 applications used to scaffold their learning (e.g., the collaborative mind-mapping application Bubbl.us) or were conscious of having used a TBLT approach. All of the learners were used to English courses in school and university which were driven by commercial language textbooks and a grammar-based syllabus.

The intensive course had a specific focus on communication and technology and expected learners to engage in daily use of CMC to develop their English ability and to explore resources for English language learning. Materials, language learning resources and lesson plans were accessible from the university's Blackboard CMS. The syllabus of the intensive course examined a number of different learning outcomes which are associated with the use of different tasks and the necessary computer applications to achieve them. A variety of Web 2.0 applications were introduced to learners in the course to: (a) scaffold the learning process (e.g., Bubbl.us, a collaborative mind-mapping tool), (b) develop learners' research-based skills (e.g., SurveyMonkey.com, an online survey tool), (c) aid learner creativity (e.g., GarageBand, an application for making podcasts and iMovie for recording and editing videos) and (d) provide an immersive and virtual learning environment for task-based learning to occur (e.g., the virtual world of Second Life).

Consequently, the intensive course was founded on TBL principles in which learners were encouraged to develop higher-order critical thinking and project skills and a holistic approach was adopted (Lai & Li, 2011). Learners were expected to work effectively in collaborative pairs using synchronous and asynchronous applications to achieve clearly identified non-linguistic and linguistic goals (see Table 18.1). The defined task cycle incorporated tasks in which learners had to work together in the role of professional researchers to design and create an interview that would be effective in eliciting data from residents about their in-world relationships. Students were responsible for planning, developing and carrying out the interview with native and non-native speakers of English in Second Life via live voice and/or text chat. The results of the survey were to be reported during a final video presentation task which learners had to produce using the iMovie application.

Adopting a task cycle, two projects were used during the intensive course: Project A (lessons 1–4) and Project B (lessons 5–12) (see Table 18.1). In Project A learners were tasked with producing a 10-minute podcast presentation to be shown to other members of the group in which they were asked to consider the history and development of Second Life. In Project B, learners were asked to develop their understanding of Second Life by developing a research-based survey of respondents, to be conducted in real-time with Second Life residents.

Table 18.2 shows the list of tasks associated with Project B – the focus of the case study in this chapter – in more detail and how it follows a pre-task, during-task and post-task cycle (Willis, 1996).

Data for Project B were collected via researcher observations, field notes, informal interviews and video recordings of the two students working in a pair at their computer screens, as well as the use of a video capture application (Jing.com) to capture some screen activity. The focus of the case study reported here engaged with two main research questions: (1) How do collaborative Web 2.0 tools and environments contribute to language learning during task performance, in terms of improved L2 identity, and (2) What challenges are faced by learners in implementing TBLT with collaborative Web 2.0 tools?

TABLE 18.1 An overview of Project A & B tasks.

Lesson	Room	Title/Genre	Computer applications used	Application function
1	Computer Lab 5	Welcome to the course Course outline		
2 ~ 5	Computer Lab 5	Project A Research-based audio podcast presentation on the topic: *What is Second Life?*	- Bubbl.us - PowerPoint / Keynote (iLife) - SurveyMonkey - Garageband - Web search engines - Second Life	- Mind mapping - Presentation - Survey research and analysis - Audio presentation creation - Web research - Synchronous target language environment
6 ~ 12	Computer Lab 4	Project B Research-based vodcast (video podcast) based on a survey conducted with Second Life residents: *What are the characteristics of residents who use Second Life? In what ways do they use it?*	- Bubbl.us -PowerPoint / Keynote (iLife) - SurveyMonkey - iMovie - Web search engines - Second Life	- Mind mapping - Presentation - Survey research and analysis - Video presentation creation - Web research - Synchronous target language environment

Findings from the project

L2 identity, Web 2.0 tools and a collaborative task-based approach

The early modelling tasks in the cycle (Task 2) immediately sought to engage learners by requiring them to explore examples of previously completed student projects. This was considered a key phase in establishing the manageability of the task. The examples aided Eri and Yoshiaki by demonstrating how previous groups had achieved task

TABLE 18.2 Project B: List of tasks

Task no.	Task cycle	Computer applications	Explanation of the task/ learner involvement
1.	Assigning pairs	Recorded with Word documents accessible in Blackboard	- Students assigned to random pairs
2.	Teacher/student modelling (*pre-task*)	All applications	- Familiarize themselves with authentic examples of previous student projects - Learn to use the Web 2.0 applications in pairs
3.	Planning the project (*during task* phase covers tasks 3–11)	Bubbl.us/Keynote	- Pair collaboration via mind mapping and collaborate multimedia presentations
4.	Designing and conducting the research project	SurveyMonkey Second Life	- Pair collaboration to design and edit an interview - Pair collaboration on Second Life and designation or roles
5.	Writing a presentation script	Bubbl.us/Word	- Pair collaboration on creating a detailed mind map of the presentation script. Focus on language work
6.	Creating the visual message	Internet research/Keynote	- Collaborative Web-based research to enhance their digital media presentations - Wide range of digital literacy skills (e.g., save, editing and resizing images)
7.	Recording the audio/video	Garageband/iMovie	- Collaborative editing of audio files supported by digital picture editing
8.	Integrating the audio and visual message	Garageband/iMovie	- Collaborative editing of audio files supported by digital picture editing
9.	Publishing the podcast/vodcast	Garageband/iTunes	- Collaborative editing in relation to the publication process

Task no.	Task cycle	Computer applications	Explanation of the task/ learner involvement
10.	Peer evaluation of podcasts/vodcasts	SurveyMonkey	- Pair-based presentations of the final recorded presentation to all groups
11.	Instructor feedback on language functions and focus on form (*post-task*)	PowerPoint/Keynote	- Reflect on the language and genre issues raised the presentation structure (e.g., use of present perfect and past simple) - Highlight errors by viewing the recorded videos again

completion, thus stimulating the pair's interest and curiosity. Moreover, the examples scaffolded the learners' initial efforts, and provided a concrete reference point to which they could return for support. By providing the learners with a model that enabled them to value and explore their own experience rather than requiring them to master a disproportionate amount of new content, the learners increased their confidence and could function at key stages in the project independently and through self-regulation (Reinders & White, 2010). Through digital media – in this case recorded videos of final presentations – peer support could be provided even though they were absent in physical terms (Jarmon, 2010). In general, it was noticeable that social presence-based peer scaffolding also took place from the more knowledgeable student during task performance (Rankin, 2008), so that the learners' differing skill sets allowed them to deal with questions internally or provided support if more difficult questions arose. Both students demonstrated peer support skills and both Eri and Yoshiaki occupied the role of knowledgeable other at different stages in the task cycle.

The planning stage of the cycle (Task 3) utilized Bubbl.us, a highly intuitive Web-based mind-mapping tool in which learners could work on two computers but collaborate on a mind map simultaneously by delegating areas of responsibility. Students benefited from each using 21-inch iMac computers which could be positioned side by side one another thereby enabling Eri and Yoshiaki to see what the other was doing during task performance. Eri was a stronger student in both oral and written English skills in non-CMC classes, but was nevertheless typically quieter in group and pair contexts. Through dialogues, facial expressions and body language they both demonstrated that they were working as a team to complete the tasks. Video data captured Eri working effectively on-task in relation to the project timeline and engaging in dialogue when clarification issues arose.

Yoshiaki, while more confident and gregarious in spoken Japanese, was less motivated in learning environments in which English oral skills were required and body language and posture would normally find him slumped in his chair. Once beside the computer, however, video data showed him sitting upright with two hands moving swiftly over the keyboard and he frequently engaged Eri in short question and answer dialogues while gesturing at images or text on either or both computer screens. A higher degree of learner equalization seemed apparent as a consequence, with both students more willing to complement the skill sets of the other. Interview responses confirmed, as Yoshiaki said, that he 'felt more interested in the lesson using technology'.

Yoshiaki therefore demonstrated that he could deal positively with the higher levels of control over his tasks that he had been given, thus supporting the idea that Web 2.0 tools can promote learner agency (Kenning, 2010). While both learners demonstrated signs of agency and confidence in their L2 identity, nevertheless both overwhelmingly chose to communicate in the virtual world parts of the task, namely, interviewing Second Life residents using text chat with a more limited voice chat engagement. Interviews and discussions with students indicated that this was because they felt more comfortable communicating via text chat with foreigners, especially using the 'cover' of anonymity provided by the in-world use of their avatars. Both learners had sufficient keyboard skills to enable them to type effectively and quickly and this may have also contributed to their preferred method of communication.

Observation of text chat and saved logs showed that Eri concentrated closely on using correct grammatical forms, whereas Yoshiaki was able to adopt a freer style and used abbreviations in the text (e.g., 'u' for 'you'). More time may have been needed as well as different physical locations for learners to become more confident in engaging more in voice chat with residents, and this is something that ought to be explored in future iterations of the project. This would seem to suggest that the multimodal environment benefited Yoshiaki to the extent that his L2 identity enabled parts of his L1 identity to manifest itself more overtly than it would have done in traditional L2 classrooms where he often reverted to a more passive subject position (Thorne, 2003).

One further aspect of their L2 identities relates to the types of skills both learners encountered in the technology-mediated environment. In addition to the linguistic skills, learners also indicated a positive understanding of the digital literacy, technology and cross-cultural communication skills they encountered, suggesting that they were useful for future employability (Lankshear & Knobel, 2011). While Eri had previously studied abroad for a short period, she saw the potential of being able to communicate with native and non-native speakers and how this could be used in ESL contexts in particular (Lamy, 2004). Yoshiaki, on the other hand, demonstrated an awareness of the benefits of engaging in sophisticated technology skills such as creating and editing sound and video files, and video recordings of the lessons showed him concentrating hard while highly engaged in this task (Task 6). As the final video task required only a recorded video rather than a live presentation in English in front of his peers, Yoshiaki was also able to maintain his interest and confidence in the project for a longer duration and this contributed to lowering in-class anxiety levels (Lamy, 2004).

The language learning tasks were set up to be learner-centred activities that attempted to develop student interaction and communication in the target language. Typically this is not the case in language learning classes with Japanese students of English at university level, and students expect to be led by teacher-focused activities in which knowledge is transmitted to them in a lecture style (Vallance, 2009). Inhibitions felt by students in typical language classrooms in Japan were discarded during the dyad's immersion in Second Life as the project wore on and it is possible to speculate that continuing the intensive course into a second semester would have continued this positive effect, especially once the initial 'wow' factor of the technology had worn off.

The 3D environment provided authentic activities and the learners experienced immersion in a range of virtual cities, locations and buildings by mastering teleporting. Both Eri and Yoshiaki took a keen interest in the design of their 3D avatars and repeatedly returned to refine their in-world images, activities that suggested a high degree of involvement with their characters and a high degree of embodiment (Jarmon, 2010). Rather than acting as mere observers of language learning activity, their heightened sense of virtual embodiment gave them opportunities to continuously participate in independent ways, adopting a first person level of engagement, rather than in the few opportunities afforded by typical classroom environments in Japan.

Nevertheless, Eri was more sceptical about the use of Second Life, and frequently referred to it as 'like a video game' in interview responses. Having previously worked together on the other collaborative tasks, the students had established leadership roles, with Yoshiaki taking an active lead on technology-related tasks such as typing at the keyboard while Eri undertook the language-based tasks, eagerly deferring to him where choices existed concerned with delegating responsibility and planning. Although Eri's English oral skills were significantly more developed, observation indicated that she chose not to correct her partner's grammatical mistakes indirectly if at all, though it was apparent she was aware of them.

Working independently with her avatar in Second Life, Eri quickly became adept at navigating the various menus and designing her appearance and changing clothing. Her virtual appearance established her creativity and in this respect she was able to act as a knowledgeable other for Yoshiaki, guiding him to locations she had visited to buy free clothing.

Both learners were also observed acting as mentors for other group members, both in smaller teams as well as in the wider class. Feedback from interviews suggested that the VW enhanced student motivation and provided them with potentially more resources online to aid them with their English language tasks. For example, access to online translation and dictionary tools was widely available and used. Learners' development as coaches, however, was restricted by their reluctance to use English and typically coaching took place in Japanese. While the adoption of multiple roles did a great deal to encourage greater interactivity, collaboration and motivation between learners, the dominance of Japanese, unless otherwise commented upon by me in my role as an instructor, tended to neutralize the acquired advantages.

Furthermore, my role as a teacher shifted between a number of different positions, enabling the learners to also do the same. Instructions to learners were directed to the whole group, smaller groups and individuals. In turn learners were able to become expert modellers of instructions and aid other learners in the process of using the technology (Warschauer & Grimes, 2007). Both Eri and Yoshiaki adopted a range of roles and taught other students as they solved various problems, both language and technology related. Through observation and interview answers, it was apparent that the pair's adoption of pseudonyms in Second Life created the cover of a new L2 identity, that this was strengthened in relation to the competence levels they experienced in mastering various digital media applications, and this resulted in a positive learner experience.

Learner challenges in using technology with tasks

Previous research on task-based approaches utilizing technologies has identified a number of potential challenges which may inhibit task performance and completion. These include a lack of technology skills or cross-cultural understanding and expectations (Hampel, 2005). Learners may also not be prepared for the types of learner collaboration required or the emphasis on using the target language (Lai & Li, 2011).

Although neither Eri nor Yoshiaki had used Web 2.0 tools before or visited a virtual world, they encountered few problems in learning to use the technology, given that the applications invited experiment and a trial and error approach. In personal comments during the lesson, Eri indicated that she did not feel comfortable with computers but this was not clear from her actual performance, which demonstrated her ability to quickly and intuitively grasp the applications she had to use. She was particularly skilled in her use of creating visually attractive and highly structured mind maps, and this allowed her creativity to show itself in ways which would normally not have been possible in non-technology-mediated classes. This finding does suggest that both learners were adept at using Web-based environments with little training, a conclusion supported by a results from a survey of all learners' experience with digital technologies conducted prior to the start of Project A.

Though previous research has highlighted the challenges posed by learners who lack digital literacy skills (Reinders & White, 2010), this was not the case for either of the two students. Using the examples of previous project work once again enabled them to imagine their own solution as well as possible routes to take in order to achieve their goals. Both learners revealed a lack of sophisticated Web search skills, typically typing in single words rather than engaging in multi-concept searching. But while the concept of a digital generation remains problematical (Prensky, 2001), both learners showed they had key skills, though Eri lacked confidence in speaking about it, a fact that may suggest more about the nature of gender relations between male and female learners in Japan (Vallance, 2009).

Spread over one week the intensive course mirrored the time typically allocated to learners during one semester. Both Eri and Yoshiaki benefited from the more focused and sustained opportunities offered by the intensive course which allowed them to learn in an uninterrupted fashion, unlike typical semester courses which consist of one 90-minute lesson every week. One of the main challenges in developing TBLT and technology modules is the reform of the curriculum needed to produce optimal environments, especially when instructors are working in foreign universities where they may have less influence on curriculum development change processes. Instructors may have the opportunity to design their own stand-alone modules, as was the case in this instance, but the influence and status required to produce long-lasting curriculum change over a whole curriculum remains a significant challenge and should not be underestimated.

Conclusions

The 3D virtual world of Second Life and the collaborative Web 2.0 digital media tools used in the intensive course provided a rich CMC environment in which authentic language learning within a task-based framework could be explored. While a number of educators have developed language learning environments utilizing new digital media tools, it is necessary to acknowledge the extent to which such virtual environments are different from face-to-face classrooms in order to develop materials and teaching and learning strategies that can fully take advantage of the opportunities for creativity and identity development which they present. In this chapter non-native-speaking students from Japan have shown that a task-based approach can be used to aid collaborative problem solving. Drawing on students' previous language classroom experience with role playing, Second Life provided the students with opportunities to utilize technology to explore language learning with a greater emphasis on authenticity and creativity – both aspects that essentialist and stereotypical descriptions of Japanese learners often fail to acknowledge. Findings suggested that learners felt more creative and engaged and more willing to utilize an approach in which they valued their experience and know-how to develop trial and error approaches. Through the use of the Web 2.0 tools, the virtual community of Second Life and the metaphor of learner as researcher, the learners developed their L2 identities in ways that could feedback positively into their academic learning contexts (Gasser, Cortesi, Malik & Lee, 2012).

While the pair overcame significant barriers to participation, and were highly active and motivated in their language learning tasks, significant challenges were also presented by the research. Most significantly, both learners preferred text chatting for longer periods in a combination of English and Japanese rather than engaging in sustained spoken discourse in English with native and non-native speakers. Second, students overwhelmingly relied on the use of their L1 (Japanese) for communicating during the preparation and collaborative stages of the tasks. This calls into question the gains made in motivation and engagement. In future developing strategies which encourage students to engage with each other in the target language in all phases of the task cycle need to be articulated to overcome this significant obstacle to meaningful collaboration in an online language learning context.

While further and more longitudinal research is required to fully examine the different aspects of how collaborative Web 2.0 digital media can be used in language learning contexts, this research suggests ways in which they can present language learners with significant opportunities to develop confidence in the L2 and learn a language by applying it in authentic situations. Findings from the study reinforce the point that research on TBLT in technology-mediated contexts should take into account the affordances of digital media and sociocultural approaches which stress that language learners are also engaged in a range of other digital literacy skills (Lai & Li, 2011). Moreover, new research approaches need to be developed to understand and analyse the focus on learner participation and collaboration in these new immersive environments.

References

Abrams, Z. I. (2003). The effect of synchronous and asynchronous CMC on oral performance in German. *Modern Language Journal, 87*, 157–67.

Bruner, J. S. (1960). *The process of education*. Cambridge: Harvard University Press.

Bygate, M., Skehan, P., & Swain, M. (2001). *Researching pedagogic tasks: Second language learning, teaching and testing*. Harlow: Longman.

Chapelle, C. (2001). *Computer applications in second language acquisition: Foundations for teaching, testing, and research*. Cambridge: Cambridge University Press.

— (2003). *English language learning and technology*. Amsterdam/Philadelphia: John Benjamins.

Chun, D. (1994). Using computer networking to facilitate the acquisition of interactive competence. *System, 22*, 17–31.

Dewey, J. (1938). *Experience and education*. New York: Collier Books.

Doughty, C. J., & Long, M. H. (2003). Optimal psycholinguistic environments for distance foreign language learning. *Language Learning & Technology, 7*(3), 50–80.

Ellis, R. (2003). *Task-based language teaching*. Oxford: Oxford University Press.

Gasser, U., Cortesi, S., Malik, M., & Lee, A. (2012). *Youth and digital media: From credibility to information quality*. Cambridge, MA: Berkman Center.

Gonzalez-Lloret, M. (2007). Implementing tasks through technology. In K. Van den Branden, M. Verhelst & K. Van Gorp (Eds.), *Task-based language education* (pp. 265–84). Newcastle: Cambridge Scholars Press.

Hampel, R. (2005). Rethinking task design for the digital age: A framework for language teaching and learning in a synchronous online environment. *ReCALL, 18*(1), 105–21.

Hwang, P. A. (2008). Linguistic characteristics in synchronous and asynchronous CMC. *English Language & Literature Teaching, 14*, 47–66.

Jarmon, L. (2010). Homo virtualis: Virtual worlds, learning, and an ecology of embodied interaction. *IJVPLE, 1*(1), 38–56.

Kenning, M. M. (2010). Differences that make the difference: A study of functionalities in synchronous CMC. *ReCALL, 22*, 3–19.

Kern, R. (1995). Restructuring classroom interaction with networked computers: Effects on quality and characteristics of language production. *Modern Language Journal, 79*, 457–76.

Klapper, J. (2003). Taking communication to task? A critical review of recent trends in language teaching. *Language Learning Journal, 27*, 33–42.

Lai, C., & Li, G. F. (2011). Technology and task-based language teaching: A critical Review. *CALICO Journal*, *28*(2), 498–521.
Lamy, M. N. (2001). Interactive task design: Metachat and the whole language learner. In P. del Garcia Mayo (Ed.), *Investigating tasks in formal language learning* (pp. 242–64). Clevedon, UK: Multilingual Matters.
— (2004). Oral conversations online: Redefining oral competence in synchronous environment. *ReCALL*, *16*(2), 520–38.
Lankshear, C., & Knobel, M. (2011). *New literacies: Everyday practices and social learning.* 3rd edition. Maidenhead & New York: Open University Press.
Leaver, B. L., & Willis, J. (Eds.) (2004). *Task-based instruction in foreign language education: Practices and programs.* Washington: Georgetown University Press.
Levy, M., & Stockwell, G. (2006). *CALL dimensions: Options and issues in computer-assisted language learning.* Marwah, NJ: Lawrence Erlbaum.
Long, M. H. (1990). Second language classroom research and teacher education. In C. Brumfit & R. Mitchell (Eds.), *Research in the language classroom. ELT Documents 133*, 161–70.
Mak, B., & Coniam, D. (2008). Using wikis to enhance and develop writing skills among secondary school students in Hong Kong. *System*, *36*, 437–55.
Meskill, C. (1999). Computers as tools for sociocollaborative language learning. In K. Cameron (Ed.), CALL: *Media, design and applications.* The Netherlands: Swets & Zeitlinger.
Molka-Danielsen, J., & Deutschmann, M. (2009). Examining the design of learning activities in Second Life through the lens of activity theory. *Nokobit Proceedings* (pp. 1–12). Trondheim: Tapir Akademisk Forlag.
Nunan, D. (2004). *Task-based language teaching.* Cambridge: Cambridge University Press.
O'Reilly, T. (2005). What is Web 2.0: Design patterns and business models for the next generation of software. Retrieved from http://oreilly.com/pub/a/web2/archive/what-is-web-20.html?page=1
Ortega, L. (1999). Planning and focus on form in L2 oral performance. *Studies in Second Language Acquisition*, *21*, 109–48.
— (2009). Tasks and technology in language learning: Elective affinities and (dis) encounters. Plenary delivered at the 3rd international task-based language teaching conference. Lancaster, 13–16 September.
Pica, T., Kanagy, R., & Falodun, J. (1993). Choosing and using communication tasks for second language instruction. In G. Crookes & S. Gass (Eds.), *Tasks and language learning: Integrating theory and practice* (pp. 9–34). Clevedon: Multilingual Matters.
Prabhu, N. S. (1987). *Second language pedagogy.* Oxford: Oxford University Press.
Prensky, M. (2001). Digital natives, digital immigrants. *On the Horizon*, *9*(5), 1–6.
Price, P. (2011). Paul Seedhouse: Learning a language is much more fun in the kitchen. The *Observer*, Sunday, 4 December. Retrieved from www.guardian.co.uk/technology/2011/dec/04/digital-language-kitchen-paul-seedhouse
Rankin, Y. A. (2008). *Design and evaluation of massively multiplayer online role-playing games that facilitate second language acquisition* (Unpublished doctoral dissertation). Evanston, IL: Northwestern University.
Reinders, H., & White, C. (2010). The theory and practice of technology in materials development and task design. In N. Harwood (Ed.), *English language teaching materials: Theory and practice* (pp. 58–80). Cambridge: Cambridge University Press.
Salaberry, M. R. (2000). L2 morphosyntactic development in text-based computer-mediated communication. *Computer Assisted Language Learning*, *13*(1), 5–27.

Seedhouse P., Ali, S., Jackson, D., Ploetz, T., & Olivier P. (2011). Learning French in digital kitchen. *International conference of the European association on computer-assisted language learning.* Nottingham, UK.

Skehan, J. (2003). Task-based instruction. *Language Teaching, 36,* 1–14.

Skehan, P., & Foster, P. (1997). The influence of planning and post-task activities on accuracy and complexity in task-based learning. *Language Teaching Research* 1/3.

Svensson, P. (2003). Virtual worlds as arenas for language learning. In U. Felix (Ed.), *Language learning online: Towards best practice* (pp. 123–43). Lisse: Swets & Zeitlinger.

Thomas, M., & Reinders, H. (Eds.) (2010). *Task-based language learning and teaching with technology.* London & New York: Continuum.

Thorne, S. L. (2003). Artifacts and cultures-of-use in inter-cultural communication. *Language Learning & Technology, 7*(2), 38–67.

Vallance, M. (2009). Beyond policy: Strategic actions to support ICT integration in Japanese schools. *Australasian Journal of Educational Technology, 24*(3), pp. 275–93.

Van den Branden, K., Bygate, M., & Norris, J. (Eds.) (2009). *TBLT: A reader.* Amsterdam: John Benjamins.

Vygotsky, L. (1978). *Mind in society.* Cambridge: Cambridge University Press.

Wankel, C., & Kingsley, J. (2009). *Higher education in virtual worlds.* Bingley: Emerald.

Warschauer, M., & Grimes, D. (2007). Audience, authorship, and artifact: The emergent semiotics of Web 2.0. *Annual Review of Applied Linguistics, 27,* 1–23.

Willis, J. (1996). *Framework for task-based teaching.* Harlow: Longman.

Yamada, M. (2009). The role of social presence in learner-centred communicative language learning using synchronous computer-mediated communication: An experimental study. *Computers and Education, 52,* 820–33.

19

CALL and learner autonomy: Affordances and constraints

Hayo Reinders and Philip Hubbard

Summary

The last two decades have seen a growing interest in the role of the individual in the learning process. We are starting to better understand the contributions that learners make to their own learning and the ways in which as educators we can build on this. This is a positive development as the majority of language learning increasingly takes place outside the language classroom. A sizeable body of general education research now exists that identifies the importance of informal learning and the ways in which this can be supported. More research is now appearing on self-directed language learning, but a lot of work remains to be done to identify the best ways to prepare learners for this. Technology has the potential to provide teachers and learners with the necessary support in this process but also in itself poses a number of challenges, especially as the successful use of technology often requires precisely those self-directed learning skills it is intended to help develop as well as presupposing an adequate level of technological proficiency. In this chapter we begin by briefly reviewing the role of learner autonomy in language learning and teaching before outlining the potential affordances offered by technology in its development. Next, we highlight ways in which technology poses constraints on this development and suggest ways in which these can be overcome. We will show that the fields of autonomy and CALL have a potentially symbiotic relationship that has important practical benefits for learning and teaching.

Introduction

Studies in individual differences, motivation and learners' beliefs (among others) point to the importance of increasing our understanding of the contributions learners make to their own learning (Breen, 2001) and the ways in which teachers can prepare learners for and support learners in making these contributions. Technology has often been seen to play an important potential role in this, both for learners to gain more control over the learning process, and for teachers to have more ways to connect with learners both in and outside the classroom. However, in practice there has long been a lack of terminological consistency and clarity and a frequent confusion between objectives (e.g., the development of learner autonomy) and the tools used to achieve them (e.g., the internet).

A common misconception for many years has been the idea that technology would single-handedly serve the pursuit of autonomy by providing learners with powerful tools that would enable them to control their own learning without the help of a teacher (cf. Levy, 1997). Partly this was the result of early optimism in the field of CALL. The promise of artificial intelligence (AI) in general and intelligent tutoring systems (ITS) in particular was such that overly confident predictions were common about the demise of the language teacher and the empowerment of learners to the point where they would be able to control every aspect of their learning. Although subsequent developments lowered such expectations, a view persisted of technology as providing learners with all the tools they would need to be successful in their learning. In this view, offering learners access to unlimited resources and language input whenever and wherever they want, would be sufficient for learning to somehow take place automatically.

Reality has of course proven to be far more complicated. Although technology undoubtedly does support learners in a myriad of ways, it is also true that without adequate preparation, practice, feedback and support, many learners are unable to make effective use of technology's affordances, and indeed may suffer from using technology inadequately (for example by overreliance on machine translation).

In this chapter we look at the relationship between the development of learner autonomy and the use of technology through exploring this tension between technology as an affordance and as a constraint.

The role of learner autonomy in language learning and teaching

Language teachers have always tried to find ways to reconcile the collective nature of most teaching environments with the (inevitably) individual aspects of learning. The development of learner autonomy, or learners' ability to take control over their own learning (Holec, 1981), has been one way in which teachers have tried to make links with learners at a more individual level, and to connect classroom learning with out-of-class language use. The theoretical and pedagogical rationale for the implementation of more learner-centred approaches to teaching is well developed and goes back many decades. Especially from the 1950s, educational psychology began to place greater emphasis on the role of the individual in the learning process. Humanist approaches considered the learner as an active participant in this process; as someone who actively shapes his or her learning experiences with the purpose of self-development and fulfilment (Atkinson, 1993; Stevick, 1980). Similarly, constructivism gave central stage to the learner by focusing less on the knowledge to be transmitted, and more on the process of constructing, reorganizing and sharing that knowledge. These developments also influenced language education, both through the development of specific teaching methods rooted in these ideas, such as the Silent Way and Suggestopedia (Gattegno, 1963; Lozanov, 1978) and – perhaps more importantly – through a general influence on language teaching towards a greater focus on the learner:

> most researchers agree that a major shift is taking place . . . in education away from the teacher-centred classroom toward a learner-centred system where the learner is in control of the lesson content and the learning process. (Fotos & Browne, 2004, p. 7)

In addition to the educational aspect of autonomy, there is also an important political element. In its original meaning, autonomy encompasses the freedom and ability to make one's own choices (Winch, 2007). Economic and political obstacles, government policies and tightly prescriptive curricula are some examples of practical impediments to learners exercising their autonomy. Nevertheless, technology can offer ways to overcome such impediments, as we shall see below.

Technology and learner autonomy

Technology can play a role in the development of learner autonomy by supporting learners in a number of ways. Free and ubiquitous access to resources for example is one way in which practical and political limitations on autonomy can be overcome. But in order for learners to be able to make use of those resources, they also need to know which resources are the most suitable for them and to have the ability to use them appropriately. Technology can help learners develop this knowledge and the necessary learning skills. This can be done *indirectly,* for example by giving students access to a learning diary to record their learning experiences and the resources they use. It can also be done by developing learner autonomy *directly* (although this is less common). For example, there are computer programs designed specifically to help students develop the ability to identify their learning needs, plan their learning and monitor their progress. The 'My English' program developed at King Mongkut's University of Technology Thonburi (KMUTT) in Thailand, for example, actively encourages students to reflect on their learning and to make decisions based on past performance and future needs (see Reinders & Darasawang, 2011). Students are taken through a needs analysis process, are encouraged to develop an appropriate study plan, are guided in the selection of relevant resources and are requested to monitor and reflect on their performance. Support is available through peers and online language advisors.

Although such programs are valuable in encouraging students to become more aware of their learning process and their own roles in this, studies into engagement levels with such software show disappointing results. For example, Reinders (2006) reports that many students had received the various prompts and alerts offered by an online support program used at the University of Auckland, but did not have the metacognitive awareness to respond appropriately and as a result often stopped using the software. Reinders concludes that in this case learners should have received more specific training, not only on how to use the software, but also on the skills necessary for self-directed learning.

Related to this, not much is known about the ways in which learners use technology *outside* the classroom (or indeed how they practise and acquire language in general). A recent special issue of *Language Learning & Technology* (Reinders & White, 2011) and an edited collection (Benson & Reinders, 2011) are two of only a few publications to specifically look at the use of technology outside the classroom. Both of these collections confirm, among others, that many learners do have a desire to shape their learning experiences, and to a certain extent do so, but that they are often not successful in this. As a result, attrition levels are often high, in particular in self-study contexts (Nielson, 2011). Almost all existing studies show the need for extensive preparation, ongoing guidance and follow-up support to ensure learners are able to make full use of resources given to them (Darasawang & Reinders, 2010; Reinders, 2006; Ulitisky, 2000; Vanijdee, 2003). Another common finding is that greater integration needs to take place between formal and informal education, and the use of teacher- and self-directed learning so that skills and experiences acquired in one domain can be built on and used in the other (Toogood & Pemberton, 2002).

The affordances of CALL for learner autonomy

CALL resources offer learners a range of affordances that are undeniable (Godwin-Jones, 2005; Zhao, 2005). Reinders and White (2010) reviewed these affordances and categorized them into two broad groups: those that carry mainly organizational or practical advantages and those that are more pedagogical in nature, as shown in Table 19.1.

Here, we are concerned with the ways in which these affordances are directly relevant for the development of learner autonomy and will now discuss each with this in mind.

Access

At a purely practical level, technology has allowed learners to gain a level of access to resources that was previously impossible. Not only do learners in rural or underprivileged contexts now have better opportunities for access to materials, but because of this

TABLE 19.1 The potential advantages of CALL

Organizational advantages	Access
	Storage and retrieval of learning behaviour records and outcomes
	Sharing and recycling of materials
	Cost efficiency
Pedagogical advantages	Authenticity
	Interaction
	Situated learning
	Multimedia
	New types of activities
	Non-linearity
	Feedback
	Monitoring and recording of learning behaviour and progress
	Control
	Empowerment

they are also less reliant on scarce or unavailable teacher support. Mobile-assisted language learning in particular offers great promise in this regard (Kukulska-Hulme & Traxler, 2005).

Storage and retrieval

An extension of 'access', technology allows for the easy storage and retrieval of learning and teaching materials, as well as learning records, giving insight into learning behaviour, both inside, and potentially, outside the classroom. This extends not only to teachers but also to learners themselves, who can not only find and access resources but also monitor their own usage of those resources.

Sharing and recycling of materials

Pedagogical materials can be easily created, shared and updated, with learners potentially contributing to this process. In relation to the development of learner autonomy, this last point is particularly important as it gives learners control that they lack in more traditional environments.

Cost efficiency

Technology is sometimes said to lower the cost of education by allowing learners to manage more of their own learning, thus relying less on teachers. Technology can reduce the cost of language materials in some cases by providing them in a readily reproducible digital format.

Authenticity

In terms of pedagogical advantages, authenticity is often cited and potentially of major importance in the development of learner autonomy (Benson, 2007), allowing learners to use real-world materials that are relevant to their (and not just their teachers') individual interests. Discussions of autonomy often emphasize the importance of giving learners access to authentic materials, and the internet provides a wealth of these for commonly taught languages and increasingly for less commonly taught ones as well.

Interaction

An important tenet of most SLA theories is the importance of opportunities for input and output, provided through interaction. Autonomy researchers have long argued for the importance of providing learners with opportunities to *use* the language, especially in settings outside formal education (Benson, 2011). Computer-mediated communication through email, chat and social networking sites allows learners to easily connect with other learners, native speakers and teachers. Tutorial software that offers students feedback on correctness (e.g., pronunciation grading through speech recognition) or input modification (Chapelle, 2001, 2005) (e.g., linked definitions, images, translations, etc.) also provides a level of interactivity that can be beneficial to the learner.

Situated learning

Related to this, situated learning is facilitated by the use of technology, for example through the use of mobile phones that allow access to support tools in real-world settings, and that allow learners to connect with peers or teachers when attempting to *use* the language. Situated learning can help to blur the boundaries between the classroom and the target language context (Hung, 2002). By setting assignments that require learners to discover language on their own, they are encouraged to take more responsibility for their learning, in socioculturally meaningful contexts.

Multimedia

Technology makes the production and distribution of multimedia resources easier, both for teachers and, increasingly, also for students. Multimedia resources may also give learners more control over the way they access target language input. For example, a movie can be watched with or without subtitles. Individual learner preferences and learning styles can thus be accommodated more easily.

New types of activities

Related to this, technology can also offer new types of activities that are difficult or impossible to replicate otherwise. Drag-and-drop exercises, Webquests, microblogging and social networking sites offer opportunities for interactive language practice that can empower students to find authentic materials and interact with them without the constant intervention of teachers.

Non-linearity

Technology allows for content to be displayed dynamically. Hypermedia gives students the opportunity to move beyond the boundaries of the materials set by the teacher. It also allows students to easily access background information or support tools.

Feedback

Technology makes the delivery of immediate and personalized feedback easier to accomplish. Natural language processing and parser-based CALL can provide feedback based on participants' prior language learning progress and their specific needs (Heift & Schulze, 2007), which can help to decrease reliance on the teacher. It also becomes easier to provide feedback in a range of different ways, through auditory, textual and visual means. At the same time, it becomes easier for students to connect with other learners to obtain peer-feedback, encouraging them to consider alternatives for teacher guidance.

Monitoring and recording of learning behaviour and progress

This is made easier with the help of technology. This not only supports teachers but also learners, who, when given access to this information, can learn to make choices about their learning process based on actual data on their progress. Electronic portfolios are an example of a tool specifically designed to encourage reflection and to support informed decision-making.

Control

Several of the affordances discussed above give students a greater degree of control over their learning. At a practical level, CALL materials can be accessed flexibly by students when and where they need to, and be provided with varying levels of support (e.g., with or without a glossary).

Empowerment

At the pedagogical level, many of the above affordances empower learners to make decisions for themselves. By allowing learners to make choices on what materials to access, how to use them, by enabling them to work with other learners, both within and outside the school, and by giving them the data they need to know how they are doing, students are encouraged to become more reflective, more critical and increasingly responsible for their own learning process (Blin, 1999).

The constraints of CALL for learner autonomy

As noted above, these affordances do not come as a free ride for autonomous learners – if they did, then the mere presence of technology should have been enough to spur a revolution in autonomous learning as it arguably has in listening to music. There are constraints, even potentially negative side effects of technology, when applied to this realm, a number of which we touch on in this section. Let us begin with the assumptions that (1) learners are working with teachers, tutors or other resources (e.g., computer programs) to help them become autonomous and (2) the learners themselves are in fact interested and motivated to become autonomous, and then discuss constraints from this idealized perspective. As with all language learning (and all education for that matter) additional issues will surface in settings where one or both of these assumptions are not met. We briefly review the preceding affordances with respect to constraints, limitations and challenges to their effective integration into autonomous learning, beginning with the four organizational categories and then continuing with the ten pedagogical ones.

Access

On the surface at least, access is a positive feature, but access has negative potential as well. Mobile learning, for example, is gaining ground for its 'anytime/anywhere' access but the mobile experience can be a degraded one due to the limited screen size (for phones, though not tablets) and the often distracting environments in which they are used. For learners to be autonomous, they need to control access and not have that access control them to keep from being constantly interrupted in tasks or being swamped with data that cannot be processed in a way that supports language learning. Rather than relying exclusively on whatever is familiar and convenient, they need to develop knowledge and skills for selecting the best available technology for particular learning objectives.

The question is basically to what extent the practical benefits of technology access extend to the pedagogical level. The simple availability of materials for self-study is not sufficient. Previous studies (e.g., Jones, 1993; Reinders & Lewis, 2006) report that such materials frequently lack the necessary support structures, such as clear instructions or even answer keys, and do not explicitly encourage students to reflect on the learning process. Materials not designed for learning purposes will offer even less guidance. Hurd emphasizes the importance of preparation for learners to take full advantage for access:

> if learners are not trained for autonomy, no amount of surrounding them with resources will foster in them that capacity for active involvement and conscious choice, although it might appear to do so. (Hurd, 1998, pp. 72–3)

Storage and retrieval

In terms of materials, the constraints lie in two areas: (1) initially indexing or tagging content for easy and accurate retrieval and (2) developing the skills in both teachers and learners to locate and sequence that material for learning. Indexing and tagging for language learning functionality can be a time and resource-consuming enterprise – ways need to be found to increase the pool of stored and indexed resources, ideally in a universal format. For the second, at the broad internet level, this means having advanced skills at searching with Google or other search engines, which many students lack (Duke & Asher, 2012). At a more localized level, it can mean having those skills within a dedicated content or learning management system, such as Blackboard, Moodle or Drupal. Besides materials, learning records may also be stored and retrieved. To do so requires first finding settings in which such records can be gathered and then ensuring that both teachers and learners have the ability to retrieve and interpret them. It is relatively easy to collect data, but data is not the same as knowledge. Both teachers and learners have to develop the skills to identify sources for such data and the means of transforming that data into useful information to support decisions and actions.

Sharing and recycling of materials

Despite its advantages for teaching, the process of distributing and recycling material sets up the potential for problems in creative language production for the learner. We live increasingly in a 'mix' culture, where repurposing chunks originally produced by others and synthesizing them into something different is taken as a legitimate form of creation. Learners must become aware of the limitations of this practice for developing and demonstrating language proficiency. Also teachers need to be aware of the limitations in their own materials development.

Cost efficiency

When we think of technology and language learning these days, the internet and apps for mobile devices come to mind. There is an expectation that everything should be free, or in the case of apps, cost very little. As a result, free material is often preferred by both teachers and learners to other, potentially better, material that carries expenses with it. But there are hidden costs to much of such 'free' material, most notably the distraction of advertising on websites, the lack of systematicity (Decoo, 2010), and the limited quality control in much of its production. Additionally, for technology at the institutional level, there are costs for hardware, infrastructure, maintenance and training, costs that may be difficult for the autonomous learner to absorb away from the institutional setting.

Authenticity

There are at least two issues of authenticity that can have negative consequences for the autonomous learner. One involves the language of social interaction found in online chat and discussion boards. The anonymity and cultural practices of many such settings support forms of discourse differing from what may be the learner's or the institution's goals. The second involves the relative level of the material. The plethora of options for commonly taught languages can readily lead learners to content that is authentic but linguistically inaccessible. If material is too far beyond the learner's level, it is not processed naturally, and thus is not useful for learning (Breen, 1985). In addition, accessing material that is incomprehensible can be demotivating. There is a temptation to rely on translation, especially machine translation, for both comprehension and production. Autonomous learners need to understand the limitations of such practices and identify appropriate material for their level and goals.

Interaction

Interactions mediated by technology may suffer from being either inauthentic, leading to a distorted view of target language use, or authentic, as noted above, but beyond the level of all but the more advanced learners. There are examples of online interactions in authentic settings that have led to apparent successes for autonomous learners, such as Lam's (2000) case study of an English learner expanding writing proficiency through postings to fan sites. However, unfettered interaction may not support sufficient focus on form, and the lack of systemization (Decoo, 2010), is likely to affect efficiency of learning as well as leave gaps in the acquired language system. There is a need to ensure that autonomous learners understand the forms of interaction that will be most useful for them. Many of the purported benefits of CMC may be limited because a very narrow range of language is used over and over. In synchronous chat in particular, there is not much *extension* and not much opportunity to focus on accuracy or complexity.

Situated learning

Despite the generally positive aspects of situated learning, a key point is for autonomous learners to be able to select the right range of situations for their learning to occur, ideally situations that are readily transferable. The range of situations in online and especially mobile settings can be limited relative to face-to-face language use, an issue common in foreign language vs second language settings in general (see Stockwell, this issue). Learners may become successful within a given comfortable range, but lack experience with key lexical, grammatical and discourse elements as well as cultural expectations outside of those settings. On the other hand, as everyday communication and professional and business interactions increasingly move into the digital realm, it is important that the learning tasks and settings reflect such authentic environments. Autonomous learners need to have the knowledge and skills to seek out such tasks and settings, rather than just pedagogically convenient ones, as often occurs when activities connected to print textbook are transferred online.

Multimedia

Combining media can be useful, but multimedia by itself does not guarantee better learning (Mayer, 2005). Multimedia may cause distractions, and the quality of online material is inconsistent. Further, learners may not take appropriate advantage of multimedia when offered. For example, a recent review of research on multimedia glosses for vocabulary learning noted the following: 'In summary, previous studies have found that L2 vocabulary is remembered better when learners look up picture or video glosses of unfamiliar words in addition to text glosses (translations in L1 or definitions in L2) but that when given the choice, learners tend to prefer and use the simple translations of words' (Chun, 2011, p. 139). Such disconnects between what has been shown to help learners and what they tend to do on their own need to be resolved for effective autonomous learning.

New types of activities

Useful new activities, such as Webquests for language learning (Godwin-Jones, 2004), are possible in computer settings. However, they may be technology-driven without a suitable pedagogical foundation. Additionally, autonomous learners may be unaware of the range of new activities and unable to discover them on their own. Needed steps include expanding and refining language learning tasks and activities mediated by technology that suit autonomous learning and developing procedures for making teachers and learners aware of their range and relative strengths.

Non-linearity

Along with the positive elements of non-linearity, there are also drawbacks. With few exceptions, both text and audio/video is linear, and textual cohesion can be interrupted by linking within a text to online dictionaries or glossaries to illuminate meaning or to resources that enrich and expand the content. Non-linearity also vastly increases the choices learners can make, and learners need to have the ability to make informed decisions regarding when breaks in linearity lead to more rather than less efficient learning. One common aspect of non-linearity in digital environments is multi-tasking, which, despite the impressions of those engaging in it, is increasingly being shown to reduce rather than enhance efficiency and quality of engagement (e.g., Ophir, Nass & Wagner, 2009). This is another example of a disconnect between many learners' perceptions and the results of empirical studies.

Feedback

Technology offers the opportunity for feedback, but the overwhelming majority of dedicated programs for language learning offer very limited programmed feedback (Reinders & Lewis, 2006). Exceptions include certain ICALL (intelligent CALL) programs, but as noted in the introduction, these have not met their original promise (see Schulze & Heift, this volume). Feedback from humans is available, but a common approach for autonomous learners is to use volunteer native speakers for this purpose, especially through tandem language exchanges (e.g., livemocha; mylanguageexchange). Feedback from programmed or untrained human sources may include information that is incomprehensible, inaccurate or irrelevant. In autonomous settings, it is important for learners to become adept at both soliciting and interpreting feedback so that it serves their needs.

Monitoring and recording of learning behaviour and progress

Touched on under the 'storage and retrieval' topic above, this affordance is often not available except in commercial learning packages. Even there, the data supplied may be of limited value, often representing only progress through the material or course based on quizzes, but not progress in language use or general proficiency. At the individual level, this is further constrained by a lack of reliable student models: one size fits all often prevails. Electronic portfolios offer an option, but autonomous learners are likely to require additional skills and knowledge to use them effectively. For this affordance to be realized, we need extensive development of learning management systems specific to second languages and more sophisticated ICALL applications, as well as greater learner understanding of how the information from those sources connects to future actions.

Control

Issues of control have been with us since the early days of CALL (Stevens, 1984). Learners first need an understanding of the control options they have for a given device or application, and often they do not have this ability at the required level (Winke & Goertler, 2008). There is arguably a need for 'technological autonomy' in both the learners themselves and the teachers who are guiding them towards language learning autonomy. Beyond this core understanding of controls, autonomous learners need an understanding at a more strategic level of when to use specific control options to serve their learning objectives.

Empowerment

Empowerment is closely connected to several of the previous categories, in particular feedback and control. All too often, learners are 'empowered' without the preparation to use that power effectively. There is also a clear connection to motivation so that the desire to build on the empowerment affordance of technology is activated and channelled. In a digital world, Dörnyei and Ushioda's (2009) theory of the 'L2 self' may hold promise for understanding and developing motivation for the connected autonomous language learner.

Overcoming constraints and challenges for developing learner autonomy

Autonomy is a growth area within language teaching and learning, and we have seen in the first part of this chapter how technology offers an unparalleled set of affordances to support it by connecting learners to one another, teachers and others as well as to programmed tutorials and rich content. However, we have also seen that there is a great potential to ignore or misappropriate these affordances. The affordances that modern technological devices, applications and networks create are only opportunities. For autonomous learners and their teachers, at least four promising paths exist for overcoming the constraints and challenges so that those opportunities can be exploited effectively.

First, there is the potential for learner training (Hubbard, 2004). We have argued that what learners do 'naturally' with the affordances of technology is often at odds with what is ideal for autonomous language learning. Teachers and developers need to begin by identifying efficient and effective techniques and procedures for using language materials or engaging in language learning tasks and activities mediated by technology. Then they need to find ways to communicate those to learners through training activities. Romeo and Hubbard (2010) suggest that learner training for technology environments should include three types: technical, strategic and pedagogical. Pedagogical training, which provides a knowledge base for accommodating new technologies and situations overlapping that of teachers themselves, is of particular importance in the development of autonomy. We are still in the early stages of clarifying the scope of learner needs in using technology, but despite the challenges inherent in language learner training (Rees-Miller, 1993), we cannot continue to ignore it.

Second, once we move away from fixed curricula, a potential area of inefficiency and frustration for autonomous learners is that of materials and task selection, especially selection of material that is too challenging to be of much use in promoting language acquisition (see, for example Nation and Waring's (1997) discussion of vocabulary level needed for text comprehension). There is a need for more information to be provided to autonomous learners in a form accessible to them so that they can make appropriate choices. Hubbard (2011) has suggested expanding the notions of Decoo (2010) regarding systemization so that the content of freely available text, audio and video resources are annotated and tagged in a way that autonomous learners can access material linked to their proficiency level and interest. In parallel to this is the propagation of more online tools like Tom Cobb's vocabulary profiler (www.lextutor.ca/vp) or various readability applications (e.g., www.read-able.com) that learners can use on their own to approximate levels for materials.

Third, at a time when collaborative learning and online social interaction are both on the upswing, there is the potential for learners to support and scaffold one another through communities of practice (Lave & Wenger, 1991). The value of peer interaction in independent learner settings has been noted previously (e.g., Lee 1998), but little work to date has focused on the specifics of the use of technology to support that. This is indeed another of technology's affordances – community building. Despite the obvious momentum from current social networking sites and 'cultures-of-use' (Thorne, 2003), making such collaborations work well for autonomous language learning will likely require the combined efforts of teachers and students, at least at the initial stages.

Finally, there is a need for more technological initiatives within CALL, or borrowed from related disciplines, that specifically target advancing learner autonomy. This includes applications that enhance learners' metacognitive development and provide support for cognitive, social and affective strategies (Oxford, 1990) *specific* to the technology environments. Like their teachers, learners need to be guided to a level of technological autonomy whereby they can embrace and incorporate new devices and applications in the service of language learning. This call is embedded in the TESOL

Technology Standards, Learner Standards Goal 3, Standard 5: 'Language learners recognize the value of technology to support autonomy, lifelong learning, creativity, metacognition, collaboration, personal pursuits, and productivity' (Healey et al., 2011, p. 252).

These four areas, combined with the prior discussion of affordances and constraints for technology in support of language learner autonomy, provide an exploratory framework for research and practice in this growing domain. It is clear that technology can play an important role in the development of learner autonomy, but it is up to the language teaching profession to help learners to be able to fully benefit from the affordances it offers.

References

Benson, P. (2007). Autonomy in language teaching and learning: State of the art article. *Language Teaching, 40*(1), 21–40.

— (2011). Language learning and teaching beyond the classroom: An introduction to the field. In P. Benson & H. Reinders (Eds.), *Beyond the language classroom* (pp. 7–16). Basingstoke: Palgrave Macmillan.

Blin, F. (1999). CALL and the development of learner autonomy. In R. Debski & M. Levy (Eds.), *WorldCALL: Global perspectives on computer-assisted language learning* (pp. 133–47). Lisse: Swets & Zeitlinger.

Breen, M. (1985). Authenticity in the language classroom. *Applied Linguistics, 6*, 60–70.

— (2001). *Learner contributions to language learning. New directions in research.* Harlow: Longman.

Chapelle, C. A. (2001). *Computer applications for second language acquisition: Foundations for teaching, testing, and research.* Cambridge: Cambridge University Press.

— (2005). Interactionist SLA theory in CALL research. In J. Egbert & G. Petrie (Eds.), *Research perspectives on CALL* (pp. 45–68). Mahwah: Lawrence Erlbaum.

Chun, D. (2011). CALL technologies for L2 reading post Web 2.0. In N. Arnold & L. Ducate (Eds.), *Present and future promises of CALL: From theory and research to new directions in language teaching* (pp. 131–69). San Marcos, TX: CALICO.

Darasawang, P., & Reinders, H. (2010). Encouraging autonomy with an online language support system. *CALL-EJ, 11*(2). Retrieved from http://callej.org/journal/11-2/darasawang_reinders.html

Decoo, W. (2010). *Systemization in foreign language teaching.* London: Routledge.

Dörnyei, Z., & Ushioda, E. (2009). Motivation, language identities and the L2 self: A theoretical overview. In Z. Dörnyei & E. Ushioda (Eds.), *Motivation, language identity and the L2 self* (pp. 1–8). Bristol, UK: Multilingual Matters.

Duke, L., & Asher, D. (2012). *College libraries and student culture: What we now know.* New York: ALA Editions.

Fiori, M. (2005). The development of grammatical competence through synchronous computer-mediated communication. *CALICO Journal, 22*(3), 567–602.

Fotos, S. S., & Browne, C. (2004). *New perspectives on CALL for second language classroom.* Mahwah, NJ: Lawrence Erlbaum.

Gattegno, C. (1963). *Teaching for languages in schools: The silent way.* Reading: Educational Explorers.
Godwin-Jones, B. (2005). Emerging technologies. Messaging, gaming, peer-to-peer sharing: Language learning strategies and tools for the millennial generation. *Language Learning & Technology, 9*(1), 17–22.
Godwin-Jones, R. (2004). Language in action: From Webquests to virtual realities (Emerging Technologies Column). *Language Learning & Technology, 8*(3), 9–14.
Healey, D., Hanson-Smith, E., Hubbard, P., Ioannou-Georgiou, S., Kessler, G., &Ware, P. (2011). *TESOL technology standards: Description, implementation, integration.* Alexandria, VA: TESOL.
Heift, T., & Schulze, M. (2007). *Errors and intelligence in computer-assisted language learning: Parsers and pedagogues.* New York: Routledge.
Holec, H. (1981). *Autonomy and foreign language learning.* Oxford: Pergamon Press.
Hubbard, P. (2004). Learner training for effective use of CALL. In S. Fotos & C. Browne (Eds.), *New perspectives on CALL for second language classrooms* (pp. 45–68). Mahwah, NJ: Lawrence Erlbaum.
— (2011). Some practical issues in systemization and autonomy. In M. Simons & J. Colpaert (Eds.), *Peer perspectives on systemization. A book review of Wilfried Decoo's systemization in foreign language teaching.* Antwerp: Universiteit Antwerpen.
Hung, D. (2002). Situated cognition and problem-based learning: Implications for learning and instruction with technology. *Journal of Interactive Learning Research, 13*(4), 393–415.
Kukulska-Hulme, A., & Traxler, J. (2005). *Mobile learning: A handbook for educators and trainers.* London: Routledge.
Lam, W. (2000). L2 literacy and the design of the self: A case study of a teenager writing on the internet. *TESOL Quarterly, 34*(3), 457–82.
Lave, J., & Wenger, E. (1991). *Situated learning: Legitimate peripheral participation.* Cambridge: Cambridge University Press.
Lee, I. (1998). Supporting greater autonomy in language learning, *ELT Journal, 52*(4), 282–9.
Levy, M. (1997). *Computer-assisted language learning: Context and conceptualization.* Oxford: Clarendon Press.
Lozanov, G. (1978). *Suggestology and outlines of Suggestopedy.* New York: Gordon & Breach.
Mayer, R. (2005). The cognitive theory of multimedia learning. In R. Mayer (Ed.), *The Cambridge handbook of multimedia learning* (pp. 31–48). Cambridge: Cambridge University Press.
Nation, P., & Waring, P. (1997). Vocabulary size, text coverage and word lists. In N. Schmitt & M. McCarthy (Eds.), *Vocabulary: Description, acquisition and pedagogy* (pp. 6–19). Cambridge: Cambridge University Press.
Nielson, K. (2011). Self-study with language learning software in the Workplace: What happens? *Language Learning & Technology, 15*(3), 110–29.
Ophir, E., Nass, C., & Wagner, A. (2009). Cognitive control in media multitaskers. *Proceedings of the National Academy of Sciences, 106* (37), 15583–7.
Oxford, R. (1990). *Language learning strategies: What every teacher should know.* New York: Newbury House.
Rees-Miller, J. (1993). A critical appraisal of learner training: Theoretical bases and teaching implications. *TESOL Quarterly, 27*(4), 679–89.
Reinders, H. (2006). Supporting self-directed learning through an electronic learning environment. In T. Lamb & H. Reinders (Eds.), *Supporting independent learning: Issues and interventions* (pp. 219–38). Frankfurt: Peter Lang.

— (2007). Big brother is helping you. Supporting self-access language learning with a student monitoring system. *System, 35*, 93–111.

Reinders, H., & Darasawang, P. (2012). Diversity in language support. In G. Stockwell (Ed.), *Computer-assisted language learning: Diversity in research and practice* (pp. 49–70). Cambridge: Cambridge University Press.

Reinders, H., & White, C. (2011). Learner autonomy and new learning environments. *Language Learning & Technology, 15*(3), 1–3.

Romeo, K., & Hubbard, P. (2010). Pervasive CALL learner training for improving listening proficiency. In M. Levy, F. Blin, C. Siskin & O. Takeuchi (Eds.), *WorldCALL: International perspectives on computer-assisted language learning* (pp. 215–29). New York: Routledge.

Stevens, V. (1984). Implications of research and theory concerning the influence of choice and control on the effectiveness of CALL. *CALICO Journal, 2*(1), 28–33.

Stevick, E. (1980). *Teaching languages: A way and ways*. Rowley: Newbury House Publishers.

Thorne, S. (2003). Artifacts and cultures-of-use in intercultural communication. *Language Learning & Technology, 7*(2), 38–67.

Toogood, S., & Pemberton, R. (2002). Integrating self-directed learning into curriculum: A case study. In P. Benson & S. Toogood (Eds.), *Challenges to research and practice* (pp. 86–110). Dublin: Authentik.

Ulitsky, H. (2000). Language learner strategies with technology. *Educational Computing Research, 22*, 285–322.

Vanijdee, A. (2003). Thai distance English learners and learner autonomy. *Open Learning, 18*(1), 75–84.

Winke, P., & Goertler, S. (2008). Did we forget someone? Students' computer access and literacy for CALL. *CALICO Journal, 25*(3), 483–509.

Zhao, Y. (2005). *Research in technology and second language education. Developments and directions*. Greenwich, CT: Information Age Publishing.

Glossary and abbreviations

ACL Association for Computational Linguistics.

ACTFL American Council on the Teaching of Foreign Languages.

AES Automatic Essay Scoring or Automatic Writing Evaluation (AWE), software that uses natural language processing to rate students' writing and provide feedback.

AI Artificial Intelligence, the ability of a computer to mimic human attributes in finding a solution to a problem.

AILA Association Internationale de Linguistique Appliquée.

ARG Alternative Reality Game, an immersive online game in which participants' actions may change the game's narrative or storyline.

ASR Automatic Speech Recognition, a branch of human language technologies devoted to the automatic processing of human speech.

ASST Automatic Spoken Spanish Test.

Asynchronous communication by email or via a discussion list, where the recipients or participants in the discussion do not have to be present at the same time.

Avatar a graphical representation of a real person, such as used in a MUVE or MMORPG.

AWE Automatic Writing Evaluation, software used to assess learners' writing and provide feedback. See also AES.

Bandwidth the amount of data that can be sent from one computer to another through a particular connection in a certain amount of time.

BBC British Broadcasting Corporation.

Blackboard a commercial Virtual Learning Environment (VLE) that integrates online communications software with content software enabling teachers to create courses online.

Blended Learning a combination of internet-based distance learning with face-to-face tuition but it may also be used to describe offline ICT-based materials with more traditional print-based materials.

Blog or Weblog, a website that contains discrete pieces of information in a diary format posted by different users such as news items, short essays, annotated links, documents, graphics and multimedia.

BNC British National Corpus, a collection containing an estimated 100 million words of spoken and written British English from the twentieth century.

Broadband a high-speed connection to the internet.

BYU Brigham Young University.

CAI Computer Assisted Instruction, used mainly in the business world. Implies a top-down, instructor-centred approach to teaching with computers.

CAL Computer Assisted Learning.

CALI Computer-Assisted Language Instruction.

CALICO Computer-Assisted Language Instruction Consortium, a professional association based in the United States founded in 1982.

CALIS Computer-Assisted Language Instruction System.

CALL Computer-Assisted Language Learning, a term which came into favour in the early 1980s, replacing the older term CALI to explore the use of digital devices in language learning and teaching.

CALL-IS Computer-Assisted Language Learning-Interest Section, this special interest group is associated with the worldwide TESOL organization.

CARLA Centre for Advanced Research on Language Acquisition.

CATE Center for Advanced Technology in Education.

CBLT Computer-Based Language Testing.

CCCC Conference on College Composition and Communication.

CD-ROM Compact Disc Read-Only Memory, an Optical Disc on to which data has been written via a laser.

CEFR Common European Framework of Reference for Languages, a scheme developed by the Council of Europe with the aim of providing a basis for the mutual recognition of language qualifications, thus facilitating mobility.

CERN Centre Européen pour la Recherche Nucléaire, the European particle physics laboratory and the birthplace of the World Wide Web invented there by Sir Tim Berners-Lee.

CIBER Centres for International Education and Research.

CLIPS Computerized Language Instruction and Practice Software.

CLT Communicative Language Teaching, an approach that foregrounded learner interaction and communication as the main goal of language teaching.

CMC Computer-Mediated Communication, a term describing the use of the internet as a means of fostering teaching and learning, especially the use of email, conferencing and social networking.

CMCLL Computer-Mediated Communication and Language Learning.

CMS Content Management System, a software package that makes it possible for non-technical users to publish content on a website.

CoI Community of Inquiry, typically a community of educators involved in a group who explore and examine issues and debates relevant to their teaching or research.

Collaborative Writing a process that involves the creation and editing of documents using Web 2.0 tools designed for use by multiple authors.

Concordance Program or concordancer operates on a body of texts (a corpus) and is commonly used for compiling glossaries and dictionaries.

COP Communities of Practice, typically a group of people who collaborate and share their experience and professional knowledge.

COPI Computerized Oral Proficiency Instruments.

COTS Commerical Off the Shelf Game, ready-made software that cannot be customized.

Courseware a set of computerized lessons, exercises, tests and reference material.

CPD Continuing Professional Development, on-going and further study relevant to one's profession in order to retain and develop one's knowledge and understanding.

CTL Commonly Taught Languages.

Cyberspace refers to communication in online environments.

DCALL Distance Computer-Assisted Language Learning, learning a language typically via computer-mediated communication (CMC).

DDL Data Driven Learning, an approach to language learning whereby learners gain insights into the target language by using concordance programs to locate authentic examples of language in use.

DECU/TUCO Deutscher Computerunterricht/Tutorial Computer.

Digital refers to technologies and devices such as computers and portable mobile devices as well as Web-based applications and tools.

Discussion List or forum, a way for sharing emails with the members of a group that utilizes asynchronous messaging.

DL Distance Learning, learning that takes place when teachers and students are in physically separate locations, using print or electronic forms of study.

DTP Desk Top Publishing.

DVD Digital Video Disc.

E-learning learning with Information and Communications Technologies (ICTs).

EAP English for Academic Purposes, learning English for integration into educational contexts such as prior to studying for a degree in the United Kingdom.

EFL English as a Foreign Language, learning English in a non-English speaking context, for example, a Japanese person learning English in Japan.

EIEGL Échanges Interculturels Exolingues en Groupe en Lingue.

ESL English as a Second Language, learning English in an English-speaking environment, for example, a Japanese person learning English in England.

ETS English Testing Service.

EU European Commission.

EUROCALL Europe-based professional association for CALL, founded in 1986.

F2F Face-to-Face, presence-based learning.

FL Foreign Language.

FLAS Foreign Language and Area Studies.

FLCAS Foreign Language Classroom Anxiety Scale.

GMAT Graduate Management Admissions Test.

GPS Global Positioning System, a satelite-based navigation system which provides real-time updates on a current location.

GRE Graduate Record Examination.

GWU George Washington University.

HCI Human-Computer Interaction, the study of people and computer technology.

IATEFL International Association of Teachers of English as a Foreign Language.

ICALL Intelligent CALL, an approach to CALL that makes use of sophisticated programming techniques that mimic human intelligence.

ICC Intercultural Communicative Competence.

ICT Information and Communications Technology, where 'C' reflects the important role that computers now play in *communications*, for example, by email, the Web, by satellite and cellphone (mobile phone).

IECC Intercultural Email Classroom Connections.

IJCALLT International Journal of Computer-Assisted Language Learning and Teaching.

ILR Interagency Language Roundtable.

ILTS Intelligent Language Tutoring System.

IM Instant Messenging, the real-time exchange of short messages typically using a phone or computer.

IRF Initiate Response Feedback, a typical pattern of response or dialogue between an instructor and a student.

IRT Item Response Theory.

ITS Intelligent Tutoring System.

IWB Interactive Whiteboard, a touch-sensitive projection screen or board that allows the teacher to control a computer directly by touching the screen.

K-12 Primary and secondary education.

L1 Mother Tongue or First Language.

L2 Second Language.

LAN Local Area Network.

LCTL Less Commonly Taught Languages.

LLT Language Learning & Technology journal, a leading open access journal for CALL research.

LMS Learning Management Systems, similar to a virtual learning environment but typically used in a corporate learning context.

LOM Learning Object Modules, a group of resources and content typically used with a VLE.

m-learning Mobile Learning, using portable digital devices such as phones or PDAs.

MALL Mobile-Assisted Language Learning, the use of portable devices such as smartphones for language learning.

Mashup a Webpage that brings together data from two or more Web services and combines the data into a new application with added functionality.

MAT Machine Assisted Translation, the use of computers to assist human beings in the process of translating natural languages.

MBA Master of Business Administration.

MITUPV Massachusetts Institute of Technology-Universidad Politécnica de Valencia Project.

MMORPG Massively Multiplayer Online Role-Playing Game, an advanced type of virtual world in which players adopt avatars to explore fantasy worlds.

MOO Multi-User-Domain Object Oriented, an early form of immersive virtual world that was text-based.

Moodle a popular open source Virtual Learning Environment (VLE).

MP3 MPEG Layer 3, a file format for storing high-quality audio files that can be played back on computers and portable media players.

MT Machine Translation, the use of computer software to produce translations of one language to another.

MTALL Machine-Translation-Assisted Language Learning.

MUD Multi-User-Domain or Multi-User Dungeon, is an early form of an immersive role-playing game typically set in a fantasy world.

MUVE Multi-User Virtual Environment, an earlier name for a Virtual World and further development of the MUD concept.

NASILP National Association of Self-Instructional Language Programs.

NBLT Network-Based Language Teaching, the use of computers which are connected together for language teaching.

NCRLC National Capital Language Resource Center.

NIAFLAR Network Interaction in Foreign Language Acquisition and Research Project.

Ning a platform that enables users to create their own social network focusing on a particular topic or catering to a specific membership.

NLP Natural Language Processing, a term used to describe the use of computers to process information expressed in natural (i.e., human) languages.

NNS Non-Native Speakers.

NPC Non-Player Characters, typically a character in a game that is controlled by the computer and not by a user.

NSEP National Security Education Program.

OHP Overhead Projector.

Open Source refers to software that is provided free of charge along with its original source code, so that it can be modified by the user.

OU Open University (UK).

PCK Pedagogical Content Knowledge, knowledge required of an instructional area both in terms of content as well as how it can be taught to learners.

PDA Personal Digital Assistant, a handheld device that combines computing, audio communication, browsing and networking features and serves as an organizer for personal information.

PLATO Programmed Logic for Automated Teaching Operations, a computer-aided instruction system dating from the early 1960s developed at the University of Illinois.

PLE Personal Learning Environment, unlike a Virtual Learning Environment (VLE), an approach to using new technologies that enables learners to develop and control their own learning environment using a range of online tools.

PMI Physical Mobile Interaction.

POS Point of Speech.

PS2 Play Station 2.

QA Quality Assurance.

QR Quick Response code, a two-dimensional barcode that can store a variety of different types of information such as a website URL or email address.

RSS enables users to subscribe to websites that change or add content regularly.

RTS Real-Time Strategy game.

SALTMIL Speech and Language Technology for Minority Languages.

SCSI Small Computer System Interface.

Semantic Web an extension of Web 2.0 whereby data available in different locations can be linked together to facilitate sophisticated sharing and search capabilities.

Simulation type of program that simulates a real-life situation, allowing users to carry out experiments which could have dangerous consequences or which are impractical in a normal learning environment.

SL Second Language.

SL Second Life, an immersive 3D virtual world originally launched in 2003 by Linden Lab in the United States.

SLA Second-Language Acquisition, concerned with the study of how people learn second languages.

SLTE Second Language Teacher Education.

Smartphone an advanced mobile phone that offers a wide range of appications including a music player, camera, GPS navigation and a Web browser.

SMS Short Message System, a text messaging service typically used on mobile phones.

Social Media used to describe a variety of Web 2.0 applications that enable people to share images, audio recordings and video recordings via the Web and to initiate discussions about them.

Social Networking a type of website where people befriend others who share their interests, find out what's going on in their areas of interest and share information with one another.

SOPI Simulated Oral Proficiency Interview, a performance-based speaking test.

SP Social Presence, the degree to which participants can represent their identity in an enviroment, whether face-to-face or via computer-mediated communication (CMC).

Speech Recognition technologies devoted to developing programs and devices that enable computers to recognize, analyse and transcribe human speech.

SRI Stanford Research Institute.

Synchronous refers to communication in a chat toom or via videoconferencing, where the participants can communicate in real-time.

Tablet Computer a compact portable computer that makes use of a touchscreen instead of a keyboard for typing and running applications.

Tandem Learning refers to two language learners who pair up in order to learn each other's language. This may take place face-to-face or via the internet.

TBL Task-Based Learning, an approach to learning in which the learner acquires knowledge of the subject that is being studied by focusing on a specified task.

TBLT Task-Based Language Teaching, the application of TBL principles in language learning, focusing on meaning and communication in authentic environments.

TCCR Tandberg Computer Controlled Cassette Recorder.

TELL Technology Enhanced Language Learning, refers to the wider range of uses of technology in language learning and teaching than the more common term CALL.

TESOL Teachers of English to Speakers of Other Languages.

TGF Tutor Group Forum.

TICCIT Time-shared Interactive Computer Controlled Information Television, an early computer-aided instruction system dating from 1977 developed in the United States.

TMA Tutor Marked Assignment.

TOEFL Test of English as a Foreign Language.

UCI University of California, Irvine.

UCLA University of California, Los Angeles.

UGC User-Generated Content, a term associated with Web 2.0 in which users can develop their own resources such as in the form of a blog or wiki.

UNESCO United Nations Education, Social and Cultural Organisation.

VCR Video Cassette Recorder.

Videoconferencing a computer-based system that allows a group of computer users at different locations to see and hear one another as if they were in the same room.

VLE Virtual Learning Environment, a Web-based package designed to help teachers create online courses, incorporating communication and content tools.

VR Virtual Reality, the simulation of an environment by presentation of 3D moving images and associated sounds.

VSTF Visual-Syntactic Text Formatting, a method to enhance online reading that arranges text into cascading lines of text.

VW Virtual World, an online 3D imaginary world or game in which participants and players adopt characters or avatars and explore the world, engaging in voice and/or text chat.

VWLL Virtual Worlds and Language Learning.

WAN Wide Area Network.

Web 2.0 an attempt to redefine the Web and how it is used based on the use of collaborative applications such as blogs, podcasts, wikis and social networking websites.

Webquest a task-oriented activity in which the learner draws on material from different websites in order to achieve a specific goal.

WELL Web-Enhanced Language Learning.

WiFi Wireless Local Area Network.

Wiki a website which allows anyone to set up a resource in which content can be edited collectively.

WOW World of Warcraft, a massively multiplayer online role-playing game (MMORPG), with an estimated 10 million users.

WWW World Wide Web or simply the Web, it refers to the huge collection of online resources which is accessed by means of a browser.

WYSIWYG What You See Is What You Get, a content creation tool which displays what is seen during editing as the completed product.

ZPD Zone of Proximal Development, deriving from the work of Vygotsky, it indicates the difference between what can be achieved by independent learning and learning with the guidance of others.

This glossary derives in part from 'The Glossary of ICT Terminology' compiled by Professor Graham Davies and Fred Riley and located at the ICT4LT website (www.ict4lt.org/en/en_glossary.htm). Extracts are reprinted here with permission from the authors.

Index